Words of War

WARTIME MEMORIES
From the American Revolution Through the Iraq War

Volume II

COMPILED BY

The Park Tudor Legacy Initiative

EDITED BY

Kathryn W. Lerch

Park Tudor School

ISBN 0-9612740-3-4
Library of Congress Catalog Card Number 2004097401

CONTENTS

FOREWORD viii

THE AMERICAN REVOLUTION

Mr. Robert Yates – Albany Committee of Public Safety
    Member of New York Provincial Congress 1775-1777 1

THE CIVIL WAR

Lieutenant John Shaw Franklin – Confederate Army
    Company D, 2nd Maryland Infantry 18

Private Joseph McClung Johnson – POW at Andersonville
    Company F, Fifth Indiana Cavalry 29

Privates Thomas Doorley and Michael Stanley – Irish cousins
    57th Massachusetts, Ninth Army Corps 35

WORLD WAR I

Private George R. Duncan – Battle of Fromelles 1916
    59th Battalion, Fifth Australian Division. 43

Private Benjamin Hendin – Jordan Valley 1918
    The Jewish Legion: 38th Battalion, London's Royal Fusiliers . . .49

Sergeant Leon C. Farmer – Mechanic & Welder
    8th Aero Squadron, First Corps, France 63

Ph.M2 Clifford Warren Williams – Assistant Surgeon
    82nd Company, Sixth Marine Regiment 67

WORLD WAR II
THE PACIFIC THEATER

Captain John W. Temple – POW at Cabanatuan, P.I.
    701st Ordnance Company, U.S. Army, Philippine Islands 75

Lieutenant Leonard Gadi Lawton – Guadalcanal
    Company F, 2nd Battalion, Fifth Marines,
    First U.S. Marine Division 86

Major Robert W. Palmer – New Guinea
    400th Squadron, 90th Bomb Group, 5th Air Force 94

Fireman 1/c Harold Lee Hunt – Philippine Campaign
    U.S.S. San Jacinto (CVL-30) 97

Ensign Robert J. Lauer – Kamikazes & Typhoons
    U.S.S. San Jacinto (CVL-30) 108

Lieutenant Llewellyn D. Halderson – Invasion of the Philippines
    21st Infantry Regiment, 24th Division, Sixth Army 120

Master Sergeant Ric Ranucci – Roi-Namur, & Iwo Jima
    Fourth Marine Division 134

Lieutenant (j.g.) John Ticusan – Mine sweeping operations
    U.S.S. Perry (DMS-17) 138

Lieutenant Alfred K. B. Tsang – B-29 Navigator
    29th Bomb Group, 314th Bomber Wing,
    20th Air Force 144

THE EUROPEAN THEATER

Major John C. Carvey – G-3 Air Liaison Officer
    36th Fighter Group, 83rd Division and Third Army 155

Major Mike Dewart – Adjutant & administrative officer
    225th Station Hospital, in Italy 177

PFC Carver McGriff – In Normandy near St. Lô, France
    357th Infantry Regiment, 90th Infantry Division, US Army . .179

PFC Ernest P. Sable – Reconnaissance Platoon in France
    Company E, 385th Infantry Regiment,
    76th Infantry Division 185

Major Joseph L. Trierweiler – Intelligence Officer
    Command Assault Bn B, Third Armored Artillery Battalion,
    Ninth Armored Division 189

PFC Joseph W. Duncan – Rifleman
    Company G, 309th Infantry Regiment,
    78th Infantry Division 203

Lieutenant Harold E. Kren – Pilot B-24
    466th Bomb Group, Eighth Air Force, US Army Air Corps 207

Lieutenant Fred Fehsenfeld, Sr. – P-51 Mustang fighter pilot
    354th Fighter Group, 353rd Fighter Squadron,
    9th Air Force, US Army Air Corps 212

Private Frank Cooney – Rifleman
    Company A, 359th Regiment, 90th Infantry Division &
    POW Stalag VIIA 222

S/Sgt Leonard Rose – B-17 crew member
    15th Air Force and POW Stalag Luft IV 226

Sergeant Ed Leitem – liberated Buchenwald
    Battery B, 995th Field Artillery, Third Army 230

Frank Grunwald – Prague, Czechoslovakia
    Memories of Theresienstadt, Auschwitz and Maulthausen 234

Private Stanley J. Fleszar – 806th Tank Destroyer Battalion
and G.F.R.S. Replacement Pool, France 1944 248

▨

KOREAN WAR

Lieutenant (j.g) Bruce Meyer, M.D. – 1951
    1st M.A.S.H. (8029), X Corps, Eighth Army 251

Sergeant 1/c Murray Freed – 1952-1953
45th Infantry Division, X Corps, Eighth Army 281

VIETNAM WAR

Sergeant E-5 William Catching – 1964-1967
First Infantry Division 288

Captain John B. Reinhardt – 1967-1968
196th Light Infantry Brigade;
361st Aerial Weapons Company 296

Warrant Officer 2nd Class, Edward Koroshetz – 1968-1971
155th Assault Helicopter Company, US Army 302

Second Lieutenant Michael T. Burns – 1966-1973
US Air Force, Thailand and POW in Hanoi 305

THE GULF & IRAQ WARS

Major John Hightower – Operation Desert Storm
3rd Battalion, 35th Armor, 1st Armored Division 318

Captain Stephen Wintermeyer, M.D. – Operation Desert Storm
46th Combat Surgical Hospital, US Army 321

Lieutenant David A. Barrows, M.D. – Operation Iraqi Freedom
US Navy, in 2nd Assault Amphibian Battalion, 2nd Marine
Division 325

Words of War

FOREWORD

IN MAY 2002, the Legacy Initiative of the Park Tudor School in Indianapolis brought to fruition its first anthology of wartime letters, diaries, oral histories and photographs in *Words of War: Wartime Memories From the Civil War Through the Gulf War*. After the publication of the first anthology, the Legacy Initiative was invited by United States Senator Richard G. Lugar to become partners with the Library of Congress Veterans History Project. To carry out this role, our students completed interviews annually with WWII veterans and civilians, and veterans from the Korean, Vietnam and Gulf Wars, from around the country.

Now, more than two years later, students, with the assistance of the faculty, have compiled a second anthology, which is even more comprehensive. This *Words of War* volume explores wartime memories – *From the American Revolution Through the Iraq War* – again through the extensive use of original unpublished letters, diaries, reminiscences, photographs, and oral histories.

Some of the very special documents in this volume include drafts of depositions that belonged to Robert Yates, who was a member of New York's Provincial Congress and the Committee of Safety in 1775. There is the diary account by a Marylander, James S. Franklin, who felt compelled to run the blockade to join the Confederate Army. WWI photographs from Leon Farmer show the 8th Aero Squadron in England and France. A veteran of World War II, John C. Carvey shares his experiences and documents relating to his duties as a G-3 operations officer in England during D-Day and with Patton's Third Army. The reminiscences of Naval officer Robert Lauer and the diary of Fireman 1/c Harold Hunt describe their experiences on the aircraft carrier USS *San Jacinto*, as they encounter typhoons and kamikaze attacks. In letters to his family, Lew Halderson describes his experiences in the steamy jungles of the South Pacific and the Philippines Islands.

There are also amazing tales of survival: from a Holocaust survivor, Frank Grunwald, as well as from WWII POWs John Temple, Frank Cooney and Leonard Rose and a Vietnam War POW, Michael Burns.

In addition to numerous accounts of ground, naval or air action, some of our letters and oral histories describe the improvements in medical treatment for wounded and sick soldiers. This is evident in the letters written by Dr. Bruce Meyer, who spent six months with the 1st M.A.S.H. in Korea, and in oral histories by two physicians, Dr. Stephen Wintermeyer and Dr. David Barrows, who served in the Gulf and Iraq wars, respectively.

Acknowledgements

The Initiative gratefully acknowledges individuals from across the country, as well as faculty and parents, who contributed letters, photographs, wartime documents or substantially supported our project: Dr. David A. Barrows, Martha Sue Batt, Joanne Black, Patricia Bozek, Harriet Campbell, Liz Day, Dr. David B. Duncan, Shirley Gaughan, Georgia L. Hollister, Carol Yates Franklin Holliday, Harold E. Kren, Robert J. Lauer, Jeffrey Lipshaw, Nancy Martzolf, Dr. Bruce Meyer, John Morton, Richard Mote, Michelle Polanco, Herbert G. Potter, Ken Rash, Harley W. Rhodehamel, Maurice L. Risch, Dr. Richard and Christine Scales, Carol B. Shumate, Shirley Temple, John Ticusan, Alfred K. B. Tsang, Martha Wharton, and Cdr. E. A. Wilde, Jr., USNR (Ret.).

The list of students who completed oral interviews for the Library of Congress Veterans History Project is too long to include here, but students and interviewees included in *Words of War* are recognized here: Kyle Bonham (John P. Hightower), Melissa Cooney (Frank Cooney), Courtney Dewart (Mike Dewart), Michael Duncan (Joseph W. Duncan), Andrew Glassman (Edward Koroshetz), Adam Holt (Carver McGriff), Brittany Ison (Frank Grunwald), Matt Lipshaw (Murray Freed), Katie Lloyd (Ernest P. Sable), Ashley Mullis (Dr. Stephen Wintermeyer), Tom Osborne (Fred Fehsenfeld, Sr.), Andrew Ragsdale (John B. Reinhardt), Neal Ramchandani (Dr. Robert W. Palmer), Jessica Ranucci (Ric R. Ranucci), Andrew & William Scales (Alfred Tsang), John Scott (Dr. Leonard Gadi Lawton), Alexa Shoff (Leonard Rose), Annette Trierweiler and Colin Stalnecker (John C. Carvey), R.J. Stuart (Michael T. Burns), and Josh Thomas (William Catching).

The Legacy Initiative is also grateful for the support and promotion of our project by Jane Kokotkiewicz, Media Specialist and coordinator for National History Day at Park Tudor, Lisa Hendrickson, our Director of Communications, and Douglas S. Jennings, the Head of School. We are also privileged to be a partner with the Library of Congress Veterans History Project and are grateful for their continued support and guidance. I am especially indebted to the history department of the United States Military Academy at West Point for selecting me as one of thirty international seminarians to participate in the 2004 Summer Seminar in Military History. This was truly an opportunity of a lifetime and something from which our students and project will continue to benefit.

A reminder to the community: the Park Tudor Legacy Initiative in an on-going hands-on history project. Its mission is to connect students with older generations and to preserve the memories of veterans from around the world by studying, researching and publishing their stories. Thus, the Legacy Initiative continues to solicit family-held, unpublished letters, and is prepared to interview veterans, because their accounts are invaluable to future generations and are a way to honor those who served, both here and abroad.

Kathryn Lerch,
Director and Managing Editor
Park Tudor School Legacy Initiative
7200 North College Avenue
Indianapolis, Indiana 46240
August 2004

This project would not be possible without the following dedicated and talented students, some of whom have worked on both volumes. Thank you to all of you!

2002-2004 WORDS OF WAR STEERING COMMITTEE

Andrew Scales & William Scales	American Revolution and Civil War
David Mossler & Josh Ring	World War I
Kemmie Mitzell & Annette Trierweiler	World War II
Kim Vawter & Andrew Ragsdale	Oral history & Post-World War II

WRITERS & CONTRIBUTORS

Hannah Bain, Matthew Baldwin, Yaprak Baran, Dana Brunette, Dana Campbell, Courtney Dewart, Caitlin Drouin, Molly Hamer, Ashley Hanson, Tom Hardacker, William Huster, Alexander Leopold, Lizzy Shula, Colin Stalnecker, Meredith Thomas, Patrick Turner, and Sarah Sondhi

The American Revolution

IN HINDSIGHT, it is too simple to look back on the Revolutionary War as a conflict that was neatly divided into two distinct ideologies of loyalists and patriots. The passage of time has fashioned the perception that contemporaries of the founding fathers were set in their ways, uncompromising in their devotion either to the fledgling United States and democracy, or to Great Britain and constitutional monarchy. As the Yates letters illustrate, the war effort was rife with suspicions of treason and the outcome of the conflict was far from decided. The Articles of Agreement and the Dop depositions respectively provide a rare look into the uncertainties of the revolution, as well as the process used in determining whether those on trial were loyal to the ideals of democracy or to the crown.

MR. ROBERT YATES
(1738-1801)

Robert Yates was a Revolutionary patriot and a lawyer in Albany, New York. From 1771 to 1775 he served on the Albany Common Council as an alderman. He was a radical Whig prior to the Revolution and was elected, along with other patriotic Whigs, to the Albany Committee of Safety, Protection and Correspondence.[1] In this capacity he was elected four times as a delegate to New York's Provincial Congress. In 1775, the Provincial Congress appointed him to the Congress' Committee of Safety, Protection and Correspondence, which officially met whenever the congress was in adjournment. From 1775 to 1777, Yates was also a delegate to the Continental Convention. While serving the New York colony, he had opportunities to make personal copies of these documents that related to his committee work.

The range of subject matter of Yates' documents is quite diverse and relates to a variety of New York colonial matters, including proposals for Provincial Congress delegates' pay, inventory lists for colonial military forces, letters to Continental Convention delegates, and drafts to the Committee of Safety.[2]

Yates, either by interest or involvement, was particularly concerned with naval issues, and his earlier efforts in 1775 and 1776 on the Committee of Safety probably qualified him for his 1777 appointment to the secret committee for the obstruction of the Hudson River against British ships. Because secret committees did not keep minutes, Yates did not make copies of the committee's activities. However, while working earlier with the Committee of Safety, Yates saved numerous documents, two of which are particularly interesting: an agreement with Thomas Blockley for obtaining gunsmiths, and a lengthy deposition regarding a Tory-owned Hudson River sloop. These documents show how New York citizens used legal means to fight the Revolutionary War.

What events precipitated the need for a new form of assembly and a committee of safety in the colony of New York? Briefly, the New York Colonial Assembly (loyal to England's monarch) was adjourned for the last time on April 3rd, 1775. Divided loyalties prevented agreement, and the Assembly failed to elect delegates for the Second Continental Congress, which was to begin in Philadelphia on May 10th. When it became apparent that the Assembly could do nothing, a committee of the city and county of New York urged the rest of the New York counties to send deputies to a provincial convention in New York City on April 20th in order to elect representatives. Once this was accomplished, the convention dissolved on the 22nd.

With the former Assembly basically defunct, a new, extra-legal governing body, the first of four Provincial Congresses, was established. The First Provincial Congress met on May 22nd, and this was none too soon. News of the battles of Lexington and Concord in Massachusetts had prompted the citizens of New York City to "burst all restraints; [they] instantly emptied the vessels laden with possessions for Boston; seized five hundred and thirty stand of arms lodged in the City Hall; took possession of the Powder House. . . . "[3] In response to this, the First Provincial Congress directed "... such measures as may be expedient for our common safety."[4] On May 26th, the Provincial Congress appointed "a standing committee of correspondence" and "the next day ordered all the counties to name committees for the counties, towns and districts," and "three days later all citizens were to sign the 'general association.'"[5] The Committee of Safety, which was to serve whenever the congress was in adjournment, had "the power to open all letters directed to the Congress and to answer the same; to examine suspect persons; take such measures as they shall think proper to carry into execution all orders. . . . "[6]

What is particularly valuable about studying the activities of the Committee of Safety and other governing bodies of this period is that one can see how they managed to carry on a revolution in an "orderly

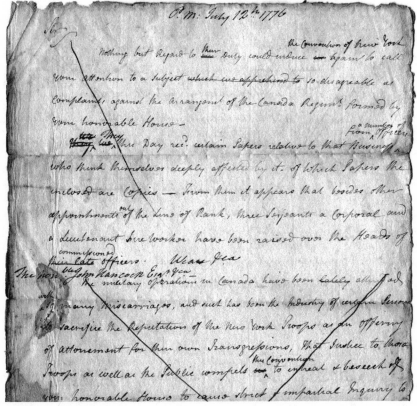

Copy of rough draft from Convention of New york regarding military matters. (Courtesy of Carol Yates Franklin Holliday)

and legal way."[7] In other words, this was a war run by committee until a regular constitutional government was created in 1777.[8]

On May 27th, in response to anti-British sentiments and potential violence, British troops formerly barracked in the city quickly boarded the HMS *Asia*, which was located in New York harbor. This was initially a precaution, but then the ship secretly prepared to depart for Boston in the first week in June.[9]

During May and June of 1775, the Second Continental Congress met in Philadelphia. At this time, George Washington was asked to organize and lead the Continental Army. As the civil conflict sharpened, there was a greater urgency to raise and train troops, to fortify New York, and to acquire powder and arms for defense. "Passes and passports were issued . . . Loyalists suppressed, and their efforts to aid the British thwarted."[10]

With the adjournment of the first session of the Provincial Congress on July 8th, 1775, Yates' Committee of Safety assumed the responsibility *ad interim* of maintaining the "military machine" and to "suppress the 'inimical.'"[11]   One of the committee's tasks was to work with the Congress' June 27th "'plan of accommodation'" regarding England, which forbade "the export of bread, flour, beef and pork" and ordered "gunsmiths...to be brought from Britain."[12] This action was timely, because the Second Continental Congress resolved on July 9th that each colony would be responsible for defending their own harbors and sea-coast. Yates' copy of the Blockley agreement details this order.[13]

[Please note that the original spelling and superscript letters, popular in the 18th Century, have been retained. Writers typically used hyphens instead of periods. Also, for greater ease of reading, paragraphs have been created in lengthier documents.]

{July 17th, 1775}
Dr Articles of Agreement Between the Committee appointed for that purpose & Thos Blockley for Importing a Cargo of Gunsmiths

Articles of Agreement Made & Concludes this Seventeenth Day of July One thousand Seven hundred and Seventy five Between {Colonel} *Leonard Lispenard, Joseph Hallett, Jacobus Van Zandt, &* {Colonel} *Alexander McDougall of the City of New York Esquires on behalf of the provincial Congrefs of New York of the first part and Thomas Blockley in New York intending speedily to go to Britain of the second part.*

First the said Leonard Lispenard, Joseph Hallett, Jacobus VanZandt & Alexander McDougall[4] on behalf of the provincial Congrefs of the Colony of New York do authorize & request the said Tho.s Blockley ten good Artificers in the Gunsmiths & Gun locksmiths Businefs to wit— to procure Locksmiths good workmen in the Trade & Businefs of making Musket or Gunlocks, other good workmen at the Trade & Businefs of forging welding & making Gun Barrells & ~~two other~~ other good workmen at that Trade & Businefs of Boreing Gun Barrells in the whole ten Artificers in number to come to the Colony of New York to dwell and reside and there carry on their respective Trades & Occupations— And the said parties of the first part do request &

Authorize the said Tho.ˢ Blockley to Advance to each of the said workmen two Guineas to defray the Expence of their removal from their respective places of Abode on Board of the Ship in which they shall come as Pafsengers.

And the ~~Leonard Lispenard~~ said parties of the first part do Covenant & agree to & with the said Thomas Blockley to repay to him or his order ~~all~~ such sums of money as shall be so by him advanced to the said workmen not exceeding two Guineas each And also to pay & discharge the pafsages of such workmen to the City of New York at the rate & price of Steerage pafsengers in any Ship or Vefsel in which they shall arrive provided that each of the said Artificers at the Time of Dr.{draft?} immediately before the payment of their respective pafsages do enter in Bond to the said parties of the first part

{page 2} the first part in double the sum so advanced & paid for each of them with a Condition to repay the Money so Advanced for each of them respectively; if the obligor shall not set up & Carry on his Trade ~~and his Trade~~ Occupation & Businefs in the Colony of New York or shall remove to dwell & reside in any place not within the said Colony.

And it is recommended to the said Thomas Blockley to Engage & send out sober prudent Men in their respective Occupations & such as will bring with them the usual & necefsary Tools of their respective Occupations that may be put into small {rooms?} or Compafs– And that as many of them as may Conveniently be had be Single Men.

The citizens and the Committee of Safety remained alert. Only a few days after this agreement, on July 21ˢᵗ, the Committee of Safety warned Brunswick, New Jersey, that "boats have sundry times loaded flour at or about your city, and have run down the west bank, and there met boats to take it from them for the use of the men of war and the army at Boston." It was essential for the colonies to be ever alert. It was especially important that their secrets did not reach the enemy. The situation became more critical when, as a consequence of the Congress' removal of cannon at Fort George, the British warship HMS *Asia* opened fire on American troops in New York Harbor on August 23ʳᵈ.[15] Also on this date, members of the Congress were "required . . . to take an oath not to divulge the proceedings. On August 26ᵗʰ business was so heavy that the

Provincial Congress voted to meet daily except Sundays."

The Congress adjourned on July 8th, at which time Yates and the Committee of Safety assumed their duties. Citizens were urged to be calm and the HMS *Asia* was allowed to purchase basic necessities. The man-of-war ship continued to be watched for the next week, and on August 31st, according to notes from the Provincial Congress, an examination was made of Jacobus Stoutenburgh, Jr., from Dutchess County, regarding Peter Dop and his sloop, which had been seized for taking supplies to the HMS *Asia*. A few days later, on September 3rd, as a result of Stoutenburgh's testimony, Colonel Lasher carried out orders "to furnish a sufficient detachment from his battalion to take and seize the sloop, and people on board which is charged with having supplied necessaries for the use of the army and navy, and now lying at anchor near the *Asia* ship of war."[16]

One individual, the Loyalist Governor of New York, William Tryon, preferred restraint —although he was virtually powerless to convince the colonists to follow his suggestions. He urged "temperate conduct" and also sent a letter to Captain Vandeput of the *Asia,* proposing some mediation. Tyron was disturbed that "a Boat which carried only some milk on Board was burnt on her return to shore as was last Sunday [September 3] a country Sloop for having put some provisions on Board of the man of war."[17] The New York Committee of Safety had questions, though. Was this sloop bringing necessities to the ship or aiding and abetting the enemy?[18] The Committee ordered that the men on board be arrested by the City Guard and charged with misdemeanors for collaborating with the enemy. On September 5th, the Committee of Safety began examining Daniel Rivers, Henry Acker, Jr., Abraham Freeligh, and Timothy Doughty.[19]

Deposition of the Dops, Berghs

Sept. 5, 1775

read Daniel Rivers– That he lives in Dutches County has been two years there– formerly lived in New York 7 years with Fredrick Rhynelander & 2 years with Cregier– That lately he lived at Esq.[r] {Mordicai} Lester's has lived there about four months– that he was a pafsenger–

That there were 13 persons on Board to wit Adam Bergh Christian Bergh David Dop Captain of the sloop Christian Dop Peter Dop two other

Brothers of the name of Dop– Hendrick Ecker {Acker}– Timothy Doughty– Abraham Freligh– John Harris who went on board of the Transport and enlisted there under Campbell and a person named Martin that he was alongside of the Transport and put six Cord of wood on Board of her– had two firkins of Butter which the man of war got.

That he came as a pafsenger– that the sloop had some wheat and wood on board when she left the man of war– that the sloop had five Musketts on Board– that the Musquetts were loaded with Bulletts– It was a piece of the Mainsail that was thrown overboard– That they expected to be taken when their mainsail was torn–

That the Men on board of the Transport are enlisted to go to Boston– That Cap^n {Duncan} Campbell asked him to enlist– That he was informed there were 50 Recruits on Board of the Transport– That there is above one hundred men on Board– That the Talk was that the men enlisted would have 50/ Sterling per month and 200 or 300 Acres of Land–That he has heard Mordecai Lester say that if the Kings Troops came over he would join them rather than join the Country–

That he the s^d {said} Rivers appeared once under & there were nine Companies on That he did not see Lester when he returnd home from on Board of the man of war has often heard Lester speak against the Congrefs and their proceedings– That Ecker & Doughty A Freligh were pafsengers–

That a Lieut.! of the man of war haild the sloop and she came to immediately that the Dops & Bergh's did not seem uneasy or concerned when the sloop was haild or bro't to, - That when the sloop came to the Lieutenant on the Transport told them it would not be safe to go the City for that the people said they would burn the sloop and hang the people on Board– the sloop came to the Transport in the afternoon– That he was informed that the officers paid for Wood and Butter– That a few nights ago they saved the life of a person who fell over out of a Petty Auger which struck ag.! the Sloop

7

discharged Six Cords of wood on board of Transport and Six other Cords on board of the Man of War that there were Cartouch Boxes & powder & Ball considerable on Board of the Sloop– That he will be 24 years of Age next November–

Sept.r 5th 1775

read Henry Acker Jun.r born at Stactsburg. Oliver Munrow– That he was a passenger on Board that there were five guns or Musketts & two pistols & Cartouch Boxes on board of Dops Sloop– That David Dop the Captain was at the Helms– That the Lieut.t Asked what he had on Board Dop answered wood & he ordered him to come to. The Transport took six Cord of Wood & the man of war four cord– That there was Butter on Board Belonging to Freligh.

That when they were haild they were about 200 yards of {f} from her– That the next day after the Sloop lay to the Transport an old man an Oyster man came on Board & told them 600 hundred Men were watching them and would burn the Sloop if she was taken– A petty auger in the Evening came alongside & struck again Dops Sloop & a man fell overboard he was taken up & after he was dried went on board of the Transport Dopps on Boards, two Berghs– ~~five~~ passengers Doughty Rivers Freligh Martin Seaman & himself.

That Capt. Campbell promised him good wages to enlist & go to Boston, & promised him Bounty & 400 Acres of Land if he would enlist for three years. That at the Training he heard them busy about Whig & Tory that Doughty & Berghs made themselves busy about those matters– That Tim Doughty drank a Health to the King & the Tories and a Downfall to the Whigs.
That he and Daniel Rivers, & Abraham Freligh {page torn} wanted to get a shore {?} and could not get Liberty to go, or be set on Shore

Sept.r 5th 1775

read Abraham Freligh– born in Ulster County lives in Charlotte precinct in Duches County near his father John Freligh– left home last Monday

week came down in Dops Sloop as a passenger– he had three firkins of
Butter on Board which Adam Bergh sold & received the money & gave
to the Examinant– That when they were haild they were nearer to the
Transport than the City– That he heard the Bergh's say they would go on
Board & see the Ship– That when they were haild one of the Dops was
at the helms– That he heard Bergh say that they were not affraid & had
been threatned by the Country people– That at the chasing of assigned offi-
cers the Berghs were there there was a Dispute between Radley & one of
the Berghs– That Bergh not want to hurt or catched by the soldiers but had
said he did not kept out of the way for fear– That the Berghs had pistols
with them– That he left the Berghs & Dops There– That Doughty was
there– That there were two or three pistols on Board of Dops Sloop– That
the Dops & Berghs are called Tories, & that Doughty was once chosen of
the Committee.

That a person who fell over out of a pettiauger {petty auger} *said he had*
a letter to a Gentleman on board of one of these vessels– his name Samuel
He said he ownd the pettiauger– he said if they came to Town they were
hard Threatned & that there was a watch of soldiers out for their sloop–
John TenBroek the Cartman said it was peacable Times in Town– That he
heard {Mordecai} *Lester opposed the people having any Committees–*

Read

Sept. 5, 1775

Timothy Doughty– Bro't upon Long Island– lives in Dutches County, left
that last Monday week came down in a sloop with wood & about 20
Bushels of wheat– had Busines with Mr. Isaac Roosevelt– That he heard
the owners of the Sloop say they would go & see the man of war & he also
intended to go to see the man of war– that the Sloop stood near the ~~ship~~
Transport Ship– The Ship haild the Sloop and on hearing what was on
board ordered them to come alongside & wanted the wood– That next
morn⁵ after the sloop arrived several oyster men told them the sloop was
known & that they would be killed if they came ashore– That a petty auger
came alongside in an Evening– A person who fell out of the Boat & was
taken up said he had a letter for a gentleman on Board this man of war–

That he was at Albertus Sickers at the Election of Officers– That he was there armed with pistols– did not join in electing officers– has not signed the afsocitation, has been threatned to be tarred & feathered & therefore went armed– That Mr Sherif Philip Livingston said Mr Grant had orders to enlist men, to give 50/ sterling & 8 per day pay & 400 Acres of Land– that he had one Gun & a Cartouch Box on board of Dops sloop – That he wanted to shoot & as he had been threatned tho' he did not apprehend that any Injury would be done to him– yet he meant to defend himself. That Harris was enlisted by Capt Campbell that he was promised 50/ per month and Land– 400 Acres as he thinks. That he had heard that any who took up arms for the Country their Lands would be taken from them & they would be made slaves– That he was in Doubt & did not therefore sign the afsociation. That he never endeavored to enlist men & never encouraged any persons to enlist has heard some people say that they would rather join the Kings Troop than the others– That he has heard the Berghs say they would rather take up arms for the King & the Congrefs– That he has heard Mordecai Lester say he would rather take up Arms ~~for~~ against the Country than for it–That the Guns were loaded on the water coming down– no Guns fired coming down– That ~~only~~ he had two Guns on Board– that there were three pistols on Board, borrowed in the Country– he understood from Mr Philip J. Livingston that he had seen Col Grant That he saw Campbell on board of the Transport & spoke to him– he was informed they were near thirty on Board of the Transport enlisted for the Kings service– but does not know where they came from– heard they were about raising a Scotch Regim^t & heard several of the men speak scotch when they were unloading the wood– That it was talked of before they left home to go alongside of the man of war, and he understood to go to see her– he expected to go to see her– some Bread sent from on Board of H–{torn page} on board of the sloop– That he has known Mordecai Lester some years has had discourse with him about the present Troubles– he said it was wrong to take up arms ag^t the King told him it would be a great disadvantage to take up arms for the Country– called it Rebellion and said they would looss their Lands who took up Arms & be made slaves.

Monday Sept. 6ᵗʰ

read

Peter Dop– came down in the sloop with his Brothers– The sloop was loaded with Wood & 21 Bushels of wheat– This is the first time he has been down with the sloop this summer– That they intended to go into the East River with this sloop– He went on Board at home– sloop loaded six miles above– his Brother is a Blacksmith & came for Iron & told him he might come in the sloop– That thirteen men came down in the sloop and that one of them enlisted– That they got no Powder on board the man of war or Transport– that they brought four or five Guns down with them. Don't know whether they were loaded– don't remember whether they discharged any Guns on the Passage down– That when the Boats came they expected to be taken– That a woman came on Board the sloop and told them a great many people were watching for them—

Morning Septʳ· 6ᵗʰ, 1775

read

Henry Eckar Junʳ· being duely sworn on the holy Evangelists deposeth & saith that he went on Board of ~~Dops~~ Berghs sloop last monday week, That Eight of them went on Board & he expected to go {to} York in her. That when they came to Dops sloop they went on board of her—That he was two or three days at Capᵗ· Radleys before he came off & got there was talking with Capᵗ· Radley about the Troubles at New York & he the Deponent proposed to go to New York that Capᵗ· Radley told him if he went to New York he would never come back again– That Capᵗ· Radley advised him not to go in such Troublesome Times—

That he heard Berghs sloop was going to N. York and asked for a passage & got provisions ready– went on board with seven persons & came down near Stoutentberghs– That this was Dops Sloop & Bergh told him they were to go down in that sloop– That when they came on Board Dop said they were loaded {page torn} —-d{?} That he asked no Questions until they were near the man of war– That he asked why they kept so far the Dock– That one of the Dops answered you need not be afraid you're not

11

Coming to the Dock– That this was before the Lieut· of the Transport called to them that when they saild along some person from the ship asked who be ye– That one of the Berghs replied don't you know me– That they then told the sloop to come to & drop Anchor– Bergh replied Ay Ay let us get a little further from you– That they dropt anchor & lowerd their Sails– The Lieut· of the Transport came on Board of the sloop & Adam & Christian Bergh & one of the Dops went with him on Board of the man of war & returned before dark That they were not gone half an hour– That they hawld the sloop a little for safety & kept watch all night & called alls well when the man of war called– That he was cook and did not watch– That next day the {faded text unclear} {the only ––ᵈ} cords of wood in the Transport & got pay for it– The man of war took five Cords but he heard it was not paid for– That he believes he was not paid by reason of the breaking his Anchor & being oblidged to set off– That five of them were very sorry that they could not get on Shore– That the first he heard of Doughty enlisting men was here in the Dungoon– That the wood & Butter was only taken out of the sloop–That Bergh sold the Butter. That there was some wheat on Board– That they got some Buiscuits & a piece of Beef from on Board of the man of war– That after they set of {f} they saw several Boats that Christian Bergh proposed if that if there was but one Boat they could stand her if they are agreed– That Abraham Freligh Daniel Rivers Seaman & the Deponent refused and Bergh then said it was not worthwhile– that Doughty staid below in the Cabbin– That when the Boat came near he Bergh said there were too many men in it & it was best to be still– That {rest missing}.

According to the minutes of the Committee of Safety from September 6th, some of those arrested (Peter Dop, age 14, Henry Acker, Abraham Freleigh, and Daniels Rivers) were quickly discharged. Next, "Martin, Simeon and Christian Dub [Dop] were respectively examined, and after a severe reprimand from the chair, and also particular advice from many of the members, were respectively discharged." [20] Six others, though, were still in custody more than six weeks later: Christian Bergh, Jr., Adam Bergh, David Dop, John Dop, Godfrey Haines, and Timothy Doughty. In late September and early October, the men petitioned numerous times for release. They argued that their financial situation was desperate: "Dop's sloop they have burned, and Bergh's sloop the *Esopus* people fetched and sold at vendue, for the use of the Congress and God knows whether they have not stripped their families of all; Dop's sloop is burned, with a great many of our wearing apparel; all which has been done before we are brought to trial, and before it is known whether we are guilty of any crime. . . . "[21] The men, who were all confined to one room, prayed for "a speedy hearing," or the chance to go home until called to a hearing.

It is not known when all of the prisoners were finally released, although Timothy Doughty was released on October 20th after the Provincial Congress reconvened. According to the Congress minutes, Doughty, who had previously "entertained designs and opinions inimical to the great cause of American liberty," had been punished sufficiently and now "promised that he [would] further demean himself in a peaceable and orderly manner. . . . "[22]

Also during the tenure of the Committee of Safety, in mid-September of 1775, it had been decided to "disarm the Tory inhabitants of the Colony and in this way to at once render harmless any opposition to the new provincial government and to procure a supply of arms at small expense," [and] further that "any persons who would not sign the General Association in support of the American cause, were to be deprived of their arms. . . . " Dop was one of many loyalists who refused to sign the General Association.[23]

The provincial government continued its defense of the colony and was no doubt pleased when the Continental Congress took measures to authorize armed vessels "for the defense of the united Colonies" and to legalize privateering by late November of 1775.[24]

The final outcome of the Revolution is of course known. Afterwards, Yates continued his service to New York State. He ran unsuccessfully for governor against George Clinton in 1777 and 1780. In 1787, Yates (now a judge on the New York Supreme Court) was elected as one of New York's representatives to the Federal Convention in Philadelphia. Yates left the Convention abruptly though, for a variety of reasons and returned to Albany.[25]

END NOTES

[1]The First Provincial Congress met from May 22, 1775, until July 8th. The Committee of Safety, which was a form of proxy committee, functioned in

the Congress' absence from July 9th to the 25th. The Congress' second session ran from July 26 until September 2nd, whereupon the Committee resumed its duties from September 3rd until October 3rd. The Congress' third session ran from October 4th until November 4th, when it elected delegates for the Second Provincial Congress and then dissolved itself. Due to a lack of quorum, the Second Provincial Congress did not reconvene in session until December 6th, 1775, yet met in committee to hear petitions, etc. See details regarding sessions and members of New York's various forms of government in S.C. Hutchins, *Civil List and forms of Government of the Colony and State of New York, compiled from Official and Authentic Sources,* (Albany, 1869), pp.64-64, 68-69.

[2] See Agnes Hunt, *The Provisional Committees of Safety of the American Revolution,* (Cleveland: 1904), Chapter II, "The Middle Colonies," pp. 64-65.

[3] *Civil List,* pp. 62-63.

[4] *Civil List,* p. 63.

[5] [New York State], *The American Revolution in New York,* "The Committee System," (New York, 1926), pp. 34-35. See also [Alexander C. Flick], *The American Revolution in New York: Its Political and Economic Significance* (Albany, 1926), p. 51.

[6] *Civil List,* pp. 64, 68-69.

[7] See the commentary on the origins and work of the Albany Committee of Safety, in the preface by James Sullivan, *Minutes of the Albany Committee of Correspondence 1775-1778,* vol. 1, (Albany, 1923), pp. iii-vii.

[8] [New York State], *The American Revolution in New York,* "The Committee System," (New York, 1926), p. 44.

[9] *The American Revolution in New York,* p. 35.

[10] *The American Revolution in New York,* p. 51.

[11] *The American Revolution in New York,* p. 53.

[12] *The American Revolution in New York,* p. 53.

[13] See *Naval Documents of the American Revolution,* vol. I, "calendar of events for 1775," p. xl.

[13] Lispenard, Hallett, VanZandt, and McDougall were all elected representatives to the First Provincial Congress. All except Lispenard were representatives to the Second Congress, and Hallett was a member of the Third Congress. Robert Yates was a delegate to all four congresses. *Civil List,* pp. 66-68.

[15] *The American Revolution in New York,* pp. 53-54. This action by HMS *Asia* had a connection to the Dop Case, which was deposed in September 1775.

[16] See *Naval Documents of the American Revolution*, vol. I, specifically the *Journal of the New York Provincial Congress*, "[New York] Die Jovis, 9 ho. A.M., August 31, 1775," p. 1278.

[17] See the complete document regarding Governor Tryon and the *Asia* in *Naval Documents of the American Revolution*, vol. 1, pp. 23-24.

[18] See *Naval Documents of the American Revolution*, vol. I, specifically the *Journal of the New York Provincial Congress, Minutes of the New York Committee of Safety*, "[New York] Die Martis 9 HO. A.M. September 5th, 1775," p. 24. The Committee of Safety encouraged citizens to observe actions counter to the good of the colony and the activities of the sloop seemed suspect—maybe because the owners were known to have Tory sympathies and had not signed the General Agreement. On the other hand, some individuals who had directly petitioned the Committee to supply the *Asia* with necessities received approval. Dr. McClean, for example, was "at liberty to supply the said ship with drugs and medicines" and Mr. [Abraham] Lott, Colony Treasurer (for several years the Agent Victualler for his Majesty's ships), was "directed to observe in supplying the said ship with beer and water." During the 1760s, Abraham Lott had applied to be a tea factor. Richard M. Ketchum, *Divided Loyalties: How the American Revolution Came to New York*, (New York, 2002), pp. 241-242; See also information on Lott's responsibilities in *Naval Documents of the American Revolution*, vol. III, the letter from "John McKesson to Richard Sharp," [New York, January 25, 1776], pp. 978-979.

[19] *Naval Documents of the American Revolution*, vol. I. See the *Journal of the New York Provincial Congress, Minutes of the New York Committee of Safety*, "[New York] Die Martis 9 HO. A.M. September 5th, 1775," p. 24.

[20] *Naval Documents of the American Revolution*, vol. I. See *Minutes of the New York Committee of Safety*, "[New York] Die Mercurii, 9 HO. A.M. September 6th, 1775," p. 32.

[21] See also Force, comp., *American Archives*, 4th, III, p. 1267, "As there are six of us confined in jail by your order, charged with misdemeanors, we should take it kind of you if you would bring us to immediate trial, or provide us in our confinement, as we have not wherewithal to support ourselves."

[22] *Naval Documents of the American Revolution*, vol. I. See the *Journal of the New York Provincial Congress*, "[New York] Die Veneris 9 HO. A.M. October 20th, 1775," pp. 541-542.

[23] See New York (State), Secretary's Office, *Calendar of historical manuscripts relating to the war of the Revolution, in the office of the Secretary of State, Albany, N.Y.* (Albany, 1868). 2 vols. Of particular interest are items referring to Dop,

owner of the Dop sloop: pp. 82, 153-154, and 156.

[24] *Naval Documents of the American Revolution,* "calendar of events for 1775," p. xlii.

[25] *Naval Documents of the American Revolution,* " calendar of events for 1775," p. xl.

The Civil War

THE CIVIL WAR is considered by some scholars to be America's second revolution. Only eighty years after the first revolution against George III, the unresolved issues of state's rights and the abolition of slavery pitted the North against the South, father against son, and brother against brother. The following is the diary account of James Franklin of Annapolis, Maryland, as he joins a

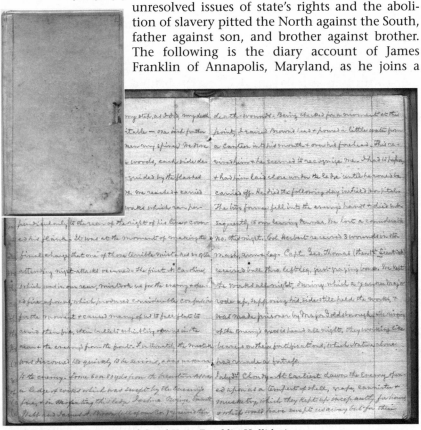

Franklin Diary. (Courtesy of Carol Yates Franklin Holliday)

Confederate unit in Virginia and is drawn north to Gettysburg, where his company fights against friends and relatives. Hoosier Joseph Johnson's tale is one of constant riding and marching, from southeastern Indiana through Kentucky, Tennessee, and finally to Georgia, where he is captured and imprisoned. There are also the Irish cousins from New

England, Thomas Doorley and Michael Stanley, who marched south and then, as a part of Grant's Army of the Potomac, fought their way through Virginia.

The Civil War was still unresolved in October of 1862, when Marylander James Franklin, then 34, left his legal practice in Annapolis. In 1860, the census showed him living next to three other younger lawyers. Franklin was unmarried and he had a mulatto boy, Lewis Turner, living with him as a servant. He also left behind his father, Thomas, a well-to do banker and his mother, Elizabeth, as well as older twin siblings.

Without the restraint of marriage and family, Franklin was eager and able to join the newly formed Confederate 1st Maryland Infantry (later re-designated the 2nd Maryland Infantry), because it comprised men of similar ilk and patriotism who valued the Southern cause and way of life. Many of the companies were recruited in Richmond, but some Marylanders, including Franklin, were distressed by the recent Confederate losses at Sharpsburg or Antietam.

Leaving the border state of Maryland was not easy, because it, as well as parts of Delaware and West Virginia, were under the control of the Union's Middle Military Department. Franklin had to plan carefully, as his diary indicates; he must have known where to go and whom to contact as he secretively made his way south. In order to get to Virginia, Franklin had to run the Federal blockade, which typically had to be accomplished under the cover of darkness and by water. He went through "B—" or Baltimore. If caught, one could be charged with running the blockade, as well as being a spy and aiding the enemy. All charges could lead to trial and then imprisonment for the duration of the war by the Federal authorities.

The first few pages of Franklin's small, oil-skin covered diary are particularly interesting. What route did he follow? Who were his contacts?

Once he made it to his regiment, Franklin continued to make notes regarding his location and movements. The smallness of the diary forced him to abbreviate his words and phrases extensively, yet because he had good penmanship and wrote with a fine pencil, it is still legible. Excerpts have been taken from his diary which focus on two significant events: his departure from Maryland and his account of the battle of Gettysburg which was possibly written just afterwards. For ease of reading, the dates in the diary have been highlighted; the spelling and abbreviations remain unchanged. (Note, in order to protect the identities of sympathetic Southerners, Franklin used long dashes where their names would have been written.)

Blockade running and joining the Maryland Line in Dixie

Augt. 11. [1862] *Left home in evg. En route for "Dixie", in company with S. F. (now Lt.) McCullough. Stopped that night at _____'s. Next day dined at _____'s, and at night left B- in sail boat in company with 17 others + started down the Patuxent. At first calm + had to row all night, but on 13th had strong breeze + whole party being in hold, came within an ace of inverting our natural position + losing "Jeff" so many recruits by the "mastery inactivity" of Capt. S. Touched at Col _____'s + proceeded down river after dark to _____'s, where we disembarked + after partaking of those things which strengthen the stomach + "make glad the heart of man", marched all night (20 miles) + reached _____'s at day-break of 15th, very tired + soaked with the rain which had fallen incessantly during the night. Dried clothes + fared sumptuously this day + the next. Expected to cross this night, but were disappointed in boat + returned + slept at _____'s.*

16th *Party clubbed in + bought a very nice yawl for $130 – Jim Railey joined party, which (now 19 —?), embarked soon after dark, + Kip deale, Tom Harrison, Ned Welch + myself taking the oars, we left behind us the soil of "Old Maryland" + struck out vigorously for "Dixie". The river here is about 9 miles wide + as we kept down the shore for some distance before heading over, we had a good 4 hrs. spell at the oars. Drew boat in march + at once marched for Westmorland Ct. H. (7ms?) (sold boat for $120 in Confeds.)*

17th *Reached Ct. H. at day-break. Hospitably entertained by Mr. _____ + his pretty daughter. Took wagons + in evg. Reached the Rapahannock, which we crossed at night where met Sam Gill + party at Cater's Ferry. Journeyed in rough wagon till we reached estate of Hon. R. M. T. Hunter, + where writer, stopping a fine horse which came a runaway down the road, passed the same into service + rode him the balance of the night.*

18th *Reached "Lloyds about 2 oc A.M. + slept till after day. Got breakfast + commenced struggle for conveyance. S.McC + self succeeded in hiring a returning carriage for $25 + expens-*

*es of boy + horses. Hospitably entertained by Mr. _____
who refused pay for dinner + horse feed. Drove all day +
reached Hanover Ct. H. at night. Put up at Hotel (honesco ref-
erens) which we left in disgust at dawn of day + reached
Ashland in time for cards*
on 19th *which (after paying 50 cts a piece to boy's Mother for
cup of coffee which she insisted on our taking before leaving)
soon brought us to Richmond.*

*In evg. Went round to Club House + met Govr. Lowe,
Capt (now Admiral) Buchanan, Maj. Griswold + other
Marylanders. A mass meeting having been called for night,
for the purpose of organizing the "Maryland Line". Govr.
Lowe + myself addressed a crowded + enthusiastic audience
at "Metropolitan Hall". Wm H. Norris Esq (now Col.) calling
the meeting to order, + Capt. Buchanan called to the chair.
After adjournment went with Govr. Lowe to his qrs. at Club
House + spent a very pleasant evg. (on the route sold Md.
money for Confed. at rate of $60 of former for $100 of latter.) Spent this day + following at "Exchange" Hotel, paying
$4 per day.*

*Met George Marden of Balt. who gave us an introduction
to Charles McIndoe + his house whither were paired + took
board at $12 per week, getting a very nice + private room +
excellent fare for the times. Marden, Tunis Bernard + Rob
Freeman (St. Marys) Edelen + Bruce, all clever fellows, board-
ing there + making the time pass very agreeably. Had a great
deal of fun in Encouraging "McI" (and little he needed) to tell
his astounding tales. Found him beyond comparison the
promptest, most amazing + plausible liar I ever met with.*
Aug. 29 *Joined the "Maryland Line" + commenced raising a
company + in a very few days got about 30 men, + in a week
more would have obtained the requisite no. for muster, but
the invasion of Maryland taking place, + activated by an
intense desire to be with the Army in the event of occupying
the State, + fearing to be left behind, waived a Captaincy +
joined forces with Jos. L. McAleer upon an agreement as to
distribution of offices, drilling the men busily in the meantime at "Camp Maryland", about 1 mile from City, on farm
formerly owned by Genl. Winfield Scott. . . .*

During the rest of 1862 and the spring of 1863, the 2nd Maryland was
largely occupied with scout and picket duty up and down the
Shenandoah Valley, with occasional forays into West Virginia to strike at
the Baltimore and Ohio Railroad. In mid-June of 1863, Franklin's unit

joined Lee's Army of Northern Virginia and marched northward to Gettysburg. This brought the war to Northern soil — Franklin was less than sixty miles from his home in Annapolis, Maryland. Franklin faithfully entered notes in his diary, except of course during the engagement from July 1st through the 3rd. He caught up with his notes on July 4th, and added some commentary, evaluating what had happened.

The Gettysburg Campaign in June and July of 1863
Marching towards Pennsylvania

. . . June 16th Marched a short distance on the Martinsburg road, and are incorporated into 3rd brigade of Johnson's Div. (Ewell Corps) commanded by B. Genl. George H. Stewart, and composed of the 10th, 23rd and 37th Va. and 1st and 3rd N.C. regts. Continue march and encamp at "Smithfield", 15 miles from W. . . .

18th Clear, hot + dusty. Marched into Shepherdstown, where we halted + out battn. Marched at shouldered arms past the other regts of the brigade at a present + take the post of honor on the right, the band playing + the rebel ladies waving flags + hdkfs. + in this order ford the Potomac and Chesapeake & Ohio Canal. . . . [?]

20th cloudy. March at 10. A.M. passing thro' "Sharpsburg" a mean old town + as union as <u>Abe</u> would desire. Women very impudent but only laughed at by our boys. Encamp 1 m. from S'bg. in woods, + walk over portion of the battle-field of "Antietam". . . .

23rd Clear. Marched via "Keetysville" + "Jones Xroads" to Hagerstown, thro' which we marched with fixed bayonets, colors flying + bands playing, + were received with strong demonstrations of Southern feeling, waving of flags + hdkfs. by the ladies &c. Cap near the "States Line", dis. marched 15 miles.

24th March at 5 A.M. thro' "Muttontown" PA, (on the line and thro' "Greencastle", where writer who had charge of rear guard, met with E. S. Riley of Annapolis. Here our brigade is detached from rest of division + took road to the left, passing thro' village of "Upton" + town of "Mercersburg", where our commissaries buy bacon, sugar, coffee, molasses &c for use of troops, paying in confeds. at Balt. prices. the men buying pipes, tobacco, candy &c continue march across North Mountain, on which some Yankee Cavy, + Militia had thrown up breastworks, but who "dusted" very quick on being treated to a shell as we advanced. Encamped at "McCon-

nellsburg", writer, guarding wagon train, getting in at midnight, + much tired from a 28 mile march. . . .

30ᵗʰ Clear. Get whiskey rations (only time) – marched at 6 A.M. repassing thro' "Shippensburg" + "Greenvillage" + taking the road to the left. Heading towards "Gettysburg". Marched 14 miles.

The Enemy Engaged

July 1ˢᵗ Cloudy. Resume march at 7 A.M. passing thro' "Fayetteville". thro gap in South Mts. + "Cashtown". As we advanced, heard heavy firing in front, and, having marched 27 miles, arrived in front of Gettysburg about sunset, where we found that heavy battle had been fought between our advance, consisting mainly of Heth's + Pender's Divns. (of A.P. Hill's Corps) and the 1ˢᵗ + 11ᵗʰ Corps of the Fedl. Army. The enemy were driven thro' the streets several miles from the town + fell back to the strong positions on the mountain heights, leaving us in possession of the field with their killed + wounded in very heavy numbers + 5000 prisoners. Pass over portion of battle-field + take our position on the left in line of battle, in which we lay down to sleep, completely tired out, at 10 P.M.

2ⁿᵈ Cloudy. Battle opened fiercely on the right + center, + the heaviest artillery fight of the war raging along the entire line, we having it is said, 160 guns playing on "Cemetery Hill" alone, + the enemy also employing it heavily. The roar was deafening + incessant – no distinguishable pause even of a second + the Heavens were literally "hung with black" by the smoke of battle. We were kept in reserve during the day in a neighboring woods, which was occasionally shelled, but "nobody hurt". saw Capt. Brown, of the Chesapeake Batty, borne from the field on litter, mortally wounded. This battery was hotly engaged & lost 17 men killed & wounded by one shell.

Just before night our brigade was formed in lines of battle, (our battn in front line) & advanced on woods covering the enemy's strong position on his extreme right & flank. Rapidly advancing, driving in the eny's skrs. before us, we crossed the creek (waist-deep) which skirts the woods a little after 8 p.m. & immediately became engaged in a fierce fight with the enemy. (It was when marching along this creek by the right flank just before fronting to cross, that I had a narrow escape, a Minnie ball dusting my coat from shoulder to *shoulder whilst looking at Sergt. Jenkin's gun which had just been struck. Had I paused for a second, whilst taking it in hand, instead of keeping up my step, as I do, my death would have been almost inevitable – one inch further back alone & it would have broken my spine. We drove the enemy steadily up thro' the woods, each side delivering volley after volley, & guided by the flashes of each others muskets. At 9 o.c. we reached & carried the outer lines of the enemy's works which ran perpendicularly to the rear of the right of his line & covered his flank. It was at the moment of making the final charge that one of those terrible mistakes so often attending night-attacks occurred – the first N.Carolina, which was in our rear, mistook us for the enemy & opened fire upon us, which produced considerable confusion for the moment & caused many of us to fall flat to avoid their fire, their bullets whistling over us in the rear & the enemy's from the front. Fortunately, the mistake was discovered too quickly to be serious, & was unknown to the enemy. Some 60 or 80 yds from the breastworks was a ledge of rocks which was swept by the enemy's fire, & in mounting this ledge Joshua Owings, Emmett Webb and James A. Brown (all of our Co.) received their death-wounds. Being checked for a moment at this point, I raised Brown's head & poured a little water from a canteen into his mouth & over his forehead. This revived him & he seemed to recognize me. I had to keep on & had him laid close under the ledge until he could be carried off. He died the following day in Field Hospital. The two former fell into the enemy's hands & died subsequently to our leaving Pennas. We lost a considerable no. this night. Col. Herbert received 3 wounds in stomach, arm & leg. Capt. Geo. Thomas (then 1st Lieut Col,) received ball thro left leg, just grazing bone. We kept the works all night, during which a Yankee Major rode up, supposing his side still held the works, & was made prisoner by Major Goldsborough. The ringing of the enemy's axes is hard all night, they working like beavers on their fortifications, which nature alone had made a fortress.*

July 3rd Cloudy. At earliest dawn the enemy opened upon us a tempest of shell, grape, canister & musketry, which they kept up incessantly for hours & which would have swept us away but for their own fortification, securely protected by which, we suffered very little loss. Had every lump of ice in a hailstorm been a bullet, the forest behind us could scarcely have been more effectually peeled, riddled + swept with lead + iron. The enemy's infantry made several advances to retake *the works, but were each time repulsed by a steady fire from our line. Shortly before 10. A.M. we were marched by the left flank from these works, formed in rear of woods in two lines of battle (the 1st Md, + 3rd N.C. being in the 1st line) at right angles to these works, + advancing to the charge of the rear of the almost impregnable hill which formed the key to the enemy's position, Gen. Geo. H. Stewart, assisted by his aid Lt. Duncan McKim, dismounting + leading the charge. We advanced rapidly driving in the skirmish line of the enemy to the base of the mountain, but when in close range of that were met by a most murderously destructive fire which sheeted down in <u>layers</u> from rank above rank of the enemy in heavy force in front + enveloping each flank, which soon broke our rank + brought the men by scores to the ground. The line was broken, was rallied for a moment + advance attempted, only to be instantly broken by a fire which it was but suicide to advance against, and reluctantly the order was given to retreat + we were withdrawn to the Creek at the skirt of the woods, losing, including the attack of the night before, one half of our officers + men in killed + wounded. (196) The gallant Maj. Goldsborough was wounded + taken prisoner. The brave Capt. Wm H. Murrary was instantly killed, with many another brave fellow in this 5 minutes fearful work, + many too badly wounded to escape, were taken by the enemy + spent many many months of captivity in their hands (**at the date of transcribing this, 4th July**, 64 Col. Herbert being yet at Johnson's Isld + intelligence recd of death of Maj Goldsborough in Baltimore). The enemy's sharpshooters kept up a severe fire on us in the evg. Morrison (Co. A) being killed, + Lipscomb of our Co. + Radecke (Co E) wounded by almost instantly successive shots. The enemy s.s. [sharpshooters] were in front + flank concealed by trees, rocks + bushes, + in the tree-tops, whilst reclining against a tree, a bullet struck closely my head, instantly after another grazed my foot, + moving some 8 or 10 paces I had scarcely seated myself when a third struck just above my head. Doubtless I had been recognized as an officer by my uniform coat + sword + had been made the target of some persistent sharpshooter. Thanks to a merciful providence, I escaped unhurt in this fearful lottery of life or death. (incident of s.s^r.) Gen. Steuart disclaimed all responsibility for this reckless charge + inept [attack] at the loss of so many of his brave men. The 3rd N.C. suffered as severely as we; the reserve line never got under fire. We remained in woods near the ck. all evg. + slept in line of* *battle, being awakened about 10 P.M. by a volley from the enemy. We advanced + gave them a volley, when they retired to their breastworks, when we again lay down, + enjoyed without further disturbance our much needed sleep till awakened at 1 A.M.* **on the 4th.**

Franklin took great pains at the end of the battle to record all of the casualties from the 2nd Maryland – there were not many officers left to do this recording. Lee brought the war to the North, but his hopes for a decisive victory quickly evaporated.

Lee's Army In Retreat

July 4th At 1 A.M. we withdraw from woods, recross the creek + march to woods on elevated ground on nearly the opposite side of town to "Cemetery Hill", rest till day-break, when we throw up breastworks + place arty in position. rains. we here await the enemy, having a fine position, but he declines to attack, his skrs. even not advancing within 400 yds. We burn a frame house in suburb of town to prevent its being made a cover for the enemy's S. Srs.[sharp shooters] being the only property destroyed at Gg [Gettysburg]. Gen. Steuart gave me his field-glass + sent me out to observe + report the movements of the enemy. Towards evg. I plainly saw that he was stealing back his skrs.[skirmishers] + saw, through gaps in the woods, whole brigades moving off – evidencing the fact beyond contradiction that Meade moved first from the field. I walked in the evg. over the battle field of the 1st, yet covered with the unburied dead of the enemy. The corpses were perfectly black, swollen, + very offensive, lying writhed + contorted in every conceivable attitude of their death agony.
5th We march at 1 A.M. 5 miles, + halt, on the Hagerstown road. rains. March again at 4 P.M., slight cannonading heard in our rear – Early shelling back some cavy [cavalry]. (It is said he did it to hurry up our wagon train). After a very rough + muddy march, camped 21 ms. from Hagerstown.
6th Resume march, cross mountains + camp at Waynesborough – 175 of our wagons were captured by enemy's cavy today, but all except 2- were recaptured by J. E. B. Steuart. The horses were shamefully cut away from our baggage wagon, when there was no necessity for it + contents all lost, including my box, overcoat, blankets, + everything I had. In consequence of this I had to sleep, or <u>try</u> *to sleep, in the cold, rainy nights, without the slightest covering, suffering*

severely + resulting in my subsequent sickness. Marched 12 miles today.

7th   Rainy. March + camp 2 ? miles from Hagerstown. Our cavy had sharp fight with that of the enemy, with sabre + revolver – the enemy getting the worst of it. . . .

10th clear. Still at same camp. At 6 P.M. leave + march thro' Hagerstown, 5 miles + camp. (3 miles from Williamsport)

11th cloudy. Take position to give battle + throw up breast-works. . . .

13th Meade, altho' his line of battle was but 1 1/2 m. dist. still declining to attack, at 8 1/2 P.M. in the rain, we quietly withdraw to Williamsport, spending a most tiresome night in its dirty streets, half-knee deep with mud, in crowded ranks, moving foot by foot as the troops in advance ford the river.

14th Reached the Potomac at day break + crossed. our corps crossed at two fords, about 150 yds apart, water nearly up to the arm-pits. Quite an interesting sight to witness the long streams of men threading the river. Writer was ferried over by John Boyl, behind him, on his horse. The other troops cross at "Falling Waters", where a fight occurred between our rear + the enemy, both sides claiming the advantage, + occasioning Meade's criticism on Lee's report. We'll bet our pile that "Uncle Bobby"'s right. Camp 3 1/2 miles from "Martinsburg", having marched 9 miles today.

The Confederate defeat at Gettysburg brought discouragement, but also time for reflection. Franklin wondered why they had not succeeded:

Thus ended the invasion of Maryland + Pennsylvania, + virtually the campaign of 1863. All conceding the splendid strategy of Lee in transferring the theater of war to the enemy's soil, and in again withdrawing his army, in the face of the enemy, over a wide and rapid river without the loss of so much as a wagon wheel, ~~the query is often~~ and the heroic + almost unrivalled process exhibited by our troops, the query is often made – why was not our success still more decided, and why were we, supposed to have the opportunity of selecting our own battle-field, forced to attack the enemy, so strongly fortified upon ground of his own choosing? To this I answer:

1st That Gen. Lee never anticipated a fight at Gettysburg, or that any fight at all would rear when it did, but relied upon the Cavalry to keep him informed of the enemy's movements in time to collect his columns, which were scattered on many *different roads, and when concentrated so dispose them as to compel Meade to fight him on terms of his own choosing. Gen. Lee <u>was not</u> informed of the proximity of the enemy. (see his official report, in which with his characteristic delicacy he states this fact) and the opposing forces met where the enemy had + availed himself of the vantage ground. Gen. Lee was thus necessitated to hurry up his forces to support those already engaged , + to attack the enemy <u>where he found him</u>.*

    2nd When we and other re-enforcements arrived on the battle-field on the evg. of 1st July, the 1st + 11th corps of the enemy were badly whipped, with a loss of 5000 prisoners + a heavy list of killed + wounded. They had not as yet got much of their artillery in position, nor fortified the heights to which they retired. Gen. <u>Early</u> strongly advocated an immediate and general assault upon the heights. Had his proposition been adopted, the already disunited enemy would have been driven from the hill, (of course with expected loss to us, but insignificant in comparison with that subsequently suffered in repeated attacks) which would have given us the key to the enemy's whole position + entirely revised the whole advantage + aspect of the fight. Unfortunately, Early was over[ruled] in led [?] (for the alleged reason that the men were tired + needed rest) the enemy occupied every moment of the night and of the next day until the attack was made, in fortifying the heights, planting his batteries, and massing his troops as they arrived. (Meade, in his official report, states that 7000 troops arrived during the night.) When the attack was eventually made, the whole range of hills, naturally very strong, was thoroughly fortified, formed with artillery, + was defended by immense numbers, so as to be impregnable to assault.

    3rd The artillery fire which we opened + continued without a second's cessation on the 2nd + 3rd was most probably unprecedented in the annuls of war. <u>160 guns were playing upon "Cemetery Hill" alone.</u> The slaughter of the enemy, crowded upon the heights, was terrific, the principal portion of his admitted fearful mortality lists being here made up. His own surgeons, who came into our lines by permission to assist the care of his wounded, represented to us that it was one frightful slaughter-pen. I have heard + believe the expressed opinion of those competent to judge – that could we have sustained this deathly fire but a short time longer, the enemy must have abandoned the position. But such a fire requiring an immense expenditure of, nearly exhausted our ammunition, of which we had then to economise the use until more *was brought from a distant base of supplies as we fell back.*

Such are the reflections of an impartial (if a participant can be impartial) observer of the Campaign upon a point which has been, + will be, the subject of a great contrarity of views, + which will furnish material to the future Historians of both sections to follow widely, divergent paths. Let facts which admit no dispute suffice: That Lee from being besieged in the outer lines which defended his Capital became, as if by magic, the sudden ——————— [?] of that of his adversaries +"gobbling" the strongly defended + important posts of Winchester + Harpers Ferry in his path, reversed the role of invader + defended with his adversary whom he had outwit-ted, filled with consternation for the safety of their own homes the deluded people who awaited with prospective delight the promised "fall of Richmond", relieved Virginia at an opportune season of the heavy burden of war, collected + brought in his triumphal train immense spoils taken from the enemy, fought that enemy in stronghold of his choice, inflict-ed a loss upon him of at least thirty thousand men, (and many put it at a higher figure) with not half that loss of his own; and leisurely recrossed the Potomac in the face of an enemy whom he had so badly crippled as to decline battle repeatedly wagered on his route, and from which he [the enemy] did not recover but sought safety in flight in the inde-cisive campaign of the following autumn. These undisputed facts ample suffice (without calling to aid still more over-whelming proofs) to place Robert E. Lee in the first rank of the world's strategists + to crown the gallant men who were the executors of his conceptions with imperishable [?] renown.

After the defeat at Gettysburg, Franklin and the 2nd Maryland fought in other engagements, including Cold Harbor, near Petersburg, Virginia, on June 3rd, 1864. Following this battle his unit took a defensive position around Petersburg in July and August of 1864. When Franklin was cap-tured southwest of Petersburg on August 19, 1864, at the battle along the Weldon Railroad, his diary abruptly ends. He was sent north to the Old Capitol Prison in Washington, D.C. on August 22nd, and from there to Fort Delaware, which was located in the middle of the Chesapeake. After more than eight months of imprisonment, in May of 1865, Franklin wrote to inform his old friend Samuel T. McCullough, who was a prison-er at Johnson Island on Lake Erie, that he and the other Maryland offi-cers imprisoned at Ft. Delaware were considering taking the oath of alle-giance.

We considered that we had done all that could be

*required; that there was no longer an armed & organized force
E. of the Mississippi; that the Confederacy is surely virtually
at an end. . . . Under the circumstances, we considered that
other duties—to ourselves & our families required that we
should no longer for the sake of an empty purpose, self-sub-
ject ourselves to the further continuance of troubles & hard-
ship, but adapt our course as readily as possible to the necessities of the Situation.[1]*

Franklin took the oath and was released on June 17th, 1865. A month
later, he applied for a presidential pardon. He returned to Annapolis after
the war, resumed his legal practice, and served as a clerk in the court of
appeals and he was a state attorney. Franklin resided with his unmarried
sister, Anne, through the 1870s and 1880s. Franklin died at the relatively young age of 54 in March of 1881.

PRIVATE JOSEPH McCLUNG JOHNSON
COMPANY F, FIFTH INDIANA CAVALRY OR
90TH INDIANA VOLUNTEER REGIMENT

Joseph Johnson was a lifelong resident of Indiana. At the age of
eighteen, in August of 1862, he enlisted in the town of Clermont,
Indiana. Johnson's regiment was responsible for scouting along the
Cumberland River in Kentucky, in the Western Theater of the war. By the
summer of 1863, though, the war became decidedly more interesting as

his regiment left its camp in pursuit of
John Morgan's Raiders in southern
Indiana and Ohio. On July 19th, the
regiment attacked Morgan's forces at
Buffington Island. From there, the reg-
iment marched on to Knoxville,
Tennessee.

From the latter half of 1863
through February of 1864, Johnson
kept a diary-like account of the 5th
Cavalry's movements. Sometime after
the war, Johnson composed a type-
written account of his experiences,
which were probably based on his earlier diary. From this account, it is possible to understand the extreme
mobility of the cavalry as his unit

Joseph McClung Johnson. (Courtesy
of Martha Sue Batt)

moves all over Kentucky and Tennessee. His family also saved some letters that he wrote in May and June of 1864. Of greater interest, though, are a couple of his letters written from Georgia in 1864. Johnson's original spelling and punctuation has been kept as originally written.

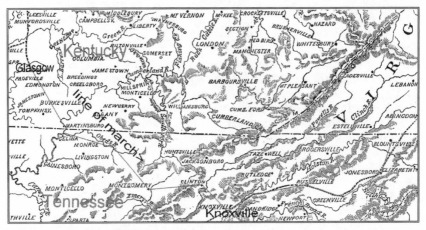

Johnson's cavalry line of march. Map adapted from *Harper's Illustrative History of the Civil War* (1866).

"Diary" Account

The Chickamauga Campaign began on August 16th, 1863. The Battle of Chickamauga lasted from September 19th through the 21st.

> *August 1st, 2nd, 3rd, 4th marched to Lebanon, 5th, 6th, and 7 lay there, 8th marched to Green River, 9th marched to Glasgow, got there at midnight, went into camp. . . . 18th, started for Tennessee, marched to Says Cross roads, 19th and 20th lay there in camp, 21st marched to Marrow Bone, 22nd marched to Mud Camp on the Cumberland River, 23rd marched to Kittee Creek, 24th marched to the Obe River, Tennessee, 25th marched 14 miles over the mountain, camped in a grove, 26th marched to the east fork of the Obe River, 27th marched 6 miles south of Jamestown. . . . 29th marched to Montgomery on top of mountain, 30th marched to Watterbury, 3 miles only, 31st marched to Poplar Creek, camped in a gap of the mountain.*
>
> *September 1st marched to Knoxville, Company F went back 9 miles, captured two prisoners and two car loads of pro-*

visions, 2nd returned to Knoxville, 3rd marched to the cross roads 13 miles southeast of Knoxville, 4th marched 5 miles past Sevierville and back there camped, 5th marched back to Knoxville, 6th marched to Severiville, 7th marched to the foot of Smoky Mountains to attach [attack] a rebel camp but they had gone, marched back to Seveirville. . . . 9th marched to Pigeon River, 10th marched to Newport crossed French Broad River and reached Greenville. . . . 12th left Greenville, went 7 miles up the river road, went into camp for the night, 13th held our camp, there Co. F sent out to look for rebs, found them within 3 miles, fired a few shots, the rebs ran, we drove them within 3 miles, fired a few shots, the rebs ran, we followed and drove in there pickets, captured 5 of them, 14th Co. F sent out with other Co. drive in the rebel pickets and came back to camp that night, we fell back 3 miles towards Greenville, 15th returned back to camp, 16th our battalion went out 2 miles met the rebs, had a skirmish, drove them, 17th lay in camp 7 o'clock that night we started on a march went about 5 miles, lay and held our horses by the bridal or halter till morning, 18th marched till afternoon, came in contact with a lot of rebs, routed them, killed one, captured several of the rebs, we got two men wounded by one of the cassions blowing up and two wounded in a skirmish, camped near Kingsport, 19th marched to Bristol, had a skirmish with the rebs, took 30 prisoners, we got one lieutenant and one private wounded, we burnt there commissary stores, turned back and marched to Bluntville and camped for the night, 20th marched at daylight towards Zollicoffers, went 2 miles, routed and drove there pickets into their main force skirmish and cannonaded same till about noon when we were ordered to fall back, we fell back a few miles and camped for the night, 21st marched towards Jonesborough, marched all day, camped, 22nd turned and marched back the same road, met the rebs about 10 o'clock at Holston River, they skirmished and fell back across the Holston and back to Bluntville where we came onto their mane force, we fought them till near night when they were routed with considerable loss in killed and wounded and a loss of 82 prisoners, our loss and killed in the fight was one and but two wounded, the town was burned in the time of fiting,. . . .

Johnson's diary ceases in February of 1864. Fortunately, he also wrote letters to his father, William, and his brother, Nelson, who were farming in Brownsburg, Indiana. In May of 1864, as part of the Atlanta

Campaign, Johnson's cavalry engaged with the enemy during the Battle of Resaca, on May the 14th and 15th and during the advance on Dallas, Georgia, on the 18th through the 21st.

Camp here in line of battle
May the 17/64

Father I received your letter yesterday. I was glad to gett a letter from home for I hadent had a letter sine we left Ky. There hasent bin a day since we left Ky. that the saddles has bin off of our horses. It is pretty hard work to fite every day and that is what we have bin at all the time ever since we gott down here. We are within 40 miles of Atlanta fiting all the time, day and nite. Yesterday there was 10 wounded in our ridgement but none killed. We have bin in line of battle 2 days and nites. We are driving them all the time but they have got to a place that they don't drive very fast know you _____ these and any of our Co. gott hurt yet there was three taken prisoners. They any byt about 25 men in the Co. at this time. The most are dismounted and sent back to parts on the railroad and some are back sick also. I haven't heard from Richmond since we started for Ky. and I should like very well to hear something that is a going on in other places and I want you to tell lme all the news that you can think of and write as soon as this comes to hand. I would write oftener if the male would go out. It is only _____ that the male goes out. We are laying behind the breast works at this time. Our horses are standing back in the roads. We are looking for reinforcements to come to releave us tonight and then I think that we will gett to sleep. We are at it fast and thick.

I shall have to close for the present. Write as soon as this comes to hand.

I am well and harty this far but don't know how long I may remain so. Think that we will be in Atlanta before a week.

J.M. Johnson

Camp of the 5th Cavalry at Atlanta, Georgia
June the 5th/64

Dear Brother:

This is the first time I halve the opertunity of setting myself to drop you a few lines to let you know that I am well this far and hoping when these few lines comes to hand that they may find you well. The boys are all well that are here.

*They halve nearly all gone back to stations on the railroad.
There is only a fiew horses in the Co. There is only 14 at this
time and there is one of two gives out every day that we
march. It wont be long till there wont be a horse in the Co.
and then I guess that we can all go a foot. For my part I ant
afraid as long as there is a horse in the Co. for I halve the best
horse in the Co but halve a good deal of riding to do as there
any but a very fiew in the Co.*

*Well Nelson we are playing hob with these John rebs. We
halve drove them within 41 miles of Atlanta. We halve bin
laying here for the last two weeks fiting all the time and the
word is this morning that they got up last night and dug out
for some other point unknown to us and we ant a caring for
we will follow them as far as they can run without they go in
the gulf and then I think that we shall stop and not before.
We halve had some pretty hard fiting to do since we halve bin
down here. A little the closest place that I halve ever bin in
was day before yesterday General Stoneman started me
through with 5 or 6 men to General Scofield with a dispatch,
the distance being about 10 miles. When we had gott out
about 5 miles we run into a squad of rebs. There was about
30 of them and they were hid in the bushes till we came up.
We had one man on ahead for an advance guard. Then they
came out in the road and took the man that was in front and
came pretineer getting the rest. Would halve gotten us all only
we happened to spy them coming out to the road side close to
us and we separated and began to get out of there just as fast
as our horses could carry us. They kept up a heavy as long as
they could see us but dident happen to hitt any of us. While
we were getting out we layed flat down on our horses then
came on back to camp and the General ordered out a ridgement to clear the road and as soon as the road was thought
to be clear we started on. Reached there about noon. Stayed
there until about eight or nine o'clock and then had to come
back on that same road that we went out on and the ridgement had left and gone on. We met with nothing on the road
till we came to our pickets and they had no orders to pass and
when we came up within about 10 steps of them and they
began to fire on us. There was one man in front that got a ball
through his pants numing his leg but not hurting him and
another ball through his back. And that is all of that.*

*Write as soon as this comes to hand for I should like to
hear from you for it has bin sometime since I heard from you*

or any of the rest and letters are so old that they don't seem
like news from home.

J.M. Johnson

At the end of July, while near Macon, Georgia, Johnson was taken prisoner of war and sent to the infamous Andersonville Prison in South Carolina. Johnson's parents saved a letter written by him to them on October 7th.

Florence, South Carolina
[Andersonville Prison]
Dear Pearance [parents]:
I am well. Tell John Duncans folks that he is well. Father
I sent for a box here the other day and know I will send for
others. One peck of dried fruit, 50 lbs. of met ham if conven-
ient, 50 lbs of pilat break, one small cheese, 15 lbs. of dried
sausage, _____ lbs of army _____ vegitable, 10 lbs. of dried
beef butes, jelly, 1 lb. of pepper and salt. Tell John Duncans
folks to make out half of the box. In the other letter I sent for
1 pare of pants, one shirt, one pare of shoes and socks and I
want them if the other letter don't gett through safe. Send
things that you think will save. I want some thread and some
stuff for patches with. Direct to Joseph M. Johnson, Co. F, 5
Cav, 30 ridgement, Indiana, Vol. Prison Camp, Florence,
South Carolina, Joseph M. Johnson respects to parents.

October 7, 64

Johnson suffered horribly while at Andersonville. He was incarcerated there after his capture on July 31st, 1864, until February 27th, 1865, when he was paroled at N.E. Ferry, North Carolina. From there he was sent to College Green Barracks in Maryland on March 5th, and then on to Camp Chase in Ohio on March 10th. Sometime after his return home, and with some strength regained, Johnson composed the following about Andersonville:

Andersonville Prison Memoirs

Anderson prison where I suffered for several months all
the woes which traitors hands and fiendish rage could inflict.
I had often read when a boy of the barbarities of the Indians
and of their cruel treatment to those whom they captured in
war, but I little dreamed of seeing and experiencing for more
crewel treatment from the hands of those who call themselves
the enlightened chivaltry of the south. Crowded together in a

narrow prison pen with thousands of my fellow soldiers, I soon realized to its fullest extent the sorrows of the last four years of cruel war. The rations issued to each man for one day were either a pint of meal or beans changed every few days for a morsel of bread and meat. On such a diet the men wasted away and died by the hundreds from starvation. I saw manly forms which once had bloomed with health and vigor grow thin and pail from desease and famine and at last dying, their victims borne by their sorrowing companies to the common burial grounds. I saw the war tears flow oeer many a youthful cheek as the young warrior bade his comrades a last good-bye and send the last sweet words to friends at home, but as he bowed his form to die _____.

Johnson stated, and this was also corroborated by other prisoners who knew him, that he suffered extensively from "cramp colic," which began to plague him in December of 1864. A starvation diet while at Andersonville, plus inclement weather conditions and a prevalence of disease, did much to debilitate and kill thousands at the prison. Johnson also believed, though erroneously, that he had "contracted disease of the stomach" and his case of "scurvy [was] caused by lying in the rain."[2]

Johnson was officially discharged on June 27th 1865, at which time he returned home to Indiana. He resided with his father for almost three years while he regained his health. In March of 1867 he married Mary W. Wright in New Augusta. They raised three children, Cora (b. 1868), Elmsley (b. 1878), and William (b.1881). Although Johnson had been a farmer prior to the war, his health no longer permitted that and so he worked as a merchant in New Augusta. Miraculously, Johnson managed to outlive many other Civil War veterans. An unfortunate accident took his life in 1932 while he was crossing a road.

PRIVATES THOMAS DOORLEY & MICHAEL STANLEY
COMPANY I, 57TH MASSACHUSETTS VOLUNTEER REGIMENT
NINTH ARMY CORPS

Two Irish boys reenlisted from Berkshire County, Massachusetts, as veterans from the 1st Massachusetts Cavalry. Would the upcoming summer of 1864 finally bring an end to almost three years of bloodshed? Doorley and Stanley would soon do their duty and support each other when their regiment joined the Army of the Potomac. Doorley and

Stanley were cousins; their mothers, Kate and Ellen respectively, were sisters. One had married Michael Doorly (also spelled Donley) and the other had married Michael Stanley, Sr. back in the "old country" (Ireland).

Michael Doorley, Thomas' father.
(Courtesy of Shirley Temple)

They immigrated within a couple years of one another to the United States, sometime between 1847 and 1852. The Doorley and Stanley families settled down in the town of North Becket, Berkshire County. The boys' letters are few and far between, and some of Stanley's letters can be found in his mother's pension application, located in the National Archives. (Note, Thomas Doorley's letters include no punctuation. Therefore, spaces have been incorporated to indicate new sentences.)

Thomas Doorley wrote some friends as soon as he joined his regiment:

Worcester Camp Wool
feb 27 1864
57th Regt Mass Vols
Dear friends   I take my pen
In hand to rite you a few lines to let you [know] that I have not forgot my Promises Dear friends I want to Let you now that I could Not have my picture Taken In Northhampton   It was late when we were Examined so we had to go Right straight abourd of the Cars for worcester   we are going to be mustered In Tuesday or Wednesday and then we will get seven or eight days furlough   you will let fathr And mother now you heard From me
I am sorry today that I cannot tell you where To rite to me   we have not Chosen our company yet   So you must not rite till you hear from me again
No more at present From your affectionate Friend
Thomas Doorley
So good by

Worcester
March the 8th 1864
Dear Parents with pleasure i embrace the presant opertunity

of writing these few lines to ye hoping to meet ye all enjoying good health as this leaves us in at presant thank god for his mersies to us all   Dear parents I received your kind and welcome letter last night and it gave me mutch pleasure to here from home   we are not mustered in yet or we don't no when we will   it canot be long for the company is almost full   we are all well and enjoy ourselves tip top   i like the soldiers   fair pretty well so far   my uncle and lackey Sealey was here and brought andrew and peter home with them   lett us no where tey are when ye write again   my hand is getting along very well   i had to laugh when I herd old brad was dead   lett me no when ye write if ye are engaged to work another year in middlefield or not   lett me no If Robert is going to work another year or not   lett me no if aney one els left the factory since or not   theire is some boys in our company that we are acquainted with   ensign Simons and frank dible and Jack casey and denis colins and pat the blacksmith . we think this regiment wont leave here before the first of June   we have plenty of fun here plenty to eat and nothing to Do onley to answer to roolcall   we have not drilled aney yet of aney Consequence i was very glad ye were content after me for all that troubled me was ye

No more at present but we all join in sending our love and best respects to ye all our friends after us   give my love to your aunt Gesack   write soon and lett me no all the particulars for i like to here often from ye

Write soon   soon   soon
soon   soon   soon   soon
When you write Direct to
Thomas Doorley Camp Wool
57 reg Worcester Mass

[names followed with stenciled letters]
Thos. Doorley
Co. 57. M.V.N.
John Jennings
John Watters
Cor. Mahoney

March the 23 1864

My dear parents i take my pen in hand to write your these few lines hoping to find you in good health as this leaves me in at present   thank god forit   I have just resieved your letter   i felt bad to heer that James was hurt i am sory that mother is poor in health i am well in health buta sore neck i have a receipt from Mr Root I will get the lieutenant to sine it and then you will get the town Bounty i would rite before but i thought i would get a furlough we got our Guns yesterday i have ben on gard fore a week the boys are all well and In good health we are on Drill every Day i am Going home some Day this week i will have to go home a lone for the boys Cant get a furlough to Geather the Soldiers down here are all got the measels There is 40 or 50 in the hospittle John Waters And Micheal Stanley Sends Their love and best respects to ye all this regament is going to leave here in a bout 8 Days this is my own riting i don't think you can reat it iwill get sow i can rite pretty well i have a very sore throte my thum is most well and drawed my months wages Tuesday i Cant Think of any more to say write soon and let me know All the particulars

No mor is at present but remain your afectionate Son
Thomas Doorley

Thomas sent another letter to his father, Michael Doorley:

Saturday Camp Woll [Wool]
April the 16 /64

With a Sory full hart i take my pen in hand to let you know that i am not Going to have a furloug Wee are going away to Day wee are going to get our bounty this after noon and i will Send mine to middlefield in Care of the Church . . . wee are going to anapolis in maryland in one of the most dangeros places & then we will be marched right in front of richmond that is where some of them will find out Soldier fun i feel bad to think that i cant go home John Waters has got back his [furlough] was the last one given out i must make up my mind to bid you good by for three years mabe for ever i little thought it was the last time i think that you cant write till I write and send my Direction to ye I must close by Sending my love to andrew and Peter and all the rest of the folks

write Soon
So good by for three years
Thomas Doorley

Michael Stanley fit the image of an Irish boy with his blue eyes and sandy complexion. He was of average height, 5' 5", and at age twenty, he was ready to rejoin the cause as a veteran volunteer. He was the eldest of five children and his generous bounty was a welcomed addition to the stretched family finances. His younger brother, Andrew, who was seventeen, remained at home to help, while his mother, Ellen, had much to do in caring for John (11), Catherine or "Katie" (6), and infant William (10 months). His father was a laborer, yet literate. Michael sent news home regarding his cousin, Thomas Doorly, and his neighbor, Michael Waters, who were marching south with him.

April the 29th 1864

My Dear parents   I take up my pen in hand to address you a few lines hoping they may find you in good health as the aspect of this leaves me at the present. I thank God for his mercy to us all my dear parents and we left here for the south 13 days ago we have been on the tramp ever since but we have not got to the place [next few lines largely illegible] *- - - any until - - - - Washington ever since - - - - I will tell you all the jabber* [?] *when — - - although we have been in Washington, Alexandria, Arlington Heights, Centerville, bulls run and Fairfax Courthouse.*

We are now at Catholics station but we expect to leave tomorrow or the day after. We are going to join the Army of the Potomac and I expect we will be in battle inside of ten days and I hope ye will pray for our welfare. We are in General Burnside's Division, first brigade and first division, 9th Army Corps.

Dear parents ye will excuse this letter as I had to march two days since I first commenced riting it. We're now on the [branch?] *of the Rappahanock river that is about 7 miles from Fredericksburg. This is what they call Rappahanock station and we are guarding it from the guerileas. There is considerable many of them hovering round here now. Ye would be surprised to se all the men that was on the march with us. There was about a hundred thousand all together.*

You will let me [k]*now in the ansr of this letter if you received the two hundred and seventy five dollars I sent you from Camp Wool. I expect we will get sixty or seventy dollars more before long. Dear father 10th and 37th are within 3 miles of us. The*[y] [are] *at brandy station. I have very good health all except my eyes they are very sore and I would like you to send me some of the best stuff you can find. Make me some eye water and let me* [k]*now so I learn to make it.*

Thomas Doorley and John Waters are in very good health at present and send their love and best respects to ye. I have a watch I bought in Camp Wool and if have an opportunity I will send it [to] *Johney. I would send it to Andrew but I don't*

think him worthy of it.
    No more at present from your affectionate son Michl
Stanley
Please rite soon. Direct your letter
Michl Stanley
Co I 57th regt Mass Vetteran Volunteers
Rappahanock Station off Washington DC or elsewhere

In the spring of 1864, Grant resolved, even if it took all summer, to engage his Army of the Potomac against Lee's forces in an effort to break the deadlock between their two armies. The Battle of the Wilderness began the first week of May, but all did not go in Grant's favor. The engagement in the Wilderness proved disastrous; the men had to fight a sanguinary battle amidst an impenetrable tangle of brush and briars that was often set afire by shells and ammunition. Neither Thomas nor Michael had time to write much news home. Thomas wrote his first letter a week and a half after the beginning of the campaign.

May the 17 1864
Dear parents i take my pen in hand to let you know my mis fortune and bad luck on the 6 of may wee was in a battle   we was cut down like grass   o deer Michael Stanley was killed Shot in the head   Denis Colins was wounded with a ball through the foot and John Waters is sick in the hospital   i am all a lone Friday i was in a nothr battle the first battle went in with 90 men in our Company and came out with 40 the last time went in with 40 and came out with 5   thank god i am well yet
Direct your leter to Washington DC
our regiment went into the first battle with 1000 men and now there is 200 and 16 left
we are driving the rebels every day   deer father and mother Dont fret a bout me i will Come home yet   I have a medel of honer for Courage in battle i did not get an answer for my last leter   i cant write any more for Sixty Days   Wee are going to fite to night good By
I feel lonesome since Michael was killed   this is writing on the ground

More than a month later, the 57th Massachusetts and various other regiments had slogged their way bloodily ever further southward and to the left around Richmond in the direction of Petersburg. They left a trail of destruction and growing losses as they moved from one engagement to the next, from North Anna, to Totopotomoy, to Cold Harbor, and finally to Petersburg, where Grant's army settled into siege positions.

Petersburg was only a short distance south of Richmond, but a long distance from ending the war. Thomas wrote home once again:

> **Petersburg**
> **June the 27 1864**
>> Deer father and mother brother and sister   i received you leter Which gave me the greatest pleasure to here from you being well in health as this leaves me in at present   thank god for his mercy to us all   i received three leters this morning   i was in a battle friday but i came out all safe that god but poor John Watres was killed in the batle   i did not get the box you sent me i cano get it now   i had a leter from Tom Waters yesterday Saing that ye was all well   one of your leters spoke of Michael Stanley   he was killed in the woods and wee had to run and leave the dead ded on the field and don't know what was done with them   i have no money   i would like if you Send me 5 Dollars we will not be paid till next fall till this campaign is over   when you write to me send me a envelop and paper in your leter for i cant get any out here   it is awfull hot out here now   i have not sene a Drop of rain this two months   it is imposible for me to get my picture taken here   i feel lonesome for my brother James   give my love and best respects to all the boys and girls   no more at present   good by   write every week
>>
>> Direct your leter to Thomas Doorley Co I 57 regt Mass vols 1 brigade 1 division 9 army Corp Washington DC
>> Send all your leters to Washington DC

Grant's army was soon reduced to trench warfare, where the troops suffered further casualties from brutal summer heat and humidity, malaria, and dysentery. These problems wer exacerbated by continual heavy marching—brutal engagements also took their toll. Desperate situations required more desperate measures, and by the middle of July, Burnside had agreed to the construction of a tunnel and mine system under the fortifications. But even this came to naught. Even more discouraging was the news sent home to Doorley's parents from the captain of his company:

> **Petersburg Va**
> **July 29th '64**
>> Mr Doorlye
>> I have sad news for you. Yesterday Thomas went to the Hospital and the same night he was worse and Died. he has not been well for some time   I never saw such a change in a person in my life as in him & went to the Dr with him and

*told him he ought to go to the Hospital and he said he would
have him go   I sent for an ambulance and he went*

*The news came this morning and I inform you imediate-
ly he was liked by all ever accomodateing and always done
his duty we have to morn the loss of A Friend, there was not
one but liked him, I will give you the particulars as soon as I
learn them*

Yours Truly
Sergt Howard
Co I 57th Mass Vols

END NOTES

[1]Kevin Conley Ruffner, *Maryland's Blue & Gray*, "The Shattered Vision,"
(Louisiana, 1997), p. 147. Comments are based on a letter from Franklin to
McCullough, April 30, 1865.
[2] RG 94, National Archives, Pension record for Joseph M. Johnson.

World War I

WORLD WAR I was the first conflict that spanned the entire globe. From its bizarre origination in Serbia to Southeast Asia, the battles raged on. The new advances in technology, such as artillery, airplanes, and tanks, only added to the mounting casualties. Many soldiers never returned from battle; or they came back in caskets, and along with them came their compatriots' letters. Their longing for communication with the world they left behind allows us to document this wartime era.

One Australian soldier who wrote intriguing letters was George R. Duncan. As he moved from Australia to the Middle East to France, he shows us how this conflict affected each corner of the globe. Benjamin Hendin, a Russian Jew, also traveled across several continents. However, he had a different cause – Hendin was fighting for the Jewish state in Palestine that the British had promised in the Balfour Declaration. Leon Farmer was not directly involved in combat, but his unit, the 8th Aero Squadron (Observation) in the U.S. Signal Corps, observed the movements of the Germans along the French and Belgium border at the St. Mihiel Salient. His story starts in San Antonio, Texas, and stretches all the way to France. Finally, there is Warren Williams, who was from Wisconsin. He was a member of both the Marines Corps and the Navy. He, like the others, witnessed all the horrors of World War I – why then was he not as eager as those others to go back to America after his duty was done? Although all of these soldiers were a part of one great cause, each one had a very different experience in the First World War.

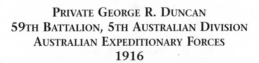

PRIVATE GEORGE R. DUNCAN
59TH BATTALION, 5TH AUSTRALIAN DIVISION
AUSTRALIAN EXPEDITIONARY FORCES
1916

George R. Duncan was the son of Watson Cranston Duncan and Frances Adelaide Duncan (neé Calman) of "Leith," Newland Street, in Waverly, which is in New South Wales, Australia.[1] Duncan wrote a number of letters to both the pastor at his local parish church (St. Barnabas) and to his parents while serving with Australia's Fifth Division in Egypt and France.

This particular letter was recopied in another hand so that Duncan's family could have a copy. Note that Duncan used the technique of carrying over the last word on each page and repeating it again on the next page so that the reader could move smoothly through the letter while turning pages.

Initially, Duncan's regiment spent some time stationed at the Suez Canal. Then, in June of 1916 it moved to France, where his unit took over the "nursery" sector near Armentieres. From there it became involved in the disastrous attack at Fromelles just the next month.

George R. Duncan (Courtesy of Dr. David B. Duncan)

Somewhere in France
July 7th [1916]
Dear Rector

This is the third letter I have written you since I left Australia and I sincerely hope that you have received them all. We have left Egypt and are now in France behind the enemy's guns and likely to go into action any day now so I thought it would be appropriate to send you a letter now and I hope that you will excuse this letter as writing material is very hard to obtain here. France is a beautiful place a regular paradise after the burning sands and heat of the Egyptian Desert. Not one iota of the land is waste. It is just one cultivated garden, vineyards, cornfields, hedges, orchards and vegetable gardens. Roses cling to the front of the peasants red-tiled cottages, which nestle snugly among a cluster of trees of beautiful green hues. Poppies grow even between the sleepers on the railway line, while grape vines in the South grow wild. The air is full of sweetness and is bracing even to nippy at night and early morn. There is a noticeable twilight and the first night here there was great laughing when Lights out was sounded as it appeared quite broad daylight after the evening in Egypt. The people here appear particularly healthy [page 2] healthy with rosy cheeks almost without exception. The French people are very good to us honest and polite and with the "Tommies" we are special guests. We have seen German prisoners who also look in good condition more like overfed than underfed by their appearance. It is very funny amusing to see our boys trying to converse with the natives resorting every now and then to their English-French dictionaries. Every night we can hear the artillery at the trenches.

World War I

The other evening we saw an aeroplane being shelled. All around it were curls of smoke and now and then the flash of a bursting shell which when perilously close to the machine which got away without being hit.

I often wonder how you are all getting on at St. Barnabas'. My mail has gone astray through being put into "C" Company 59th Battalion. If I am a casualty, only my name and number will appear I believe. No. 4770 [number 479] Private G. R. Duncan. I do hope that my letters turn up as they are worth their weight in gold.

While in Egypt we saw neither Cairo, Heliopolis nor the Pyramids being camped firstly at Tel-el-Kelier and then Ferry Post and Ismalia in the heart of the Desert. Some of the natives were [page 3] were dirty and lived only in mud huts but others were clean, ~~gentlemanly~~ intelligent and very ~~intelligent~~ gentlemanly in their manners, while without exception the Europeans at Ismalia, who where almost exclusively French lived in little palaces. So far I have had no sickness, of course the most severe test of all is to come and I pray to God to give me more than my normal strength when the time comes and if he is willing I will come back and see St. Barnabas and hear another sermon preached from the pulpit. If I do not come back I hope that people who knew me will be able to say that my character was good and then I will be content. I always made it my object never to willfully hurt anyone's feelings and I am sure the influence of Army Campaigning will not alter my determination to keep up to this ideal. I do hope that our people come out of this War a more serious, industrious and religious people, taught by the lesson of bitter experience and above all I believe that religion or the Spiritual side of life is going to be the most important element in human existence. You'll excuse me trying to preach a sermon but at this time of death and destruction I think that everyone should be more serious and not [page 4] not frivolous. Already I have noted how the French people can teach us many things in which we laud ourselves without fear of contradiction. Well dear Rector I know that you are praying for me, for all of us over here at the Front and we all need your most earnest prayers for success to come our way.

We have just finished a most strenuous route march, which broke up the Brigade for miles along the Road, but I am glad to say that I stuck to it to the last. Blistered feet, chafes, and other complaints are universal today and we are now starting again after a night's bivouac. May God help us now, as we will be subjected to most severe tests. I haven't been sick since I left Australia and I have got plenty in me yet for the trenches & I don't see that there is any reason why my chance of survival is less than any of the others in my Battalion. I will now close asking you to remember me always in your prayers as I know you are doing. I have not seen or heard of George Lamam yet but you never know when we may bump each other. I suppose Andy Pedrana will be on his road here by now and on the whole Sydney must be getting full of soldiers [page 5] [soldiers] *all anxious to participate in the great "World War" – well dear Rector remember me to all at St. Barnabas. Wait till I come back to the Debating Club, I'll talk you all out of the door with news (censored just now) with love and respect*

From George R. Duncan
"Australia's sons let us rejoice for we are young and free.["]

Duncan's next two short letters, which were written to his parents, are in pencil and although at times they are almost illegible, they still convey a premonition of what was to come for the Australian troops as they moved into position near the French-Belgian border town of Fromelles.

Somewhere in France
10th July [1916]
   My dear Mother,
      We are now under fire from the enemy just behind the trenches & so far there have been no casualties. The time has come at last when we must one and all face the enemy and may God help us for the sake of those we have left behind for I know you will be most anxious and I don't want you to worry. Even if I should not come back what is my life along side say Lord Kitchener's or thousands of others mothers' sons who have died on the battlefield? So far your prayers and Isabel's and all who have prayed for me have not been in vain for I haven't had a day's sickness since I left "fair" Australia and the last two days I lasted out a rout march which was reckoned as most severe and which proved too much for many of us. One of our section told me that I surprised him and stuck to it well and dear Mother there is no reason whatever why I shouldn't go right through the ordeal and come back and see you all again. Now I can see you all only in imagination. Isabel's smile and Jean's merry little prattle, says "Where George and Georgie gone away." I know you will all [be] *scanning the newspapers and news you will only find my rank name and number that's all that [?] appears. I haven't*

had any letters for such a long time, nor any papers or parcels. Well if they cheer some poor wounded chap in a hospital I'll be content. We can see aeroplanes being shelled continually and also villages where troops are billeted. Well dear Mother keep praying and keep happy. It's no use of being sad, there's too much sorrow in France. May God bless you and keep you with love from Your Loving Son, George XXX

My dear Dad,
Am so far well and uninjured just behind the trenches. We are likely to be shelled if observed but so far no casualties have been observed. What little money you are drawing on my behalf use for yourself if bad times come. If I happen to fall there is also a little pay £5.00 owing to me out of my 2/- per day which you ought to receive as I've made out my will in my Pay Book leaving everything to you. Whether you get it or not is a matter of pure chance I think. Don't forget to claim my 1/- deferred pay also, every little bit helps. I have just come through a severe route march which caused many to fall out and some to break down. It's a matter of spirit. I've got some whopping blisters for sale now but is a mere introduc-tion to what is to come I can plainly see but I've still got plen-ty left in me enough to shoot a couple of Germans [illegible words] themselves. If I am wounded I will see "this royal throne of kings, this sceptered isle" and if the wound is seri-ous enough they ought to send me home. We have just had [?] good news from the British Front north of the River Somme & [——?] from the Southern Front also. The French people give [?] very good tours and — - matter of buying and selling arti-cles [?] ——-trust us to a remarkable degree [?] it is very amusing to see [?] our [?] boys fall back on the French hand back ———now and then while hotline [?] —— France has suffered by the looks of mourning in every village. Every able bodied man is ———[needed?] except the Railway men — —- My dear Dad, God bless you and all of [?] faith and —— hope to come back soon [?]

From your loving Son, George

The Battle of Fromelles

At 6:00 P.M. on the evening of July 19th, the 15th Brigade, which con-sisted of the 58th battalion on the left and George Duncan in the 59th bat-talion on the right, waited for the signal to advance across No Man's Land. To their right was the 61st British Division. Beginning earlier in the day at 11:00 A.M., and for the next seven hours, the Allies pounded the

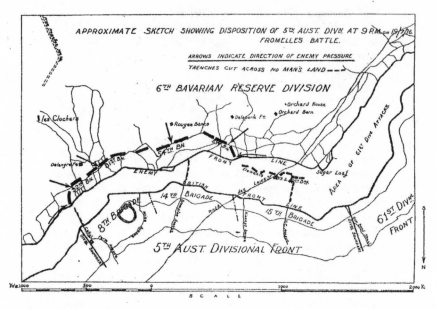

Map from *The Story of the Fifth Australian Division.*

Germans with shells to "flatten the enemy front." In addition, they feint-ed a series of assaults, in order to entice the enemy out of their bunkers and to expose the enemy to shells and shrapnel. It was reported along the 61st Division's frontline that the enemy's parapet had been "'shattered all along the line.'"[2] This intelligence unfortunately proved wrong and had disastrous consequences. Meanwhile, the Bavarian Division was entrenched in front of a ridge known as Aubers Heights. From this posi-tion the Germans watched and waited for the anticipated attack. The Germans also manned rifles on a high point referred to as "Sugar Loaf." From an account of this attack published in 1920, one learns details of the fatal assault, which enfiladed Duncan's battalion:

> *Punctually at 5:45 p.m., deployment into No Man's Land commenced, and it was hoped that the artillery barrage would be sufficiently intense to keep enemy heads down until the deployment was completed. . . . On the extreme right . . . the 59th Battalion was scarcely over the parapet before a little desultory musketry fire was opened on it, coming chiefly from the Sugar Loaf. Before the men had gone 30 yards this fire had grown in intensity and a machine gun added . . . to the rapidly increasing fusillade. The waves pressed forward steadily, but just as steadily the enemy fire grew hotter and hotter and the enemy front lines were seen to be thickly*

manned with troops. The losses mounted rapidly. . . .
Thirty-five out of 39 of the assaulting officers were
already killed or wounded, and with them most of the
N.C.O.s.[3]

The Sugar Loaf was never taken. The assault broke off on the morning of July 20th "after the 5th Australian Division had lost over 5,000 officers and men. It was the first serious engagement of the Australian forces in France, and the only one not to achieve success."[4]

While over 400 Australian soldiers were found on this battlefield, not a single body could be identified. Therefore it was decided that the Australians should be buried in a common grave and Duncan's and the rest of their names should be added to a memorial there for the 1,294 Australian casualties in that sector of France.

PRIVATE BENJAMIN HENDIN
THE JEWISH LEGION: 38TH BATTALION OF LONDON'S ROYAL FUSILIERS IN EGYPT AND JORDAN, 1918

Benjamin Hendin was born to a Jewish family in Krasnopol, a small town in the Bialystok district of Byelorussia or Poland, in about 1894. When he was two, his family moved to Nikolaev, a bigger city in the southern Ukraine, about 150 kilometers from Odessa. In 1906, after pogrom rioters destroyed the family grocery store, the Hendins immigrated to the United States, where they became citizens. The family moved first to St. Louis, then to Tyler, Texas, and then back to St. Louis. In 1916, Benjamin's older brother Max and sister-in-law Nettie moved to Detroit, where Henry Ford had just begun the $5 day. Twenty-two and still unmarried, Benjamin joined them in Detroit, where he worked in and then bought a small shoe store. By the time the United States entered the war, Benjamin was largely supporting Max's family (now including daughters Frances and Esther) because Max had been blinded on the job.

In 1968, at the age of 75, Benjamin wrote, by hand, a 268-page autobiography. What follows is the account dealing with his experience of leaving Detroit to fight with the Jewish Legion of the British Army in World War I. The source document is a thirty-year old photocopy of the autobiography; in addition to being barely legible in some places, and despite Benjamin's command of English (in addition to Yiddish, Russian and Hebrew), he never bothered to learn spelling other than phonetically, and capitalized and used punctuation only randomly. To make the account readable, the spelling and punctuation has been corrected to the extent that the original style of writing has not been lost.

WORLD WAR I

The War

The War started in 1914. America entered the War in 1917. The Allies were in a sore state – as Russia quit the War when the Bolshevicks came into Power. Germany was victorious as the war was not in Germany. France was partially occupied as well as the Low Countries. England was being shelled by Guns from the French Coast. The German submarines played havoc with shipping from United States & Canada to Europe. Soon after U.S. entered the war, every able young man had to register for the draft. I as well as other people. In the Spring of 1917, the Government of England came out with the Balfour Declaration favoring the establishment of a homeland for the Jews in Palestine. As it proved after the War when England had the Mandate of Palestine, the Balfour declaration was like the Indians say made with a forked tongue. However in 1917 the statement was greeted by the Jews and a movement started led by Vladimir Szabotinsky [Vladimir Jabotinsky] & to form a Jewish Army to fight in Palestine. Due to at that time unknown to the world the British Army and government were against forming a Jewish Army. Their opinion was backed by assimilated rich Jews in England. Also the Zionist organization whose headquarters were in Berlin at that time did not favor the forming of a Jewish Army. Of course all of that was inside diplomacy known by few.

After many meetings by Szabotinsky & other Jews with the British Army it was agreed that Jewish Battalions should be formed by Russian Jews residing in England & Volunteers from other countries. Eventually 10,000 Jews from England, United States, Canada, Argentina, later Jewish prisoners from the Turkish Army formed the Jewish Battalions under the Royal Fusiliers regiment.[5] Later the volunteers from Palestine joined.[6]

At the rich widow['s] I mentioned previous [one of Benjamin's shoe store customers who had taken an interest in him], I met a Colonel from the [United States Army] Quartermaster Corps. He wanted me to join. I would immediately be made a top Sergeant and remain in United States during the War. My duty to train men as shoe repairers, also as inspectors where shoes were made for the Armed Forces of U.S.A. and its allies. I was torn between the duty to the family and my wish to join the Jewish Legion. Finally late in fall of 1917 I joined the Legion and got 4 months time to arrange my business. I left Max assisted by Nettie to run the business.

World War I

They had hired shoe repair man and they were the buyers and salesmen.

The Army

After leaving Detroit just previous to my draft call I went to Windsor, Nova Scotia for training, first stopping over in Montreal for assembly and more recruits. In the City of New Brunswick the small Jewish community gave a dinner and reception for us. I was close to 200 lbs. when I came to Windsor. The Barracks were rundown, wet & cold, the shower wooden floor. The first thing we marched, got canvas bags & filled with straw. Given 2 blankets. Assigned your platoon & Company & marched for Supper. Worse food I never tasted. The food was terrible all the time we were in Windsor. Next day we were given uniforms but no Guns and our training started. It consisted of marching, Saluting and calisthenics, with lectures of Military behavior & difference between a soldier who was like a mechanical man & the officers who were Gentlemen.

I was offered to become a non com but would be lost upon arrival in England. I declined and remained a private. Within time a small kosher style restaurant opened near the Y.M.C.A. As I had plenty of money, whenever I could get off duty, I would eat supper there. At one time we were called to fight a forest fire & spent a few days on the firing line. Despite the restaurant food, I kept on going down in weight. Within 4 months I was down to 145 lbs. but that was in England.

One day we were confined to barracks & told that we were going to embark for England. That night we left for Halifax [Nova Scotia]. Kept in solitary away from all civilians. In the evening we embarked in boats. There were 11 boats in our convoy, old tramp ships & anything that could float. In the convoy was a cruiser and several Japanese small destroyers. The destroyers returned in a few days. The boat I was on Stank. In the hold 4 tier of Bunks were built. You had to crawl in as there wasn't enough room to sit in the bunk. The food was given right where the bunks were in an empty spot. I thought the food was bad in Windsor, it was much worse on the boat. Due to the slowness of some boats the trip to England took 12 days. There was a bar selling crackers & drinks & candy top side. Most of the trip that was what I ate. There were constant drills on boat that gave us a chance to inhale fresh air. At night the entrance to the hold was closed. We all had to stay in the stinky hold. I was sorry I didn't *accept the non com status as Sergeants had cabins top side, about 10 to a cabin. We had several scares from Submarines but no attacks. During the voyage some soldiers died. There were Canadian troops also on boat. They were buried at sea.*

Finally one afternoon we saw some English Destroyers come to meet us as well as dirigibles.[7] We landed in England late in the afternoon. We were taken by train to Hounslow Barracks. Next day we were given medical examination, delousing, Baths, soldiers kit & new uniforms & sent by truck to our barracks in Croton Hill near Plymouth where outside of leave we were all the time we were in England.

The food was much better. We had a dining room, library, canteen. Our training started in earnest. We had bayonet training, how to arm your Gun, proper military bearing, running, marching, sentry duty, wrestling & boxing, also lectures.

The only day of rest for those not on duty was Saturday when we marched to the football grounds. A square was formed, the officers and men forming 3 sides of the square. The front of the square was occupied by the Chaplain and on top of Drums was box holding the Torah. After a services of about 45 minutes we were dismissed & were free for the rest of the day, some getting passes to go to Plymouth. There wasn't much you could buy at that time in England but you could go to a restaurant for fish & chips, get photographed, flirt with the girls and enjoy being away from camp. But be on sharp look out for Officers to salute. You could get by without saluting from a major up but it was tough if you didn't salute a lieutenant. Some men were discharged being too young & parents wanted them back. One for not coming on parade as kept on praying in tallis and tefillin [Jewish prayer shawl and phylacteries], sort of a conscientious objector.

However, we were formed into soldiers fast, taking pride in our Company and regiment, finding muscles where there were none. Hike 15 miles with a pack and Gun over 100 lbs., the Captain riding, the others hiking. One officer who had the eye of an eagle & very strict but on hikes he always carried several Rifles for soldiers that were pooped.

Our officers were a mixed lot. Some Gentiles & others Jews. The same went for the non coms. Our Colonel who was a Christian, Peterson [Patterson] of the 38th Battalion, Royal Fusiliers, was more Jew than most of us. He was a Zionist and probably commanded the Zion Transport Corps in Gallipoli. There were Palestinian Jews. Some of our Christian officers were not happy to be in a Jewish Battalion and some were outright Anti-Semitic, but until after the War showed only by riding the soldiers with too strict of a discipline.

However, men were needed badly in the field and one day the battalion was confined to barracks & told that we were getting ready to ship out next day. Next morning the kitchens were closed, the quartermaster supplies all packed, the camp leveled. We ate from rations that day, cheese, bully beef & hardtack & tea. Towards afternoon we were assembled again. After being in the ranks, two companies were marched away for the train. 2 companies remained for next morning. No supper that night. When I got to my pup tent I discovered that someone stole my blankets. I went to the Quartermaster Sergeant. He told me that everything was packed. He asked me how long I was in the Army. He then told me that in the Army it is not a crime to steal only to be caught at it. However, I still couldn't steal and didn't have blankets until we got to Cherbourg, France.

Next morning without breakfast we were put on lorries & then on the train. About 7 a.m. some women came on the train and gave each a cup of chocolate & small roll & that was all the food we had for 36 hours.

Southampton. On arrival we were put in embarkation cages. Sentries watching that no one should speak to Civilians. We were real prisoners. Towards evening several companies of U.S. troops came. They were given Bread, Beans & Hot Dogs & Coffee. At that time I sure was sorry I didn't join the U.S. Army.

In darkness we embarked on a small boat. Usually room for 200, there were 1000 troops on the boat. English, American, there was no room to sit or lay down. I finally crawled under a bench near the Gunwale. The English Channel lived up to its name – it was a very rough trip. Now & then waves came over the side. I got good & Wet & miserable. No camp ever looked so good to me as the one in Cherbourg. We got warm breakfast, all we could eat. The army rations tasted very good that morning. I got two blankets finally. Like a real soldier I swiped them from my Bunk when we left after several days for Egypt.

The whole Battalion left Cherbourg together on several trains of freight cars marked 8 horses or 40 men. The Transport which had horses was in one train and so was the field kitchens & all the quartermaster goods.

The other trains had the officers & men and one field kitchen for making tea. The officers were in third class passenger cars. All the rest in the 8 x 40 cars. Our journey ended in Taranto[8], southernmost point of Italy. It took us nine days to cover about 1200 miles. There were several rest stops on the way with showers & warm food in which we spent several hours. The rest of the time we had Jam Cheese Bully beef Hardtack & tea. We replenished the food with vegetables, fruit & wine bought from the natives at stops in villages & small towns. As soon as we stopped, the natives came out offering their wares, asking for Bully beef, meat was very scarce to them. We traded and bought for cash.

Some of the deals on both sides were not exactly kosher. At one stop one of the soldiers said let me fool an Italian. He took out the meat put sand in the box & covered the top with about 2 inches of bully beef. At the next stop we started trading, he with an Italian for a bottle of wine. The Italian wanted to see the can of beef first, he the wine. Finally as the train was pulling out, the Italian handed him the wine for the exchange of the can of bully beef. When the soldier opened the bottle, it had Water instead of wine. The Italian had Sand instead of meat.

We decorated the outside of the cars with Branches and wild flowers that we collected on our stops. The people as we passed waved their hands at us & were happy to see more English soldiers come to their defense. Several times we had to hide in tunnels during air attacks but on the whole it was a pleasant journey.

Taranto

We embarked on a large boat still in the hold but a lot more air than the Atlantic crossing. The food was better or we probably got used to army fare on boats.

However it was very crowded with several thousand troops. Our Batt. as well as other troops. We were in one section. When call for food was made, instead of looking for our own mess tin, we took whatever was on hand. The same thing happened on drill. We just grabbed a Rifle so that before landing all troops went upside with the Rifles. Then the officers called the number of the Rifle in their hand. If it was your Rifle number you got it & gave the other one back so that we landed each with his own.

Egypt

The Journey took five days and one afternoon we landed at Port Said, Egypt[9].

WORLD WAR I

In Port Said, we officially became a part of the Egyptian Expeditionary Force[10] short E.E.F. We were put in the reception center. Next morning after kit inspection, we left by train to Tel El Khebir[11], a historical battlefield. It was about 40 miles from Cairo near the Suez Canal. It was a huge camp containing nearly 40,000 Turkish War Prisoners & more coming every day. Our battalion of about 1500 men took over the sentry duty from an Indian brigade of 5000 men. The Indians were Sikhs, tall, bearded and very strict disciplined by English officers. The Sikhs would not eat any meat but what they killed. They were very clean in dress & bearing. Besides their Rifles, they had long spears, at when not in battle.

Back to our camp. It had the largest mosquitoes. We were put 8 to a tent and huge tents for other purposes. There was no dining tent. We lined up for food & ate at our tent, cleaning our utensils at the kitchen entrance. There cold showers & plenty of water. Also Egyptians came over for which we paid to do our Laundry. The life for us was very hard. We had to do sentry duty for 24 hours, get 4 hours rest & then training till evening. It made us ready for what was to come later on & hardened us.

Once when I got off sentry duty, just laid down on the ground. We had no bunks from the time we came to E.E.F. until our return for discharge in England. Over a year. Anyhow as soon as I undressed – on sentry duty you had to be completely dressed for 24 hours – my sergeant called me for kit inspection. I told him that according to Army regulations I was excused for 4 hours from all but emergency & refused to go. Then my lieutenant came me an order to dress & go for the kit inspection. I started dressing very slowly. He called in 4 men & told them to take me to the Clink under arrest. There is such a ruling in the British Army as silent contempt for an officer. By dressing slowly, I showed contempt. I was marched to the Clink with my Rifle, 2 Grenades, 140 rounds of ammunition. I had no time to return the ammunition to the quartermaster. With all of that I could kill half of the company. Later on I was taken before the Captain who fined me $5.00. He said I was right in my complaint but in the army you first obey orders & then complain to your superior. I think that the sergeant also got a bawling out for ordering me for kit inspection.

Reading now about the savagery to Prisoners of War, I must say that we were very humane. As soon as prisoners arrived & processed, the sick ones were taken to the prison hospital staffed by English & their own doctors. They were given very humane treatment. The other prisoners after being given a receipt for personal property, however some remained in the hands of the staff, were issued old repaired and cleaned uniforms as dyed black with a P in the back. Underwear, blankets, shoes, cooking utensils, but no razors. Other prisoners from the campground cut their hair very short, were given a shower, left all their old clothing & got the new outfit. Then assigned their tent & then from then on they were under their— [page missing].

I got a 48 hour leave to go to Cairo. I stayed in a hotel owned by a Greek near the Esbekia Gardens. Cairo in the main streets was modern, however, the poverty of the people was shocking. Near the finest stores you saw at night people sleeping on the sidewalk. The famous Shepherd Hotel was filled with French, Italian & British officers and rich civilians. I attended services at the big Cairo Synagogue. It was richly decorated. After the Sabbath Service, a lunch was served to the visiting soldiers. At that time, there were a lot of rich Jews in Egypt.

At the hotel I stayed, I couldn't sleep on the bed because of the spring. Having been used for months to sleep on hard ground, had to put mattress on floor & then sleep like a baby.

Went sightseeing to the Pyramids & camel ride. Also visited Esbekia Garden – at day time luxury plants & trees, at night the largest prostitution center in the world. Women of all races & shades. A Jewish prostitute from Poland as a patriotic gesture offered me for free but that part was in the European Center. In the native section orgies were shown that even now I am too bashful to describe. Hashish was smoked & many English soldiers were doped by hashish in their water smoking pipes or knock out drops in their drinks, then robbed and thrown out on the street. It was out of bounds for troops, but troops went there anyhow.

My leave was for 48 hours but I took an extra day. My platoon sergeant, an Irishman, loved drinks, especially Richen Wine. I got him a bottle. When I showed up a day late, he fixed up so that I wasn't fined nor put against my record.

Finally the time came for the Jewish Legion to go to the front.

In June, 1918, Hendin and the 38th Battalion arrived on the front lines where they were inspected by General Allenby. A couple of days later, the 38th took up its position along a three-mile line "between Jiljilia (some three miles west of the Nablus Road) and Abwein," where they began their job of digging trenches and patrolling "a most trying part of the line in the Jordan Valley. The seven miles for which they were responsible stretched westward from the Jordan above Jerico . . . ." In late September, the 38th Battalion, joined by the Anzac Mounted Division, took part in an attack with Allenby against Turkish and German troops. The enemy was outflanked and Patterson's troops occupied the road between Tel Nimrin and Es Salt (Ramoth Gilead). After the Turkish collapse, the 38th Battalion, assisted by the 39th Battalion, returned to Jerusalem with a large number of prisoners.[12]

The Jordan Valley

My battalion, the 38th, also the 39th, had the most dangerous spot in Nablus & Jericho valley. The heat was 100 in shade. We were only a speck in the Allied forces of British, Australian, New Zealand, Hindu Gurkas & West Indian troops. Also French & Italian. Opposing us was Turks and small detachments of (Jäger Battalionen) and aviators. Austrian artillery. The Germans and Austrians were well fed & had the best of everything. The poor Turks who the Germans called the Lousan Buben hardly had any food or clothing but plenty of ammunition that the Germans supplied for taking everything else away from the Turks.

We did not lose many men from battle, about 30 killed. Our biggest enemy was illness. At one time 2/3 of the battalion was unable to muster due to dysentery, malaria & skin rash.

Due to the fact that we had Turkish-speaking soldiers who talked the Turks into surrender, the Jewish Legion captured the most prisoners for the comparative amount of troops. We also captured a large cannon and a lot of booty. At one time we went over the top but the Turks were gone from the trenches. The Jewish Legion were the first troops to cross into Transjordan. Right behind came the Australian Cavalry who played havoc with the enemy. The Australians were fine men & very good soldiers but discipline and saluting was not their meat. That they left to the British & Indians.

The plight of the Turkish prisoners was terrible. They were starved & in rags. Many of them died after eating a meal. Their stomachs could not stand the cheese & bully beef. Chicken soup we didn't have nor milk. They were so disorganized that Hundreds of them marched to the rear as prisoners with only 2 or 4 soldiers as guards.

The Germans were well fed & in fact we captured very fine food in their quartermaster supplies. Who were supposed to have been so brave gave up like sheep and addressed the soldiers 'ja, mein Herr", "no, mein Herr". They also needed very few guards to march to prison camp. However as soon as they were safe in camp their cockiness returned. Their songs "Deutschland über Alles" and other patriotic German songs resounded. They were treated better as prisoners as after the armistice they worked in the Army machine & railway shops, they got paid and upon giving their word that they will not try to escape, they were even taken out of the prisoner compound 5 or 10 at a time with a guard & went to town. They kept their promise; as had one escaped all privileges, [it] would be revoked to all.

After the armistice, the 39th battalion was stationed in Sarafend close to Rishon Le Zion, near Jewish settlements. Orange groves near. We in the 38th battalion had the hard luck to be sent in Rafah, a desert, the present Gaza Strip. There was a small prison camp there, a lot of ammunition dumps, railway shops staffed by German prisoners & English technicians. Our job was to watch all that and the R.R. tracks and stations. We spent the hardest time of our military life there. The sandstorms were nearly a daily occurrence. There was no water near. It had to be brought by water tanks. Our daily ration consisted of the water bottle plus 2 cups of tea a day. Some times we got lime juice & Lemons. When real thirsty we chewed on pebbles. The only road was a chicken wire cover on sand. As soon as you stepped off the wire you sank in sand. There was one Water Well & Pump but that was reserved for the British Engineering Corps and the Prisoners who had more water than us.

After the Armistice

With the end of the war, the Anti-semites in the Armed Forces began showing their dislike for us as our food was getting worse. Despite the fact that during the War many of us got decorated and we were mentioned in dispatches by General Allenby for the good job we did, we started to be treated as stepchildren of the Army. Instead of British Military Police we were put under Egyptian Military Police. The higher military echelon started putting pressure on our officers with more & more duties for the Jewish battalions. It is customary that ample warning is given for a General inspection. With us the General dropped in without warning for inspection and then reported that we were not as spic & span as other units.

In the meantime, we ate Sand & slept Sand. When the wind started the fine Sand went through everything. All you could do when not on duty was to lay on the ground & cover up over your head for some relief. The sick list was getting bigger & bigger. Most men away in the hospital but the high command kept on increasing our duties. We were spread for about 50 miles guarding the R.R. tracks & stations.

Then an order came for us to go to the [am]munition dump to dismantle Shells & Bombs. We only worked at it 2 days, only working when an officer was nearby & then stopping. The officers were with us as such work was to be done by experienced Engineering Corps. Finally seeing that we didn't do the Job, we were relieved from it.

A detachment of about 50 men were in El Arish. Finally things got so bad for them that they refused orders. They were surrounded by Gurka troops and arrested. They all got heavy sentences. Probably they would get off lighter were the Court Martial of English regiments but they were officers of Hindu regiments.

Also in Rafah things were getting rough. Our Captain Starrs showed his dislike for us openly. One morning a detachment was called to work in the Supply Dump. I was one of them. The sergeant there told us that if we can complete the job without killing time we can go back to Camp & have the rest of the day off. While we had lunch at Camp the whistle blew and the same detachment was called for another work job. In the meantime a Sand storm started. You couldn't see 10 feet ahead. We told the corporal that we were excused for the rest of the day, but his order remained. One of our men we called Bab A Golo or Coach Driver started to argue with the corporal. The outcome, the corporal called an officer and Bab a Golo was put in the guardhouse. In the meantime the detachment slunk away. Several weeks later he was held for Court Martial. His defense att[orney]. was Lieutenant Samuels, a very intelligent English Jew. He was tall & looked like a Lord, which he was, Lord Samuels' son. He remained in Palestine & still is there a citizen of Israel, the only British Lord who is not a resident of England. At the Court Martial, we testified as well as the Dump Sergeant that we should be free the rest of the day if we do our job. However it was English & Hindu officers of Indian troops again. They sentenced the Bab a Golo to 5 years hard labor & dishonorable discharge.

In the meantime, Lieutenant Szabotinsky [Jabotinsky], the organizer of the Jewish Legion, not agreeing with the soldiers of El Arish, was their defendant. After the Sentence he protested to the Court Martial for the hard sentence & busted because they were men of the Jewish Legion. As an outcome he was cashiered out of the Army. Later on in 1921 he was put in jail by the British. His ideas were not mine, but he was a wonderful orator & writer. Spoke 9 languages but he told us his thought was Russian, which he translated in his mind. When unrest broke out due to the sentence in El Arish he spoke to us & quieted us down. The Legion was composed of one extreme to another. We had people of every standard, including some men that later became famous architects, Poets, writers, musicians, doctors & President of Israel Ben Zivi & Ben Gurion. Mostly just people & some crooks & adventurers but we all made good soldiers.

At one General inspection which we were getting about four times as much as other units, while the battalion was lined up for inspection, in front of us about 100 yards was the Transport Unit. Horse drawn. Somehow one team got scared probably due to the music of our regiment. They started a runaway, the driver trying to stop them. Finally the team with heavy wagon stopped about 10 yards away but the ranks did not break. We all remained at attention none moving. Had the horses not stopped in time there would have been Killed & wounded. I think that that General must have given a good report about us.

While some of our men were on leave in Petah Tikvah, Simah Swatitski, her maiden name Hendin, asked if there were any Hendins in the unit. As it happened they were from my platoon & told her I was from Detroit. She wrote a letter to Colonel Peterson that I was her younger brother who she never met as she left for Palestine before I was born. She advised me of the letter. I was called before the Col. who granted me 3 days leave to go & meet my sister. I met Simah, her husband David & daughter Shoshanna who was a baby. Also met Abraham Hendin, his sister & mother. I left them some gifts & money to Abraham & sister.

Eventually an Australian cavalry regiment was sent to Rafah as a punishment. An Australian sergeant was found murdered & robbed in Camp. The Arabs used to come to camp for Laundry & sell vegetables, fruit. The footprints in the Sand led to a nearby village. The Australians asked the (Muktar) head man to give them the murderer. They surrounded the village so none could escape & gave them 24 hours. When the 24 hours were up they removed the women & children & shot every man there & destroyed the village. That started a Stink and General Allenby himself came to the regiment. When all were on parade he told them they were

Murderers. They yelled back that if they were murderers it was people like him who made them murderers so they were banished to Rafah, the Siberia of the Army, where we were stationed for months.

As soon as they got there, about 3 miles from our camp, they were near the Sea shore, they started digging for Water. There was plenty underground Water. Made hot showers & a beautiful camp. Our condition got better as we had water near. They wanted us to come & take showers & have all the improvement of their camp. The diggers were very friendly people, no saluting except when on duty. Officers & men dressed the same. No ceremonies but they were good when it was needed – fighting. The present Israeli army is patterned after the Australian Army.

Shortly after, a detachment was sent to Salhia, Egypt. I was one of them. There was a small P.O.W. camp there. I was the regimental M.P. My duty to keep [page missing].

[A?] *bridge, which was cemented on came off. As there were no Dentist in the hospital I was given 48 hours to go to Jaffa to have the bridge cemented on. I asked the Dentist to write a letter that he had other work to do & spent 4 days. Also visited Petah Tikvah. Upon my return with the letter, I was fined two weeks pay for not reporting to the proper M.P. force in Jaffa. As I had plenty of money sent me from home, in fact $500, during my service I didn't mind that.*

At the end of June our Company was transferred to Sarafend, which was heaven. Close to all the Jewish communities. We could buy all the food we wanted. Also the Army food improved. I was attached to the Quartermaster sergeant. When he was discharged I became the Quartermaster. Lived like a king, had a tent to myself and the stretcher to sleep on. Whenever I went to Petah Tikvah I filled up my Pack & knapsack with Coffee Tea Sugar & bully beef. Also big chunks of cheese & passed it out to the family there. Also helping Abraham with money now & then. Next to Simah had a girl friend, a real beauty. Dark & big black eyes. I got a crush on her & spent more time with her than the family, but I was too slow in popping the question.

Going Home

In the meantime, orders came for my demobilization. I was one of the first because of business reasons. I made my last visit to the family, leaving them large amounts of provi-

sions & gave Abraham's sister another $10. Next day I left for Cantara. Eventually boarded a ship. Still in the hold but not crowded. I slept in a hammock which took me several tries to master. As my eye got inflamed went to see the ship doctor & was on top deck where life was elegant. I saw Justice Brandeis who was returning from Palestine but due to my dirty clothes I was too bashful to approach him. The doctor gave me Boric acid & cotton to wash my eyes & told me to see the doctor in England.

After several days the boat landed in Marseilles, France. During the stay we were outfitted with new uniforms, the kind that actually fit, given our service ribbons.[13] The few days I was in Marseilles I made up for all the lost Army days. It was one big bang up, girls and all.

Finally started for England, this time in a 3rd class coach eating in the dining car, getting to Calais, & then by boat across the Channel, but this time I had a hammock. Arrived Southampton again, but in a reception center & then proceeded to Winchester which the repatriation center for Soldiers overseas. After medical inspection was given a week's leave to go to London which I enjoyed very much. Had another flame with a Jewish girl & kept her picture. Corresponded for a while and then forgotten. The English girls were easy pickups & a good time was had by all as long as you had money of which I was not short of. Returned to Winchester, given the discharges, a trip all paid to Detroit. I embarked in London on the Scotian this time in a Cabin served by stewards. Food in a dining room. It probably was not first class, I am sure it wasn't, but it seemed like heaven after Army days. We landed in Quebec & by train to Montreal & then to Detroit.

At that time I was in peak of condition, straight as an ramrod, 175 lbs., 44 chest, 34 waist, could wrestle my weight with tigers or so it seemed to me.

It was early Oct. a beautiful day when I got to Detroit. Didn't have much to carry as one of my Kit bags with all kinds of souvenirs was stolen. So had just a kit bag with a civilian suit & personal things plus Just a few souvenirs. When I approached the store, Esther was resting on a step. She ran to me & jumped in my arms, probably recognizing me from pictures she saw of me – as she couldn't remember me when I left.

WORLD WAR I

In all I served in the Army nearly two years. Experience worth a million, but as the saying is, it wasn't worth a nickel to give for it.

❖

SERGEANT LEON C. FARMER
22ND COMPANY, 1ST DIVISION, SECOND ARMY
8TH AERO SQUADRON (OBSERVATION), U.S. SIGNAL CORPS

Leon Farmer, born and raised in Indiana, was a skilled welder and mechanic. His abilities to reconstruct broken and crashed bi-wing airplanes were essential to the war effort because of the newly developing field of aviation warfare. The 8th Aero Squadron (Observation) was one of the first American Squadrons to be organized, having been formed on June 21, 1917, at Kelly Field, San Antonio, Texas. He traveled from Indiana to Texas for training, from there to Thetford Flying Field in England, then to Amanty, France, and finally to the Allied-occupied Germany. This squadron was engaged with the First Army for approximately two and a half months in the following sectors in France: Toul, Chateau-Thierry, St. Mihiel, and the Argonne-Meuse. Farmer's treasured leather-bound album of World War I vintage photographs also provides an eyewitness perspective of wartime Europe from the air.

Leon Farmer. (Courtesy of Shirley Gaughan)

San Antonio, Tex.
Camp Kelly
8th Aero Squadron
July 28, 1917
> *Dear Mother and all:*
>> *I received your letter yesterday with Inez letter enclosed. I was mighty glad to get both of them. I also received one from Inez and Grace sent directly to me. Was very glad to hear that they arrived alright after a good trip.*
>> *I should have written you before but have been quite busy with drill and work together. They are building about twenty mess halls and sleeping halls to accommodate ten or fifteen thousand men, so we get a chance to unload lumber etc, once in a while. There are always plenty of men so that we are*

Chow line for 8th Aero Squadron at Camp Kelly, Texas. (Courtesy of Shirley Gaughan)

relieved often. The little bit we do is really good for us. The carpenter work is contracted by a civilian firm.

Since I last wrote we have been issued more clothing that we needed. So that I have three good pair of shoes, two felt hats, and two suits and an extra pair of pants, besides underwear, socks, etc. We were also issued our rifles, Cartridge belts, new mess kits, Canteens, etc. We were issued our pistol holster, but will get the pistol later. It is to be of the Colt automatic type. The equipment is very complete and all new. Will get a picture of the stuff and send it home.

Capt. Wheeler, our squadron commander is to have charge of the new aviation field at Detroit. We have orders to leave not later than the 8th of July for Detroit. We will be equipped with 36 airplanes, about the same number of trucks, several machine guns and shops tools for setting up and keeping the machines in running order. The field at Detroit is to be for the training of young aviators. I do not know yet what my job will be.

This squadron is about as strict as a military school. The Capt. and first sergeant have tried to make this the best company in camp, so there have been about 50 transferred out of it into other companies. It has been the survival of the fittest. As the incompetent men were put into other companies, good men would be put in to take their places.

World War I

We have to take great pains with our dress to have our shoes shined, our trousers clean and neat, and must have all shirt buttons butoned. We must wear a black neat tie at all drill and other formations aside from fatigue. As this is the only company that wears ties and

A DeHaviland bi-plane of the 8th Aero Squadron. (Courtesy of Shirley Gaughan)

takes such pains, we attract some attention. It was hard at first to get out of our tents dressed properly on the spur of the moment, but we have gotten so we would rather do that than the old way. The first sergt. is very considerate of his men in every way. If they do their work they get along alright. If they don't they go out of the company.

Our address will be: 8ᵗʰ Aero. Squadron, Selfridge Aviation Field, Detroit, Mich.
I am feeling fine and hope you are too.
We had a pay day the 21ˢᵗ. I was paid $7.00. We get another pay day just before we leave.
Saturday P.M.

I was interrupted yesterday. The company which is [to] help build a camp road. This morning we had general inspection after which we had our picture taken as a company.
You asked about our sleeping. We still sleep on cots (canvas covered). Have been issued two blankets and a tick to be filled with straw. It is warm enough, so we do not need the tick, so we did not fill them. Nobody sleeps on the ground.
We are getting fine rations now too. This morning for breakfast we had, Post toasties with sugar and milk, bread and butter, coffee and meat stew consisting of potatoes, gravy and beef.

This noon for dinner we had bread and butter, baked beans, green onions, cabbage, and Lemonade, also bread pudding with pudding sauce.
For Supper, last night, we had bread and butter, potatoes, and

gravy, boiled ham and ice tea. I am living better now than I did in South Bend. We did not get such good eats before the squadron was formed, but it hasn't been bad at all.

You asked about a mending kit. We are issued a needle book arrangement containing thread, needles, pins, buttons, and scissors, so we can do quite a deal of mending. I made me a bracelet watch case for my watch out of some leather taken off one of the new leggings.

We had a little rain yesterday. The first good shower since we've been here.

Will have to stop now, hoping to hear from you as soon as we get to Detroit.

Lovingly your son, Leon

I received the paper and enjoyed it very much. It was a very beautiful wedding this summer.

Farmer's first stop in Europe was Thetford, England where he remained only a short while before moving to France.

France
American E.F.
8th Aero Squadron
Nov. 30, 1918

Dear Father;

I wrote to Mother a short time ago so will answer your letter tonight. I just received a letter from Mother saying that you all had recovered from the Influenza. I am certainly glad to hear such good news, as the epidemic is very serious in some localities.[14]

I am in good quarters and am enjoying the best of health. We had a fine Thanksgiving dinner consisting of: Fried Oysters, Beef steak, Mashed Potatoes, Bread, Coffee, gravy, Potato Salad, Cabbage Salad, Pumpkin and Apple pie, Chocolate Cake, Grapes, and Nuts. We have some very good cooks.

Hoping to hear from you again soon. I am, lovingly, your son, Leon

I wish you all a Merry Christmas and a Happy New Year . . . .

Farmer returned to Indiana in 1919. He, along with his squadron, received a commendation for their service in France. The 8th Aero Squadron clocked up 900 hours of flying; total losses were eight killed, three injured and six missing.[15]

WORLD WAR I

Margaret (Peggy) Williams Johnsen

❖

Ph.M2 Clifford Warren Williams
Assistant Surgeon, 82nd Company
6th Marine Corps Regiment

Warren Williams hailed from Wisconsin. Williams was more fortunate than many front-line participants – he did not suffer the horrors of trench warfare. Instead, he was responsible for putting the survivors back together again. His first letter home was written the day after Mother's Day; for the first time ever, he was not home to celebrate.

Somewhere in France
Monday P.M. [May] *14/18*
Dear Mother:

Yesterday was Mother's Day & even if I could not go to church I remembered it & thought that it was a great deal different than any I have ever had before. That is in a certain way, but at the same time you saw all the boys that are over here wearing a flower of some kind that showed that they knew what day it was, even if they were a great many miles from home & out of the States.

I tried to get a cable off when I got here, just to let you know that it was all O.K. But you have to go through a great deal of Red tape, so you might just as well wait for a letter to get to you, as it will get there just as soon.

I have met a bunch of Corpsmen that left the States before I did and they sure are looking fine in every way, & I guess that by the way they drill you here, etc. that they sure ought to stay in good condition as to their physical & mental side of life. I have just about considered that a many could do anything if he had to & if he got used to it.

I am feeling fine in every way & I guess that I sure shall stay that way if I have anything to say about it.

If you do not hear anything of my allotment it is because I took it out after my Record had left America, but as I can take our cut here it is all O.K. I will let you know as soon as I find out for sure.

France sure is one durn healthy country & I know this, that it sure is a fine country for plenty of fresh air. The trees have been all leaved out a long time & the fields are all about 2-3 feet high & look fine, & just about all of France is put into cultivation or is raising food it is all cultivation here . . . .

WORLD WAR I

Oct. 14, 1918
France
> Dear Mother:
>
> Your welcome letters came to me this time, while things were very hot & while I was reading them, there was just about as many shells & machine gun bullets going around us, as possible. It sure was one warm sector, just about as hot as I have ever seen. It was the "Champaign" sector, our first & I hope our last time there. We sure gave the Dutch [Germans] more than they expected though and the French think that there is no one quite like the American Marines.

After Williams wrote his mother, he shared more details with his father:

> **Later.**
> Dear Dad:
>
> I will answer your letter also on this page, as paper is a little short. Your said in your letter that from what you have heard that I have sure seen a fine taste of Hell. Well I have but I want to say this that we have not seen half the Hell, & do not expect to see it that the Square heads have. They are sure catching the Devil & the U.S. Marines are giving them a darn good share of it.
>
> Dad letters from me may seem far between & not very full of anything interesting but you know you can not write a letter here like you can [at] home. So if they are few & far between & all they say is that I am all right just let it go at that, & leave the rest for me to tell when I get back to the good old U.S.A. for I sure will be able to tell it there . . . .

Oct. 17, 1918
Some other place in France
> Dear Folks:
>
> I got some real paper tonight & a good place to write . . . .
>
> Everything is going fine here and the Allies are continuing to give "Fritz" all they have coming, & hoping that each day a victory will bring the war just that much nearer the time when we can all go back to the States, with the Kaiser licked & licked good. They sure have been launching it to him lately & I do not think that he will stand for a great deal more, with out finding he has "bit off more than he can chew." He knows it now [?], but is just bull headed enough to try and fight.
>
> . . . I am also sending in the letter a ribbon like the Germans wear on their Iron Crosses, & a German mark that

you would very likely like to see, & of which we see plenty of here. The kids can have them for a souvenir if they want to, or you can do any thing else you want to with these. . . .

Everything here is going fine. It is getting like fall, but we have a good place to sleep, with plenty to eat. So don't worry at all for Uncle Sam is sure looking out for us here. We wear our overcoats now after supper & it feels pretty good.

. . . Will hit the hay now, write often & send pictures if you can.

Love to all, Warren

Oct. 28 / 18
France
    Dear Folks:

It has been some time since I have had much of a chance to get a letter of any kind off home, & the way things are going here now, every one is still pretty busy, but I can get a short note off at least, & leave the rest of the war to talk of later after it is all over.

Everything is going fine, & as it is getting a little cold, we are doing our best to keep the "Squareheads," as warm as possible, & are making out fine in all places. Things are beginning to look now as if we were making it a little too warm for him, for he sure is putting up a fine line of talk, and we are all hoping that before long we will not have to address our letters U.S.A.

Well as I said starting this I just wanted to make it short & everything to let you know that everything is all O.K. After things are over here & it is not as busy as it is at present, we will be able to write a little better letter, but until that time this will have to do for a real letter.

Love to all, Warren

Warren Williams (following the Armistice on November 11th) identified his unit's location as LeMans. He was detached from the military hospital there and worked in a casualty camp nearby. With the armistice, there was also the great opportunity to travel more freely around both France and Germany. For Williams, the race to get home at the end of the war was quite different from the majority of the Doughboys.

Le Manns, France
A.P.O. 762
Dec. 13, 1918
    Dear Folks:

Not much news of any kind, but you can sort if try & say some thing, to let folks know that you are all O.K. at least.

WORLD WAR I

I am still at the same place & I do not know what they are going to do with us & when they are going to do it, just trusting to luck that something will happen in the near future. I sent to the Co. about ten days ago & expect any time to get some of the mail that I have missed for the last two months. Very likely when I do get that I will be able to answer a few things that you very likely have asked. We will not be in the States by Xmas. I know that for sure, but from all you can get here now, we may be any place. Personally I would rather go over in Germany with the Marines for I sure would like to see what I can of Germany while I am here, as when I do get back, it is hard telling when I will have a chance to see it again. Very likely I will have a fine language when I do get back. English, French & German all mixed up, what do you think of it? So you see as long as I have been with the "leath-ernecks" through the worst of things here, I sure want to go through the better part of the time here. They will have things coming that they rate, & I sure do hope that they do get theirs . . . .

With love to all & a Happy Xmas as ever, Warren

By January 1919, Williams' Marine unit was moved to Leutesdorf, along the Rhine River, where they became a part of the Army of Occupation. He was billeted with a German family and with the war over, developed some new opinions regarding his former enemies. Germans.

Leutesdorf (o. Rhine)
March 24, /19
    Dear Mother,
        . . . .You ask what parts of France I have been in & where I have been. Well Mother to put it all together we have been in all parts of France, North, South, East, and West, also in a great many cities. Have not had the pleasure of a Liberty in Paris yet, but have been through there two or three times. I have seen all I want to of France, & after this it is going to be see America first. The trip home will also, as you say be a great deal different than coming over, as we can see things in a different way. . . .

Leutesdorf (o. Rhine)
April 4, 1919
    Dear Mother:
        . . . Yes, we live at the same house as the [German] girls, right across the hall from them & have our sick bay (Co.) downstairs. There is no war on now, & with the women there

never was & although they are Germans, they sure are fine people. Seems more like home than any thing I have had for a long time & it also makes life a great deal more like it should be. We eat at the same place, just a private mess is served. The lady of the house cooks for us and we draw our eats from the Galley. Little extra things we can get, which are quite a few, we buy and as she has cooked in a restaurant for nine years, we are getting heavy, getting real home cooked eats & plenty of them. Don't much care if they send us home for a while or not as I still have two years to serve, & at present I am having a better time than I ever had . . . The girls are fine girls, straight as a string as I am good looking (but we are not allowed to fraternize with the Germans (?) they say . . . .

Well my time is up for the sick bay, so I think I had better cut this short . . .

Write often & with love to all, Warren

April 23, 1918 [1919]

Dear Mother,

Well folks, with the help of God & a few franks [Francs] I sure am having one fine time taking in all the different placed of France I can see.

I started out on the 18ᵗʰ of April on a 14 day leave, & have sure been doing some traveling since. We had our first stop over as usual in Paris. It sure is some town & when it comes to dressing etc., a variety etc., the people of America sure will have to come to Europe. I have been many places & many styles since I got here but in the summer time, this country sure is a regular place in that line. We saw most of the things of interest there & one of the most wonderful thing that I ever expect to see, is this new picture painted for the Allies. It was called the "War Pantheon". It is about 150 ft long I should judge & thirty or forty high. I can't explain it very well, but I will try to get a booklet on it when I go through Paris on the way back to Germany.

We left Paris & came south, first to the city of Lyon. That is a fine place also, & has just about everything there that a fellow wants for excitement.

Leaving Lyon, we came still farther south, to Marsailles, Cannes & are now in Nice. Cannes. . . . Nice is situated right on the Med. Sea a very short ways from Italy. It is near & if there ever was a place in Europe or where America called God's Country, it is Nice. I never was taking up with any place like Nice. Palm trees, ripe oranges, mountains, Med. Sea & one of the "fastest" little (?) towns I have ever seen . . . .

World War I

*We are going out to Monte Carlo tomorrow & from there
over into Italy a little ways. I very likely will have plenty to
tell you when I get back to Germany, but now I will just state
a few of the things that are here, & what I see on the different trips.*

*I do no know where we shall go after leaving here as the
only thing you can plan ahead on is keeping enough money to
get back into Germany.*

*The was sure was a "sar bon Sector" but if a fellow can
get a few trips like these he forgets there ever was a war, & if
they would send all the soldiers home from this S.O.S. & just
have a small army of Supply, then leave us in Germany &
grant us leaves to France. I would not much care if I got home
for a year or more, for it sure is a fine sector here in Nice.
Wish you would be here to enjoy it with us, as it is a trip that
you will remember all of your life & Nice accordingly to what
I have seen is a great deal better than Paris all in all.*

*Will write again in a few days & until I get back to
Germany I will have to wait for mail from Home.*

Love to all, Warren

Cliff. W. Williams

3rd Bn, 6th Regt.
U.S. Marines
A.E.F.
Germany

End Notes

[1] The family information for George R. Duncan comes from the [British]
Commonwealth War Graves Commission, which has a database for
commonwealth soldiers who are buried in Europe. http//www.cwgc.org
(March 6, 2004).
[2] A.D. Ellis, *The Story of the Fifth Australian Division: Being an
Authoritative Account of the Division's Doings in Egypt, France and Belgium,*
(London, 1920), p. 95.
[3] *The Story of the Fifth Australian Division,* p. 96.
[4] The same Commonwealth Graves Commission also summarized the
events of 19/20 July 1916.
[5] The 38th (Service) Battalion: Formed at Plymouth, 20 January 1918,
from Jewish volunteers. 5 February 1918, left England, arriving Egypt
March 1918. 11 June 1918: attached to 31st Brigade, 10th Division. 25

WORLD WAR I

July 1918: unattached from Brigade; during September 1918, attached to Australian and New Zealand Mounted Division, in Palestine. *The Royal Fusiliers (City of London Regiment) in 1914-1918.*

[6] The Jewish battalions became the 38th through 42nd Royal Fusiliers. The battalion was "chiefly intended for the reception of Russian Jews, to be enlisted under a special convention with M. Kerensky's Government. Permission to use Kosher food was granted with the assurance that the battalions would be employed on the Palestine front, and would be granted a Jewish name and badge if they distinguished themselves. About 2000 Jews joined from England . . . [but] their enlistment was stopped with the fall of M. Kerensky's Government and the victory of the Bolsheviks in Russia; but, in the beginning of 1918, a widespread movement of voluntary recruiting began in the United States and Canada. . . . The recruiting campaign in the United States, Canada, the Argentine, and especially Palestine, evoked unprecedented enthusiasm, both Zionist and pro-British. The 38th Battalion, under Lieut-Colonel J. H. Patterson, landed in Egypt in January, 1918, to complete their training, and went to the front in June, 1918." From H.C. O'Neill, *The Royal Fusiliers in the Great War,* (London, 1922), pp. 26-27.

[7] A dirigible is a self-propelled, lighter-than-air craft which frequently floated virtually silently above the front lines in an observation capacity.

[8] The capital of Taranto is a province on the Gulf of Taranto, which is an arm of the Ionian Sea. It served as the headquarters of the Italian fleet and as a chief naval base.

[9] Port Said is on the Mediterranean Sea at the entrance of the Suez Canal. Founded in 1859 by builders of the Suez Canal, it served as a military hospital for wounded troops from Gallipoli.

[10] Egyptian Expeditionary Forces referred to the British Army in Egypt. Formed in March 1916 and established at the Port Said headquarters, it was formed to command the growing British forces in Egypt.

[11] Tel El Khebir is a military fortification sixty miles east of Cairo and the site of a victorious British battle in 1882, in which the British gained effective control of Egyptian affairs by defeating the insurrectionary Egyptian army.

[12] *The Royal Fusiliers,* p. 27.

[13] The 38th wore a purple sleeve badge with the Shield of David in 1918. Later, in 1919, Hendin's unit and the other Jewish battalions "were given the name 'Judeans' and a special badge, the 'Menora' . . . with the Hebrew word, *'Kadima'* ('Forward and Eastwards'). *The Royal Fusiliers,* p. 28.

[14] The first wave of enfluenza cases began at Ft. Riley, Kansas in March

of 1918. Incidents of the flu were greater at military bases and coastal ports. The second wave spread world wide as troops began to return from the European front in the fall. The deadliest month for flu fatalities in the U.S. was October when there were an estimated 195,000 deaths. There were over 500,000 fatalities in the U.S. and twenty million world wide before the pandemic declined in June of 1919.

[15] Commendation from Headquarters Air Service, Second Army A. E. F., February 18, 1919. From personal papers belonging to Leon C. Farmer's family.

World War II:
THE PACIFIC THEATER

THE WAR IN THE PACIFIC represented the first front by the Allies against the tyranny of Japanese totalitarianism, against their attacks and subjugation of millions of people. Before the tide turned against Japan, its empire reached from New Guinea and the Malay peninsula in the south where it threatened Australia, to the seven thousand Philippine Islands, and across countless Pacific atolls to China and Manchuria, as well as the far reaches of the Aleutian islands.

After Pearl Harbor's "Day of Infamy," the American forces regrouped, trained, built, and then deployed navy, infantry, and air forces on a massive scale. These forces island-hopped through the Solomon, Admiralty, Caroline, Marshall, Gilbert and Mariana islands. The Americans reclaimed the Philippines in late 1944 and early 1945; they used B-29 bombers to fire-bomb Japanese cities from the air, and they also threatened invasion by sea and land.

Diaries, memoirs, letters and oral histories from the men who fought in the Pacific theater are a testament to their courage and determination to do their duty no matter how difficult, whether it was landing on Guadalcanal, going ashore at Leyte or Iwo Jima, surviving sinking ships, kamikaze attacks, killer typhoons, or enduring years of Japanese imprisonment.

LIEUTENANT JOHN W. TEMPLE
701ST ORDNANCE COMPANY, 5TH AIR FORCE

"One of the Expendables"

Temple began his service in April 1941, when he was called to duty from his job in Milwaukee. John W. Temple, a graduate of Lehigh University, was raised a Quaker, yet he and his two younger brothers were all participants in World War II (his brother Bill was a pilot and his youngest brother, Henry, was in the Navy). In October 1945 Temple wrote an account of his wartime service, which took him to the Philippine Islands, prior to Pearl Harbor – and eventually to the infamous POW camp at Cabanatuan on the island of Luzon.

World War II

In Temple's account, he spoke of the initial preparations for a potential conflict:

John Temple. (Courtesy of Shirley Temple)

. . . Our new army was definitely in its infancy. There was practically no modern equipment. For the school we had but one each of the 20 mm, 37 mm aircraft cannon, and a few aircraft machine guns. There was no opportunity for practical bomb handling and little for ammunition handling and gun maintenance. All of these we later learned when we had to 'play for keeps.'

Temple's account, which was written after the liberation of the Philippines, is best read along with an earlier eyewitness report written by Major V. C. Huffsmith, Ordnance Officer, in the 5th Air Force. Huffsmith's report, which was submitted in November 1942, detailed the initial deployment of Fifth Air Force men and material in the Philippines from October 1941 until the American force's surrender in April 1942.[1] Because his report is a first-hand account, it adds significant details related to Temple's later report, including the deployment of the 701st Ordnance unit, the outbreak of war with Japan, and later activities in defense of Mindanao.

Temple begins his own account from the time he was called to active duty with the 701st Ordnance Company. He arrived at Clark Field in the Philippines in early October 1941, where ominous signs of potential conflict with Japan increased every day:

A short time after the school I became a casual officer to supplement the 701st Ordnance Company Aviation Air Base, when they embarked from Ft. McDowell, San Francisco, on October 4, 1941. . . .

First, there was a brief four hour stop at Honolulu, and then westward. We could then first see the growing gravity of the Japanese situation. . . . We had a brief look at peaceful, unprepared Guam where we took on water – then Manila harbor landing October 23, and its modern huge pier.

At the end of November, Gen. Brereton had just arrived to head the Air Force, and he spoke to the officers at the base, saying that by the first of April we would be prepared for anything. Apparently, the Nips realized that too. Some anti-air-

*craft artillery arrived and was set up in defensive positions. I
visited one 37 mm gun position – they had no ammunition.
Also, we were digging protective air raid trenches and foxholes, armed with ancient Lewis machine guns.*

*The 19th Bombardment Group had arrived with thirty-
three B-17s. Most were in need of engine changes and repair
after a strenuous cross-Pacific hop. . . . On top of that, they
were obsolete and vulnerable, being without tail guns. Besides
those there were a few P-40s, P-35s and B-10s and
B-18s. . . .*

The Escape Hatch of the Philippines

December 1st brought orders for them to move to Mindanao in order
to establish a new air base at Del Monte. Two-thirds of the men and
equipment had arrived there prior to December 8th. Preparations proceeded at a normal pace, and Temple's unit was established by December
4th.

*On December 2 the 701st was moved to the newly estab-
lished Del Monte Air Base in the Province of Bukidnon,
Mindanao, the southern island. It is in rolling limited plateau
country, surrounded by rugged unexplored mountains and
interlaced by deep narrow canyons that make trucking a haz-
ard. Barrack construction was just underway and also an
underground hanger and some underground tunnels for headquarters, etc.*

*We arrived on December 4, and a day later 400 tons of
bombs arrived at the nearby port of Cagayan. They were
placed in small piles throughout the airfield area.*

*We were still in the process of getting settled in neat vul-
nerable rows of pyramidal tents when 'it' happened December
8 (December 7 in the States) – Pearl Harbor and Clark Field
'got it.' Luckily about half of our 33 B-17s, the only bombers
in the Philippines, had been sent to safety at Del Monte,
while those at Clark Field were pretty nearly knocked out on
the ground. We sent a few B-17 missions out from Del Monte,
but things were too hot for them so, to save what we had, they
were sent south to Java and Australia, places already being
threatened.*

On December 8th, some of the remaining men in the 701st and 440th
Ordnance units were still in the process of departing Manila for
Mindanao on a couple of small ships. According to Huffsmith's account,
when the news of Pearl Harbor arrived, "only dire threats of martial law"
could convince the skipper of the *Samal* to sail with the rest of the troops

– he preferred "evacuating to the hills." It was too dangerous to stay in Manila's harbor. Eyewitnesses aboard the *Samal* saw Japanese planes bombing nearby Nichols Field. Finally, with supplies of ordnance on board, the *Samal*, accompanied by the *Pisquataqua*, set sail on the 10th of December and cleared the minefields around the island of Corregidor. Both ships prepared to zig and zag their way to Cebu, should Japanese planes appear. Once safely to Cebu on Mindanao, the men unloaded the ordnance in record time.[2]

Meanwhile, those already at Del Monte Air Base anxiously awaited further developments. The ordnance account reported on the preparations:

> *Only a portion of the ground* [crew] *for the Air Base . . . had been able to reach there. . . . Anti-aircraft protection for the aerodrome and camp areas appeared as an almost insurmountable task. No anti-aircraft artillery or machine guns existed on Mindanao and none appeared to be forthcoming. . . . The only sources of cal. 50 machine guns were . . . [from] salvaged aircraft.*
>
> *[In addition] . . . pits had to be dug, gunners trained, and maintenance performed. . . . In as much as the Japanese did not wait until we were ready much of our training was carried on by actually firing at Japanese strafers. . . . As time permitted now pits were dug and guns emplaced. . . .*
>
> *For weeks the only ground troops near Del Monte were approximately one battalion of Filipino troops . . . and in as much as a landing was momentarily expected in the Buga area, it was decided that the Air Base troops at Del Monte would be melded into an emergency rifle battalion for the purpose of defending the Aerodrome against paratroops. . . . Every Ordnance and Air Corps soldier put out as though his whole life had been spent in an Infantry outfit. . . .*

Temple continued his account:

> *We, at Del Monte, didn't see anything of the Nips until December 17. The ordnance outfits were eating their evening meal before sunset at our mess setup in a scattering of scrub trees near the airfield when we heard the roar of motors and saw three or four single engine planes coming in low toward the field. 'God they're coming awfully fast for a landing,' someone remarked. They sure were, and Nip zeros let fly with all guns and worked over all we had on the airstrip. A couple of B-17s, a B-18, and some trucks manned by our 50 cal. machine guns for anti-aircraft fire were ineffective. Two days*

later 27 medium and dive-bombers worked us over, followed by eight 4-motored flying boats. The bombing was ineffective, due to the way we dispersed, and we had but two deaths and only a few wounded. We were beginning to wonder where in Hell was the Navy and why no planes from Australia? News from Luzon was not heartening, and the Nip advances in the Indies were meeting no opposition. The house was falling about our ears – Singapore fallen, Manila taken, and our troops with their backs to the wall in Bataan. Dispatches read that the Nips were continually taking 'unimportant' islands in the East Indies to establish air support for further advance. Even Davao, on the southern part of our own island of Mindanao was taken. What a mess!

As they listened to the news of islands that had been captured by the enemy, Temple and his comrades were no longer optimistic:

After the January promise for aid had failed to material-ize, we could see the hopelessness of Philippine defense. [It was] just a matter of time. It seemed a shame – the engineers' airstrip developments in Mindanao were abundant and well hidden. I, personally, saw eight air trips in just Bukidnon, and there were numerous others in other sections, – plenty of space for planes by the hundred. The Nips kept the air constantly patrolled, forcing us to keep most of our road traveling at night only. . . . The air bases depended completely on the land for sustenance. . . .

Huffsmith corroborated Temple's assessment of preparations:

Initially camp life was a nightmare. The well-planned camp was abandoned when war started, and after the first strafing raid men were forced to hide like animals. Meals were very poor and were prepared before dawn and after dark. Bread, butter and fresh vegetables were absent from our diet. Men and officers slept in trucks and under tarps. It rained nearly every night. Beds, although little used, were very hard and often very wet. Sickness became prevalent. Malaria and dysentery resulted in the hospitalization of many men and officers. Hospitals were little better than camps. Quinine was so scarce that prophylaxis treatment of Malaria was impossi-ble. Mail ceased to reach Mindanao shortly after the outbreak of war. Clothing and shoes became worn out. Nerves reached the breaking point. . . . This was our situation about the first of February [1942].

WORLD WAR II

In the new state of the war, old planes had to be abandoned and new ones quickly created. Could they hold off or even delay the inevitable? And for how long? Not wanting to sit around and wait, Temple and others in his unit took action:

> *A Nip destroyer raided our nearest port on the Inland Sea and lent a feeling of weakness to our situation, so we began moving bombs inland to the side of a big natural barrier, the Mangima Canyon. Over there too we hid our Ordnance Company with its shop trucks. It was doing valuable work in devising land mines, converting salvaged 50 cal. B-17 machine guns to ground guns and anti-aircraft guns, and repairing the rapidly deteriorating automotive equipment. The number of trucks began shrinking as we robbed from one to repair others. One of our clever automotive sergeants even constructed a truck from the parts of six other makes. It was affectionately named "the six and seven-eighths."[3]*
>
> *It fell to my lot to be officer in charge of the guard of our secret airstrip, which the Nips never spotted. There we had the largest American air force in the Philippines. The collection was tragically comical – a P-40, which dared only risk reconnaissance, the 'Duck' an old Navy amphibian, used to fly to beleaguered Bataan, a defenseless Waco, an antique unarmed biplane P-12, a P-35 . . . , and a civilian Beech craft. We had had several other P-40s, which had cracked up, resulting in killing the nerve-wracked pilots. We did have one satisfying thrill. One day the P-40 returning from reconnaissance came across a Nip seaplane and cleaned him up with a couple of short bursts of his guns. Other than that, all we did was to sit and take it.*
>
> *Perhaps the most important mission of Del Monte Air Base was to operate as 'the escape hatch of the Philippines.' Pairs of B-17s or B-24s would fly in at night from Darwin, Australia, to evacuate important personnel. From there we saw General McArthur and President Quezon go, as well as airplane mechanics and pilots needed for resisting the threat to Australia.*
>
> *In the middle of April we made our last air blow in the Philippine Islands; ten B-25s and three B-17s were flown up from Australia and stayed for several days at the different air strips in Mindanao to make a few missions. Two of the B-17s bombed Nichols Field in Manila, and the B-25s worked on some shipping near Cebu. Cebu was taken at the end of April when my Ordnance Company moved into the center of Mindanao taking bombs and equipment. Then we were*

stymied; when you are at the center there is just no other place to go.

Despite being in heavy jungle, the 701ˢᵗ was dive bombed with casualties. Their spies were on the job.

Then Bataan fell [April 9ᵗʰ]. Soon after Nip landings were made on new fronts, a third front near Davao having existed since the first of the war. We gave the Philippine Army all of our 50 cal. ammunition and rigged up more ground machine guns from salvaged B-17 weapons. Also made firing pins for Mindanao's artillery . . . two to each front.

By April 29ᵗʰ, 1942, Major Huffsmith was ordered to evacuate to Australia, and he was one of the last officers to leave Mindanao. He recognized that "the defenses of Mindanao were none too good," but that "they would hold out for a few months until we were able to move most of the Air Base units out by air." However, this scenario would not occur.

With the surrender at Corregidor on May 6ᵗʰ, only days remained before the Japanese would overwhelm the American forces:

Fighting was hardly under way on the new fronts when Corregidor surrendered, followed by Mindanao on May 10, 1942. The story we had was that General Sharp, in command of the southern islands, was inclined to fight on with guerilla warfare, and that is what the base personnel, of our own volition, were mentally prepared for, but General Wainwright was forced to include us in the surrender. Otherwise, the Nip General Homma would not accept the surrender of the already disarmed Americans on Corregidor, that is: they would be liquidated.

Davao

After the 1942 surrender at Malaybalay, many American soldiers, including Temple, were sent to the Davao Penal Colony near the southeastern city of Davao on the coast of Mindanao.

About 2,000 Americans and 8,000 Filipinos reported to the surrender area at Malaybalay. After five months about 1,000 American technicians were shipped to Japan, and the rest of us Americans to Davao. Our treatment up to then had been excellent, – the Nip colonel in charge was quite a gentleman. The small group which surrendered at Lanoa, however, had a rough deal — three were shot as reprisal for escapes, and the rest were made to do a 43 kilometer walk wired together and with very little water – one died.

WORLD WAR II

The complexion of our treatment changed at Davao. There we were joined by a woebegone lot of 1,000, who had been shipped down from Luzon. While we at Malaybalay were being so well treated, about 5,000 Americans and 27,000 Filipinos on Luzon died as a result of the 'death march', starvation, mistreatment and disease. . . . However, all of the 2,000 of us in the Davao Penal colony soon reached a mean of health condition. . . . More than 90% in camp had malaria as the quinine was inadequate. Food given us was not sufficient for the work we did, although there was enough lying around. In groves right near our compound bananas, in excess of what the parrots could eat, and coconuts lay rotting on the ground. We became adept at smuggling in small amounts of food foraged when out working, – items such as snails, snakes, dogs, parrots, sweet potatoes, anything which could be classed as edible.

It was quite evident that the Nip policy was to feed us only enough for a bare existence and no more. I dropped, with the aid of malaria, from 165 pounds to 115 pounds, never to get back to more than 125 pounds, of which much was water swelling and edema. To top that malnutrition showed up, beri-beri, pellagra and protein lack, causing swollen legs. The latter made one feel as though they were walking around with a pair of heavy boots. We were hardly in shape for the farming work we were doing. Food became an obsession – the topic for all bull sessions was food. Everyone made notebooks listing countless recipes and also eating places in the States where we planned to go whenever we got back, – hungry day in and day out, month in and month out, year in and year out. Would we ever have a full belly again? The prison became a monotony of work, sleep and hunger, but we were always hopeful. Rumors were always plentiful and we just kept dully waiting for "the Yanks and the tanks."

Japanese punishment was inconsistent:

. . . Sometimes the guards, who were Taiwan (Formosan), would treat us decently and other times would take pleasure in overworking, overloading and beating the fellows. Quite a few developed ruptures by being forced to handle loads beyond their capacity. As one example of many: I and three others with clubbings as an incentive, carried a litter of corn weighing 660 pounds barefoot for a mile and one-half, a tough job for a healthy man much less scrawny, sickly ones such as we. . . .

WORLD WAR II

In the spring of 1944 a group of 750 officers and men were sent to work at an airstrip at Lasang. That bunch was on a prison ship which was sunk by an American sub, – 80 escaped. I avoided that detail by being retained for helping in the planting of sweet potatoes. No one else had taken the trouble of identifying the vines of the seven different varieties we had.

Cabanatuan

Temple wrote, "in June the Davao camp Philippine Prison Camp #2, was terminated and we 1350 were shipped to Luzon, one of the northern islands of the Philippines" and then on to Cabanatuan, located towards the southern end of Luzon. According to Temple, "[i]t was a miserable month-long trip in a freighter hold – [it was] hot, but little water, packed like sardines, – it came damn close to duplicating the black hole of Calcutta." Unbelievable as it was, conditions continued to get even worse; yet the American POWs remained resourceful:

The food situation was the worst ever. To indicate how little we ate I had one bowel movement after ten days and that was unnecessary - the next time was another nine days. Fortunately there was but one death, but one of our doctors said that if we had been on the boat a few days longer we would have begun to die like flies.

We were sent through Manila to the Cabanatuan prison camp. In passing through the streets we could observe American Red Cross items for sale on push carts - apparently that had been sold to the Pinos by the Nips. We had . . . received two Red Cross packages per man in 1943 and four in 1944, really godsends. We started to blossom out a little as we partook of them. We certainly could have used more, but the Nips told us bluntly that they would follow International Law only if it was convenient to them and that condition apparently never existed.

At Cabanatuan the diet was as slim as ever, but the Nips were at least listening to our complaints of mistreatment and now and then would do something about it. We were not surprised at their change of attitude as we knew the gist of what was going on in the outside. We had some very clever lads repairing civilian radios for the Nips, and they stole enough parts to construct a small set that they hid in a canteen. With that they could hear American broadcasts, which news was passed by mouth.

WORLD WAR II

Liberation

By September 1944, after five months of imprisonment, Temple and the other prisoners become more hopeful when they heard approaching American planes. Liberation would come, but it was not known how soon:

> *... The morning of September 21st – no work that day and everyone was in the compound. The sun was coming through fleecy clouds over the hills to the east when a slight steady hum became perceptible. As it grew steadily in volume, we looked at one another and thought 'Boy here it is!,' and it sure was. Out of that golden glow we could see weaving pairs of Navy fighters escorting a tight formation of dive-bombers. Then, nearby, two other groups appeared and headed west across the central plains of Luzon. [W]e could hear the dull rumble of bombers as they pasted hell out of Clark Field. Everyone came out of their barracks patting each other on the shoulder and being quietly jubilant. The Nips had forbidden demonstrations but were too upset to attempt enforcing the rule.*
>
> *Thereafter we had weekly visitations of Navy planes, even working over the airfield near our camp.*

However, September turned into December, and there were still no prospects for rescue:

> *In December the Army planes showed up, B-24s, P-38s and A-20s and then we heard about the landing in Lingayen January 9th. We could see artillery flashes at night and the Nips seemed to be very confused and disorganized. One day a unit would head eastward past the camp and the next day back.*

Men of the 6th Ranger Battalion are shown advancing toward the Japanese Prisoner of War camp at Cabanatuan, Luzon, Philippine Islands, January 27th, 1945. (National Archives)

WORLD WAR II

Our permanent guards pulled out and left the camp under the lax jurisdiction of Nip commanders in the area. We then had 500 left in the camp. In October and December groups had been moved out to go on ill-fated prison ships where most of them perished. Only the sicker ones were left and I fortunately had become quite ill in October. We looted the Nip camp area, collected forbidden vegetables from the garden and killed Brahma steers that were roaming wild nearby. For three weeks we did nothing but eat. I gained thirty pounds in that time – others gained fifty.

Two prisoners of war were rescued and liberated from Jap prison camp on Cabanatuan, Luzon, P.I., by the 6th Ranger Infantry Bn. They are left to right: Navy pay clerk Paul Jackson, and 1st Lt. Willard Smith, US Army, January 31, 1945. (National Archives)

Finally, in January 1945, rescue came for Temple and the other survivors at the hands of U.S. Army Rangers:

On the pitch dark night of January 31 at about eight o'clock a group of us were sitting outside the barracks when shooting began all around the perimeter of the camp. We hit the dirt and thought the jig was up, looked like the Nips were going to do away with us, when the shooting stopped and someone shouted 'the Americans are here.' They were the gallant Rangers. We ran out of the camp posthaste over dead Nips, then stumbled across the rough dry rice paddies and streams to the nearest barrio, where the Filipinos furnished carabao carts to carry the forty percent who could barely walk. Later the moon came out making the walking easier. We passed safely through the Nip lines and after a total of twenty-three miles hit American lines.

Homeward Bound

After about three years of grueling prison work and illness, Temple and the other prisoners were finally on their way home:

From then on it was a story of quick evacuation, a pleas-ant trip to the States and a hero's welcome in Frisco on March 8, 1945, three and one-half years after that fateful trip west-

ward. We then began to catch up with the three year void in our lives, the vast amount of new American equipment, WACS, WAVES, this new man Truman, women running streetcars and taxies, women in men's work, rationing, new slang, new songs and cold weather, – what we had been missing in our Rip Van Winkle past. A sobering thought contrasts the rejoicing, there are damn few left to enjoy this rebirth. Out of approximately 20,000 Americans in the Philippines in 1941 about 5000 survived, a 75% loss.

This was the price America paid for unpreparedness in the Philippines. We were indeed 'the expendables.'

After liberation from the Japanese on January 30th, 1945, Temple was promoted to captain, and, at the time of his discharge in 1947, was a major. Five years after he returned home, John Temple married and began raising a family. He became a successful metallurgical engineer, and eventually became superintendent of one of the mills, from which he retired at age sixty-two. In retirement Temple was active as a conservationist on the Monterey Peninsula in California.

LIEUTENANT LEONARD GADI LAWTON
COMPANY F, 2ND BATTALION
5TH MARINES
1ST MARINE DIVISION

Not long after completing Officer Candidate School, Gadi Lawton enlisted in the Marines on July 21, 1941. Little did he know that the attack on Pearl Harbor would occur less than six months later and that he would be called upon to serve with the 5th Marines in the South Pacific. Lawton remembered distinctly he heard "the first rifle shot fired by an American in World War II – it was on Tulagi. I heard it. I didn't fire it, and I don't know who did, but that was . . . the very first offensive action of World War II anywhere."

As a warm-up exercise, Lawton "went to Fiji Islands . . . and stopped for a little practice landing. We had never landed. So we had a practice landing in the Fiji Islands. [We] loaded again and took off for the Solomon Islands." The Marines' strategic objective was to capture the Japanese airfield on Guadalcanal before it could be completed and used against American forces. This required successful landing assaults on the nearby islands of Gavutu[4], Tanambogo[5] and Tulagi, the capital of the Solomon Islands[6].

Lawton remembered how a series of "miracles" helped the Marines in their efforts. "Our flotilla passed by the southwest corner of

WORLD WAR II

Guadalcanal at Cape Esperance[7] – we were spotted by the Japanese lookouts, but the lookout's message was never received at the Japanese headquarters 600 miles away on Rabaul." Another miracle was that the airstrip construction crews were two days behind on construction; if the Japanese planes had been there when they landed on August 7th, 1942, "we'd never gotten to shore." In addition, when their landing craft were coming into shore, the enemy cannons "were never fired once."

Landing on Tulagi

Lawton landed with the "Raider Battalion, the Parachute Battalion, and the Second Battalion, [of] Fifth [Marines] . . . on Tulagi, . . . the capital of the Solomon Islands." As Japanese troops had occupied the island since May 1942, the Marine landing was met with opposition and also surprise. Lawton recounted the unexpected situation on Tulagi:

> So we landed under fire . . . and then it stopped. I thought,
> 'What's going on here? Do you win a war in two hours?' . . .
> So we took up positions. . . . We spread out over the whole
> island. A mile long, and a half mile wide. Tiny little thing.
> And two smaller islands Gavutu and Tanambogo. . . . So we
> took . . . those three islands. . . . But, what happened is that
> the enemy force had moved into caves. These were honey-

US Marines wading ashore at Tulagi, August 7th, 1942. (US Navy photo, National Archives)

combed with caves. At night, midnight, they came out. The Japanese never attacked in daylight. Never. They are night-fighters. . . . The only time they fight in the day is if we attack them.

Thus, the Marines were in a difficult situation – how could these still-green Marines rid the island of the Japanese? Their equipment was "terrible. . . . our rifles were 1903 Springfield single-shot bolt-action rifles. . . . We had a few machine guns. We didn't have any tanks. We didn't have any flamethrowers. We didn't have anything to clean out a cave with – except grenades." Thus, the dilemma was partially resolved the next day when one Marine suggested that they throw hand grenades into the caves. The first attempt failed, to their amazement, because the grenade was thrown back at them. They learned quickly, and tried a more successful delaying tactic. This same Marine now "pulled the pin, let the handle fly; held a live grenade for three seconds or four seconds and threw it in. That's how we cleared out caves down in Tulagi," bragged Lawton.

Landing on Guadalcanal

A couple of days later, on August 7th, while under the cover of darkness, Lawton and the Fifth Marines crept across the water from Tulagi to Guadalcanal. Additional forces landed at Lunga Point on August 9th.

We jumped off and got ashore. I suppose I learned one of my greatest lessons in my life that night. It was dark. We had just landed helter-skelter. Our battalion was mixed up with paratroopers and raiders and everything else . . . and it was black. And I was standing there on the beach with four or five of the men and said, 'My God. We got jumped off it' And here comes a . . . a guy and he shines a little light on his collar and it's a full colonel . . . and he's the regimental commander. And he said, 'Who's in charge of this group?' I said, 'I am. I'm dead right about that,' and so on. And he said, 'What did you do?' I said, 'Nothing. We're just standing here. We don't know what to do.' 'Well,' . . . he said in a loud tone of voice, 'any idiot can do nothing. I expect more than that from a Marine officer.' I guarantee you, that night I was an officer from that moment on. I made decisions. I did something. Yea. That's when I became a Marine, if you want to know the truth about it. That very night.

With the arrival of daylight, the Marines got organized. Lawton's unit was held in reserve while other paratrooper and ranger units moved into positions where they could observe the Japanese.

WORLD WAR II

[We] *did a lot of patrolling because the enemy kept landing troops at night . . . around us. They could've landed in
daytime. In fact, they were still landing in the morning. We
could look down a few miles and see them unloading. They*
[the Japanese] *chopped a trail all around our perimeter.
Guadalcanal is eighty to ninety miles long; twenty miles
wide. The Marines held . . . six miles. So they could land
wherever they wanted. We didn't have any artillery that could
reach them. We didn't have any airplanes. We didn't have
any ships. So they just landed. . . . They cut a path through
that jungle called the "East-West Trail" – or we called it*
[that]– *so that they completely surrounded us with that trail.
So we had to . . . send patrols out and find out where the trail
was and where the enemy . . . might be. . . . Many of the
patrols were ambushed . . . Division Intelligence decided that
they're coming down Bloody Ridge . . . 'cause it led from their
trail right to the airstrip . . . So we lined up there to meet
them. . . . We were not on the original front line, but our battalion was reserved for the whole outfit. Now, reserve is good
and bad. You don't get the initial attack, but, where the
attack is heaviest, and they're breaking through, that's where
the reserve goes.*

Japanese attack on August 12th

"Well they did come down the night of the twelfth. . . . Boy the fighting – we could just hear it going like mad and we were . . . the only
reserve there was for that home perimeter. Everybody else was on the
line. . . . So we knew we were just waiting to hit. Well, . . . they were
breaking through . . . and it was almost morning." At which time General
A. A. Vandergriff ordered the reserve unit to move up the ridge to rein-
force. "Well, we got up behind that ridge . . . where we had to cross the
top of that, and work our way quickly up to the . . . where the fighting
was. But as I say, it was almost dawn, and at dawn they quit fighting . . .
which is a blessing."

Lawton told how a man from E Company and a man from F
Company "lined up" close together "and somebody gave a signal, 'You
both run across the top of that bridge . . . try to get cover . . . in the jungle off the top of Bloody Ridge and move up.' Well . . . came my time and
a boy from E Company . . . and they said, 'go!' and we jumped up and
ran. A shot rang out, and that boy fell with a bullet right in his head. . . .
So I crawled up there and we got in position and then the next night of
course they started again. So we had two nights . . . pretty heavy fighting
here. By that time, we had used up almost all of our ammunition and
what little food we had. The Navy came to supply us and the *Wasp* was
lost."

World War II

The Japanese suffered heavy losses in their struggle to hold the East-West Trail. They also were low on rations, according to Lawton. "They had no supply. When they used up their rations, they're done. [If] they were wounded, [if] they didn't have any food . . . more of them I expect died on the East-West Trail than we killed that night. . . . They were a motley crew. So we were hungry, but they were starving, and there is a difference."

The Matanikau River

Marine operations on Guadalcanal continued unabated into October, by which time Lawton was the company commander (due to casualties). In October, in order to rid the west side of Guadalcanal of the Japanese, Lawton recalled:

> . . . we planned to start going down to the Matanikau River – which is on the west side, (that's where we were all the time – always on the west side of that six-mile perimeter). We got ready to cross the river. There was only one way across it at that point. Right at the mouth of the Matanikau is a sand bar that just nearly concludes that river. There was a spillway – a natural one . . . oh, fifteen or twenty feet across . . . but a small . . . area of water that you could wade across. It would be about waist deep. And then there was about a three or four foot embankment there. You had to jump up on that embankment before you could . . . start down the coast. Paul Moore . . . was . . . the B Platoon [leader] there. . . . So, here I was – a clean, bean, second lieutenant . . . had three . . . 400 men under my command. I said, 'Paul, you take . . . you take your boys . . . send four . . . five of them over there . . . get them up there . . . so they can set up a protective part for the rest of us to come.' Well, those boys got up there, and the minute they got on top, the enemy opened fire. All five of those boys were wounded. Both sides had to retreat. But, Paul . . . went over there five times and brought a boy back every time.

[Lawton found out after the war that "the same day we had planned to cross and wipe them out, they had planned to cross and wipe us out. We met at the Matanikau."]

> My company was up higher on the river, and that's where the engineers put that little floating bridge across. And we . . . crossed there into the jungle, and . . . we were to take the ridge – the ridge that ran parallel to the coast . . . and move down it – protect the flank, that larger, main body that was going

90

along the coast. . . . There's undergrowth all the way down to it. There's not an open area by any means. A few palm . . . a few . . . coconut palms, but most of it's just . . . rough undergrowth. . . . We moved along and finally the main body was held up.

The Beach Road

Lawton was ordered by Major Walt to move down the hills a few hundred yards "[to] cut down to the ocean, and to cut off the Japanese who were holding them up. So, we did. We fortunately found a place that was maybe thirty or forty yards wide . . . that was fairly clear. . . . So, we went down there . . . and . . . we cut off that whole outfit. They didn't know we were there. . . . I knew that the enemy was on . . . further west, so that *we* were surrounded. We surrounded them, and they had us surrounded. So I divided the company into two groups . . . [one] facing one west and one east," and Lawton waited to see what would happen next. At this time, another Marine discovered a "handful of electrical wires." Lawton ordered the lines cut, and

> *Boy, it wasn't three minutes until the troubleshooters . . . came along. They couldn't figure out what had happened to their system of communication. Well, our boys . . . were walking along with their heads down, looking at the wires. They came from both sides. [They] . . . shot them immediately and of course one or two of them bound to have gotten away, so they knew we were there. So then, we started getting activity from both sides coming at us. Those on . . . farther along to the west pulled up a small cannon . . . like our 37 mm cannon – a little cannon on wheels. They were blasting down what we call the "Beach Road." . . . But at any rate, they couldn't shoot at us through the jungle. They'd just hit trees, so all they could fire at was that down the road and then they'd send a few troops down there. They didn't know how many we had; we didn't know how many they had. It was kind of, 'I'm scared and you're glad of it,' . . . That's the sort of situation we were in. But, still . . . we were getting peppered pretty good and getting some casualties . . . and . . . I was very apprehensive about that night, because they attack at night. And I thought, "Oh, my." We are not very strong as one company here facing two directions . . . But, all we got was a few [Japanese] men sneaking around trying to . . . get through at night . . . [and] even though it was terrifying – wasn't that hard of a battle . . . during the night.*

WORLD WAR II

The next day, Lawton and his men were in the same position. They radioed for some supporting artillery fire, which he hoped would drive out the enemy. While making a reconnaissance of the area where some shells might have landed, Lawton went looking for his friend Paul Moore.

> I walked along and I saw some leaves moving like that (wavering in the air like normal leaves), and there wasn't any breeze blowing. So I stopped. Here stepped out from behind the tree was the enemy. We were staring at each other face to face . . . both of us went for our firearms and I happened to go faster. That's the only man that I know that I killed face to face, but that's not a good feeling. When you're shooting at 200-300 yards away, that's an impersonal war, but when you see somebody face to face, and you shoot them, that is different. That's different. I've often thought about that boy. His parents had no way of knowing where, when, or what happened, because we had them in a trap and nobody escaped from that trap. That's just not a good feeling. Not a good feeling.

For a brief moment Lawton thought, ""Hey I have won,' but it didn't take long to regret. I think about it every once in a while now – that boy. Sure am sorry I've got that on my résumé. That's just not good. You're in war to kill somebody but you do it and then you think, 'I did wrong.'"

By the next morning, Lawton's unit was low on ammunition, and therefore more desperate measures became necessary. At this time, he received orders from the battalion commander to form his men into a skirmish line that was to come down the hill and push the enemy "into the ocean."

> So as soon as it was light enough to see, we spread out and started down that hill. Well, they were ready for us. About 8 o'clock we hadn't gotten very far. We were down on flat land, but that was about it. And . . . they had some machine guns and they nailed at us and we were losing people. And I saw Paul Moore go down. Right through the chest – all the way through. He went down like ton of brick. And I thought, 'Boy I have to crawl over there and see if I can say goodbye.' And there was a corps man there . . . a navy boy who is trained to be a medic in the field, and he and I crawled on our bellies like a snake . . . Got over there where Paul was . . . and he was putting compresses on him and doing whatever he was trained to do. And I saw another boy beginning to move in[to]

a position where he'd be . . . right where that gun had caught Paul . . . and I sort of half way raised up and I said, 'Don't go there!' and a bullet came right across . . . and went through my left shoulder. I don't know if it was a stray bullet or someone had me in their sights, but if I'd have been an inch closer to the ocean, I would never be telling this story.

. . . I dropped back down and the corpsman said you have been shot. And I said, 'Well, all I felt was a jar.' It wasn't hurting at all. So I dropped down and he said, 'I can't do anything for you, I am trying to keep Paul alive. You're apparently not hurt too bad.' . . . So he gave me a little bit of sulfa. . . .

Lawton, in spite of his injury, quickly got back into action, helping some men roll a 37 mm gun into position.

There were . . . two or three guys [who] were trying to pull it, and it was through that underbrush and everything. And I went over and grabbed one of the wheels . . . and I just about wrecked my right shoulder and both of my shoulders weren't worth a nickel. But we got it up there because I knew where they had to shoot, so I said, 'All right boys, here is where we gotta shoot.' Well, we shot with that thing until we ran out of ammunition, but we quieted down . . . [the enemy's] machine guns and things. Then we could all begin to move forward. And we moved forward and actually pushed them into the ocean. They jumped in the water and tried to swim or run through the water and to get further to the west where they knew they had reinforcements, but of course they ran into the boys that had relieved us, so none of them . . . none of them got out of that. So, by that time it was about 12:30 or 1. . . .

Following the assault, Lawton was evacuated with some of the other wounded to a hospital that had been set up near the airstrip. Since he had not been seriously injured, he talked the driver of a Jeep into letting him "ride the spare tire," until he "got across the Matanikau. [and] . . . got further back into our territory.

Lawton received numerous medals for his service, including the Silver Star and Purple Heart, as well as a Presidential citation and commendations for his and his unit's accomplishments on Guadalcanal. Yet Lawton does not "put much stock" in such rewards for bravery and hasn't even read his citation. "Maybe they thought because I was shot and went ahead and fought for another four hours or so. Maybe that is why.

I don't know. . . . I wasn't any braver than anyone else. We all marched down that hill. We all pushed them into the ocean and a lot of guys were shot worse than I was."

HEADQUARTERS OF THE COMMANDER
SOUTH PACIFIC FORCE
OF THE UNITED STATES PACIFIC FLEET.

The commander South Pacific Area and South Pacific Force, takes pleasure in COMMENDING

SECOND LIEUTENANT LEONARD G. LAWTON
UNITED STATES MARINE CORPS RESERVE,

for service as set forth in the following

CITATION:

"For conspicuous gallantry and intrepidity in action against the enemy in the British Solomon in the period of October 31 to November 3, 1942. Lieutenant Lawton had command of a company during the offensive action of his battalion from the 31st of October to the time he was wounded on the 3rd of November.

During this period of time Lieutenant Lawton was outstanding in the tactical handling of his company, both in the approach to the enemy and during contact with the enemy. On the morning of November 2, Lieutenant Lawton was ordered to move his company from its position on the left of the Regimental assault line to envelope and cut off an enemy strong point of about one battalion which was holding up the advance of the right flank of the regiment.

Lieutenant Lawton maneuvered his company into its position out the enemy's communication wires and set up a back to back defense on a front of approximately two hundred yards in order to secure the break in the enemy's lines of communication.

As a result of this maneuver Lieutenant Lawton's company received a strong counter attack of the enemy from both the east and the west. With the aid of artillery and machine gun fire each of these attacks were repulsed and his company maintained its position until relieved late in the evening, suffering few casualties and inflicting heavy losses on the enemy

W.F. HALSEY,
Admiral, U.S. Navy.

Certified a true copy:

E.S. CARRIGAN,
Marine Gunner, USMCR.

Letter of commendation to Lt. Lawton.
(Courtesy of Dr. Leonard Gadi Lawton)

MAJOR ROBERT W. PALMER
400TH SQUADRON, 90TH BOMB GROUP, 5TH AIR FORCE

"I enlisted on the eighth of December 1941, the day after Pearl Harbor. I was driving a truck, I was saving money to go to college. . . . I was driving from Chicago to Minneapolis [where he lived at the time], [and when] I heard on the radio that Pearl Harbor had been struck, and I didn't know quite where that was, but I knew that . . . it had belonged to us. And so, I pulled in to the place, I parked my truck, went in the office resigned before I even knew whether I could get in the service . . . ." Since Palmer was neither a college graduate nor twenty-one years old, his enlistment was delayed until March of 1942. He had always been fascinated with the idea of flying and Lindbergh had been one of his childhood heroes, so he was thrilled to qualify to train as an aviation cadet. In fact, he remembers how his "first ride in an airplane was my *first* lesson." Since he was short in stature, he was sent to fighter pilot school, where he initially learned how to fly P-40s and P-51s. "We were hotshots. We flew upside down mostly. We flew up as high as we could, dove straight down and see how fast we could go, we were crazy." But because the need in the Pacific required more B-24 pilots and few fighter pilots, Palmer ended up training with B-24s. This "probably saved my life, to be sent to B-24s," because these planes could not be flown recklessly.

As soon as Palmer qualified to pilot a B-24, he was sent to New Guinea, where he joined "the 90th, Bomb Group, Fifth Air Force, 400th squadron." He remained with this group until the end of the war and flew a remarkable 175 missions (versus the more typical 30-40 missions). "I was there because they kept me. My crew went home after a year. They kept me because I had the most combat hours in the group, the most instrument hours in the group. I had flown instruments more than anybody else in the group. [The Pacific region] had awful weather and they kept me there to be an instrument instructor pilot."

Palmer remembers how his bomb group literally mission-hopped from one island to the next across the Pacific. "I started out in New Guinea at Port Moresby[8], went over to Nadzab. . . . Then we went up to Wakde, which was an island, then we went to Biak, which was an island. Then we went to Morotai, then Mindanao, and then Luzon, and then Ie Shima, which is northwest of Okinawa, and we were up there getting ready to invade Japan" when the war ended.

Flying conditions were far from pleasant.

> *We didn't have any sonar. No nothing, these were very primitive airplanes. The wind whistled through them, like the wind whistled through a crap house. It was amazing, forty below zero up there; you would freeze your butt. [It was] 130° on the ground and up there 40° below, 130° above on the ground in New Guinea or 120°, and you would put on those wool suits to fly at high altitude and lose ten pounds just taking off, just ringing wet.*

Palmer flew countless hazardous long-distance missions, such as when they bombed "the oil fields in Balikpapan on the island of Borneo." At this time they were flying "from a base on Biak Island, northwest of New Guinea. We weren't supposed to be able to fly that far. But we flew that far and we lost a few planes in the ocean on the way back. They ran out of gas."

One of Palmer's most memorable experiences occurred in December 1944, when his plane was shot up and disabled while flying near Manacorri, in northwestern New Guinea.

> *I didn't have time to think about much. My right landing was shot off, my right fourth engine – number four engine*

*was shot off. Number three engine was on fire, but number
one and two were running. And we were at 19,000 feet, about
500 miles from home. . . . We had 500 miles to go – had my
plane was all shot up, my engineer was killed. A piece of ack-
ack caught him right under the jaw and tore off half of his
head. He was standing right behind my shoulder, and he was
always running the airplane [and an] anti-aircraft explosion
right under the airplane – a piece of shrapnel came up through
the bottom and got him right there and killed him. But there
we were with all that problem, and a dead engineer. And
what we did was stand on the rudder as much as we could,
to keep the plane that we didn't power over . . . except number three had a little power.*

*The right landing gear was shot off, right engine was shot
off. Everything on the right mostly was badly destroyed. I
had a dead engineer and everybody was having a hard time.
I had to bring the thing in because I had a dead body on
board. He couldn't jump out. . . .*

As he came into his base at Nadzab, he managed "to keep that side
of the plane up, we lost altitude gradually, went over the strip, got
home." The crew jumped out at 5,000 and "I brought it around and
crashed it." This was not particularly heroic, "because those old clunkers
went pretty slow and I got it down to about eighty miles an hour and I
got down near the ground. I just kept pulling up the nose, until "fump"
in the Kunai grass, which is about ten foot bull rushes . . . and I just
plopped it into the kunai grass."

Palmer reflected on both his apparent good fortune and the down-
side of leadership: "I am very lucky, I have always been lucky." In contrast to this, in the spring of 1945 his responsibilities as squadron commander depressed him. As "a squadron commander the night before the
next day's bombing, I had to make up the list of what airplanes we were
going to fly, what pilots and crews were going to fly, and where we were
going to go. I *hated* that job, I didn't want the job, but the reason I got it
'cause I had been there longer than anybody else. And I had to send my
friends out on bombing missions and they got killed, and that's not very
nice. You don't ever get over that."

These were onerous responsibilities for men so young. Palmer
remembered that " . . . we were just kids. My whole crew was average age
[of] twenty-two. I was twenty, when I started flying with them. I was
twenty-one when I was flying combat. I grew a mustache, told everybody
I was twenty-three. I was twenty-one. But I didn't want anybody to know
I was twenty-one. . . . I don't think they believed me, but in those days
we were just a bunch of kids. . . . "

Following the war, Palmer was more mature and motivated to complete his undergraduate college degree quickly and then he went on to medical school thanks to financial assistance of the GI bill. Palmer looks back with pride on his military service and on the life experiences he gained from it. "It made me. World War II was the center of life. . . . It made me believe that I could do anything, and I can, and I do, and I did and I have been very lucky. I have four fine sons, a wonderful wife, a good profession, good health, lots of friends. What more can you want?

FIREMAN 1/C HAROLD LEE HUNT
CVL-30 *U.S.S. SAN JACINTO*

Harold Lee Hunt was born in Kansas City, Missouri, January 5, 1916, and was raised in Nebraska. His father was a sales clerk, and his mother was a church organist, who then ran a rooming house after being widowed with three young children. Hunt left behind his wife, Mae (Fleharty), and his almost two-year old daughter, Georgia Lee, when he enlisted in Belleville, Kansas. He joined the Navy and was rated fireman first class. Hunt served on the U.S.S. *SAN JACINTO* (CVL-30, "The Little Queen") in the South Pacific, coincidentally, at the same time as George H. W. Bush, who was an ensign in flying group VT-51. Hunt's "diary" was handwritten on onionskin paper; he recorded his thoughts on various dates between August 7th, 1944, and May 19th, 1945. His diary has been supplemented by the ship's official history, *A Short History of the U.S.S. SAN JACINTO: 3 May, 1944 . . . 15 September, 1945.* [9]

Hunt sailed from san Francisco on August 7th, 1944 and arrived at Guadalcanal a month later, during the latter part of September the SAN JACINTO sailed for the U.S. port at Ulithi.

> *Oct. 11, 1944 – Arrived at Ulithi Island in the Mackenzies Group* [Western Carolines] *and this is pretty dangerous territory. Always having air raid alarms. Wrote to Mae to-day.*

The *SAN JACINTO* was headed back to Ulithi for replenishment when it was recalled to action on October 23rd upon receiving word that the Japanese fleet was moving in the direction of Leyte. As a part of Carrier Task Force 38, the *SAN JACINTO'S* Air Group 51 launched air attacks against Okinawa, Formosa and Luzon.

> *Fri. Oct. 20. – Still here and still on this tub. The fleet's due in to-morrow. I should write more but there is absolutely nothing to write about. My thoughts are all on Mae and little Georgia Lee. If I could just see them for a little while making it wouldn't be so bad. It's Hell too. People at home wouldn't believe it so why not forget it.*

WORLD WAR II

The Second Battle of the Philippine Sea began on 24 October, during which the *PRINCETON* was damaged (and later had to be sunk by American forces). Finally, on October 31st, the *SAN JACINTO* headed again towards Ulithi and arrived there on November 2nd, 1944.

> ***Monday Oct. 23.*** *– Still here but don't think it will be long now. Just finished writing to Mae. That's all for now I guess (Sure am losing weight.) It's now seven P.M. on Monday Oct. 23, 1944 at home. Air raid.*
>
> ***Sat. Oct. 28.*** *– Still here but was assigned to a[n] aircraft carrier, The San Jacinto on the 25th but it isn't here yet. Took on 600 survivors of the Princeton yesterday. Some of them not in too good shape. Wrote to Mom to-day. Feel better than I did but still weak.*

The *SAN JACINTO* docked in port at Ulithi from November 2nd to 5th, 1944, and Hunt boarded the ship.

> ***Fri. Nov. 3*** *– Went on S.P. [shore patrol] duty Mon. Oct. 30 and Tues. Oct. 31 on Mog Mog island. Came aboard San Jacinto there Nov. 2. Worked like hell to-day (Friday) loading supplies. Quite a ship and seen lots of action and going to see a lot more. Here's hoping. wrote to Mae and Mom to-night letter no. 5*

The *SAN JACINTO* set sail on November 5th for the Leyte-Samar area, but the destination was changed to the San Bernardino Straits.

> ***Thurs. Nov. 8*** *– Just off the Philippines and boy is it rough. Plenty of trouble as soon as weather clears. Our planes went out yesterday. Wrote Coop and Ellen to-day. Wish I was home. Wonder how Mae and little Georgia Lee are. God bless them.*

The *SAN JACINTO* arrived and was in action with combat patrols off Leyte, P.I., on November 11th, working to intercept and destroy a Japanese bomber and torpedo plane. The action of this fleet also destroyed four transports, a light cruiser, and three destroyers west of Leyte en route to Ormoc Bay.

> ***Sunday – Nov. 19*** *– Been too busy to write here lately but we have had quite a time. Had these attacks last week and one this A.M. Looks like we are heading into trouble again to-day. Wish I could put down in words, my true feelings but I don't know how. I know it's hell and sure wish I was home. We will*

probably go home in the Spring unless we get hit and have to go back for repairs or something. I wonder how Mae and Georgia Lee are. I just wrote to them and Mom and the folks. Hope they are getting along okay.

On November 20th, the Task Group retired towards Ulithi and arrived there on November 22nd.

Sat. Nov. 25 – *Wrote to Mae and G. Lee. We are in Ulithi Islands & had our Thanksgiving here. We were lucky. Pulled in Nov. 22. I'm on boat duty. Not so bad here but wait until the water gets rough. Plenty lucky on our last raid too. Hope our luck holds.*

On November 29th, the *SAN JACINTO* headed toward Guam (minus Air Group 51, which was replaced with Air Group 55), where there was a week's intensive training for the new air group.

Wed. Nov. 29 – *Left to-day for Guam. I'm dead tired. Just finished writing to Mae and Georgia Lee and Mom.*
Thurs. Nov. 30 – *Left Guam for? Beautiful island but torn to hell.*
Thursday Dec. 7 – *One year ago today I joined the Navy. If I could write well enough to express myself & say what my thoughts have been, the things I have seen & did, I could write the most wonderful book that was ever written. We are going back into Ulithi & are scheduled to drop the hook at 0915 in the morning. Had a very quiet and peaceful little cruise this time breaking in our new squadron. Wrote Mae and Georgia Lee to-night. Sure wish I was home.*

The *SAN JACINTO* headed back from Guam to Ulithi on December 8th, to prepare for its return to sea duty on December 11th, whereupon it set sail for eastern Luzon in order to support the capture of Mindoro by pinning down air operations on Luzon from December 14th to 16th.

Thursday–Dec. 14 – *Day before yesterday I received word Mae's father had died. Launched our attack to-day at sunrise. Five of our planes failed to return. Japs haven't come out after us yet. Must be scared or planning something. Attacked Luzon. I'm dead tired and going to try and get some sleep.*

Hunt reported losses (also mentioned in the ship's history) involving fighter pilots, one pilot who was rescued from a water landing, and two more pilots who crashed into the ship's barriers.

Harold Hunt (row 2, 3rd from right) with most of "A" division fire crew on flight deck of the *SAN JACINTO*. (Courtesy of Georgia Hunt Hollister)

> ***Fri. Dec. 15 –*** *Made another raid to-day but still no Japs out after us except subs. Had two torpedoes this A.M. One across our bow and one across stern. Both missed and no damage done. On the mid-watch this week.*

On December 17th, the ship moved to a refueling zone, but rough seas and adverse weather forced discontinuation of this operation. On the 18th, "one of the most severe typhoons ever to be encountered and survived by naval units in the Pacific . . . reached its maximum intensity about 1030 with many ships suffering varying degrees of damage, three destroyers being lost. The *SAN JACINTO* suffered severe though not crippling damage when the excessive rolling (42 degrees) and pitching caused a plane on the hangar deck to loosen and snap its heavily reinforced mooring lines. The runaway smashed into other parked aircraft, loosing them in turn, and in short order the hangar deck was a sliding mass of planes, engines, tractors and other heavy equipment which was smashed from side to side, ripping open and carrying away air intakes and ventilation ducts. Small fires broke out and were quickly extinguished and, by the valiant efforts of repair parties and volunteers, the hangar deck was secured by 1600. . . . " The ship returned to Ulithi for repairs from the 21st to the 30th of December, 1944.

On December 30th, the *SAN JACINTO* advanced again, with units of the Thirty-eighth Task Force, in order to spearhead an amphibious assault led by General MacArthur on the Lingayen area of Luzon. For this purpose, the ship launched air strikes against airfields in central Formosa

Rolling seas during typhoon, Jan. 5, 1945 and overturned TBP (Torpedo Bomber Plane), *SAN JACINTO,* Jan. 5, 1945. (National Archives)

and northern Luzon from January 3rd to the 6th, 1945. The 9th of January was designated as D-Day for Lingayen on Luzon and MacArthur's landing. The ship's flight crews resumed attacks once off the "mine-laden" waters of Formosa and destroyed enemy planes on the ground.

> *Tuesday Jan. 9* – *It's been a long time since I wrote here. Dec. 18 – Off Formosa we ran into a typhoon and it tore us to hell. We lost six or eight cans [destroyers] in that storm. Lost about 16 of our own planes. We are lucky to be afloat. Went back to Ulithi and tied up to a repair ship. Left about Dec. 27 for Formosa, Luzon and the Leyte Sea. Sure weren't in any condition to go to sea. First two days of this operation we destroyed 16 enemy planes. Lost two ourselves. That was Formosa again. Don't know yet what happened on Luzon. I know we covered the invasion & it was a hell of a battle. We are now on our way back to Formosa and will be there in the A.M. I sure wish the next few days were over because I know we are going to have one hell of a fight on our hands before to-morrow is over. I wish I could write down the strange*

thoughts and feelings I have. It's 3:15 A.M. I have the mid-watch and we are getting damn close to Formosa now. I hope Mae said a little prayer for me last night. Just wrote to her a while ago and to Hasly [Harly?] Hall.

Thurs. Jan 11 – *Made air raids were not attacked. Last night about 1:00 P.M. [A.M.?] we sailed through the straits of Formosa into the China Sea. We are now about 200 miles from Hong Kong China. We are after the Jap fleet. To-morrow we fuel [?] —– in French Indo China. If no Jap fleet between here and there we head back and go to Hainan [Island] after them. From there we go to Hong Kong and from Hong Kong back to Formosa and from Formosa its hard to tell where we will go if we are still afloat. A[nd?] he's the farthest west any American ships have been since the war started.*

Fri. Jan. 12 – *Still in China Sea. To-day we destroyed 32 Jap ships. Last one of [by?] our own planes. Pretty good hunting but I sure will be glad when we get the hell out of here. Wrote Mae, Coop & Frances to-night.*

From the 15th through the 16th of January, the crew continued striking airfields on the China coast and Formosa area, as well as the Hainan-Takao shipping lanes south of Hong Kong.

Mon. Jan 15 – *Believe we are going thru Formosa straits to-night & sure hope so. At least we will be out of this China Sea area. Had two attacks to-day but no damage done. It's 11:25 P.M. and my watch is over at 12:00 Midnight. Wrote to Mom and Mae tonight. Lots of rumors about us going back to the states after this operation. Boy, I sure hope so. Keep your fingers crossed.*

Wed. Jan. 17 – *Still in China Sea. Heading into a storm. Hope it isn't as bad as last one. Almost ran aground yesterday. Had only fifteen ft. of water under us. Huge swells rolled us and knocked planes over board. Three in blisters and 1 cat walk and mashed them. Don't believe we lost any men. The planes were worth over a million dollars. Lost in about ten seconds. Rumors still thick that we are going back to states.*

Adverse weather hampered further operations on the 18th of January. When the weather improved, the fleet changed plans, exited the Balintang Channel on January 20th, and resumed its strikes against aircraft, shipping and installations. The fleet, including the *TICONDEROGA* and the *LANGLEY*, were attacked off the east coast of Formosa on January 21st; the *SAN JACINTO*, returning from Formosa, shot down enemy aircraft in this action.

WORLD WAR II

Mon. A.M. Jan. 22 – It's 5:30 and reveille just blew. Day before yesterday we were attacked by planes from 4:15 P.M. until midnight. Again at 2:45 A.M. No damage done. Yesterday they came at us at 12:00 noon and were at us until 8:30 P.M. Yesterday they hit the LANGLY [Langley] once and the TICONDEROGA twice. TICONDEROGA is on bad shape and went back. Also hit YORKTOWN and two destroyers. Lots of men killed & wounded. Cost Japs plenty of planes. Probably lost our chance of going to the states for quite a while. We sure are lucky they don't ever hit us.

On January 22nd, crews flew from the ship to obtain reconnaissance photos near Nasei Shoto and also to carry out attacks on enemy shipping and grounded aircraft. On the 26th, Hunt's ship arrived back in Ulithi for a two-week long replenishment and recreation period on nearby Mog Mog Island. On this island , the men could enjoy "cool drinks and base-ball, swimming and shell-hunting, horseshoes or volleyball" and even a late Christmas celebration.

Mon. Feb. 12 – Arrived back in Ulithi Jan 29. I was put on the captain's gig as engineer here. Left on Sat. Feb. 10 after the longest stay ever have had in one place. Met Clyde and Jones on the beach. Had a lot of mail and a few packages. One from Mae and one from her mother. Also one from my mother. We are covering the invasion of the Bonin Islands this time. Will make two strikes there and then go on to the Bay of Japan area. Probably have plenty of trouble too. Took on a few new men this time in, but we are still short a few. Decorations were awarded this time. Silver Star, Bronze Star, Purple Heart etc. all a pain in the ass. Took on a new executive this time too.

While back in Ulithi, the *SAN JACINTO* was detached from the Third Fleet and reassigned to the First Carrier Task Force in the Fifth Fleet. On the 10th of February, their fleet moved to approximately 150 miles off the southeast coast of Honshu. From there on the 16th, the flight crews began their first attacks against aircraft engine plants at Ota and Koizumi, Japan; on the 17th they attacked Tokyo. Because of inclement weather, though, further attacks were cancelled, and the *SAN JACINTO* moved southward into position for the anticipated assault and landing on Iwo Jima, which were scheduled for February 19th.

Fri. Feb. 12 [16] – Well, here we are – 75 miles off the coast of Japan and are we ever giving the Japs hell. To-day we destroyed 28 planes in the air and whipped out an aircraft factory on the island. Raised hell with all the air fields around Tokyo too. The Japs haven't come at us yet but will I suppose. I'll never forget this. It's colder than hell and I worked all day during G. Q. [General Quarters] in that damn whale boat. About froze to death.

***Sunday** – **Feb. 25** – Hit Iwo Jima and covered invasion in Volcano and Bonin Islands last week. To-day we hit Tokyo again. No trouble. Headed for China Sea again after Jap convoy. Sure am getting home sick. Wish I was home.*

On February 27th, the *SAN JACINTO* was rammed by a refueling tanker, which required that it be repaired back at Ulithi. Meanwhile, the fleet proceeded westward again towards Okinawa, where flight crews destroyed more enemy aircraft and ground installations. On March 2nd, the *SAN JACINTO* left for repairs in Ulithi, arriving there on the 4th.

***Went into port** [Ulithi] **March 4** – tied up to repair ship and repaired damage received by tanker ramming us. Went and got skipper a new boat. Japs attacked several times while we were in port. Randolph was hit bad here (Ulithi).*

The *RANDOLPH* was struck by one of two Kamikaze planes on March 11th. The Okinawa Campaign began on March 14th once Task Force 58 departed Ulithi. "Okinawa was the strategic key to the whole Pacific tactical situation" and was a bloody campaign. On the 18th and 19th of March, flight crews destroyed enemy aircraft and assembly plants at Miyakanojo and Kagoshima respectively, and shipping at Kure Harbor south of the Shikoku coast. During these assaults, various ships in the fleet (the *FRANKLIN*, *HANCOCK*, *HALSEY*, *POWELL*, and the *ENTERPRISE*) were hit by kamikaze attackers and/or bombs. A carrier, the *WASP*, was also hit, and the *SAN JACINTO* was sent on March 22nd to replace the *WASP* and was assigned to another Fast Carrier Task Group, Task Force 58.

***Left port March 13**. So far we have hit Shikoku, Iwo Jima, Nagasaki [Nansei Shoto?], Yokohama, Keto Iowa [Kerana Retto?], & I don't remember what else. The last few days have been bad. Japs attack all the time. Every carrier in our task force have been hit but us. BATTAN, BELLEAU WODS, ENTERPRISE, FRANKLIN. When big E was hit we changed task forces and took E's place [the WASP actually]. Japs have strafed us and hit us with shrapnel but have missed us with bombs and suicide planes. They have been using army planes & better pilots. Don't seem like out luck can hold out much longer.*

World War II

On the 23rd and 24th, operations began in support of the invasion of Kerama Retto, Okinawa and Ie Shima, flight crews destroyed ground installations and sank a ship convoy in the East China Sea. Attacks resumed against the Okinawa area on March 27th, while on the 28th the *SAN JACINTO* planes sank cargo vessels coming from Kyushu.

[continued from March 13th] *We have destroyed lots of planes including one of our own that we shot down ourselves. Also destroyed Jap convoy of troops. Three troop transports, several cans and S.K. [?] We were the first to take on ammunition at sea. Worked O.K. to-day when we re-fueled took on ammunition, stores and mail. We'll probably be a long time out this time. They say we are going back in June. Sure hope so. Made my rate this time at sea but hard telling when I'll ever get it. That was the biggest rawest deal I ever had pulled on me. Wish I was home. Seems like my nerves are going bad on me lately. I'm nervous and jittery all the time. I think some good rest would help a lot. Had a letter from Mae and one from Mary [?] to-day. Everyone is O.K.*
Sun. April 1 – It's 12 midnight, we are about 75 miles off the islands of [O]kinawa. To-morrow at dawn or to-day I should say, we invade [O]kinawa. It's about 60 miles long and 35 miles wide. Probably be the toughest invasion of the war. It's about 250 miles from Japan proper. We are putting ashore the first and sixth marine divisions and twenty-seventh and seventy-seventh army divisions, about sixty thousand men. It will take some time to get them all ashore. Have been hitting [O]kinawa for the last month, softening them up. If and when we secure [O]kinawa, the war will be practically over. We will be right in the Japs front yard. This is where they almost got us about two weeks ago. Glad I'm not in the Army or Marines on that landing. Latest dope is that we will be home in June. Here's hoping. Took another man off and sent him back to the states yesterday that went nuts. They call it sico nervosas or battle fatigue. We call it just plain nuts. I think if we ever get a bad hit about half the crew will crack up. Seems like a lot of them are just on the verge. Sometimes I think I'm a little off myself.

During action on April 2nd to 3rd, six men were lost and one was rescued from the aircrews on the *SAN JACINTO*. On the 6th, the Japanese "launched an all-out air offensive against all American forces in the vicinity of Okinawa. An estimated 500 planes, nearly all Kamikazes, attacked . . . [and] over 300 of them were shot out of the air by our fighters and anti-aircraft fire." After noon on the 6th two Kamikaze bombers singled out the *SAN JACINTO*. "Our guns shot a wing off one and plummeted him into the sea off our starboard quarter. The second dove at us from astern, was repeatedly hit by our anti-aircraft fire and flamed up when about 100 yards away, crashing out of control in our wake. . . . A few minutes later another . . . burst out of low clouds less than four thousand yards away and began diving at our bow from dead ahead. Our guns opened concentrated fire at short range and poured repeated hits into him, but he came on in, finally crashing into the sea less than fifty feet off our starboard bow. The ensuing explosion splattered the flight deck and bridge with pieces of plane, Jap pilot, shrapnel, oil and water."[12]

> *Fri. April 6 – Off Okinawa. Japs come at us at 10:50 A.M. and really gave us hell all day. The Texas longhorn was credited with twenty-six and one half planes to-day plus one sea gull. Ship itself shot down four. One missed us less than fifteen feet. We all thought we were hit. Pieces of Jap bodies and plane all over the flight deck. One man killed and one wounded. We certainly showed the big boys how to-day. No runs that I know of were made on another carrier. I don't know whether we are lucky or just plain good. Something – I wonder if we are leaving the task force group to go home to-night. Hope so. Dogged the watch to-night and I'm on the eight to twelve. Wonder if I'll ever get any sleep. Damn Japs haven't let me sleep all week.*

On the 7th, the Japanese fleet sent out their battleship, the *YAMATO* and a screen of support ships. Planes from Task Force 58 sank the battleship, and the *SAN JACINTO* planes sank one of the three retreating Japanese destroyers. From that point on, the duty of the Task Force was to provide tactical air support for the troops on Okinawa and to smother "the violent but spasmodic Jap air counterattacks."[13]

> *Sunday – April 8 –We were at G. Q. all day yesterday again. Shot down several more planes and destroyed a Jap task force. SAN JAC. is credited with one cruiser sunk, 1 battleship – 2 cruisers, 3 destroyers left – 2 badly burning and two got away. Pretty good day's work. Day before yesterday our fleet (5th) destroyed six hundred Jap planes over Okinawa and the fleet had several casualties on Friday and early yesterday morning funeral services were held aboard ship. To-day we are fueling and taking on ammunition. Hope we get some mail. Hope we go home before long. These seem like the longest operation we have ever had.*

WORLD WAR II

Japanese counterattacks resumed on April 12th and 14th, but with little success. On April 13th, members of the fleet learned of the death of President Roosevelt, which was "heightened by the knowledge that his youngest son, Lt. John Aspinwall Roosevelt, was attached to the Task Group Commander's Staff."[14] A silent prayer service was observed for the late President at General Quarters on the 15th of April. Only a day later, at the invasion of Ie Shima, the *SAN JACINTO* was attacked once again by Japanese fighters. Once again the crew shot them down before they could hit the ship. For the next week and a half, operations were rather routine, and B-29 bombers began to eliminate the airfields on Kyushu, which virtually eliminated enemy raids.

> *April 18 – Still off Okinawa and it has turned out to be a gritty good battle. Best yet or worse I should say. Have been under attack every day but two so far. Have had bombers, Kazi[kamikaze] boys and torpedoes but so far haven't been hit. Some G.Q.s last for hours. Sunday we were under attack continually for nineteen hours. Came at us all night & drop flares too. Wish I was home.*

On April 27th, the *SAN JACINTO* retired toward Ulithi, arriving there on April 30th after forty-eight consecutive days at sea. The out-going Air Group 45 was replaced with Air Group 49, while the ship's crew was given time to rest and relax before returning to sea on May 8th.

After a short rest, the *SAN JACINTO* was redeployed with the 58th Task Force to launch more strikes against airfields on Kyushu on the 13th and 14th. On the 15th, the force retired southward for a quiet week with only one air strike launched against Tokuno on the 19th.

The Okinawa Campaign began May 18th and lasted until June 10th, 1945. Strikes were launched against Tokuno, Kikai, and Amami O Shima, which resulted in heavy damage to ground and harbor installations. By May 27th, the *SAN JACINTO* had returned to Okinawa to provide support for the 10th Army.

> *May 19 – Hitting Okinawa yesterday and to-day still the same old ear bangin shit. Never saw anything like it. Be glad when the first of the month comes and I get out of the diesal gang. More later.*

After the war, Hunt returned to Belleville, where he worked as a butcher at Safeway and raised his family.

WORLD WAR II

※

ENSIGN ROBERT J. LAUER
CVL-30 *U.S.S. SAN JACINTO*

Robert Lauer graduated from the U. S. Naval Academy at Annapolis mid-World War II. After a three week crossing on the escort carrier U.S.S. *CASABLANCA* (CVE-55) to the Admiralty Islands in the Pacific, Lauer finally went aboard the *SAN JACINTO* on September 21, 1944. Lauer spent the remaining thirteen months of the war aboard her. After the war, Lauer wrote a memoir about his experiences on the *SAN JACINTO*.

The *SAN JACINTO*, which was a part of Task Group 38.4, "came into the anchorage of Manus Island in the Admiralty Islands, about 4 degrees South of the Equator and North of New Guinea . . . ." These islands, which had "recently [been] taken from the Japanese by General MacArthur's forces," were tropical, with hot days and cool nights. Lauer remembered the spectacular view that he had down to the bay from outside his Quonset hut. On the fifth morning after he arrived at Manus, he was reassured:

> *During the night Task Group 38.4 had entered the bay and dropped anchor in orderly rows. . . . There were 4 fast aircraft carriers, 2 new fast battleships, 3 cruisers and probably 12 destroyers. And this was only one fourth of the total of Task Force 38. In addition there were numerous units of the Service Squadron which had accompanied the task force. I remember thinking then that there was no doubt about the outcome of the War, only a question of how long it would take. The hundreds of us who were awaiting our ships were directed to pack our gear and head for the boat landing area. I said good by to several of my classmates who had made the trip out with me and found the motor whale boat from the SAN JACINTO waiting to take me and a few others out to the ship. I came up the accommodation ladder with my sea bag and other gear, requested permission to come aboard, and then spent the next 370 or so days and nights aboard, interrupted only by an occasional few hours liberty on a Pacific atoll or Philippine island.*
>
> *We left Manus on Sept 25 and went on my first war operation, the tail end of the invasion of the Palau Island group. On October 9 I had my first experience of enemy action when the Task Force was attacked by Japanese Judy type dive bombers. One started a dive on the carrier Enterprise but swung off and dropped a bomb, which hit the carrier Franklin 2800 yards on our port bow. The whole thing was very excit-*

ing, but it did show they played hardball. After the action we had a critique and review in the wardroom, which was done after every enemy attack. It was interesting to me how many different opinions were expressed about which direction the enemy planes came from, where they attacked, and who shot them down. After about three weeks we arrived at what was to be our operating base for about nine months, Ulithi Lagoon, about 900 miles East of Mindanao.

At this time the decision was made that the next event in the Pacific war would be the invasion of the Philippines. Our next operation, as Task Force 38, with Admiral William Halsey as Commander Third Fleet and Admiral McCain as commander of the fast carrier task force, was to destroy as much Japanese air strength as possible in the Philippines and Formosa, as well as in southern Okinawa, to minimize resistance to the invasion scheduled to take place in late October 1944.

There was much enemy action against our task force during this operation. Perhaps the most spectacular took place off the coast of Formosa in mid-October one evening as we were at General Quarters just before sunset. The sky was overcast and the sea was a dull gray color. Without warning from radar or the combat air patrol we were attacked by 13 low flying twin engine "Bettys", Japanese Mitsubishi bombers all carrying torpedoes. My battle station was on the starboard side aft where I was responsible for the 20 and 40 mm machine guns. The first I heard was the chunk-chunk of the guns on the port side. I could look across the flight deck and see the tracer rounds going out, but at first didn't know what they were shooting at. At once all the carriers were firing their machine guns almost horizontally. Then I saw a greenish Betty with her bomb-bay doors open coming directly at us from below the horizon, the nose gunner firing at us like crazy, and the plane in flames behind him. They dropped the torpedo when less than 1000 yards from us, and I couldn't see how it could miss, even though the task force was moving at over 30 knots, turning together in formation. The torpedo hit the water, dived down to get going on its course, and in the process passed directly under the SAN JACINTO! The plane crashed in flames just astern of us. By then a second one was coming at us in the same manner and dropped its torpedo. As that plane went down in flames the torpedo passed just astern of us, and I could see its path as it crossed into our view on the starboard quarter. By this time all 13 torpedo planes were flaming bright orange in the water and creating a weird, almost Halloween like scene or seascape. Some of the Japanese aircrews were floating on their wreckage, but when our destroyers tried to pick them up they simply jumped into the sea and drowned.

The task group just north of us wasn't so lucky. Our sister ship, the U.S.S. PRINCETON, had been struck by Japanese bombs and exploded alongside the cruiser BIRMINGHAM in the process of abandoning ship. The cruiser U.S.S. HOUSTON, which had been built from funds from the same bond drive that had paid for the SAN JACINTO, had taken a Japanese torpedo and her stern section, deck awash, was barely hanging on. She was towed over a three day period back to Ulithi. Over 400 men were lost on these ships.

The next operation was the actual invasion of Leyte in the Central Philippines on Oct 20. The story of the Battle of Leyte Gulf has been told in many books. The San Jac was in Admiral Davison's Task Group 38.3 and we were involved on Oct 24 in the pursuit of the Japanese carrier task force coming down from the North, which our planes completely destroyed.

Kamikaze

Shortly after these monumental events we received a message that the Japanese had performed several suicide attacks by aircraft on some of our ships in Leyte Gulf, and that we should be alert to this possibility in the carrier force. No one took the warning literally, but assumed it meant a series of low level daring dive-bombing attacks. On Oct 30, about 60 miles off the East Coast of the central Philippines we learned to our dismay that the word "suicide" meant just what it said. We had been operating flights covering Army operations on Leyte, since they had not yet established their own air bases. Due to the light prevailing wind from the West we gradually moved in toward land a good bit closer than normal. I recall that at one time in the forenoon I could make out the dim outline of land to the West. That was a disconcerting feeling. Shortly after noon we were called to General Quarters since the radar had picked up Bogies approaching from the Northwest. The combat air patrol identified them as Bandits (enemy) and reported several Splashes (shot down), Then we heard a "Heads Up" which meant one or more had gotten through the CAP (Combat Air Patrol).

What happened in the next ten minutes is something I will not forget. We were searching the sky in the direction from which we were advised the attack was coming. A single plane appeared and dived on the Enterprise while anti aircraft guns from all over the task forced opened up. The pilot aborted his attack on the Enterprise, did a wing over and crashed into the starboard quarter of our sister ship, the BELLEAU WOOD, at exactly the spot where my battle station was on the SAN JACINTO. There was a huge explosion followed by volumes of black smoke and flame as the BELLEAU WOOD attempted to keep station and fight the fires. Seconds later another Japanese plane appeared in a straight uninterrupted dive at about a 45 degree angle straight into the flight deck of the FRANKLIN, just abreast of her island structure. Again there was explosion, black smoke and flame, as two of our four carriers were crippled within a matter of seconds by two small aircraft.

When the BELLEAU WOOD was hit I thought it was the worst bit of luck, that the plane had been shot down and accidentally crashed into her. When the FRANKLIN was hit it became obvious that these were truly suicide pilots and they intended to dive into the ships.

No sooner did this awful realization take place than from my sector on the SAN JACINTO we spotted a third one coming down directly at us, neither altitude nor bearing changing, only the wing span getting larger by the second. We were firing every one of our 20 mm and 40 mm machine guns and we could see the tracers going into the plane. It was a greenish Zeke carrying an ominous brown bomb under the fuselage, and it had an orange meatball under each wing.

At the last moment we could notice the elevation angle move up, and he shot over our heads and crashed in the sea just off the port side, missing the ship by no more than a few hundred feet. I am sure the pilot was killed in the last stages of his dive.

We had not a moment's reprieve when yet another Kamikaze appeared in exactly the same position in the sky as the previous one. At least we knew it was possible to avoid them so we fired every gun we had directly into him. It appeared he might overshoot also, since the force was steaming at emergency flank speed (30 knots) and turning during this entire episode. The pilot made a right turn and dive, attempting to hit the island structure, but narrowly missed it and crashed just off our starboard bow with a huge explosion. Finally a third one started a run on the SAN JACINTO but we concentrated our fire on him and he veered over and headed for the ENTERPRISE but was blown apart in the middle of his dive.

That was the end of the attack. We headed East at full speed with two smoking and flaming carriers with great holes in their flight decks. In the meantime our own planes that had been attacking Japanese positions on Leyte were returning. Neither the BELLEAU WOOD nor the FRANKLIN could recover aircraft. We recovered all of ours and then began to take aboard those of the BELLEAU WOOD. It became necessary to throw planes over the side as soon as the pilots and crews were removed, since we had no room to stow them all. The same was true of the ENTERPRISE recovering FRANKLIN planes. Mercifully no more attacks came out as we steamed away from the Philippine coast in the late afternoon. During the night we headed for Ulithi with a universal feeling of disbelief and shock. Thus began the era of the Kamikaze, which was, with few exceptions, the standard method of attack used by the Japanese against our naval forces until the end of the war more than 10 months later.

Typhoon

On December 1, 1944 we proceeded to Apra Harbor in Guam and unloaded Air Group 51, which had been aboard the San Jac for over a year and had spent the last nine months in combat. We said Good Bye to George Bush and his fellow heroes, for such they were, and brought aboard a new group, Air Group 45. . . .

We then headed back toward the Philippines to provide air cover for U.S. Army forces invading the island of Mindoro. The need for our support was so great that we stayed a few days longer than was advisable in view of the deteriorating weather. . . . The need to refuel was very great and an attempt to do that was made, but the mounting seas and increasing winds would not permit it. With conflicting information of exactly where the storm center was, we actually passed through the eye, where the sea was calm and the sky blue, but not for long! This experience was overwhelming. I was glad to have had it, but I did not want to go through it again, although the following June off of Okinawa, that is exactly what happened.

The December typhoons off of the Philippines caused more damage to our ships than the Japanese had been able to do. We lost three destroyers, which simply disappeared in the storm. All aircraft on the light carriers and a great number on the large carriers were lost as the ships rolled, up to 45 degrees, and pitched in a manner that seemed as though some giant crane were lifting the bow up and up and then releasing it to go crashing down into the sea. We had holes punched in the boiler uptakes and in the ventilation ducts. Electrical equipment was shorted out and boiler damaged by the incursion of seawater.

After three days the storm had passed. Task Force 38 was spread all over the Philippine Sea. We finally reassembled, filed damage reports, and headed wearily back to Ulithi. During those three days it was almost impossible to sleep. Eating consisted of passing out cold sandwiches and some fruit and cold drinks. While walking from one spot to another one often had the option of walking either on the deck or the bulkhead, bracing against the other surface with tired arms. In this typhoon 790 lives were lost.

In Ulithi the Commander of Service Squadron Ten came aboard to inspect our damage and within hearing range of several crew members said that we would have to return to the States for repairs. It took about 45 seconds for this to be spread throughout the ship, and morale skyrocketed! Captain Kernodle, however, had other ideas and said no way was he going to take his ship out of combat for storm damage. So they sent our sister ship, the MONTEREY, back to Pearl Harbor to be repaired and had us go alongside the U.S.S. HECTOR, a repair ship, where we stayed till after Christmas and had all of our damage repaired with both crews working around the clock for ten days. Before the MONTEREY left we took what we could from her. My assignment as a boat officer was to help carry items from the MONTEREY to the SAN JACINTO. I was told what to take by the first lieutenant of the Monterey, Lt Cdr Gerald Ford, another future president of the USA.

Kamikaze II

On the 14th of March, 1945, as Task Force 58, . . . we sortied from Ulithi and proceed north to participate in the coming invasion of Okinawa. We were now part of the 5th Fleet under command of Admiral Raymond Spruance. Whenever we changed fleet admirals we changed the numeral designation of the fleet, presumably fooling the Japanese.

After refueling on March 16th, we deployed off the southeast coast of Kyushu and started a series of air strikes against Japanese air and military installations in preparation for the landing of Marines and Army troops in early April. Antiaircraft fire was intense and we lost our air group com-

*mander on the first sweep. We attacked shipping in the Kure
Harbor and on the island of Shikoku. After a day or so the
Japanese finally launched a full-scale attack against us on the
19th of March.*

*I remember it well because I had just gotten off the bridge
in the morning and was coming down on my way to breakfast in the wardroom. Halfway there the alarm gong sounded. I looked across the sea at the nearest carrier,* the U.S.S.
FRANKLIN, *just in time to see a dive bomber, not a
Kamikaze, come out of the clouds and drop two 500 pound
bombs which hit her dead center of her flight deck. At the
time this happened the FRANKLIN was just starting to
launch fully loaded planes, and on her hangar deck they were
loading bombs on her TBMs. There was a massive explosion,
and flash explosions starting forward on her hangar deck
going directly to her stern, and then flashing back again as
her planes exploded one after another. She was almost invisi-
ble in dense black smoke and was maneuvering to avoid col-
lision. She was quickly designated as guide so the rest of the
ships in the formation could avoid hitting her. Two other
attacking Jap planes were shot down, one right above us.
Watching the FRANKLIN in her agony no one thought she
had a chance. The task force commander called her on the
voice radio (TBS) and said "You have permission to abandon
ship", To our amazement her skipper, Captain Leslie E Gehres
USN, replied, "I think I can save her!" And he did. But the
price was heavy.*

*The cruiser SANTA FE went alongside her to take off sur-
vivors and in turn lost people when further explosions erupt-
ed on the FRANKLIN. When the attack subsided the Cruiser
PITTSBURGH took the FRANKLIN in tow astern and started
pulling her slowly to the south. For the next two days the
whole task force zigzagged southward to protect the
FRANKLIN, which was clearly identifiable to the Japanese by
her trail of smoke that was visible for fifty miles. As a result
of this the next day we were attacked by over 100 Japanese
planes. This was a wild day. One Kamikaze dived on the carrier HANCOCK directly across our bow. Our machine gun fire
and that of others flamed the plane and he missed the carrier but crashed into a destroyer that was fueling from her. Two
other planes attacked the ENTERPRISE, the other large carrier in our group. The first plane dropped a bomb but missed
the ENTERPRISE, then scudded away and was not shot down
till it reached the edge of the formation. A second suicide then
made a run on the ENTERPRISE and hit her in the flight deck*

causing great damage. This attack finally put the old ENTERPRISE out of the war. She had been in the Pacific from before the war up till this incident, but could not be repaired soon enough for her to get back into action before V-J day.

As the day progressed the Kamikazes kept attacking. The adrenalin was flowing at record rate, but we had begun to develop a certain degree of confidence that if we spotted them soon enough, and if we kept up our fire until they were on top of us we could pretty much count on killing the pilot and diverting the plane to avoid hitting us. Two more made dives on us this day but we shot them down before they hit us. Unfortunately as one was attacking another carrier our gunners followed them with the same intensity, and an-overzealous F6F pilot in hot pursuit of one was caught in the crossfire and was himself flamed and crashed. Fortunately we were able to rescue the pilot essentially uninjured.

I think it is fitting to inject a note about the U.S.S. FRANKLIN. She was undoubtedly the most brutalized aircraft carrier of the War. I saw her when she was hit by a dive bomber in September 1944, hit in the middle of her flight deck by a suicide plane in October 1944 causing her to return to the United States to have her flight and hangar decks rebuilt, and then finally I watched her when she was struck by two 500 pound bombs in March 1945 which totally disabled her and came close to abandoning her off the coast of Okinawa. She was towed, and later on her own power proceeded through the Panama Canal to the Brooklyn Navy Yard where she was completely rebuilt, but too late to get back into the War. A grim irony is that her hull number was CV-13. Her commanding officer during the episode in March, 1945, was Captain Leslie Gehres USN, who declined to abandon ship when authorized by the task force commander. I have not seen an exact count, but I would assume that because of these three attacks she probably suffered nine hundred crewmembers killed and twice that many wounded.

The word "Kamikaze" translated into English means "Divine Wind." It is a reference to a battle in early Japanese history when the Japanese Fleet was fighting a much larger force of Mongol invaders and miraculously a strong wind arose to destroy the enemy and do no harm to the Japanese ships. Apparently the term seemed to express the hopes that the powers in Japan had for their suicide program when they initiated it in October of 1944.

I always believed that the Japanese never truly understood the potency of this weapon, or the potential of it when properly employed. The reason for this undoubtedly was that they never had the benefit of reports or critiques of their attacks, since none of the participants ever returned to tell them how well it went or what they could do to improve their effectiveness. At any rate, during the last 10 months of the war, when the Japanese military power was fading fast, they inflicted more casualties on the U.S. Navy with the Kamikaze weapon than were inflicted during the entire war by any other means. With the exception of Pearl Harbor, Kamikazes immobilized more U.S. naval vessels than any other weapon used in the war. Had they known the effectiveness of certain tactics that they used on single occasions but never repeated they could have done much greater damage. . . .

Invasion of Okinawa

On March 30th we began direct support of the invasion of Okinawa by American Forces, which started on Easter Sunday, April 1, 1945. Marines and Army units went ashore and established footholds as the Japanese army forces fought ferociously.

On April 6th the Japanese air forces launched an all-out attack against U.S. Naval forces in and around Okinawa. The day was cold and the sky was gray with dark streaks between clouds. My battle station was on the bridge and my function was to keep station on the guide ship. The Navigator always took the conn, or O.O.D., and the Captain was free to "fight the ship". The official record says that on this day over 500 Kamikazes attacked our task force, south of Okinawa. Our combat air patrols shot down over three hundred before they could get to our formations. Nonetheless we were attacked all throughout the day, never leaving our battle stations. The Kamikazes always went for the aircraft carriers, so they took a lot of antiaircraft fire from the other ships as they came at us, since the carriers were on the inner circle of the task group formation.

Every one of our four carriers was a target off and on this day but we managed to shoot them down without a direct hit. On the SAN JACINTO, we had been attacked by two during the morning and they crashed in the sea nearby. The big carrier, BENNINGTON, narrowly missed being hit, as did the BELLEAU WOOD. Everyone was scouring the sky to find the next one in time, when almost without any warning a bomb-laden Zero came out from between two low clouds no more than 4000 yards ahead of us at an angle of about 30 degrees, heading straight for the bridge where I was standing. For me, this was the moment of truth, because his wingspan just kept getting bigger and he didn't change his bearing or elevation, even though the tracers were pouring into him. At the last second his wheels dropped down and he dipped just out of sight about 50 yards off the starboard bow. He hit the water with a tremendous explosion. We all hit the deck as pieces of airplane came flying through the

Crew aboard U.S.S. *SAN JACINTO* (CVL-30) cleaning up the remains of the Jap plane Kamikaze, which crashed near starboard bow near Okinawa in Ryukyu Islands, [photo developed on April 7, 1945.] (National Archives)

bridge windshield and fell on top of my back. When the smoke cleared there was a green belt with a silver belt buckle swinging on the crane in front of us and parts of plane and pilot were all over the flight deck. Two men were killed in the forward bow 40mm gun crew and five others wounded.

. . . Tension was pretty high, and when damage reports had been taken we started cleaning the debris off of the bridge. A piece of a piston from the plane had come through the windshield and fallen on my back and rolled over into a corner. The Navigator, before getting back up off the deck had, without anyone noticing it, used the yellow grease pencil he had in his hand to write on the piston, 'To Cdr Geo. Winne from Hirohito'. As the quartermasters were cleaning up one young sailor yelled, 'Holy S—-t, Mr. Winne, this thing has your name on it!"

After this violent day the Japanese recognized that the picket destroyers 15 or so miles away from the center of the formations with their own CAPs were getting early warnings and sending out their fighters to intercept before the kamikazes could get into the carriers. They then began a campaign to attack the pickets, which were more easily hit. During the next six or seven weeks the Navy suffered more destroyer casualties than in any other period of the war.

I recall a beautiful sunny day in April when the sea was so calm you could see reflections in it and we were operating south of Okinawa with four carrier task groups in a line, sep-

arated from each other by about 25 miles, center to center. We could barely hear the TBS radio traffic from the group to the northeast. It became apparent from the liveliness of the voices, and from the anti-aircraft fire visible on the horizon, that they were under attack. We then saw a flash and smoke go up between the two groups, followed by a desperate call for help from a destroyer saying he was being attacked by several kamikazes. Our group was ordered immediately to his help at flank speed, and within about twenty minutes we were surrounding him, but it was a pitiful sight. He was sitting with his fantail just under water, both stacks and part of the superstructure missing, smoke coming up from several places on the ship, and looking generally like a wet firecracker. He was eventually towed out, patched up, and got up power to proceed to Ulithi. The Captain was Gordon Chung-Hoon, a former Naval Academy football star, Class of 1934, who had been born in Hawaii and who eventually retired as an Admiral, having received the Navy Cross for defending and saving his ship after being hit by three Kamakazes.

On April 7ᵗʰ the Japanese sent their massive new battleship YAMATO into the Inland Sea with intention to proceed to Okinawa and destroy the American invasion force. Our task force carrier planes attacked in waves and sank the hapless battleship, along with its destroyer screen. The SAN JACINTO planes were credited with sinking the lead destroyer.

Throughout the rest of April each day was like the preceding one as we cruised back and forth southeast of Okinawa, sending fighter CAPs further up toward Kyushu to intercept kamikazes coming down from Japan. Hardly a day went by that we were not attacked somewhere in the task force, but we had continually improved our defensive tactics and suffered only occasional damage, except for the picket destroyers who were still being heavily brutalized On the 27ᵗʰ of April we headed south and finally arrived at Ulithi for a nine day stay at anchor. We had been at sea off of Okinawa for forty-six days.

The ultimate readiness condition was Condition 1, or General Quarters, when every man aboard was at his battle station, all watertight doors were dogged except for those necessary to fight the ship, and all hands were in anti-flash dress. We always went to general quarters when in enemy waters at one half hour before sunrise and remained there until one half hour after, and also from one half hour before sunset till one half hour after. This was because the Japanese were known to try to attack just at sunrise or sunset. Breakfast in the morning and dinner in the evening was served immediately after securing from general quarters.

GQ was signaled by bugle call in the morning and evening, but any time attack seemed imminent it was signaled by the general alarm, which was a penetrating gong heard throughout the ship and had the effect of a shot of electricity enough to make a stone statue run for his battle station. In the middle of a meal it could clear the wardroom in about ten seconds. Once we knew about kamikazes the intense awareness of the need for speed in response to their presence in our area was uppermost in everyone's mind. Lookouts scanning the sky could spot an aircraft when it was no more than a speck. Trigger fingers were commonplace. Any number of times some ship would start firing like mad until they discovered they were shooting at Venus. Most people go through life not realizing that you can see that planet in the daylight if you look hard enough.

The most insidious effect of the kamikazes was the ultimate wear-down on the crew because of the constant tension during the day. Many people who had had more than their share of action during the war without any visible effect on them became so tensed up that they lost their appetite, Some people lost ten to thirty pounds during the last ten months of the war for that reason alone.

The one relief was that they could never attack after dark, even though on certain occasions they would send out a plane or two with flares which they dropped that would seem to light you up like Main Street on Saturday night, but apparently the pilots could not see us because they never came close at night.

As soon as the sun went down you could relax, go to dinner, and then hit the sack, because there were no night owls aboard.

Nagasaki

The SAN JACINTO had been in the Pacific War Theater in continuing action against the enemy for 16 months, and by August 1, 1945, she was overdue to return to the US for overhaul. Rumors of this great event had been floating around for several weeks, but Admiral Halsey, sensing evermore effectiveness from his carrier operations had delayed sending ships back as long as possible. We knew we were next in line, but we didn't know when we would be sent home.

World War II

On August 9th the first atom bomb was dropped on Hiroshima. When we heard the news in the early evening of that day the big question was "What the hell is an atom bomb?" The captain, wanting straight answers, called Lt. Commander Winne to the bridge and asked him. I had the OOD watch at the time and listened to Winne's lecture on nuclear reaction theory. One would have thought he had been working on the bomb instead of navigating the SAN JAC around the Pacific! Peace rumors then abounded, still nothing happened. We continued to launch attacks on Shikoku, Kyushu, and into the Inland Sea of Japan. I had the midwatch as we were proceeding northwest to launch in the morning when we received an urgent message to the task force directing us to reverse course and proceed at full speed to the southeast. We were in the line of flight of the plane carrying the second bomb, which was dropped on Nagoya the next morning, but we were not advised of the reason for the course change.

The next day as we proceeded southeast I was standing in the middle of the flight deck talking to some of the other officers. There was nothing going on at the time, since we were only operating combat air patrols, which usually lasted two to three hours. Then we heard a peculiar noise, which sounded like a cross between a rumble and a gust of wind. We all looked around to identify it, since all noises were of great interest in our situation. There was no explanation so we dismissed it. That evening we received the news of the second bomb having been dropped, on Nagasaki. One of the officers on the bridge with me said, 'What time did we hear that noise on the flight deck this afternoon?' We all gave our opinion and found that it was just about the time that the news said the bomb was dropped. I have always been convinced that I did hear the detonation of the bomb as the sound carried over the open sea to the ship.

LIEUTENANT LLEWELLYN D. HALDERSON
COMPANY E, 21ST INFANTRY REGIMENT,
24TH DIVISION, U.S. SIXTH ARMY

Lew Halderson, born in 1914, was not content to remain behind a desk doing lab work for the Army at the Edgewood Arsenal in Maryland with a war raging in the Pacific and Europe. Thus, he requested active duty, and, after receiving additional training at Ft. Benning, Georgia, was shipped off to the Pacific Theater. It was certainly a long way from his boyhood home in Newman Grove, Nebraska, where he had graduated from the local high school and then graduated from the University of Nebraska in 1936.

Halderson, who was not married, wrote numerous letters to his father, Helmer or "Pop," his Aunt Inez, his Aunt Gertrude and Uncle Ira, his brother, Max, and Max's seven-year-old daughter, Joanne. His letters were treasured by his family and relatives – not only was his penmanship wonderful, but he had a great sense of humor and a way with words which was especially appropriate for his young niece and aunts. He often included trinkets or souvenirs in the letters that were intended for Joanne.

Lieutenant Llewellyn D. Halderson. (Courtesy of Joanne Black)

Anti-Japanese emotions ran very high in the United States after Pearl Harbor, and were raised to an even higher level once US troops became involved in the bloody campaigns in the Pacific. Consequently, it was not unusual to have soldiers vent their emotions in letters to their fathers or other male friends or relatives. Halderson was no exception and Max was certainly aware of Lew's detestation for the enemy – parts of these letters were certainly too unsuitable to share with the women in the family then (or even now, and for this reason ellipsis replace the most objectionable portions).

Halderson served first in Hawaii in April 1943, and from there he went to Australia in September 1943, where he had an opportunity to get closer to the war effort. He served in the New Guinea campaign in the spring of 1944, where the battalion executive officer, Major Dayle Bolliett, praised the caliber of Halderson's work and the fact that he "prefer[ed] to lead a platoon," rather than work as a guard officer or in a chemist's job.

Eventually his leadership skills helped him get more involved in the action – this time in the invasion of the Philippines in October and November 1944.

The following letter, written from Hawaii, accurately reflects Halderson's unforgettable sense of humor as well as his initial impression of his work with the 21st Infantry. What makes it doubly of interest is his rather optimistic tone toward his involvement in the war, which undergoes a radical change in later letters to his brother.

World War II

[Company "E", 21st Infantry
A.P.O. #24, c/o Postmaster
San Francisco, Cal.]
Hawaii
April 22, 1943
> Dear Max:
>
> We had a good trip over on a good boat, and I was assigned to the 21st Infantry Regiment shortly after arriving. it is a good outfit and the work is much more interesting than recruit training – and also a good deal more rigorous.
>
> I am in a special unit commanded by a young (24) major. He is an excellent officer and also has the rare faculty of being thoroughly entertaining. He eats at our Company mess and has the table in a continuous uproar. One of the legendary characters over here is Major "Spike" Knave, a burly, bow-legged Irishman who graduated, by the grace of God, from West Point. He is said to be the only officer in the U.S. Army who can belch and fart at the same time – in the presence of women – and get away with it. His exploits seem to be innumerable, but one, which took place in Washington when he was a Lieutenant, is particularly choice. It seems that he turned up at some swank bar or other, the only other customer at the time being a woman, who later turned out to be a general's wife. As he came up, he heard the lady order a Horse's Neck. The Lieutenant straddled a stool and bellowed "give me a Horse's Ass, then we'll only have to kill one horse." The general's wife thought it was just too cute.
>
> I spent my first 24 hour pass in Honolulu early this week and had a good time. Everything was crowded, of course, but it was a change from camp life.
>
> I sent a few mementoes to you and the family last week which will probably not reach you for some time.
>
> The weather here is really wonderful – exactly the opposite of the blistering summers and numbing winters in Nebraska.
>
> *Best regards to all, Lew*

In a letter written on September 4th, 1943, from Australia, Halderson comments on its exotic wildlife. He writes, "Australia is, of course, noted for its strange animals. I have seen a number of them, Kangaroo, wallabies (like kangaroo only smaller), four-foot lizards, winged lizards, koala bears, and a few others." In the beginning of his next letter, he comments further on living with some of these animals while simultaneously showing his loving affection for his niece, Joanne. He later offers some interesting comments on Australia's culture as well as on the war effort.

World War II

[Australia]
October 15, 1943
Dear Max:

I enjoyed your letter of September 24 received a few days ago. While your living arrangements do not appear to be so good, at least you have the family together again.[1] I would like to send Joanne a little kangaroo, but it can't be done. They make ideal pets until they grow to full size, which takes some time. We have several here in camp. They are practically no trouble, as they sleep most of the day, and go out to feed at night. We also have a koala bear, and a few other miscellaneous animals around. . . .

Since coming to Australia we have seen a good bit of the country. It is a good 20 years behind the states in almost every respect, although the people themselves are treating the American soldiers with every consideration, and I am obliged to admit that the latter are a bit trying at times, particularly when on pass and drunk. Although not many of them are – just that inevitable few who would be the same anywhere.

Practically all of the ? million population of Australia is concentrated in the several coastal cities on the eastern coast, the hinterlands being very thinly occupied if at all. Consequently, if one gets away from that narrow eastern strip, wilderness prevails. Wilderness is prevailing.

Our training has been mulled up somewhat by the old army form of non-combatant combat known as "fighting inspectors." It is due, perhaps, to the experience in New Guinea that sick soldiers can't fight – but healthy soldiers can't fight either unless they know how. However, I believe we will have sufficient time to correct any considerable deficiencies.

. . . Your conversation with the Guadalcanal Marine was interesting, although the Marines don't deserve a great deal of credit for the Guadalcanal Campaign. The[y] made an unopposed landing, occupied Henderson airfield practically without firing a shot, and sat tight, fighting a few defensive engagements until the Army took over and cleared the Japs out. It is true that they took quite a drubbing from the air, but so are a lot of civilians these days. While back in our old location, we heard an excellent talk by General Sproggins, who was chief-of-staff for the ground forces, after the real fighting began in Guadalcanal, and the main part of the offensive action which cleared the Japs from the island was done by the Army forces there.

By the way, I am now in the 24th Division, 1st Corps,

WORLD WAR II

Sixth Army, of the United States Armed Forces in the Far East (USAFFE). Why the censor allows that to go through, I don't know exactly, unless it is for the morale effect. I censor the mail of my own platoon, and all of them are very anxious for the folks at home to know what outfit they are in. After all, the anonymity of fighting an unknown battle in an unknown, far away location, would be a bit disconcerting.

I am enclosing a couple of Australian coins for Joanne for souvenirs.

Best regards to Louise and the youngsters. Lew

By the time Halderson wrote his next letter, there had been, in his own words, a "general quickening in the military situation in this theater." Apparently, he is beginning to realize the true realities of the war, implicit in the opening paragraph.

Australia
December 19, 1943
Dear Pop:

I have been quite remiss in writing. Conditions are pretty much militated against settling down to write a good letter. Then too, it isn't like a job in civilian life, where one can quit at 4:30 and call it a day. Here there is always something that can be done, and should be done, even after one turn in at night. Not that I object to that, though, in the least. The only way to be in the Army is <u>busy</u>. However, as I say, it does get in the way of writing letters. . . .

My activities here in Australia have been pretty much confined to camp and training areas. I did visit Sidney, which turned out to be quite a town, although considerably behind towns of comparable size in the States in most respects. The Australian people are most friendly, although the merchants are inclined to take the Yanks over in a good many cases.

You have, of course, read of the general quickening in the military situation in this theater, most notably the establishment of a beachhead on New Britain by elements of the Sixth Army, of which this Division is a part. That was, of course, the curtain-raiser for the New Britain Campaign, the most important objective being Rabaul, and the New Britain Campaign as a whole being the most ambitious yet undertaken in this theater of operations.

When and where the 24th Division will be committed is, of course, a closely guarded secret. We are most fortunate, however, in having the opportunity of benefiting by the experience of other divisions who preceded us in this theater, namely the ones that won the Buna-Gona and Salamana campaigns. The terrain and the enemy will be much the same wherever we may go in this theater. . . .

I'm surely glad to hear that you're feeling "in the pink." If everything goes ok we'll go duck-hunting in the sand hills in a jeep after the war, and great as your prowess as a hiker is, I think I'll be able to hold my own with you after several years in the Infantry.

Sincerely, Lew

By May 1944, Halderson and his regiment had moved to New Guinea where they remained until October 1944. The battalion's executive officer praised Halderson's leadership skills in this letter to Halderson's father:

May 26, 1944
Dear Mr. Halderson,

I have just left Lou [sic] up in northern N.G. I was his battalion executive officer for the past year and only recently left him under orders to return to the states.

Undoubtedly he has told you about the life up there – it is a miserable situation at the best. Lou has been the battalion S-4; and without tossing compliments I would like to tell you that he is about tops. He was put into a job at my recommendation because on our trip to Australia I got to know the caliber of his work, as he worked under me as a guard officer. I knew he did not want the job, loyalty and efficiency – and his battalion c.o. is quite profuse in his compliments. I thought you would like to know how he is regarded by his superiors. Personally I believe Lou is far more valuable in the . . . chemist job than in the infantry, but he prefers the latter.

The living conditions as you can guess are miserable. We have been on ? and 1/3 rations much of the time.. . . . [two words illegible] and without a change of clothing for 3 weeks – that has eased up now but it was pretty tough while it lasted. However the bombings have quieted down now and there is not need to worry.

Please don't bother to answer this letter – I promised the fellows I would write to their families and let them know how they are – Lou is fine.

Sincerely,
Major Dayle Bolliett
Dayle Bolliett
Augusta, Wisconsin

When Halderson came into contact with enemy troops in New Guinea, his language became more vitriolic, but he only shared it with his brother, who was probably not offended. [The most offensive parts of the letter have been deleted for this reason.]

June 8, 1944
 Dear Max:

  The situation has quieted down here and we are now engaged in the routine of camp building, rehabilitation and similar activities. We are still sending out a few patrols into the hills to round up small parties of Japs reported by the natives, but it is pretty tame hunting as most of the Japs by this time are half starved, sick and about ready to throw in the sponge anyway.

  This operation area is taking shape rapidly. More has been done since our landing than the Japs were able to accomplish in the two years they held it.

  The second front is, of course, the leading topic of conversation here now. The reports we have received so far have given only the bare facts and the meaningless statement the operation is "proceeding according to plan." At any rate it has been a great morale booster and has relieved a "gnawing anxiety" almost universally felt here about the second front. According to the President's own statement, the European operations will have no affect on the gathering offensives in this theater.

  You have no doubt read that our forces ran into unexpectedly heavy resistance at Biak Island. Just the reverse of what we encountered here. There will no doubt be some tough spots on the road to Tokyo, but the American soldier is so far superior to the Jap in most respects that the ground fighting will invariably find the Japs at a disadvantage. These representatives of the Sons of Heaven are diminutive. . . . They are obsequious and servile to a disgusting degree and I find it quite impossible to regard them with anything but the deepest contempt. [The enemy] . . . at first flushed with cheap victories over undefended peoples behaving with inconceivable violence and brutality toward their captives, now bowing and scraping and begging for mercy leave me as cold as hell. This should be tempered, however, with the fact that the Japanese troops we encountered here were not first line combat troops. We will no doubt meet some stiff opposition in our next operation.

  Best regards to Louise and the kids. Did Joanne get the Australian souvenir I sent?

              Lew

126

WORLD WAR II

July 7, 1944
Dear Max:

I surely enjoyed the picture of the family. You are all looking fine.

Apparently my letter of about two months ago was delayed or lost, in which I said we had just completed an operation against the Japs. It was a pretty tame affair, however, as they didn't put up much of a fight. In fact, we have seen more action in the subsequent mopping up than we did during the active campaign. The first time I took my platoon on a patrol mission we killed three Japs, but haven't run into any since. All of the Japs carry "invasion money" intended for

Japanese bill intended for use during the occupation of Australia (Courtesy of Joanne Black)

use in Australia. Why the devil they lug it around with them now is a mystery, but they all have some of it. I am enclosing a shilling note and a piece of bona fide Jap money. We took a good deal of other stuff from the Japs we got including six good watches and a couple of little flags.

All in all the Japs we met were pretty sad affairs, but from our casualty reports on the Saipan operation, which is not yet completed at this writing, they still have some tough combat outfits.

We run into a good many natives during patrolling missions. They are friendly and bring us papias [papayas], bananas, eggs and melons for cigarettes (which, by the way, we have very few of). They are expert at various types of handicraft, from making dugout boats to fish spears. They hate the Japs.

We have been out of touch with any sort of civilization for many months, and have been eating preserved rations of one sort or another for nearly a year. As this sort of fare is by this time becoming somewhat more than monotonous, I would like to have you send me some things that would vary the menu a bit and give it some badly needed zip. Such things as pickles (both dill and sweet), catsup, mustard, Miracle Whip, Tabasco sauce, Worcestershire sauce, olives, shrimp, canned chicken, dried beef, salami sausage, pickled red peppers and like items would help make the fare we get if not

WORLD WAR II

sumptuous, at least edible. I don't suppose all this stuff is available, but a small box once or twice a month would sure-ly be appropriate. The containers should be small and well packed, as mail takes quite a beating somewhere along the line. Pop is taking care of my cash, so let him know what it costs and he will send you the money. In the first box you might also throw in six handkerchiefs, two hand towels and a bath towel. Also 100 sheets of good air-mail stationery and 50 stamped envelopes (air mail).

I will try to send you some more Jap souvenirs if we ever get to a place where I can wrap them.

Sincerely, Lew

The following two letters were written to Joanne. What makes these letters of particular interest is Halderson's ironic display and juxtaposi-tion of love and hatred within these consecutive letters. This irony is augmented by the fact that his vehement feelings are not expressed to his seven-year-old niece.

July 10, 1944

Dear Joanne:

I am sending you some Dutch coins. The small ones are one tenth of a guilder and the larger ones are one fourth of a guilder. A guilder is worth 53 cents in American money. All soldiers in my regiment are now being paid in Netherlands Indies money.

From time to time I will send you some more of these coins. Perhaps you can persuade your Dad to take them to a jeweler and have a bracelet made out of them for you, when you have enough.

Affectionately, Uncle Lew

August 2, 1944

Dear Joanne:

I am sending you a few Japanese pencils. The pencils are not bad but the people who make them are.

We have captured many things from the Japanese soldier here. While hardly any of it is as good as the American's, we use many of their things while we are waiting for our own to come across the ocean from America. We have eaten much Japanese rice, which their soldiers left here when they ran away. The Japanese soldiers are afraid of Americans and unless they have many more soldiers then we do they run away or blow themselves up with a grenade.

Affectionately, Uncle Lew

WORLD WAR II

The next few letters indicate that Halderson has been profoundly affected by his role in the war. His tone has totally shifted from one of optimism and excitement to one of cynicism and deep-rooted anger.

August 2, 1944
Dear Max:

Your letter of mid-July came today. I was glad to hear from you. It does seem as though the mail is snafu; however, I'm glad to hear that Joanne got the souvenirs. I sent her some money from another country, and said I would send some more, but since then a recent censorship regulation prohibits sending that kind of money. I'd like to know if what I did send got through. I suggested you might have a bracelet made for Joanne with the coins, as it would no doubt be attractive to a youngster.

The situation here is beginning to pall somewhat and the men are bitching like hell. I do think it is a serious mistake to keep an organization overseas as long under these conditions. Since Pearl Harbor the division has been overseas continuously and has seen only four days of action against the Japs, that is, a small percentage of one battalion saw a few hours of fighting. Aside from patrolling of minor nature, that completes the combat picture of the division during the war with Japan. Aside from our training we have been primarily a group of labor battalions. As one man wrote, "Don't worry Mom, I'm in a non-combatant outfit." In obscene Army vernacular the men wish to hell this division would shit or get off the pot. The pot, unfortunately has become so glued to this organization's posterior that it has taken on all appearances of a permanent anatomical appendage. I'm obliged to agree with them, albeit silently, as when I became an Infantry officer, I did not contract to act as a foreman of a labor gang in a stinking New Guinea jungle. So here I am bitching, something I hate to see in myself as much as among the men, but it's no use saying everything is lovely with things the way they are.

. . . The War picture looks highly promising, but it will no doubt be another year before things are wound up on this side. I do not expect to get back before it's over.

Best regards to Louise and the family.   *Lew*

P.S. I'm sending Joanne a few Jap pencils.

August 11, 1944
Dear Aunt Inez:

. . . Everything is quiet here by this time. A few strag-

gling Japs put in an appearance occasionally, but there aren't enough around. As usual the infantry is doing all of the dirty work, such as unloading transports, building roads and various kinds of labor for nearly everyone. The men are pretty well fed up with unloading iceboxes, beer, and fresh meat for the Air Corps and higher headquarters when the infantry is still on 2/3 of a K ration. We do have our kitchens now, but the food is nearly all canned stuff which comes from Australia and it's very poor grade stuff. In fact about the only items made in Australia that are any good are beer and wool sox. It's about time somebody in the War Department woke up and gave the Infantry an even break with the other branches of the service, or see to it that theater commanders do so. The Infantry has the toughest, dirtiest, more disagreeable job in the armed forces, but they get the poorest food, the worst facilities and the fewest furloughs. The plain fact is that the Infantry gets what's left over after all of the other branches have had their pick.

Best regards to all, Lew
P.S. I'm enclosing a few Jap coins.

August 16, 1944
Dear Max:

Things are going along here pretty much as usual. We are starting another training schedule, but enthusiasm for training at this stage has been worn down to a nub. However, it is necessary to go through the motions to keep the men busy.

I am enclosing a few Australian coins you can give to Joanne. Let me know if there are enough for a bracelet. I am also sending some Jap coins for souvenirs.

The rainy season is just about over here, so the weather is a good deal more pleasant than when we arrived. This New Guinea heat, however, is something different than any I have

Joanne's bracelet made of coins from New Guinea, 1941-1943. (Courtesy of Joanne Black)

ever encountered. I didn't realize it until one day when we had to fight a grass fire. After twenty minutes of vigorous exertion the men as well as myself were nearly out and a few became unconscious from heat prostration. It was a good lesson and I'm glad I learned it in a non-tactical situation. You can't push men to the limit in this climate without serious consequences.

Have you had any luck with the camera? I could get some fine pictures here of the natives and local scenery. If you can't get a camera, I could use as many V127 films as you could get. One of the officers has a camera this size. The pictures are too small, but they are better than nothing.

I was promoted to 1st Lt. some time ago, but it will no doubt be the last for a long time, as all position vacancies are being filled by base commanders who got their promotions in some training center in the States and are now being sent overseas as replacements. The same applies to non-coms. A good many of our privates have forgotten more about field soldiering than the replacement non-coms ever knew. It makes everyone sore as hell but nothing can be done about it.

News is scarce here. We heard that Allied troops have reached Paris, but it may just be a rumor.

Lew

P.S. Am also enclosing a poem.

On October 17th, the invasion of Leyte Island in the Philippines began with the ultimate purpose of reclaiming the island as a stepping-stone to northern Mindanao and Manila.

There were three tactical phases to the operation: the first was to secure rapidly the entrances to Leyte Gulf (October 17-19). The second phase, on October 20th was more complicated. Halderson and his 21st Infantry Regiment started off the operation when they landed on Panaon Island and rapidly gained control of the strait. Then, an hour later, the amphibious assaults began on the coastal strip of land from Tacloban to Dulag. Once ashore, the next task was to secure the central valley of Leyte. Phase three was much more daunting, though, because the mission now was to destroy all remaining hostile forces on Leyte.

Simultaneously with the landings at Leyte, the battle of Leyte Gulf took place when the Japanese fleet engaged our Third and Seventh fleets from October 24th to 26th, during which a large part of the enemy's ships were sunk. In spite of this, the Japanese were not going to give up easily and reinforced much of Leyte with their crack Imperial 1st Division, believing that "the battle of the Philippines would be won or lost on Leyte Island."[16]

World War II

[Leyte, Philippine Islands]
October 31, 1944

Dear Aunt Inez:

We made another landing recently. There was no opposition. We were sleeping in hammocks the next night. There were several sporadic, single plane air attacks but we had no casualties, and knocked done one of the planes to boot.

Several days ago I took my platoon on patrol about 20 miles from base camp. It turned out to be a pleasant trip.

Our patrol route led by the guerrilla GHQ in this area. I was, however, completely unprepared for the reception they gave us. The GHQ itself was a model of organization, complete with desks, typewriters, field radios and other HQ paraphernalia. They cleared out a schoolhouse as barracks for the men, and put is in the officers quarters. (There was one officer along besides myself). We slept between <u>sheets</u>!, had showers, they washed all our clothes after we went to bed so they would be ready in the morning. We were carrying rations for 3 days, but never had to touch them. We had eggs, sunny side up every morning, roast pig for the noon meal and chicken at night with all the trimmings. We stayed there 3 days.

The guerilla organization was an amazing piece of work. We knew that guerrillas were active in the area, but had no idea that they were so completely organized. Considering that it was built up after the Japs came, and without equipment, communication or supplies in any quantity it was a truly remarkable achievement. They had killed many Japs and had those that were trapped in their garrisons.

Their will to fight was something I have never seen before. Their one hope is that they will be taken along with the Americans to fight the Japs farther up.

Of course there is a reason for that. The Jap atrocities against civilians, women and

Natives of Dulag village greet 1st wave at Leyte, October 20, 1944. (National Archives)

children ~~are~~ *were so vicious and barbarous as to be almost unbelievable. There is little need to repeat the sort of things the Japs did. You have doubtless read of their activities in Nanking and other places. They did all of these and more.*

One Jap garrison was located in an old brick house on the coast. The guerillas had had it surrounded for several months, so that the Japs were unable to move out of the house. Because of a lack of heavy weapons, the guerillas were unable to attack. However when we came, one of our gunboats shelled the house. The Japs were able to escape under cover of the shelling, but the guerillas were hot on their trail. They tracked them down and killed all 28 of them. On the day we visited the place they had killed 25 and had the last 3 cornered in the mountains. I met the Lieutenant commanding that company of guerillas. He was a fierce, intense person and I noted mentally that I was glad these people are on our side when I met him. The Japs had taken his wife, holding her as a hostage until he surrendered. He did not surrender. He does not know whether his wife is alive or dead, or where she is.

One day while we were there the guerillas brought in 2 Jap prisoners who were survivors from a Jap warship recently sunk. They were luck to be alive, now though the guerillas had strict orders not to kill them. One of the Japs was from Tokyo. He didn't want to fight anymore. He wanted peace. He said all the men on his ship wanted peace. He believed that America started the war.

I met a good many remarkable people among the guerillas, but one of the most distinguished was the niece of the commanding officer. She was barely 5 feet tall, but had more energy and determination than a dozen average women. She was the general manager around the GHQ. She ran the house, the hospital, and had organized more than 1000 girls and women for making clothes and equipment, growing gardens, raising pigs and chickens for the guerillas. She was well educated and intelligent, speaking English well and fluently. She was our hostess there, and I would like to have you buy something and send it to her. Of course the women here have been without all of the things that could be bought in a department store for more than 3 years. I don't know just what to suggest except cosmetics. Maybe you could think of something else to make up a variety of things that a woman in those circumstances would like at a cost of about $10.00, and send the bill to Pop.

I can't give you her address yet, as we are not permitted to say where we are. God knows why because they have

announced it many times over the radio, but I will send it as
soon as censorship is lifted.

Sincerely, Lew

By the 3rd of November, the American forces were moving up the central valley, and advancing in the direction of Ormoc, which was held by the Japanese. The operations at Leyte, though, became protracted and bloody. Japanese reinforcements were rushed in to engage the 24th Infantry Division, of which the 21st Infantry was a part. The difficulties of movement and engagement were exacerbated by the rainy season (including a typhoon in late October) and the mountainous, jungle-like terrain. Acquisition of every inch of ground was painfully slow. As Haldlerson's company headed towards Ormoc, they encountered stiff Japanese resistance, and they "fought one of the most bitterly contested battles of the war," which was centered around Breakneck Ridge. This was not a "ridge," but actually a "series of knobs," surrounded by "shoulder high cogon grass, [and] the pockets between the hills thickly wooded." It was here that the Americans met the crack Imperial First Division.

From November 5th through the 16th, the Americans learned how to clear "connecting trenches in terrain impassible for tanks." Halderson and his men in E Company would have found the fortifications "impossible to spot . . . because of the grass and excellent camouflage." Hundreds of "spider holes" were "dug flush to the ground" and "remained undiscovered even after troops had searched the area." For Halderson and others, this type of combat was exhausting – with the incessant rain turning Leyte into "one big mud hole," where resupply was almost impossible," and the men were often "fighting by day and hauling supplies at night."[17] Sniper fire by the Japanese also took a heavy toll, and battle casualties were especially severe among officers. The casualty list, tragically included the name of Lew Halderson, who was killed on November 12th, as he continued his efforts to secure Breakneck Ridge. The ridge was finally secured November 16th, and subsequently hastened the end of the Japanese occupation of Leyte.

MASTER SERGEANT RIC RANUCCI
4TH MARINE DIVISION

Island Hopping: Roi-Namur, Saipan & Iwo Jima

Ric Ranucci did not wait for the draft board to call him. "I enlisted. I was in my senior year of high school, then I quit school and I enlisted in December of 1942. I enlisted in the Marine Corps." His training for the Marine Corps began on January 9th, 1943, in Parris Island, North

WORLD WAR II

Carolina. From there, he was sent to Camp Lejeune, North Carolina, to train as a telephone operator and later to Camp Pendleton, California, where he became part of the 4th Marine Division, which was specifically used to string telephone lines.

On January 2nd, 1944, the Fourth Marine Division shipped out of San Diego, California. From there, Ranucci says, "we made a beach head in the Kwajalein Atoll: namely, Roi-Namor in the Marshall Islands. We were one of the first divisions ever that went directly from our native country into combat. That operation on Roi-Namur lasted approximately a period of four to five days, and it was the first taste of combat for all of us, most of us. We had some veterans in our organization from Midway and Guadalcanal. They formed a nucleus of our veterans, and they trained us and took care of us until we got our feet wet in combat." Although the period of combat for the Fourth Marine Division was short, it was their duty to clean up the island. We "had bulldozers that dug out great holes in the sand. We would throw two, three, four hundred dead bodies of Japanese in them and we would cover them up. It was unpleasant duty, but we were evacuated from that island and the day we evacuated, that night we were hit by a Japanese air raid . . . it was a horrible experience. Believe me, there's nothing like being bombed from the air when you can't do nothing about it."

Saipan

After Ranucci left the Kwajalein Atoll, he returned to Maui in the Hawaiian Islands, to rest, train, and add replacement recruits to his division. In June of 1944, the Fourth Marine Division headed to the island of Saipan, in the Mariana group. "That operation took a period of about thirty to thirty-five days. It was day and night, night and day, and it was a horrible experience for the whole time we were there." Landing was always arduous, because after circling in Higgins boats, Ranucci remembered:

> a lot of people would get sick . . . but then you hit what they
> call the departure line, and . . . about six Higgins boats would
> head for the beach. . . . When you hit, you could bet your life
> that there's all kinds of incoming rounds, . . . and it's all con-
> fusion. Well, my job and the people I was with . . . was to
> string lines between whatever it was – from division down to
> regiment, from regiment to battalion, battalions to company,
> and companies out to what they called OPs [observation
> posts]. . . . At night time it was brutal for us people – when
> we got a line that went out or there was a short (what they
> call an open or a short), it was our job to lay another line,
> which we didn't do because we couldn't see where we were
> going, so we had to trace the other line, which was precarious

because you're moving and you could be shot at either by the Japanese who were waiting for you, or by your own people. It was very dangerous.

Ranucci remembered one such event in particular:

They said there was a line out at battalion. All our other people were gone, so Mascal and I took off on that line. When we got back to battalion there was a line out. We didn't even know who strung the line or where it went. . . . We were following that line, and when we got back to regiment they said they had a line out to division. Now mind you, we have come a long way from where we started and we didn't know where we were at, Mascal and I . . . Well, we took off and kept going and going and we didn't know where we were. We lost the line, we didn't know where we were at. We were just in a great big open field but we knew that. All of a sudden, the sky just seemed to light up and we hit the deck real quick. . . . What it was artillery that went off. We were silhouetted before we hit the ground. Before we knew it, there was machine guns firing at us all over the place. Well, we were hollering like mad 'We're marines. Quit Shooting. We're marines. Quit Shooting.'

We knew they were our own people. We were that far back. They finally quit shooting and all of this 'come up with your hands high' and all this. . . . When we started off the next day, we didn't know where our organization was. But we kept walking and whatnot and finally we asked here, asked there, and we eventually got back to our original outfit. They had us listed as MIA, which is called missing in

Marine Division on Roi-Namur in the Kawajalein Atoll, February 1-2, 1944. (National Archives)

action. And I said 'We're not missing in action, we're still here!'

After a brief rest and additional training in Hawaii, the Fourth Marine Division left in January of 1945 for the island of Iwo Jima. Iwo Jima, they were told, was only about ten square miles and would be easy to take over. Ranucci himself thought, 'boy, this is going to be an easy one.' When they hit the island, however, the fighting became brutal. Because of the terrain, there was no way for the troops to dig into the ground.

That night, instead of digging foxholes, my buddy and I, who I was with on this trip by the name of Des Roberts, we used to call him 'Canuk,' we put in a great big shell hole. It was either made by a bomb or naval artillery, a big, big hole. . . . Before dawn, we started getting ready for that day's action and a shell came over . . . Des and I heard it. We hit the deck immediately and it landed at the further end of that shell hole. We looked, and the guys at that end were all dead and we knew it and the incoming [fire] was tremendous again. Des took off, I gave him a little count and I took off. When I took off, I saw another hole and I jumped for it and I got hit in the back of the right shoulder. It didn't break the skin but it numbed me to death. Anyway, I came to find out that Des was in the same hole. We weathered that, and that barrage let up. Des and I got out and we went about our business again. We started moving forward with the troops. We couldn't do much while we were moving, just moving by the frontline troops and that's it. That day, we did string line and when we did, one line was open. In other words, it wasn't working right so Des and I located the problem . . . somebody had ripped it open. We were bent over and the shell landed behind us and Des got hit real bad. So did I, I got hit on the inner left thigh. I had to take Des down to battalion aid where I had to leave him—he had a chunk of shrapnel through his left arm, through both ends, and it had sealed itself it was so hot. . . . I left Des there, and I had to go on my own. I did this for a period of two to three days after the fact.

After this adventure, Ranucci was tired of combat. He was alone, but still fighting. He was stationed on the north side of the island when the American flag was raised. That picture became famous across America; for the troops, it was proof that their work and losses were worth something. After the war ended, Ranucci returned to Hawaii.

Ranucci lived briefly as a civilian and enjoyed his time playing soft-

World War II

ball and semi-pro football, but when the Korean War broke out, he realized that he was wasting his life. He enlisted, again, in the Marine Corps. Eventually, he was assigned to Able Company, First Battalion, First Marines on the 38th parallel in Korea. As Ranucci said, "I heard the first shell go over my head and I thought 'are you crazy, what are you doing over here? Didn't you get enough in World War II?'" . . . You were there in a dumb hole in a hill and they'd shoot at you and you couldn't do [anything] about it, just take it. . . . At any rate, I stayed up in the lines there for nine months." After those nine months, he got relieved. At twenty-six, he was considered too old to fight on the front lines, so he was transferred to Maison, North Korea, where he acted as a motor pool sergeant. Ranucci was eventually sent back to the United States and was discharged in January of 1953.

Lieutenant (j.g.) John Ticusan
U.S.S. *PERRY* (DMS-17)

John and his wife, Sally, wrote hundreds of letters back and forth to one another as a way of staying close, if only in spirit. They were newlyweds, and wartime separation, as well as the events in the Pacific, made the war years a very anxious and distressing time. In John's absence, Sally lived in San Francisco, where she, like so many other "single" spouses, worked in the war effort and patiently waited for her loved one to come home.

Virtually every evening after work, Sally took the opportunity to share her thoughts and family news. She often referred to herself as "Mamie" and to her husband as "Johnnie," "Papie," "Tic-boy," or "Sug." All of Sally's letters are very special, as they provide an intimate look into the personal lives of two people very much in love. These letters are certainly the opposite of the infamous and demoralizing "Dear John" letters! Rather, these uplifting letters are written conversations that include expressions such as "Boogies to you dear from the one who loves you most in world," and there is the promise of "bear hugs" and sweet dreams with "our faithful sandman."

Far away in the South Pacific, Ticusan served as an officer on the U.S.S. *PERRY*. In September of 1944, the *PERRY* was operating as a minesweeper off Anguar Island, in the Palau group of the Caroline Islands, in the South Pacific. This was a dangerous business, because "minesweeps . . . spearhead an invasion; it is always the minesweeps that open up the vital gap through which the amphibious forces pour their massed weight. And it is almost always the minesweep that gets sunk first."[18] So too for the U.S.S. *PERRY* on September 13, 1944. Naturally, Sally's letters reflect the highs and lows of emotions when the news reaches her.

WORLD WAR II

September 20, 1944

Dearest Papie,

Your Mamie sends you all kinds of comforting love. I learned this morning what happened September 14th to the Perry through a very wisely worded night letter from Ham and Trudie in Indianapolis.[19]

It was telephoned by Western Union and I happened to answer myself about 8:00 A.M. When she started reading me the message I wondered if I heard correctly and called Helen to listen downstairs.

Last night Trudie and Ham were listening to the radio when loss of the Perry was announced. She told me no lives were lost and I shall be eternally grateful to her and to Ham not to have come suddenly upon the newspaper article at work.

Of course I was very upset but decided I better go on to work. I was comforted in the knowledge that the Navy and all

Lt. (jg) John Ticusan (row 1, far right) with the officer complement of the U.S.S. *PERRY* (DMS-17) aboard the *U.S.S. CLEVELAND* (CL-55) after their ship was sunk on 13 September 1944. (Courtesy of John Ticusan)

newspapers do not publish losses unless every family is first notified.

I pray that "very small casualties" is an accurate account, and I thank God that no lives were lost on our ship. Since it was a landing operation I presume other ships came alongside quickly.[20]

Please remember honey that I have always asked you to tell me the whole truth no matter how drastic it might be. Troubles are ours to share as well as joys and I should not appreciate it if you failed to tell me about any injury minor or major in quality.

Tonight I wrote Margaret Steward because I am certain Seattle papers must have had the same information. I promised to telephone her if I heard anything definite and I am glad to be able to count on her doing the same thing.

Jump saw it in the paper and has some Navy friend trying to get more details. Ann's friends have ears open, Jane Pickett called, Charley (?) called, and I called K.C. Wallace. K.C. was out, but his Mother was very reassuring. She believes you will get a 30 day survivor's leave. If that is true and you are not harmed in anyway I shall be so happy.

Boogies to you dear from the one who loves you most in all this world. I shall wonder where you are resting your tired head tonight and every night until I hear from you yourself.

Helen wrote Captain Gaddis in Pearl and he may be looking you up if you get to his neighborhood.

It would be wonderful to be where you are to help you share this. Since I am here please think of me very close to you for I have never left your side since we were married.

Mizpah   All my love, Little kisses and bear hugs Sally

September 21, 1944

Dearest Johnnie

Many little kisses and soothing caresses I bring to my dear Papie. How I wonder where you are Sug and if you are all right.

In last night's letter I told you how I learned of the loss of the Perry from a night letter telephoned from Western Union yesterday morning.[21] *Ham and Trudie had heard the news broadcast on Sept. 19th. It was very thoughtful of them to let me know in this way. Trudie had it worded so wisely that after the initial shock of hearing something had happened to our ship I was not too alarmed.*

Of course I realized nothing would have appeared in the

papers until every family had been notified if there had been that necessity.

A wire cane today from Aunt Marne saying "Learned about John's ship. Is he alright? Please write us. Love"

I sent Trudie and Aunt Marne night letters of 25 words tonight.

It has worried me about whether I should write or try to wire Mary. Actually I know nothing to tell her and I think a wire would frighten her so I have done nothing. I am not certain whether this is what you would want me to do. I hope something in the way of news of your location and condition reaches me very soon. Just as soon as I hear from you I will write her air mail special delivery which I believe wouldn't take her so much by surprise as a wire.

Your Mamie is right there beside you every minute. I pray that you are unharmed and on your way to the States.

Goodnight dear. I hope that wherever you are you are resting well tonight and dreaming of the one who loves you most. Mizpah   All my love, Sally

September 22, 1944
Dearest Papie,

Tonight I send an extra large amount of boogies and little kisses because it is serenade night once more. Honey do you realize when you get right down to figuring that we have been married eleven months? I love you much, much and pray that we might be able to celebrate October 22nd together.

Letters came today from Floss and Margaret Steward. They, too, have read about the Perry and ask news of me. I have no news to relay but feel certain since I have heard nothing that you are all right.

The waiting is grim because of the uncertainty, but I do hope for a cable or a letter early next week saying you are well and safe.

Floss was so upset she couldn't get herself to write me much about her baby.

Johnnie back in June you told me to remember that you will always lean on me for love, comfort, and faith. I do hope you have remembered dear. There is nothing I want to do more than comfort you in time of trouble and love you always.

I know your ship is gone, maybe some or all of your belongings, but honey you must remember nothing – absolutely nothing matters if you are safe.

My whole being longs for you. I cannot squelch the rising

hope that you will reach the States soon.

All kinds of bear hugs and irresistible winks are yours. My love is strong and true for you are my Sunshine and my all.

September 24, 1944
Dearest Papie,

All my love and little kisses are yours dear. I love you much, much and yearn to squeeze you in a powerful bear embrace.

This morning I was awakened by Western Union telephoning a wire from Mary. She evidently had wired the Navy Department to find out if you are or are not a casualty.[22] The answer is no – which is a fact that I was thoroughly convinced of previously, yet it is good to have it confirmed.

I had talked it over with Ann and knew I could not obtain further information so did not attempt to wire Washington myself.

How are you Sug? I wonder and wonder where you could be and what ship picked you up. Do take care of yourself and write your Mamie just as soon as possible. I promised both Mary and Margaret Steward I would telephone them as soon as I hear anything from you.

I love you with all my heart and soul Tic-Boy. You are my sunshine.

I hear your Marne calls and remain right here to answer each and every one of them. Boogies.

Little kisses and busters I send to you in never-ending supplies. Remember that you are my everything and I yearn for your return.

September 27, 1944
Dearest Papie,

. . . Sug, he [K.C. Wallace] told me his Dad checked the casualty list. You were not on it nor was anyone whose name K.C. knew. He also said he thought you probably were picked up by an assault transport.

I guess one of these days I will hear from you. I am trying to be patient honey. . . .

All my love, Sally

October 2, 1944
Dearest Johnnie

My prayers have been answered. Now I know that you are safe and well and on your way home. I am extremely thank-

ful for all our blessings darling.

Three letters came this morning. Helen made a special trip to bring them to me at noon. As we waited for our lunch at Edy's I read the letters you wrote Sept. 16th, 18th, and 24th. We're all terrifically excited at the prospect of a recent visit from you!

Your Mamie is just about to bust with gladness. I love you so much. Boogies and many little kisses.

Of course I knew why I didn't get mail promptly. News of the Perry was in our papers and even Bud knew it in England Sept. 21st.

Tonight I telephoned Margaret Steward at Seattle to let her know you are all right. I was sure Jack was O.K. too and told her his initials appeared on our envelopes. I do hope she gets mail tomorrow. Probably it takes a day more to get to Seattle.

This past week I did have many extra hard tugs at my heart. The very night it all happened I was discussing you with Jane Pickett at her apartment.

Every night you are in my thoughts but that night you were uppermost even more than usual!

I know from the papers, only that the ship was lost off Palau. To say you had a "rough" time I am sure is putting it mildly. I am so thankful that you are well. And I want you to know I understand that you cannot write any information about the circumstances.

Just the other night I read Helen your telegram that you sent me a year ago about getting my duds together – What a coincidence that you would write that same phrase in your letter!

I'll say things look bright! They never looked better Sug!!! I am trying to be patient but I can scarcely hold still.

October 7, 1944
Dearest Papie,

. . . I am very happy Sug knowing you are on your way home. May you arrive quickly and safely. I must confess I am getting impatient. How the days and nights drag until I can one more hold you ever so close to me. You are my very Sunshine.

. . . I am sorry you are without clothes – did someone loan you a shirt & trousers? I thought that was probably the case but honey loss of mere possessions means absolutely nothing – just so you are safe. . . .

John Ticusan finally returned in October on thirty-days' leave, which he spent with Sally and their families in Indiana. This was a joyous time for all, but much too short, as he soon had to return to active duty. Once the war was over, though, John, Sally and their infant daughter, Jean, settled in Indianapolis.

Lieutenant Alfred K. B. Tsang
29th Bomb Group, 314th Bomber Wing, 20th Air Force

Alfred Tsang was born to Chinese immigrant parents in New York City. During his early childhood, though, he returned with his mother to China. He remained there until the threat of war in the Far East became too ominous, and he returned to New York in 1938. At that time, Tsang lived with his father, and he attended for a brief time Public School 23 in Chinatown, and then enrolled at Haaren High School.

With the attack on Pearl Harbor, though, his secondary education was interrupted. Tsang felt a moral obligation to drop out of high school in 1942 in order to enlist. "I was raised by my mother who was taught by a Confucian scholar who was also my tutor. It was the

Lt. Alfred K. B. Tsang. (Courtesy of Alfred Tsang)

Confucian ethics to uphold the society above one's self, accepting personal responsibility, humility, respectful of authority, and be fair to others. I enlisted instead of waiting for the draft because my mother would be ashamed of me if other women's sons were to bear my responsibility to the society that gave me refuge from the war." Tsang was convinced that being "enlisted in the Air Corps was better than being drafted into the infantry. I enlisted on October 20, 1942 at the Grand Central Palace on Lexington Avenue in New York." Since Tsang had completed fewer than three years of high school, he expected that he "would go to cooks and bakers school or general duty." However, tests indicated" Tsang was well qualified for "radio school." Consequently, Tsang completed training at the advanced navigator school, where he had training in physics, math, meteorology and Morse code. Tsang recalled how it was "the navigator's job to fix the position of the vehicle by methods such as pilotage or map reading, celestial by taking elevation angle of celestial objects, taking bearing or direction of the vehicle in relation to radio stations, but not over hostile territory. RADAR and LORAN were advanced technolo-

WORLD WAR II

gies we learned later in the war."

Tsang was proud when he stated that he "graduated on May 20, 1944, nineteen months to the date after I enlisted, and became a second lieutenant in the Air Corps." This was unusual, especially for a Chinese-American.

> *The U.S. Army was racially segregated during the war. I was the only person of color (not the term then used) among the flight crews. I also thought the Army was an equal opportunity employer. How could it be for an ethnic Asian like me, a high school drop out to have become an officer at the age of twenty, not even old enough to vote? It was a bewildering experience at the same time. I was often asked how I got assigned to a combat unit against Japan because I would be more harshly treated if captured. I got there because they were looking for a last minute replacement and an instructor at a combat crew training school would fit the need. I had that previous assignment not because of combat experience that I didn't have, but because the Chinese Air Force was being trained for the B-24, and that my linguistic skills might help. Somewhere along the way, they forgot the unwritten policy. . . . It didn't matter that I didn't have any combat experience nor much operational experience in navigation. . . .*

Once the Pacific islands of Guam, Tinian, Saipan and Iwo Jima were secured, the B-29 bombers, for which Tsang trained, were ready for operations. Fighting had not even ended on Iwo Jima in February 1945 when crippled bombers returning from Japan began making emergency landings. Tsang was indebted to those Marines who died to secure Iwo Jima; he would not have survived the war without their sacrifice.

Baptism of Fire

> *The first mission that we launched on March 9 and dropped bombs on March 10 was the most fearsome for us and for the people on the ground in the target area. The B-29 was made for high altitude precision daylight formation bombing. When we assembled for briefing, the first for my crew that [had] arrived on Guam less than a week earlier, and we had never so much as . . . [taken] off with a B-29 from the North Field (now Andersen Air Force Base), the first item in the announcement was target Tokyo. We were to bomb at an unheard altitude of 5,000 feet using incendiary bombs, carried no guns, and used no running lights. Many history books report that leaving the guns behind was to be able to*

145

carry more bombs. The real purpose was to keep us from shooting at one another in the darkness of night. Some books also indicated that we left the gunners behind. That should have been done in common sense. There was no point in taking them along just for the ride. In the esprit de corps sentimentality, it was one for all and all for one. We flew as a crew so that we finish our tour as a crew, or perish as a crew.

Of the thirty-six B-29 combat missions I flew between March 9 and September 1, 1945, 23 were incendiary, commonly referred to as Fire Bombing, and all but three of them took place in the darkness of night. The other daylight missions were general duty or explosive bombs most of which caused instant destruction. The complete missions took anywhere from 14 hours to as long as 18 hours and 40 minutes (Koriyama). Each mission took part involving two calendar days. We took off one day and landed the next.

Finding Tokyo was not a difficult job. By the time we got there, the city was in flames and could be seen more than a hundred miles away. It was fearsome – our baptism of fire.

Three bomb wings from Guam, Saipan and Tinian launched 325 aircraft, 279 reached the primary target while 20 bombed alternate targets. We lost 14 aircraft. Fifteen and one half square miles of Tokyo was burned out. Casualties on the ground were in the upper tens of thousands. They were closer to, more or less, the number that perished in Hiroshima.

Encore

After the initial shock, we went on to other major cities such as Nagoya, Kobe, Osaka, Yokohama as well as smaller ones, and back to Tokyo more times. By June it became such a routine that we called our missions milk runs. At one of the briefings, we were informed that they had loaded some delayed fuse fragmentation bombs and we asked why. 'For the benefit of the fire fighters.' We guffawed. It seemed to make sense that if we had intended for those cities to be burned, we certainly didn't want the fire to be put out. Sometimes, the reason given for the target was [that] the population [was] over 100,000.

The Human Toll

After the shock of the first mission, bombing Japan was more like shooting fish in the barrel. We had losses, but not very obvious. Our crew didn't have a B-29 assigned to us as our own. It happened three times when after we flew other crews' aircraft twice, they were not to be seen again. We were not superstitious, of course. But we finally have a B-29 of our own and were apprehensive about flying our third mission in it. Three crews we shared our hut with also didn't come back. Their personal effects were quietly removed. There was never any announcement on what happened to them. We never saw the seriously damaged aircraft nor wounded crew members. The seven-hour return flight from the target was too long for the seriously damaged or malfunctioned aircraft to survive.

It was brutal to drop bombs on defenseless civilians. We tried not to think about it. We kept to our own thought, at least for myself. Some older and more educated guys talked about philosophical things. I stayed away from those bull (albeit serious) sessions lest I betray my ignorance and illiteracy. It was to our advantage that they were defenseless. Earl Russell and Joe Franklin in our hut told us not to foolishly think that we will come out of this. My thought was someone will always come back from each mission, and I would be that someone. Earl and Joe didn't come back. Were they pessimist? What else could we expect when we were out to do so much destruction and killing? I have read the Germans had prisoners of war camps of as many as eight and ten thousands of Allied officers. I suspect they were mostly aviators.

The flames in the target [were] intense from the burning napalm and magnesium-so intense that the thermal draft caused turbulence for our aircraft. During one mission, I thought we were hit and was about to bail out, and I didn't even have the chest chute pack snapped onto my harness. Cold chills run over me when I think about that foolish and embarrassing close call. The radio operator yanked me back into the cabin: "Lieutenant, we are not hit. We need you to navigate us back to Guam." And I also have nightmare over that event waking up in the middle of the night with soaking perspiration.

Hanging bombs

The B-29 bomber was normally configured to carry 40 500-lb. bombs. When we carried the one hundred pound incendiary bombs, five of them were held together by cable and shackled to a release mechanism. Each bomb had two fuses. The tail fuse was a spinner type and wired for safety. Upon released from the aircraft the safety wire remain with the aircraft, and the tail fuse would spin through the air and thus arms the nose fuse. Upon impact the nose fuse would detonate the bomb.

On the night of June 28, 1945 we were to bomb the City of Nebeoka with incendiary bombs. Upon release over the target, the bombs shackled to one of the lower racks failed to release. This failure blocked the bombs in the higher racks from leaving the aircraft. Since those top bombs had left the shackle, the tail fuse were free to spin and they were spinning by the heat from the burning target below. Any striking of the nose fuse would cause the bomb to detonate.

The radio operator alerted me of the situation. I went out to the bomb bay and tried to release the shackle with a screw driver that I was trained to do. However I couldn't access the manual release of the hung-up bomb rack. Lt. Herb Small, the bombardier, was right after me and started kicking each of the several released bombs through the vacant spaces toward the ground below.

In order to do what he did, Lt. Small had to shed his flak jacket and parachute pack. The B-29 didn't have a center catwalk like the B-17 and B-24 heavy bombers. He had to walk

Lt. Tsang, (2nd row, 2nd from right) and crew with "forced" smiles, prior to bombing mission over Japan. (Courtesy of Alfred Tsang)

along the bulkhead and hold onto the structural members. While shoving the bomb with one foot, he could have easily slipped and fallen through the bomb bay.

To be in the light

The B-29 was the product of high altitude precision bombing doctrine. It was the first production aircraft with pressurized cabin with remote controlled gun turrets so that four turrets with ten 50 caliber machine guns could be trained on a single target. But we didn't know much about the wind velocity above the weather. That was how we got to use a sophisticated machine for low altitude fire-bombing. At five to eight thousand feet, we were too low for the heavy anti-aircraft artillery unless a shell actually penetrates through an aircraft. However, the automatic weapons could be lethal if an aircraft is sighted. The Japanese were not unprepared for night bombing because we saw some of our airplanes were caught by searchlights and were brought down. We had seen them at a distance, and the light beams looked like they were supporting the aircraft in the air. Eventually, we were caught by fourteen of them on one wing and fifteen on the other. It was an eerie feeling to be in the spotlight.

Coup de Grace

Two days later, we were called to be briefed for another mission. . . . Tokyo in broad daylight! Here we go again. After many milk runs, the war returned to us. But why did we have to take on a high-risk mission so late in the game that had already been won? There were four strategic targets for which each of the four wings was responsible. Our wing, the 314th, was assigned Nagoya. It was taken out early in the campaign. Tokyo was 73rd's on Saipan. . . .

Formation flying was very demanding on the pilots. However, it was for a short duration. We were to rendezvous at some distance offshore from Honshu. Then form up and proceed toward the initial point, and the target. A tight formation was the objective. The bomb pattern would be more concentrated, and so were the defensive fire power. On the other hand, antiaircraft shell could easily find a target. The aircraft immediate to our right was hit at a time when the war would soon end. The incredible thing happened. The flight engineer, a big strapping man with flak suit still on him managed to get out of the smallest window right next to the number three engine. That window was intended as escape hatch upon ditching. Bud Greenness right heel was clipped by the prop in his bailing out. We were quite anxious for him. His wife was pregnant when we left the states.

One day later, the second atomic bomb struck Nagasaki. Then the waiting began again for the surrender.

Once more we were called to another briefing for another nighttime incendiary strike. Our target was Kumagaya in Northern Honshu. Our instruction was if surrender should come, we were to salvo our bombs at sea, and return to base. Lately we were having passenger joining us for the ride. It was so safe that our passengers were willing to sign waiver. The passenger on this mission was an intelligence officer, a

Bombing run over Japan. (Courtesy of Alfred Tsang)

lieutenant colonel joining us. He was non-rated, meaning an officer had not been qualified to perform aerial duties. We had no heart in dropping the bomb load, but we did. The sunrise was the best part of the mission for me. Most of the time, most of the crew were asleep except the flight engineer and me. The fear and the difficult and fearful work was behind us. It was great to be alive. Forty minutes before we landed, the intelligence officer received the message that the war ended.

Finale

There was another briefing two weeks later. No guns, no ammunition and no bombs. We didn't need the full length of the runway to get the aircraft airborne. Our target was Nagoya. Ostensibly, it was to be a reconnaissance mission to look for POW camps. Actually it was a triumphant tour de grace, also a treat to see our handy work. We had waited two weeks after the final combat mission for this to be certain that it would be safe. Our crew would get combat credit for this mission, our 35th and thus completing our tour. We were the lucky ones to have completed a combat tour. Customarily *upon returning from a final mission, the crew would buzz the field, i.e., come in low at tree top level over the runway before entering into the traffic pattern before landing, but we decided not to do it.*

I volunteered for a reconnaissance mission to southern China to search for POW camps with a crew on Tinian. We were overnight for rest at a base on the Philippines. It was gut wrenching to see the Filipino boys (girls stayed away from the military) eating our discard from the garbage cans. They were too afraid to come too close to us for handout. It was not the first time I saw beggars. We flew over Canton and Hong Kong where I grew up. My mother and grandmother were down there somewhere. I didn't tell my Tinian crew about that.

Self-reflection

Tsang commented, "in the Tokyo 50th anniversary essay, "Sorrowful Fiery Reminiscence," I wrote: 'For the grieving survivors in Dresden, London, Coventry, Cologne, Chungking, Tokyo and many other places, it was all the same whether their loved ones were killed by atomic, smart or fire bombs or the V-2 rockets.' My emotion has been at the bottom of the pit for so long that it has not seen the light of day. I have been told to get over it, and it happened so long ago. If only I could."

The fire-bombing of Tokyo and other Japanese cities took an great emotional toll on Tsang. For him, "innocence lost is forever gone. The memory and my sorrow of the Tokyo conflagration will remain till the last of my days. I have collected sample of soils from Tokyo, Iwo Jima, and places where my parents are interred, and have asked my family to mixed them with my ashes; and to cast part of the mixture into the Pacific where many B-29 went, and the remainder in the columbarium at Arlington."

For the most part, members of Tsang's squadron "in the B-29s either came back unscratched or not at all. We were one of the few crews that completed the tour of 35 missions. We forewent the R & R leave that was allowed after 22 missions. Our entire crew received the Distinguished Flying Cross and the Air Medal with three Oak Leaf Clusters."

END NOTES

[1] "Brief Account of the Philippine Service of . . . the 701st and 440th Ordnance Companies" recounted in a letter to Brig. Gen. Earl McFarland from Maj. V. C. Huffsmith, Fifth Air Force Ordnance Department (APO 929), November 20, 1942. A copy of this letter is in possession of the

World War II

Temple family.

[2] Huffsmith, "Account of Philippine Service," (1942), p. 1. In John Temple papers belonging to Shirley Temple, his wife.

[3] Huffsmith corroborated this story. "Maintenance of transportation became a major problem. All stocks of spare parts were quickly exhausted and it became necessary to salvage vehicles and trade parts to keep others in operation. . . . Sergeant Edmonds . . . built many cross-breed vehicles from salvage parts. One in particular was notorious. The vehicle, a cargo truck, consisted of a Diamond T motor and steering gear, a Dodge front end, a Ford rear end, a Chevrolet cab, and an Ordnance bed . . . and was christened the "six and seven eighths."

[4] Gavutu Island was a main base in the Solomon Islands, first for the Japanese who invaded it in April, 1942, and then for the American 1st Paratrooper Battalion, and was recaptured on August 7, 1942. The Japanese were entrenched throughout the island. The Marines suffered when they were shelled and bombed by their own forces. After the island was secured, the U.S. Navy used Gavutu as a PT boat base. Before the war, Gavutu Island was used as a Royal Australian Air Force seaplane base. The Japanese captured it in May of 1942.

[5] Before the war, Tanambogo Island was used by the Royal Australian Air Force as a seaplane base. It was captured by the Japanese in May of 1942. A small Marine attack on Tanambogo had failed on August 7, 1942, and that island was still in Japanese hands well into the following day. During the morning, fresh Marines arrived from Gavutu to help complete the fight there. After a heavy bombardment from Navy ships, landings began on Tanambogo, led by a pair of tanks, and by nightfall the island was basically in American hands. Again, as on Tulagi, "mopping up" of the well dug-in Japanese continued for some time afterwards. The cost of taking Gavutu and Tanambogo was 70 Marine lives. There were only a handful of Japanese survivors when the Americans finally gained complete control.

[6] The Guadalcanal to Tulagi invasion was during August 7-9, 1942. Tulagi is a small island (5.5 km by 1 km) just off the coast of Florida Island and Guadalcanal. The Japanese occupied Tulagi on May 3, 1942, with the intention of setting up a seaplane base nearby. The next day, the ships in Tulagi harbor were raided by planes from the U.S.S. *Yorktown,* in a prelude to the Battle of Coral Sea.

[7] Cape Esperance is located on Guadalcanal. A battle occurred here on the night of October 11-12, 1942. The Japanese lost a heavy cruiser and a destroyer. The U.S. Navy lost the destroyer, the U.S.S. *Duncan.*

[8] Port Moresby was a port off the coast of New Guinea that US forces occupied during World War II; also on New Guinea is Nadzab, which was developed by American forces as a massive air base. Wakade, Biak, and Morotai were islands held by the Japanese and used as communication centers and airbases. The Americans needed to take and hold these islands in order to begin the American advance towards the Philippines in 1944. Mindanao

was the first objective in the Philippines.

[9] *A Short History of the* U.S.S. *SAN JACINTO*, published for the ship's crew, lists no editor, publisher or date of publication. Hunt's diary sections have been introduced with information contained in the ship's operations report, specifically Chapter 5, pp. 12, 14-18, 20, 22, 24. Specific citations have been noted when the information is quoted directly.

[10]Possibly referring to the Aiea Military Reservation *(1941 - unknown), Aiea Heights* Battery Aiea (1941 - 1944) two 240mm howitzers was built here to support the Kunia and Kalihi batteries. Also here was a 3-inch AA gun battery (1942), and a AA brigade-level command post (1942) (which still exists). See American Forts (West) – Hawaii. http://www.geocities.com/naforts/hi.html (January 15, 2004).

[11]For information on the troop ship AP-133, see the *Dictionary of American Naval Fighting Ships*: the *General O.H. Ernst* sailed from Seattle 27 August 1944; and, after embarking more than 3,000 fighting men at Honolulu, she transported troops to Guadalcanal Manus, and Ulithi before returning to San Diego December 4th. Underway again 10 days later, she carried troops to Guadalcanal and promptly returned to the West Coast, reaching Seattle January 20th, 1945. Following a round-trip voyage during February to Honolulu and back to San Francisco, the busy transport made a round-trip voyage between March 17th and May 22nd, carrying troops from San Francisco to New Hebrides, New Caledonia, New Guinea, Leyte. and the Admiralties. http://www.ibiblio.org/hyperwar/USN/ships/dafs/AP/ap133.html (January 15, 2004)

[12] *A Short History,* p. 22.

[13] *A Short History,* p. 22.

[14] *A Short History,* p. 22.

[15] Max Halderson resided in Bartlesville, Oklahoma. Letter from L.D. Halderson to M.H. Halderson, May 28, 1944.

[16] William J. Verbeck, *A Regiment in Action,* [A history of the 21st Infantry Regiment, U.S. Army], (n.p., 1946), p. 12.

[17] *A Regiment in Action,* p. 16.

[18] Excerpt from W. Karig, R.L. Harris and F.A. Mason, *Battle Report: The End of an Empire* as compiled in *The U.S.S. Perry (DD-340/DMS-17): An Illustrated History, 1922-1944,* which was compiled by Cdr. E. A. Wilde, Jr., USNR (Ret.), 1997. (Hereafter, E.A. Wilde, *The U.S.S. Perry).*

[19] Sally had very little information regarding the sinking, which actually took place on September 13th.

[20] The *Perry's* fast minesweeping ability made it an ideal ship for the island-hopping campaigns of the Pacific. After leaving the Mare Island Navy Yard in November of 1943, Ticusan and his crewmates participated in numerous naval actions, including the Marshall Islands campaign [December 1943-February 1944], the Hollandia operation, the invasion of the Marianas, and the capture of Anguar and Peleliu Islands in the Palau Group [September

World War II

1944]. Source is E.A. Wilde, *The* U.S.S. *Perry*.

[21] Excerpts from Lieutenant Ticusan's ship's log summarize the ship's activities for September 13th" 1400 [hours] secured from General Quarters . . . 1407 changed course to 230 T and (pgc) and 228 (psc), executed column formation astern. 1411 changed course to 255 T and (pgs) and 253 (psc). 1414 Formation changed course to 030 T and (pgc) and 029 (psc). 1418 . . . in 70 fathoms of water a violent explosion occurred starboard side amidships. Lost all steam to main engines and both fire rooms flooded. Ship took 30° list to port increasing slowly. 1420 Commanding Officer ordered abandon ship. About 1425 boats from the U.S.S. *Preble* and U.S.S. *Guest* commenced recovering survivors from the water. . . . " E.A. Wilde, *The U.S.S. Perry*.

[22] There were casualties aboard the U.S.S. *Perry,* and these included the five men stationed in the Number 1 fire room, which received a direct hit from the mine. "It was believed that the five men were instantly killed by the force of the explosion. All means of access to the space were checked. Steam and rising water made escape impossible. . . . and their bodies lie with the ship." The men were Joseph J. Brand, Arthur W. Schieber, Ottice C. Joplin, Henry C. Edgell, and Dan J. Wersebe. For more information, see the Memorandum (1/6/45) in E. A. Wilde, Jr., *The U.S.S. Perry*.

WORLD WAR II
THE EUROPEAN THEATER

FOLLOWING THE COMMENCEMENT OF THE WAR IN THE PACIFIC, the war in the European Theater began in North Africa and Italy. The lack of Allied progress in Italy required that another front be opened, and so a grand-scale invasion, otherwise known as D-Day, was planned for the day of June 6th, 1944. Though the cost of human life was high, the Allies succeeded in taking hold of the Normandy beaches. This was a significant turning point in the war in Europe.

The Allies then proceeded through Europe, liberating occupied countries, including France, on their way into the heart of Nazi Germany. Indeed, the Nazis proved to be ruthless. The Allies were met with stiff opposition in the last German offensive, the Battle of the Bulge, which began on December 16th, 1944, and lasted through January of 1945. The Allies, however, triumphantly defeated the Nazis, and began liberating the many concentration camps throughout Germany. Though Germany surrendered on May 7th, 1945, and May 8th was declared V-E Day, the war continues to live in the hearts and the stories of many veterans, soldiers, Holocaust survivors, and prisoners of war who contributed so much to the fight for humanity.

Major John C. Carvey
G-3 (Air) Liaison, 36th Fighter Group
and 83rd Division, Third Army

John Carvey began his early military training at Culver Military Academy in Indiana. He went to Columbia University and was in law school in Texas when he was called to active duty. During World War II he wrote more than a thousand letters to his fiancée, Carolla Jean Flentke, a student at Indiana University. He also shared his memories of service in an oral history interview. These accounts have been meshed to give a better picture of significant events in the European Theater of Operations from 1944 to 1945. Carvey's positions varied according to the unit to which he was attached: he served primarily in the 83rd Division, but was loaned out as a liaison officer to the 36th Fighter Group, and he was also a part of Patton's Third Army.

WORLD WAR II

Arrival in Europe

My division sailed on a ship called the S.S. GEORGE WASHINGTON. This was a liner that had been captured from the Germans in WWI, and renamed the S.S. WASHINGTON, and when Woodrow Wilson went to the peace conference in 1919 in Europe, this was the ship he selected to go on because it was supposed to be a really, a very, very luxurious liner of its day, but when I got on it, all that stuff had been ripped out and about one third of the 83rd Division was on this ship and the division in those days had about 14,000 men. We docked at Liverpool after a fourteen-day voyage in which we had several submarine alerts. . . . I went there – to a place

Major John C. Carvey
(Courtesy of John C. Carvey)

. . . in England called 'Keele Hall.' This was a British estate, that had been converted into a British Army base. That was the headquarters of the 83rd Division. . . . Then, I was sent to a school in Sunning Hill Farms, and eventually to the Royal Air Force School of Army Cooperation in Old Sarum. . . . And then when I graduated from that school, I came back to Keele Hall and was told I had to report to General Patton. . . . I was attached at that point to the 36th Fighter Group and I was to be the ground officer for them. . . .

At this point, Carvey was sent to "a field called Kingsnorth, which was about three miles from Ashford, the county seat of Kent County. The importance of Carvey's duties quickly became apparent in May of 1944.

Invasion Planning

. . . We were taken to a briefing in Sunning Hill Farms . . . early in April [1944] . . . I was a captain at that point, so, we went in the manor house and they had all these maps up on the wall, but they were covered up. Everybody filed in there that was attending. They didn't even have chairs in there for captains. We stood, but if you were a major, you had a chair. And General Patton was there and I think John Bradley was there, and I know General Ridgway was there, and General [Maxwell] Taylor (these were airborne officers) and General Gavin, he was an airborne officer. The purpose of this meet-

156

ing was to brief everybody on the D-Day invasion. So they took the paper off the maps, and there was just a lot of detail, all the underwater obstacles and all the casements, and all of the big German guns were shown on this, and . . . I'm saying to myself, I just got here today! And they're getting ready to go on an invasion – it sounds like tomorrow! I thought that I had at least a couple weeks before I had to do anything like this! And it was pretty scary because you know the Germans had that place fortified and they weren't expecting us to come, but still they were ready when we got there. So then, we had a briefing session at Uxbridge, which was after I graduated from the British Royal Air Force School. And all of the GLO's, as we were called, meaning 'Ground Liaison Officers,' only I think we called them ALO's meaning Army Liaison Officers. . . .

We were in this theater and boy, they locked the doors after inspecting . . . you had to identify yourself, and go off this checklist and so forth, and then they told us that we were going to be given the field order for the invasion, and that we were to become biased because of this information and so they explained what they called the 'bigot system.' You know [what] the word, B-I-G-O-T spells? If you had access to all of the invasion information, and a right of access, you had a card that said 'C' on it, a big blue 'C', and your name and identification and physical description. That was the complete 'Bigot Card.' That meant you were entitled to talk about any phase of the invasion with anybody else who had a 'C' Bigot Card. So, we were instructed that . . . if we wanted to talk about something with the invasion, we had to identify ourselves. . . . You would say to the other officer, 'Are you bigoted?' If he didn't know what that meant, then you knew very well he wasn't bigoted. If he said, 'Yes, I'm bigoted,' you'd say, 'Are you partial, or complete?' If he said 'Partial,' or 'Complete,' then you asked to him to show you his card, which he would of course. So there were only two people of this Air Corps group that were bigoted, that was Colonel McCroskey who was the A-3, and myself, so we couldn't talk to anybody else, including a group commander about the invasion. Only Mac and I could talk and we were afraid to talk to anybody else for fear we'd let something slip.

In a letter to Carolla, written a year after D-Day, Carvey added to his account of Operation Neptune and Overlord preparations. This was so secretive that "I did not even tell my assistant Capt. Watson and Major McCroskey was tight lipped. I think all in all it was a well-kept secret

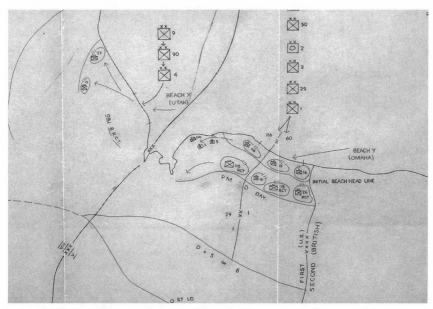

Operation Overlord plans of Utah and Omaha Beaches. (Courtesy of John C. Carvey)

throughout the Army."

> *Well, four days before the invasion, through the Army Ordinance, they sent an order down to this fighter group that they had to paint alternating stripes, black and white, on the fuselage of their airplanes. That's so the ground people . . . wouldn't shoot at them, [be]cause, when an airplane goes over at 200 to 300 miles per hour, it's pretty hard to see those stars on the wings. You know particularly if they're up a little high, or if they're coming so low that they go by fast, so if they could see that black and white stripe, they would realize that was an allied airplane. Well, we had aerial supremacy on the beachhead, and in France, and so there wasn't much Luftwaffe intervention, but it was good to know that you had those stripes, because nobody would shoot down our own aircraft, which would be easy to do otherwise. Since they only put those on there four days before invasion, the Germans didn't have a chance to figure out what it was all about, and if they had, . . . they would have put it on all of their planes, you see. So they, what little air force they had, w[as] flying around without that identification. So, they were targets. . . .*

WORLD WAR II

In the same letter to Carolla, Carvey described the last hours before the invasion began:

> . . . *We knew that when we received a message telling us that "Operation Doorbell" was to begin as the go ahead signal for "Operation Neptune" to begin. That Evening (June 5) about seven p.m. Major McCroskey and I were setting around discussing some details watching to make sure that no one else would walk in his office and disturb us. At that moment one of the enlisted men came up and saluted before handing Major McCroskey a message. He read the message and then handed it to me without a word. All it said was "operation doorbell tomorrow."*

When it was finally announced that the invasion of France was underway, after all of the planning and preparations, all that the Supreme Allied commander, General Dwight Eisenhower, and the ground and air liaison officers could do was watch and wait with great anticipation and anxiety. Carvey had a unique opportunity to be an eyewitness and he described a scene that has remained with him since the war:

D-Day Activities

> *I got in an airplane. It was called a B-26. It was a strip down airplane, meaning the armament and the armor plating had been taken out of it, and there [were] no guns on it. This was a really kind of a super taxi for this Air Corps group. And so, Colonel McCroskey, who was bigoted along with me said, "How would you like to go up on a ride?" This was on D-Day, and I said, "I sure would." So we got in this airplane with about six other officers, and we flew from what they call the Wash, which is a piece of [land that] sticks into the ocean. We flew down, all along the shoreline, we were two miles back in, [be]cause we knew if we got out there on the shore line, we'd be probably fired at. So we were back about two miles at about 3,000 feet and we flew all the way down to Southampton and back. So I could see the armada that went out there. It was the greatest scene, probably I'll ever see in my life. It looked like there were so many ships that a man could walk from ship to ship, all the way to France. And they had the balloons on the fringes, you know the aerial balloons, which were to keep the Luftwaffe away, if possible. And I could see the gunshots, the twinkle of the German firing on the distant shore. So that's what I did on D-Day, [be]cause the group I was in had some missions and we'd already*

*briefed them on what their missions would be, so they came
back in at intervals, after having been in France and done
what they had been assigned to do. We'd interrogate them
and they could tell us what they'd seen or done and then
they'd go back out. So, I didn't have any particular role that
day, thank goodness! I've read enough about it that I'm glad
I wasn't on that beach.*

Six weeks after the successful invasion, Carvey recounted his first
opportunity to see France personally.

July 26th, 1944 8 p.m.

> . . . *I awoke at 0700 this morning and found the Colonel
wide awake. So we dressed, shaved and hustled off to breakfast. There we found Major La Roche who asked where we
were bound. In no time at all we "checked out" and were off
to France to see the War.*
>
> . . . *Of course I suspected to see lots of shipping in the
English channel but still it almost stunned when I looked
down from several thousand feet and saw all the ships of all
shapes and sizes. It gave you an idea of the immensity of an
invasion. But when we got to the French coast there were
ships, it seemed, everywhere. It's plain now to me why Hitler
did not invade England right after Dunkirk. For an invasion
must be sustained by boatload after boatload of supplies once
you get a foothold. The shipping lines are its very blood-
stream. Adolph, I believe, just did not have the ships, barges
etc. that a slam bang invasion requires. Perhaps I'm forget-
ting that we were faced with a formidable array of troops
when we landed whereas the Nazi army, fresh from its French
triumph might have had much less resistance from the defeated, and somewhat disorganized British.*
>
> *Well we flew over the French coast and I began looking
for the tell tale signs of battle. We flew over a low tide and I
saw some of the "dreaded" underwater obstacles on the tidal
flats. At low tide they looked relatively harmless but I am sure
that when covered or partially so, they would be nasty. The
next sign I saw as in the area where I knew some of our gliders had landed. You could see scars on the green grass where
a glider had rested and a few skeletons, looking like a chick-
en from whom the meat had been removed leaving only the
bones. This I believe is due to the fact that salvage crews save
all the gliders that can be used again by having a "tug" come
down low and hook on to a Nylon rope stretched between two
poles. The glider is thus air borne. I have never seen this done*

*but the "Illustrated London News" for July 15th, has some
photos and an excellent description of the process. Gliders not
worth saving are "robbed" of parts (instruments, etc.) and the
residue is burned. This accounts for the skeletal appearance
and the brown scar on the ground.*

*. . . One look at the highways and the fields convinced
me that the "Yanks had come to stay." The Yanks are everywhere with every conceivable item of equipment. We put
down a nice field where before the Yanks came was just
another French farm. Now it's a full size airdrome doing quite
a "nice business."*

*We had told Major Whipple and Jimmy Watson to meet
us, but it was 30 minutes before they arrived. Later I learned
why. I asked Jimmy to drive me thro[ugh] a couple of French
towns that had figured in the early fighting. They were torn
up somewhat but not demolished. Two things made me
uncomfortable. (1) Driving on the right side of the road once
more. (I almost screamed in protest when we rounded the
curves on the right hand side.) (2) The M.P.'s which abound
in the countryside but which are doing a bang up job of keeping the heavy traffic moving.*

*Most of the houses in the towns had the French Tricolor
hanging from the second story windows. I noticed a tricolor
with the Cross of Lorraine in the center. I saw many French
people . . . in general they were all old or just children. . . .*

Later in June he recounted his first impressions of France. In his
duties, he was responsible for listening to radio reports from pilots and
reporting their findings to the Third Army's headquarters:

*. . . the beachhead had been secured and the American
forces had pushed inland quite a bit, and so, you could see
some of the effects of the bombing. You could see some of the
German vehicles that had been pushed aside . . . as the
Americans went in. We started flying missions. . . . By this
time, the Third Army was . . . just about through the . . .
German lines. . . . That happened on July the 27th, and when
we got the breakthrough, then this group was busy trying to
keep up with the ground forces that were going to the east as
fast as they could go, and with as little opposition as they
could encounter.*

*We got across France rather quickly, . . . and we got to
Paris I think around the 1st of August. There wasn't a whole
lot of German opposition for several weeks, because once . . .
what they called the Falaise Gap had been captured – the*

WORLD WAR II

German army disintegrated on the Western front. Of course General Patton wanted to go as fast as he could go to the Rhine River and he couldn't get the green light for that, so that was one of his biggest disappointments.

August 8th, 1944

. . . *The other day I stopped in a little French city and a little French boy of six or so patted my knife (he had crawled right into my jeep) saying "Pour Les Allemanges?" (For the Germans?) "Oui jeune homme," I replied (yes, young man.) Then he made a motion as if with drawing my knife from its holder and he then drew his imaginary knife across his throat making a rasping noise. Thus did this young French man indicate his attitude towards Germans.*

Our young hero then crawled over to my right side and patted the holster, wherein lay my pistol. Once again he enquired "Pour Les Allemanges?" and I replied "Mais Oui" Which is a strong way of saying "Yes!". Perhaps "You Bet" our slang for "You can wager your money on it, is a rough equivalent. My guest then withdrew an imaginary pistol from my holster, held his palm as if a gun, and shouted "Boom! Boom!" Just like we boys played Cowboys and Indians in my youth. . . . I deduced from this performance that this young, lusty Frenchman and I were "on the same team."

In England the kids used to say "Any gum chum?' here they say "Avez-vous des chewing gum?" meaning "have you some etc." So my little pal asked me if I had some, but he was disappointed.

. . . *Your French word for today is "CIDER" pronounced as we say cedar chest. It means a light wine made from apples. Well my darling, this letter must end so that I can obtain some sleep. However, before I drop off I shall look at your pictures and tell you that I love you very much. In the event that you are unable to hear me say it, Ill write it here, "I love you, Carolla, and will as long as there is a young man named John whose head is full of visions of a lovely lady named Carolla.*   *Your John.*

Paris was liberated on August 25th, 1944 and a month later, Carvey described his impression of the city:

I paused for a time at the Arc de Triomphe, which was built to commemorate the many victories of Napoleon. Underneath it lies the tomb of the French Unknown Soldier of World War I, the most sacred spot in France. A bronze bra-

162

zier was supposed to contain the "Eternal Flame." But there was no flame for there was no oil. How symbolic that the Flame should have gone out with the arrival of the Allies so that we can help rekindle a new flame for France.

I talked to a Frenchman while standing there and asked him if the Germans had dared to parade under the Arch itself during their stay. He said no that they had only marched around it.

According to him, the Germans used to parade around and around it and then on down the Champs D'Elyssee to the Place De Concord. The Parisians who were in the area were forced to watch the parade. So most Parisians contrived to be elsewhere at the hours the Germans paraded. My friend gracefully invited me to have a glass of cognac at the corner bar. I refused equally graciously.

In the afternoon I left Paris and drove on here. The trip was beautiful and historic. It is ground that Americans should know much better than we do. School children are not impressed with the fact that thousands upon thousands of American boys already lie sleeping in French soil. There are huge American cemeteries here and they are to me holy plots of ground. The title to the land is in the United States of America. Yet I heard no outcry in America when the Germans seized the country in which our sacred dead lie.

It is my observation that little if any desecration was practiced upon our National Cemeteries in France. In 1940 the Germans moved fast and in 1944 we moved even faster so that there is a minimum of battle damage. The French employees who tended the cemeteries with painstaking care were devoted to their jobs during the German occupation. The cemeteries are well kept and show how truly devoted the employees. . . .

In October, Carvey moved with Patton's Third Army to a temporary headquarters position at Nancy, France. En route to Nancy, Carvey passed recently created cemeteries, as well as famous ones from the Great War.

October 4th, 1944

. . . Traveling down one road in the country I came across the sad stor[y] of 17 French soldiers. They were officers and men who died, according to the dates on the little wooden crosses, in 1940. That was during the German blitzkrieg of France. These 17 men, lay in an isolated spot off the highway in a long trench. A few dried flowers were the only sign that France cared for those brave men who lost their lives in an

attempt to stem the Nazi tide. The inscription on the grave was "Soldat inconno. Unknown soldier." Whose son was he? Has his family in France given up hope that he might be in some German prison camp? Does he have a fiancée waiting for him? These are some of the thoughts that I had. I took a picture of the spot and before departing I saluted to honor those brave men. For the German conquest of France was quick. [T]here were casualties, a few among the victor and many more to the vanquished French. The heroes of a victorious people receive some homage and are not forgotten. The dead of a conquered, enslaved people are only further reminders of the futility of the struggle against might. . . .

I remember a story on that same hillside of "those who came to conquer and remained to die." While I was looking at the Marne I noticed a small German cemetery to my right on the hillside. In the center was a cross of wood in a little grass plot. Immediately in the rear were two rows of 20 wooden iron crosses, which serve to mark the German dead. While the soldiers of France, England, and the U.S. sleep under the "Cross of Jesus Christ," German dead lay sleeping under the iron cross and swastika as I have tried to indicate by my drawing. The inscription carried his class or year of birth, his name and his date of death. These 40 men all died in 1940 during the "Blitz" of France. Immediately in front were two rows of crosses, twenty each, showing that the comrade had gone to "Valhalla" in 1940. But there is more to our story. These iron crosses had been stained or varnished to protect against the weather, and a little fence of stained wooden pickets had been built to enclose this Nazi shrine.

But alas some additions to our cemetery were evident as some more of our Master Race became weary of this world. Some time in 1942 five additional bodies were added thanks to some F. F. I. activity and a large number were added in August 43. It seems that some of our planes had dropped in. This upset the German plans a row was added in front of a row behind the original four rows. These iron crosses were not varnished or stained and the little wooden fence had added unpainted sections in front and rear to fully enclose the enlarged plot.

1944 was defiantly a bad year. Perhaps it was the F.F.I. [Forces Françaises de L'Intérieur or the Resistance forces]. Perhaps it was too much feasting and drinking, but the Germans had deceased for every month. August, their last month, was the most miserable. Thus Valhalla had four extra rows in front and four rows behind. Most of the dates were Aug. 44. In the last row the Germans had left part of their trench unfilled in their haste to depart from France. Method of burial revealed that they dug a trench five feet deep, six feet wide and fifty feet long. Bodies were laid in side-by-side and a wall of limestone rock erected to wall off the last buried body from the open end. There was room in the last row for three to four more bodies and the limestone rocks that walled off the recently buried must have been scanty for some of the largest flies hat I have seen were going in and out. Dying for the Vaterland is not always so beautiful. Too bad that the Hans and Fritz lying there could not have known how he looks now. . . .

October 6th, 1944

. . . *After leaving Aisne-Marne Memorial I journeyed to the American Cemetery at Bellau. It is beautiful. From the main road one enters a long, tree lined drive with flowerbeds on either side, and well kept lawns. The broad entrance is flanked by shrubs. At the head of the entrance are two chateaus. These chateaus are well built modern quarters. One is for visitors and the other for the caretaker.*

Behind the two chateaus after passing thro the beautiful wrought iron gates one comes to the burial grounds. The cemetery is shaped in a partial circle. Perhaps I can draw it.

. . . *I walked around the perimeter of the chapel and to my dismay I found the chapel badly scarred from some sort of gunfire or bombing. There were also the marks of small caliber ammunition in the stone. I knew that by the time the Gunman who broke thro at Sedan in 1940, reached this general neighborhood French organized resistance was negligible. I feared that perhaps we might have erroneously bombed-strafed our own chapel.*

On departing I asked the caretaker just what caused the damage. He told me that in 1940 the Germans shelled the chapel tho the nearest French troops were six miles distant. Later some German officers came to the cemetery and grew very angry when they saw some of our soldiers were buried under the "Star of David" stones. (You've seen how Christians are marked ✝ & Jews are marked ✡). The caretaker managed to dissuade them since the U.S. and Germany were not then at war. So they went up to the chapel and fired their pistols at the chapel. These my darling, as you must never forget, are the "Master Race."

I asked the caretaker who paid him and he said that the Resistance had paid him after France was cut off from the U.S. His pay was 2000 francs per month ($40). He had five assistants who were paid 1500 francs per month. The head *caretaker was a World War I veteran. He showed me where a rifle ball hit him in the shoulder and came out his back. One of his assistants had lost a finger.*

Just how they kept the grass clipped so closely is a mystery to me for they told me that the Germans would not give them petrol for their gasoline power-driven lawnmower. So they were forced to pull and push like you will see your John do on our lawn someday. . . . Yours, John.

Late in the fall of 1944, there were indications that the 36th Fighter Squadron was going to be transferred into the Ninth Army. Carvey, though, hoped to continue working with his contacts in the Third Army in Nancy, France. At this time, on December 10th, 1944, he received his long-awaited promotion to Major. Carvey was with the Third Army when the battle of the Bulge began on December 16th, 1944. In order to be closer to the action, Patton moved his Third Army out of the luxury of Nancy to Luxembourg. His headquarters "took over a building that had been an old folk's home and they used this building until Easter Sunday of 1945," according to Carvey. Carvey's letters were much less frequent during this period, because he was busily engaged in coordinating air support for the beleaguered ground troops.

Battle of the Bulge Action

I was at the Third Army headquarters during the Battle of the Bulge, and I was charged with some coordination. We got a radiogram from General McAuliffe that they were in need of blood plasma and bandages and serums and stretchers that the 101st Airborne Division in Bastogne, which was surrounded by Germans, was in sorry need of those very things. So, I went to the air corps opposite, whose name was Lt. Colonel Allen, told him about this need, and he could try to get this plastic pod it was called. It was about eight feet long and maybe this big around, and we loaded it with bottles of serum and plasma and stretchers folded up and bandages and then we strapped iron straps around it to keep it together. These were attached to the undersides of the P-47 aircraft, where you'd normally have bombs. So then this group — there were twelve airplanes — flew over to Bastogne. And what happens is, the air corps people, unless you were very careful sometimes, when the first aircraft would drop [their] bombs, the others would see this, and they'd think it was time to bomb too . . . and nobody had any idea what kind of trajectory that this pod would have. . . . ([A] bomb is nose-heavy, and it goes over and has fins in the back, so it goes fairly straight down, of course it'd be at an arch because of the momentum of the aircraft.) Well, these pods, they were very erratic, and so we got word back from General McAuliffe's headquarters, that said that the Germans had gotten over 80% of them. I'm sure they enjoyed those things, and so I quickly went back over to the Air Corps and we devised another mission and we also arranged that we would have the Americans, when these came in sight, to fire red smoke flares, and that they were not to drop their bombs until they had cleared the smoke. You know, of course, even that's going to drift on you, but at least it's going to [a]light in the town some place. So we had a little better success the second time around and General McAuliffe didn't have to call in and complain.

Well, General Patton heard about the mistake (the first one) and he came down to my office. I'd already laid on this second repeat mission I just described and I didn't want to talk to him really, because I knew he'd be angry as he could be. I could hear him coming, because General Patton marched every place. He never loafed. He marched in military cadence every time I had anything to do with him. And I could hear these steps coming, which I recognized and also I could hear the toenails of this bull terrier he had that went with him, called Willy. And I thought, "Oh, I just hope he doesn't stop out here in front of my office." And all the sudden the door bursts open and there he was, with all his stars on, his pearl-handled revolvers and his helmet, and what he called his war face. And he looked at me and he said, "Major," in this high pitched voice he had (he did not have a bass voice), "Your mission was a G— D— failure," referring to this first trip that went over. And I managed to stutter out, "Yes, sir." And he said, "Well, what are you going to do about it?" I'd already done about it, but I was so frightened and I was stammering, and of course I was standing at rigid attention, with my hands on my trousers. . . . I'm looking straight at him, and trying to tell him. I finally got it out that I'd done it. He looked over at me, when I got the explanation out and he said, "Are you frightened of me, major?" and I said, "Yes, sir." He said, "Tell me, are you married?" and I said, "No, sir." He said, "I want you to make me a promise, when you get back to the states, the first thing I want you to do is get married. After you've been through the hell of married life, nothing I can say will ever scare you again!" With that, he about-faced and out he went. So you can see, he was a character. He was an actor. Now you know I told that story to everybody that I ran into, you can imagine. You knew you had to be on your toes because George Patton would find out if you didn't.

Carvey's responsibilities kept him very busy through Christmas and the week following; Patton and his operations staff were "following very closely the developments of the German's attempts to break out of the ever-tightening ring" and with the onset of very cold weather. Except for the men in the foxholes, the cold benefited those men, who were flying support missions or transporting materiel. "This hardens the mud & clears the air of fog & haze. . . . Mud is always a problem for an army."

30 Dec 44

. . . This like so many recent days was one of great activity. But American and British forces are all busy. From the amount of activity, you might imagine it was summer when weather is not such a problem. But both in the air & on the ground our soldiers are flying and fighting in unbelievably adverse weather. If the Germans can do it, we must be able to do at least as much.

I have never seen the pilots more eager to fly than recently when they realize that everything they do directly affects the German capacity to drive on. They are doing a magnificent job and fly constantly in weather conditions that would ground U.S. planes. But even so their dangers & hardships are not to be compared with the rough life of the infantry. Several of our pilots who have been up to the front lines will readily attest to that. One visit & they are happy that they are in the comparatively comfortable life of the Air Corps.

. . . I am afraid that I look a little war weary these days. I've suffered little but I've seen so much that I feel for my friends who have been far less fortunate. I hope so much that this Nazi effort is their last for every day that passes adds to the sorrowing homes of the nation.

Please do not forget to thank Our Father for his watchful care over both of us. May we be reunited soon!

All My Love Your John

31 Dec 44

. . . The present attack of the German Army in southern Belgium & Luxembourg should somehow make the people at home & the soldiers who are inexperienced, realize what a dangerous & capable soldier the present day German has been trained to be. Even now when they scrape the bottom of the man power barrel the German that is produced is a half

trained soldier thanks to Nazi Labor Service & civilian organizations of a semi-military character. It is this reservoir plus the desperation of a cruely wounded yet strong bear brought to bay that has assisted the Nazis in this December bid for victory.

We are all glad that the Germans have decided to come out and fight. They have less advantage out in front of their Siegfried Line. They are more vulnerable to ground attack & much more vulnerable to air attack. It is up to American soldiers to prove they are the German equal and throw them out of the area with as great a losses as is possible for us to inflict upon him.

I shall be thinking of you in thirty minutes when our clock strikes 12 & 1945 begins. My hope is that we may be fortunate enough to see 1946 in together. Pray that we may, my darling.　　　　*All My Love Your John*

By mid-January 1945, the last German offensive was crushed and the war in Europe was rapidly progressing towards its desired conclusion for the Allies. Post-war preparations were made by the Allied leaders, Churchill, Stalin and Roosevelt at Yalta in the Crimea from February 4 to 11, 1945. Details from the Yalta Conference regarding the dismemberment of Germany and the occupation of post-war Europe were of great interest to Carvey.

15 February 45

I have been thinking much of the conference held by Churchill, Stalin & Roosevelt. Never has such an important meeting of three men been held unless one thinks back to Lloyd George, Clemenceau & Wilson in 1918.

Comparing the men I fancy Churchill over Lloyd George, & F.D.R. I believe superior to Wilson. The enigma is, of course, Josef Stalin. He is the man few people know tho F.D.R. & Churchill are familiar personages to the Anglo-American peoples. There is much about him that reminds me of what I know of Clemenceau.

. . . If the Russian armies can launch further attacks I think that we ourselves will break across the Rhine with a speed that will startle you & the folks back home. The German line becomes thinner each day in manpower. The next time we break thro its "curtains" for "Jerry" . . .

My hope is that such a favorable event can happen soon. . . .

. . . I have been reading, as has most of the world of the important meeting that the three Allied leaders just complet-

ed in southern Russia. . . . I hope that the beginnings of a world structure which will lay the foundations for a lasting peace were laid down by the three Allied leaders. Pray, we should, that the spirit of world brotherhood has found that the future will be one of opportunity for the Christian ideal.

Churchill, Stalin & Roosevelt's momentous meeting had perhaps its predecessor when Lloyd George, Wilson & Clemenceau met at Versailles to plan a new world. I don't think that Mr. Wilson talked the language of his two cohorts. He apparently lived on a superior plane in his own eyes and the other two settled down to bargain as the best solution.

I don't believe that Mr. Churchill, & with his intimate knowledge of history & F. D. R. student of the past as he is were unmindful of the errors of 1918. This time I suspect they worked in closer collaboration than aloof Mr. Wilson. The document produced seems to reflect a great deal of F. D. R. & considerably less of Stalin & Churchill. I rather expected Mr. Stalin to do a little more dictating.

There will be arguments about unfortunate Poland no matter the solution agreed upon. Poland's claims & desires were not without blemish for she annexed from both Russia & Lithuania in the 20s while Russia was in the throes of reorganization. Russia's claims were also disputable, & at the moment Russia was in possession of 100% of the Polish region. The compromise reached seems to have arrived at a solution which gives & takes something from both viewpoints. Considering what Stalin could have demanded (& who were Britain & the U.S. to say nay) I think those who label the solution as a "Fourth Partition" of Poland are likely to be those who have always condemned the U.S.S.R. On the other hand it does remain to be seen whether Stalin allows an independent Poland or whether thro some Russian sponsored Polish party he achieves the same end by subterfuge.

I am most heartened by our own indication that this time the U.S. will not shed the blood of its young men & thereupon retire to its shores & tell Europe "to stew in its own juice." We have an investment in Europe & its peace. That is the blood of those soldiers who will forever rest here, both from 1918 & 1943-4-5. May this sacrifice have not been in vain.

All of this means so much to us & our children. That is why I so pray that something constructive will come of this. . . .

Carvey and the Third Army finally left Luxembourg on March 10, 1945. They established new headquarters, first at Idar-Oberstein, and eventually in Frankfurt. Carvey remained in Frankfurt for only five days; then he went on to Hersfeld and finally to Weimar, where he visited Buchenwald.

Headquarters Third Army
2 April 45

. . . So here it is just before supper and I am writing to the one and only fiancee that any man could ever desire, from the homeland of the nation that said "Today we own Europe, Tomorrow the world." After France, Belgium, Holland and Luxembourg, where we were friends and liberators we are now self-announced conquerors. It is not a welcome change yet a most necessary one if we are to stamp out this creed that spawned this war and all of our troubles. May we be able to complete the task soon.

Along the route I drove yesterday the Germans had many road blocks made of steel gates, with a wheel on the open end that allowed them to be rolled into position. They were not inexpensive and of course were all constructed after March 1936 when Hitler (with his then 2nd rate army) defied the nations of France, England, and the U.S. by reoccupying the Rhineland with military garrisons. I have seen modern military barracks as large as our own old Ft. Benjamin Harrison in cities the size of Bloomington. Why do all the cornerstones say 1937 and 1938? What did we think Hitler was building these for? Our blindness becomes more inexcusable as the evidence mounts. Even the friendly postman in Germany is a soldier in a uniform closely resembling the Army. The railroad engineer, the fireman, all are soldiers! All have had basic military training and are organized in military grades. I will not excuse our stupidity by saying "who sold us this bill of goods?" meaning who convinced us Germany meant no harm? Rather I ask, will we always be so selfish in our outlook that we can tell the other nations that we are not interested in assisting in corraling aggressors and what's furthermore we are too poor and too busy to keep an adequate military strength.

. . . From our recent rapid progress we can draw much encouragement. The magnificent performances of General Patton's forces has surely reduced the time considerable. As you know once we reached the Rhine we did. . . .

On the same date as Carvey's Easter letter to Carolla, there was another remarkable event, which made a lasting impression on him:

World War II

When I got to Idar-Oberstein on Easter Sunday, 1945, my sergeant came in my office and said, 'Major, there's three men out here that insist on seeing an American army officer.' I don't know how the sergeant read into them, but he did and he brought in these three men. They looked in terrible condition, you know, physically, and I said, 'What do you want?' And they, I'd been told they were all American soldiers from WWI, and they told me that they had been in the Army of Occupation in 1919, and I guess it was July 1920 when they brought the American Army [of] Occupation home, (which we didn't do this time, thank goodness), and they had married German girls while they were in the Army [of] Occupation. And apparently, they had some sort of commitment, that every other year, they would take their wives back to Germany for a thirty-day vacation type of thing. They had done this apparently, and in 1935 it must have been, they were not allowed to leave. ([It] could have been 1937) [and] in any event, they went over in good faith and they were not allowed to leave. Well, when the war came on, they were all interned because they were aliens and Americans. Their children, their boys particularly, had been brought up in the German Nazi youth movement [and taught] to despise Americans and British and French people. Anyway, so they didn't look with any particular approval on their parents, and after the war began with America, which was December the 9th or 10th, after Pearl Harbor, they began to receive real privations, because they were in concentration camps. They were not in prisoner of war camps. And so they were even scorned by some of the Germans that were in these concentration camps. So here we are on Easter Sunday, 1945, and I said, 'Well why are you here? How'd you get here?' They claimed to have walked all the way from this German concentration camp [from] which they were released. The American Ninth Army or the British army had liberated them, and just turned them loose, and so they walked down to the American army sector, which was quite a few miles, maybe over a hundred. And I said, 'Now that you're here, what do you want me to do?' They said they wanted food and they wanted some place to stay. And I said, 'Well, you're not in the American service, but certainly we can see to it that you're fed and we can probably use you in the kitchen to do some work around there a little bit, or they could do anything in the world.' Well meanwhile, of course, I got in touch with our American Red Cross representative, and in due time, they were repatriated to the US, and I remember asking them if they wanted their wives

notified, or their children, and they said they didn't care.
Their children had never come to see them in the concentra-
tion camp and their wives, of course, they were thoroughly
Nazified and so as far as they were concerned, their family no
longer existed. So that taught me, don't marry any German
girls in the army occupation.

After leaving Frankfurt with the Third Army, Carvey witnessed evidence of German brutality against American pilots who had been held in
German POW camps:

I saw American prisoners of war that were liberated after we
crossed the Rhine and some of these people, their weight had
been reduced under a hundred pounds. They hadn't been fed
at all. And under the Geneva Convention . . . they're supposed
to be fed. The only thing you could say in defense of the
German authorities was that nobody probably in Germany
was eating as well as they had been, and so they weren't real-
ly worried about feeding the P.W.'s. And these were soldiers
that in the most part had been captured in the Battle of Bulge,
in the first days of it in Luxemburg. So consequently, they
were very happy to be liberated, as you can imagine.

"Before the war was over," Carvey commented, "I had been to
Buchenwald, a German concentration camp. It was a terrible thing. . . . "
Eventually, Carvey rejoined his 83rd Division on April 16th in
Bavaria, so that he could be the G-3 in the XXI Corps and in the 36th
Fighter Group. He remained with the XXI Corps and General Milburn
until the end of the war. For a brief time, Carvey and the XXI Corps
maintained their headquarters in the Messerschmitt aircraft factory,
which had produced war materials for the Germans.

Hqs XXI Corps
May 1, 1945
         . . . This is the day that in former years the Nazis used
to hold tremendous rallies in the Nuremberg stadium.
Originally it was a Communist Rally Day and the Nazis in
order to overshadow their rivals for power in Germany adopt-
ed the same day. (I seem to be repeating myself) . . .
         I saw the room where Hitler was imprisoned by the
Weimar government today. It was about 15 feet long and ten
feet wide. It had a wooden door, a rug on the floor and a com-
fortable bed. Though incarceration is not pleasant he certain-
ly had no complaints. His autographed picture hung from the
wall!

WORLD WAR II

Not more than thirty minutes away I had seen a horrible concentration camp where men were burned alive and beaten and starved. The contrast was too plain—and I sometimes wonder how I can ever like Germans again.

All My Love, Your John

I have not received a letter from you since 14 April. Moving too fast I guess.

The war appeared to be coming to a quick resolution.

2 May 45

. . . Last evening the German radio announced that one A. Hitler, was dead. It hardly caused a ripple of emotion. Six months ago, such an announcement would have met with considerable speculation and comment. Now it is very much anti-climax.

This morning I saw one of the Nazi's most evil geniuses. Field Marshall Gerd Von Rundstedt. Had we captured him in December or January, what a sensation it would have been. Today, he was just another old man we took prisoner.

Yesterday we found Admiral Horthy living quietly in a huge mansion deep in a firred forest. He was the Hungarian "Regent" (for a non-existent Hungarian Monarch) who as Hungary's dictator tried to run with the Axis boys Adolph and Benito. For a while it was very remunerative and Hungary gained slices of Czechoslovakia and Rumania. But as more and more Hungarian legions were siphoned away to die in Russia, the bargain proved a sorry one. When the US-British offensive broke out into France, then Admiral Horthy tried to call a halt. So Adolph removed him and placed a more reliable Nazi in power.

The bonds of Europe are breaking and soon "the light will come. . . ."

Today we heard that the German Armies in Italy had surrendered at noon. Just a few more days to run down the organized resistance, though the real work of peace is just beginning. . . .

Perhaps I should write more about the beauties of Southern Germany. It is a pretty country and the chalets are picturesque homes. But I have just had my fill of Germans and Germany. After seeing the monstrous things they have done in the name of National Societies and seeing the absolute lack of sympathy for the hundreds of thousands of miserable people they have created, I am not given to admire their landscape.

174

Their "political prisoners" tramp the highways in their filthy rags. Somehow it seems that God-fearing fold would bring them into their homes and give them a suit of clothes and a bath. But I have not seen an act of kindness or sympathy for them or for the thousands of foreign refugees that throng the country side. As far as I can see the German are indifferent and feel no responsibilities. . . .

All these stories and rumors of peace have not caused much of a stir here as I think most of us expect to go on until all of Germany is overrun. If the Germans decide to quit anytime before then, most of us will be happily surprised. . . .

Carvey recounted with a bit of bluster "that he was all set to bomb Hitler's birthplace [Linz], but "they called off the war." Thus, with Victory in Europe, or V-E Day, on May 8th, the end of the war had finally arrived.

9 May 45

. . . Yesterday was officially "Victory-in-Europe Day". To say the war stopped yesterday is hardly accurate. The fighting just dwindled away until the Germans agreed to recognize an accomplished fact, i.e that they were incapable of further organizing opposition. The war was also a war of ideas. It was a war of two philosophies of the individual. Under one, the individual was created to be the slave of the leader, & to him went their full devotion & energy irregardless of the ideas he represented. Under the other the leaders were the servants of the people, who reserved the right to replace them if their ideas failed to meet the moral & political standards they supported.

That war may well go on for many years. Those two ideas are incompatible & can not exist in a world so closely knitted as our own. Japan still represents that alien philosophy- alien to Anglo Saxons.

One phase of the "Great Crusade" is finished. The other is yet to be accomplished. I wonder what my part will be in it. . . .

With the war over, Carvey recounted one of the strongest impressions he had of the defeated Germany:

The greatest sight I guess I saw . . . I went over a brow of a hill. I was headed east in my jeep and I could see for about three miles. It was down a valley to a bridge and then up the other side, and it was on an Autobahn, and they had this median strip which was about forty feet wide or more, that was solid with German soldiers coming to the west, no guards, except I went about a half mile and there's an American chief with a corporal practically sitting on his gun. . . . All they wanted was to get out of this war and get food and they were marching under their own directions to the west, and . . . that was quite a sight after these guys had been shooting at you to see. I must have looked at maybe 5,000 Germans at that point in this caravan and there was no threatening gestures towards me or any Americans, but I did notice that as some of the trucks went by, they were doing this. And later on, I got acquainted with some German P.W.'s after they were released and they said the thing that was most impressive to them was the mechanized American army, because the Germans had a lot of horse drawn artillery, and all of their hospital wagons and their quartermaster were all horse-drawn. They were not a fully mechanized army like we were.

You understand, of course, that Hitler had never been in Britain, had never been in France until after France surrendered. He had no idea about the industrial might of the democratic nations that could be brought to bare on him. That's why I think his delusions undid him. Of course, before he committed suicide, he blamed the lack of will and character on the German people for the surrender. That didn't have anything to do with it.

5 June 45

. . . Today a year ago was the day before "D"-day. It's hard to tell anyone who was not a participant in the events that led up to it how vivid one's memories still are of the things that happened. . . .

Well here it is a year later and I am not far from leaving Europe. I really thought then that I would be lucky to be going home in a year and a half, if I were one of the lucky ones to go home at all. But coming home I am. I sent all my correspondents not to write to me until further notice. . . .

I have been able to let you know that I was coming before I ever started. You have really been (as we say in the Army) "alerted." Let me type those words again, they are such fun. "<u>I am coming home!</u>" In the event that you haven't heard or still can't believe what your eyes discern, "<u>I am coming home!</u>" YEAH MAN!! (Pardon a little exhilaration this time.)

Following the war, Carvey returned to Indiana, where he married his fiancée, Carolla.

176

WORLD WAR II

MAJOR MIKE DEWART
MEDICAL ADMINISTRATIVE CORPS
225TH STATION HOSPITAL

" . . . [My friends and I] were singing on a radio station up in Kokomo, Indiana . . . when it came in on the ticker tape that Pearl Harbor had been bombed," Mike Dewart recalled. Just over two years later, Dewart left Pier 17 in New York aboard the S.S. *HENRY GIBBONS*. Now a drafted member of the 225th Station Hospital, he was headed for Oran, Algeria, to begin his duties.

"Oran was but a staging area, but it will make a livid mark on the memories of everyone who was there . . . the sun beat unmercifully one day and the rain would beat unmercifully the next. The water was almost undrinkable and the wine was little better. The people, the sights and the smells were a constant source of wonderment," read the *Station News*.

Dewart was not in Oran long, however. On the 25th of October 1943, the 225th Station Hospital was called to duty in Europe. Dewart sailed out of North Africa on a Navy transport and arrived in the harbor of Naples, Italy, the day after it fell. Dewart described the experience: "We climbed down rope ladders over the side of the ship to get to little boats to take us to shore; all of the piers and port equipment had been bombed by the Germans. . . . We set up [the hospital] in a World's Fair ground that Mussolini had built . . . commemorating the conquering of Ethiopia."

The World's Fair of 1940 was to have been held in Naples, but never opened because of Italy's alliance with Germany. Now the 225th Station Hospital was set up in one of the spectacular buildings that Mussolini had ordered built for the occasion.

Major Mike Dewart - Adjutant of the 225th Station Hospital. (Courtesy of Mike Dewart)

177

It had huge murals of Ethiopia, a marble floor with a mosaic globe in the center, eight feet in diameter, showing all the Italian colonies. On one wall was a great mural of Caesar's triumphant march into Rome. On the other wall was a slightly larger, more prominent, Mussolini riding on a white horse over a prostrate Ethiopian. One wall allots a few lines to each of several ancient writers speaking of the glory of the Italian race. This not-so-subtle propaganda was to impress the visitors to the fair with Mussolini's comparison to Caesar.

By January of 1944, World War II was well underway, and soon the hospital was filled with victims. " . . . There were so many casualties that there was an ambulance train . . . [that] came down almost every night from the front lines to our medical center. Instead of 500 patients, we ended up with 1,500 patients in our hospital. It was crowded, big, and busy." The hospital was so full, in fact, that tents were set up outside to accommodate the wounded. Though this was a necessary move, it was also extremely risky.

Naples was a very dangerous place to be. " . . . The Germans bombed Naples harbor almost every night. They would drop bright . . . magnesium flares by parachute, and they would float down and light up the whole countryside . . . They would bomb mostly the harbor and the water front, but we were close to it and occasionally, some of those bombs would drop in the wrong place. . . . We had two of them drop in our hospital area; killed a lot of patients that were out in the tents."

These bombs were not the only threat. "When [the Germans] were flying over every night, the town . . . was surrounded by American and British anti-aircraft guns, and they would shoot up into the sky . . . [at] those Germans . . . [the sky] would light up like the Fourth of July; the whole sky was just a light of tracer bullets . . . we had a lot of shrapnel from the anti-aircraft shells . . . fall back to earth and you could hear them falling around you . . . They came down and they would just cut you to pieces if they hit you."

The last couple years of the war were especially difficult, as the fighting came to a crescendo. But it was through these trying times that Dewart and the rest of the hospital staff learned the most. In a letter to the Commanding Officer, Dewart wrote, "Our staff and personnel have been constantly busy month after month, which has not only resulted in the production of a large volume of work, but which has educated all of us to a higher degree of medical and administrative ability. In giving to others, the patients, we have gained a great deal for ourselves." The 225th Station Hospital stayed in Naples for almost a year and a half, until it was moved to northern Italy.

The hospital was taken by boat to Ancona, on the northern shore of Lake Maggiore. Then the hospital staff traveled an additional thirty-five miles to a little town called Fano. Here, Dewart and the staff hurriedly set up the hospital in forty-eight hours. "We set up a hospital in a school building there, in order to service tactical fighter planes at an airfield that was . . . close by. . . . We were very busy and had a lot of . . . injured pilots."

The hospital was in Fano for about two months, until it was moved further south to an area just north of Florence. Soon, though, the 225th Station Hospital was needed in the war-torn Pacific. As July drew to a close, the unit was reorganized, and in early August the hospital staff, along with their equipment, boarded a ship and headed for the South Pacific. Dewart recalled how their plans changed once again: "After we got halfway across the Atlantic, the atomic bomb was dropped on Japan and they diverted our ship to Boston Harbor; we got to go home early." About hearing this news, Dewart commented,"we were overjoyed, obviously, very happy, and very proud to have participated in the war."

PFC CARVER MCGRIFF
357TH INFANTRY REGIMENT, 90TH INFANTRY DIVISION, US ARMY

While Major John Carvey's air and ground liaison duties kept him from going to France until well after D-Day, replacement soldiers was needed quickly. McGriff saw the preparations for D-Day and had a premonition of what was ahead of him.

McGriff recounted his arrival in Europe:

> We were sent over to England and I was at that point what's called a 'replacement,' which was what most of us were. And we did advanced combat training in England for two months. And, of course, we didn't know there was going to be a battle of Normandy because it hadn't happened yet and it was very secret. But one day we were marching – actually we were riding in trucks and we saw hundreds of planes going overhead pulling gliders. And we didn't know that we were at that point seeing the glider troops going in to land in Normandy. And so that night, really the night of the 5th of June, the 102nd [101st] and the 82nd Airborne Divisions dropped their paratroops into Normandy, and also the gliders landed. And so we suspected, of course, that's where we were going.

McGriff and the others in his replacement unit were green troops and therefore "didn't worry" because they were naïve. They learned fast, though.

World War II

We had to board ships that took us across the English Channel. And then when we arrived there, we were formed up and told that we would be assigned to an infantry division. And the first night that we started marching and we had hardly gone any distance at all. . . . I saw a dead man lying in a ditch, and he was wearing the insignia of a sergeant in the 101st Airborne Division. So when I saw him I knew this was the real thing. We marched quite a distance and passed several gliders that had been crashed in the open fields. So, we knew that's where the airborne had landed.

Finally that night, we were exhausted. We were dead tired and we stopped in a field and they said that we would sleep there that night. Now, sleep meant you were going to get maybe three or four hours – I think it was about three. And to do that, you were to dig a hole and sleep in that hole and the ground was as hard as this floor. It was really terribly hard to dig a so-called foxhole. In fact in World War II, they had what they called foxholes, which was originally a deep hole that you could stand up in and still be fairly safe, but the ground was so hard that nobody could dig a real fox hole – what we dug was what we called a slit trench – and it might be a foot deep if you were lucky. Anyway . . . we found some trenches that had been dug by somebody else and we slept in those. And when dawn broke we got up and found that they had been used by another unit that day which had been shelled by enemy mortars and had suffered terrible casualties. And I remember one of the men had found an unused field jacket and had put it on and the next morning when he looked at it, it had a big hole right over the heart. So that he knew then that the man who owned it had been killed. The next day . . . we were each one assigned to the unit that we would serve in for the rest of our time.

McGriff became quickly initiated to combat. He reminisced:

I was in an infantry company in Normandy during the fighting . . . and we had just captured a position. And about a hundred yards from us was a hedgerow and behind that hedgerow were some German soldiers and they were firing at us with machine guns . . . and we were ordered to attack the hedgerow and we didn't . . . do it. We just laid there so we wouldn't get shot. And a major walked up, standing full height, pulled out a .45 pistol and said 'I'm gonna shoot anybody who's still lying on the ground. Now get up there and move.' And we moved. . . .

WORLD WAR II

Once the invasion forces landed and McGriff's replacements moved further into France, a number of events occurred that remain as clear to him today as when they first happened. The first memorable experience occurred not long after D-Day, while his unit attempted to move through impenetrable hedgerows:

> We were moving up to begin an attack that was to open up the whole front lines of the war. In fact, it was around the town of St. Lô and the American forces had been stymied. We had taken weeks to accomplish what the original planners thought we could do in a day or two. And so after this vicious fighting through the hedgerows – see, Normandy, France, is composed of thousands upon thousands of fields of varying sizes, each one surrounded by a hedgerow and each hedgerow is probably anywhere from five feet to eight feet high so that you could capture a field, maybe a hundred yards across then you had to do another one and another one. So, it had taken us weeks to move across. Then finally we reached a point where we were to engage – we being the entire army really – to engage in this big, ferocious battle.
>
> Well, we were on the verge of that and on the edge of a field and we were taken by a mortar barrage and the Germans had a field piece or a cannon they called an eighty-eight, this 88 mm cannon and it was usually on tanks or on a movable base so that they could fire them and then by the time we could pinpoint them, they'd moved. Well, they opened up on us and we had to hit the ground and when the barrage ended, I got up and look and the man to my left – well, first I should tell you while we were waiting there a little, white puppy came walking over and I like dogs, so puppy walked up to where I was sitting and I began to pet him. He was a cute little puppy. I picked him up, cuddled him and everything. And when the explosions started we immediately hit the dirt. When it was over I looked over and the man next to me was dead and the puppy was dead, and for some strange reason, the death of the man didn't bother me, but the death of the puppy did. And the only thing I can explain from that was that somehow I had become used to death. I had seen so much of it, but some how a puppy – the innocence of a puppy. . . . It didn't fit that a tiny little puppy, who knew nothing about what was going on should die. And that kind of . . . was, I guess, the numbness that beset men in combat. And you reached a point where you just tried to ignore it. Now, now, let me say this one thing. If it was a close friend, which this was not, then that was a different matter.

WORLD WAR II

A second story involves a small trophy of war:

The Silver Box

Well, I was in this infantry squad and we had just taken a little town and all the structures were destroyed except one. And the sergeant came along (he was a friend of mine) and gave us orders not to do any looting. But then we decided (he and I decided), this house seemed to be deserted, so we would go and see what we còuld find. And we broke into the house, and it wasn't like breaking into a house here, of course. The place seemed deserted and so we took many things that we found in there. And one of the things that I took was this little silver box. It says Lourdes on it. . . . For Catholic people to make a pilgrimage to the city of Lourdes, is . . . important – [it] can be an important part of their religious experience.

Well, we had found some food in there, not much, but we were all hungry because we had very little food. And we went down to the barn that adjoined this house and were fixing beans and . . . and we were making soup, and we needed more water so I said, 'well, I'll go back up.' I saw a pump outside the house.

And when I went up to the house I saw a shadow move inside the house. And so I had brought several canteens to fill and I set the canteens down and took my rifle and I put a shell in the chamber and I walked over to the door and I thought it could be a German because the Germans were right down the road from us. And I shoved open the door and when I did, a man walked out and he was a Catholic priest wearing a black robe. And there I stood, holding a loaded rifle pointed at a Catholic priest and I spoke no French and he spoke no English. So, I didn't know what to do so I just took off and ran back down to the barn. And I said 'For gosh sakes guys, we just robbed a Catholic priest!'

So, we were debating what we should do and a moment later in walked the priest bringing the rest of his food. We had not only taken his food, but he was giving us what little he had left and I felt terribly embarrassed so I went to the men while he was there visiting – there were probably eight or nine of us there – I said, 'come on guys, give me everything you took and give me some money.' So I collected all the money I could get from the guys and everything that all of us had stolen. And while they talked to the priest, I sneak[ed] back up to his house, to the window we had broken and I put everything back. And I put all the money that we had collected in

WORLD WAR II

there too, but the one thing that I forgot to return was this lit-
tle silver box. And when we had gone on and marched down
the road quite some distance, I reached in my pocket and there
it was. So, it – and it had some coins in it, which are still
there also that had belonged to the priest. And I felt bad about
it, but I couldn't return it, so this is one of my souvenirs.

Captured by the Germans

Allied forces continued to pursue the Germans from town to town, from hedgerow to hedgerow, until they reached a stalemate around the French village of St. Lô. Here the situation became especially dire for McGriff and his unit:

> *I was there for about a month in combat and toward the*
> *end, our unit was under heavy artillery fire. We were running*
> *out of ammunition and the Germans had gotten in behind us*
> *and we were fighting a German parachute battalion. And . . .*
> *our own people were unable to get more ammunition up to us.*
> *So, for about twenty-four hours we were engaged in a battle*
> *that . . . had expended most of our ammunition and once we*
> *realized [it], . . . they came in with a Tiger tank (and that was*
> *the largest tank ever made at that point.) I think it was as big*
> *as a house and it had one of these big .88 artillery pieces and*
> *we were looking right down the muzzle. . . . The Germans*
> *were moving in on us. Finally, we were in a ditch that was*
> *maybe fifty yards long and firing at them. And finally we*
> *agreed to surrender and one German jumped in to the end of*
> *the ditch, raised a machine gun, and we thought he was going*
> *to execute us and one of our men (a friend of mine named*
> *Castille) shot the German. . . . Then, the rest of them [the*
> Germans] *took us prisoner. We put our hands up and we were*
> *made to walk into the little town we had just come through*
> *and they lined us up in the middle of the street. Well, our pla-*
> *toon leader, Lieutenant Harvey, had already called in an*
> *artillery barrage on that town because we knew the Germans*
> *occupied that town and the town was a small village. . . . And*
> *when the artillery barrage landed, it hit both Germans and*
> *Americans. . . . I got hit by an artillery shell, I was knocked*
> *unconscious as . . . most of us were and many of the Germans*
> *as well.*
> *And a little story that will explain a lesson that I learned.*
> *There was a Mexican soldier in our unit and I didn't like him.*
> *I didn't like the Mexicans. They talked – most of them spoke*
> *Spanish when they were together. They had some English but*

not much, but they were still [privates] – *I was a PFC, Private First Class* – *that's one step above a private. But they hung out together and most of us didn't like them. They had a silly game they played that caused them to yell in Spanish at night. So I had taken a dislike towards this man and I didn't have anything to do with him. And . . . he had a little guitar he would play and sing sad songs and we knew he was home-sick for his home in New Mexico. After the barrage had hit us and I regained consciousness (I had been wounded on both legs, so I couldn't walk) and I felt somebody picking me up and carrying me, and I looked up into the face of this Mexican. The shells were still exploding around us. He had risked his life to come out and carry me to safety* – *the guy I didn't like because he was different from me. So I learned a lesson from that. I learned not to judge people just because they're different.*

Well, he dragged me over up against a wall where I would be safe and the next man they dragged up was my squad leader, a sergeant who had become a good friend (Brewer) and he looked up at me and I looked down at him and he died. And then they brought the other sergeant . . . (I was in a machine gun section, which had two squads) . . . the other squad leader, Jackson, up and he looked up at me and then he died. So I had lost – *my platoon leader was dead, my squad, or my platoon sergeant had disappeared (we never knew what happened to him), our section sergeant was wounded, and both of our platoon or squad leaders were killed. And most of the other men in the squad were either wounded or killed.*

So, I was carried then into a small bar — tavern that was along the street there. We stayed there through the night while the shelling continued and then the next day the Germans came. And a German sergeant walked into the room where we lay . . . There were probably thirty or forty of us wounded in various degrees — he walked up to me and offered me a drink (and when you are injured you become very thirsty). So he offered me his canteen and I drank everything I could drink. It turned out to be hard cider and I got roaring drunk. I'd never had an alcoholic beverage before, but it impressed me that this German sergeant whom we'd been trying to kill and he'd been trying to kill us, now came in and showed us mercy — took care of us.

I was taken then to a hospital in France with the other men. I was there for a month. At the end of the month, that battle I mentioned where we were trying to break out and tear into France, had finally taken place. We had captured the city of St. Lô and American troops were racing now and . . . I was in a little hospital, and having been there a month, we could hear machine gun firing in the distance. We could look out the window and there was an anti-aircraft battery and the . . . the Americans, were flying the fighter plane sorties into the town and they didn't know that there were Americans there. They had warned the French to vacate the town and so we could see. . . . [the Germans] shooting at our planes. When we heard the machine guns, we knew they were coming and so there was a pitched battle around our little hospital and it was hit seven times by our own artillery. And one of our men risked his life, escaped from the hospital and broke through the German lines and into our lines and told them that we were there, and so they quit firing at our hospital. As a matter of fact, one of the men who had been in the hospital wrote a book about it later and that's how I got that story. And so then we were released and taken back to hospitals in England.

After several months of convalescence in an English hospital, McGriff was reassigned to limited duties in a mailroom in England. He would have preferred to have a less embarrassing task, but international law prevented him from going back into combat. Once he "had been a prisoner of war and they had gotten your name and number, then you dare not fight again."

▨

PFC ERNEST P. SABLE
COMPANY E, RECONNAISSANCE PLATOON
385TH INFANTRY REGIMENT, 76TH INFANTRY DIVISION

Ernest Sable was drafted into the Army and immediately put into the infantry's basic training. He remembered, "Everybody wanted to be in the service. It was a time in our life [when] it was very patriotic to be in the military and every – all the kids in my neighborhood went in the service and everybody *wanted* to be there. . . . "

I did apply for pilot training, so when I finished my seventeen weeks of infantry training, I went from the U.S. Army to the U.S. Army Air Corps . . . [but] because of the impending D-Day landings in Europe, they were short of manpower and so . . . they shipped all of the privates and the PFCs out of the 76th Infantry Division and . . . the 200 of us, along with other people from universities, special training units in the Army Air Corps cadet class. So that's how I ended up in the 76th Infantry Division.

World War II

I was a rifleman and I was assigned to E company. In the infantry division there are approximately, I think around 14,000 people and it's divided into three regiments and I was in one of the three regiments in that division and I was in a rifle company and they asked for volunteers to join the regimental reconnaissance platoon, and I volunteered for that. . . . [It] comprised twenty-four people and we were mobile in that we had two squads and we had Jeeps. We didn't have to walk and in that unit I went overseas to England. We were there in November of 1944, and then in December of 1944, the Germans launched what is known as the Ardennes Campaign, or the Battle of the Bulge, and our division was sent to France and then to Belgium (actually to Luxemburg), and we participated in that campaign.

The Ardennes Campaign of the Battle of the Bulge

Sable was still stationed in England when the Battle of the Bulge began in mid-December. Two weeks into the battle, his unit arrived in Luxembourg, where it conducted reconnaissance. Unfortunately, Sable and most of the other units lacked the basic necessities for the winter season:

When we went over to Belgium during the Ardennes, or Battle of the Bulge, we did not have winter clothing. We had leather boots and we did have overcoats, but we didn't have any winter jackets or any winter gear and the end result was that we had a lot of casualties from frostbite and that included all the people in the Battle of the Ardennes. I had frostbite on my feet that caused bloodspots on my feet that lasted for ten years after the war. A lot of people had more serious cases of frostbite and actually, were evacuated, but the problem was that we were fighting in the wintertime in that area, and we didn't have winter clothing, so at that time we didn't have a good supply situation. . . .

Company E

On a more positive note, Sable appreciated the camaraderie of his unit. He recounted how almost all of the members of his platoon were very young, "18, 19 years old, with the exception of the sergeants and the lieutenant . . . my sergeant was 25 (and I thought he was an old man)." They were also well-educated and an "exceptionally nice group of people . . . from all walks of life, and . . . everyone in the platoon was friends of each other . . . so we got along pretty well."

186

WORLD WAR II

This camaraderie was essential, because on reconnaissance duty, good teamwork was essential. The recon platoons provided crucial intelligence, according to Sable, and when they were "in defensive situations, [they] manned observation posts, listening posts, and went on four-man patrols into enemy territory and . . . when we were attacking, we sometimes went ahead of the regiment and sometimes to each flank to contact adjacent units, and when we would run into the enemy, we would just get out of there, as a matter of fact, and just report where the enemy was to the regiment and they would send rifle companies in that area." Their intention was not to engage in direct combat, but "to find out information and report it back to whoever needed it." Consequently, Sable's unit, unlike rifle platoons, suffered few casualties.

The men in his company also kept their wits about them. Sable felt that having a positive attitude was crucial, because "if you . . . dwell on the people laying around, the dead, the incoming artillery fire . . . [and] if you don't have a sense of humor, it becomes pretty grim." Sable recalled that everybody in his "platoon had a sense of humor and we survived. We would make fun of things quite often that were very serious and that's, I guess, part of survival."

Sable remembered two particularly memorable reconnaissance missions:

> On one occasion, the regiment was in the defensive position along the Mosel River and the Germans were on the other side of the river and they wanted to have some prisoners to talk to — to interrogate. So, being a recon platoon, I and three other guys went across the river with the objective of capturing some prisoners. . . . We went across the river and captured four Germans and brought them back to our side.

On another occasion, the situation was a bit more complicated, and had serious implications for the regiment:

> One instance when we were . . . in a defensive situation along the Saar River and there was a town (I can't think of the name of it) that we didn't hold and the Germans didn't hold and we both had listening posts in that town. And on this occasion, we went in at night. There was probably about a ten man patrol and . . . we went to three different houses in this village and we would drop off two people at each house, and in turn, pick up, or relieve, two people at each house, and we would stay for twenty-four hours and then, [it was] strictly a listening post, and we had telephone communication . . . later on that night, we'd lost communication back to the regiment – we were probably . . . a couple thousand yards out

in front of our lines and we lost communication between the other two houses. So the whole day, we didn't know what was going on.

That night, when we were to be relieved — we (actually it was dark, but it was sort of moonlit) . . . could see, instead of that small patrol approaching to relieve us, we could see a large group of people, and we were very apprehensive because . . . we didn't know the situation. Finally, they gave the password for the night before and we acknowledged it, and we then discovered what had happened. A German patrol had gone through our lines and caused a lot of casualties to one of our companies and in turn had cut all the communication lines that we had, and that's why we couldn't — we didn't hear from our people and they didn't hear from us. So to relieve us, they sent a rifle company with . . . over a hundred people. . . . They didn't know what was going on either, but it was a very apprehensive day because we didn't know what was happening and . . . we were a couple thousand yards in front of our own lines.

MAY 7 1945 – THE DAY THE WAR ENDED

The day the war ended for Ernest Sable.
(Courtesy of Ernest Sable)

By the end of the war, Sable's regiment had seen combat in Belgium, Luxemburg, and Germany. The division also participated in the Central Europe campaign. It went from Luxemburg all the way across Germany to the Czechoslovakian border before the men were sent home.

In July 1945, according to Sable,

> . . . they broke up our division and several people from our platoon went to Marseilles, France, and we were there for about a month or so . . . and then we were going to be scheduled to go to Okinawa. . . . When we were three days out of Gibraltar, they announced over the loudspeaker that they had – that the Japanese had capitulated as a result of the atomic bomb. . . . So . . . with the advent of the atomic bomb, I got out of the army and the war was over for me a lot quicker. . . .

World War II

It's been sixty years . . . since I was in the service and things . . . fade out a little bit. I would say this, during World War II, everybody was patriotic. It was a war that everybody was for. There weren't protesters, people against the war, in those days. It was the thing to do. It was, as I say, very patriotic.

▨

MAJOR JOSEPH L. TRIERWEILER
INTELLIGENCE OFFICER
3RD ARMORED ARTILLERY BATTALION, 9TH ARMORED DIVISION

Joseph Trierweiler was living in Montana with his wife and young family when World War II began. He had completed ROTC training years earlier, and while in college he had joined the Colorado National Guard. He was in the reserves from 1936 to 1942. With his recall at the outbreak of the war, he left his job at the Montana Soil Conservation Office and went for more training, which prepared him for leadership roles with the Combat Command A unit (CCA) of the Third Armored Artillery Regiment.

Trierweiler was deployed with the 9th Armored Division to England in August of 1944. In October of 1944, the Division crossed the channel to France. From mid-October through November, his Division made strong progress towards the Luxembourg-German border. At the end of November, Trierweiler assumed responsibilities as an intelligence officer for the 3rd Armored Field Battalion. He wrote numerous letters home to his wife, Edna, and their four children.

September 27, 1944
> *Dearest Edna, Jack, Jim, Joan & Ruth:*
> *Today was rather nice again. The sun was out most of the afternoon and it was windy but I don't mind that even if the wind chapped my lips a little bit.*
> *It looks like you had quite a lot of company. How were the watermelons? But don't mention the potatoes. We have them every day and I am rather tired of them.*
> *How does Jim like school? Also Jack? Do you feel half way free to do the housework etc with two of the children out of the way in part of the day.*
> *This English beer is bad stuff. One glass in the evening and I have to get up one or twice during the night. This is bad on a windy night. I had to give up the evening glass (When we could get it).*
> *I forgot to tell of a sight that I saw in London that*

amused me. On one of the busiest streets a woman picked up her little girl and hold her over the curb while she wee wee ed and in the mean time her little boy stands along side of her doing likewise on the side walk. At least they had their mothers consent and she did not seem to be at all embarrassed nor the others passing by disturbed. I guess its "When you gotta go you gotta go." I some how can not imagine you doing the same thing. Ha.

Sending all of my love to you all. Daddy

By late November, Trierweiler, was located with his CCA unit near Echternach along the Mosel River in Luxembourg. His command base was at Hallar.

December 10, 1944

. . . The stoves they use here are quite the affair. They look something like my drawing. The smoke follows the arrow from one side to the other. They are hard to start hard to keep going and throw very little heat. Sure nothing like that oil burner of ours. And do they smoke. They put out far move smoke than heat.

They are collecting mail now so had better stop and get this off.

Sending all my love to you all, Daddy

Somewhere In Luxemburg
December 15, 1944

. . . This is quite early in the morning. One fifty five to be exact. I just finished grabbing a few hours so that I could work tonight rather than this morning.

I still have a crink in my neck this morning. I guess I need you here to work it over for me, but then probably if you were I would have one in my back. Ha.

From your last letter it seems that you are not keeping the house warm. It's heck of a lot cheaper to buy gas than it is to pay a doctor and I dislike doctors. You have to get Joan over her cold too. I know that I would not stand for a cold house if it can be helped, so you act accordingly. One of us being uncomfortable is enough, and I mean that.

. . . I know that Dad will manage to keep busy. He always has. If he is going to keep that many hens, he will get more eggs than he needs. You should be able to get nice fresh eggs then shouldn't you. What is the price of eggs there now? I understand that they are seventy five and ninety cents a dozen in places in the States. That's high but some of the boys

here would give that much and more for them.

The things I would like to have is home made soup, Spanish rice, hamburgers and SALADS. Nice Crisp Lettuce and fresh tomatoes. Oh Boy. I would eat a tub full right now. I betcha.

This is all making me hungry so I think that I had better close for now and see what I can dig up.

Sending all my love to you all, Daddy

December 15, 1944

. . . I have already written my letter for today but after receiving four air-mail and one V-mail letters from you this evening I think I that I am justified in writing again don't you think.

It is now nine in the evening and this is the first night I had off for some time. I am looking forward to a good nights sleep. We have no beds here but have lights, water and good shelter. It is at times like this that the old air mattress proves its worth.

Yes, I can imagine the children's delight after the first snow. You know I used to look forward to them myself. Even when older. I never had a bought sled. I always made my own, which of course had wooden runners. I guess I had just as much fun with it tho as any of the other kids. I made a new one each year.

I had thought that you had at least two pairs of shoes for each of the children, and was surprised to know that you had to make the trip to town with Jack. I do not know when I shall be able to go to town again or what they have in the line of children's shoes. Let me know what size it takes and if I see any that will do perhaps I will send them home. Let me know the size for all of them. It seems that Mrs. Carroll is quite a nice neighbor. You write so much about her keeping the children or the two of you going shopping together.

The lights just went off, they do that frequently, I am now using a flashlight to see by. . . .

I do not know why the censer cut out the Luxemburg. We are permitted by our division and higher headquarters to state it. I think they are probably behind the times in their office. We are permitted to say that we are at the front also. I have never knowingly put anything in my letter that is forbidden. It makes it hard to write about the times because we are restricted and there are items that I know you would be interested in. Your letters are never touched. . . .

I have not said all that I want to but had better crawl in as its getting too cold to sit any longer. The beds the warmest place.

Sending all my love to you all, Daddy

From the 16th of December until his letter on the 22nd, Trierweiler had no opportunity to write. The Germans began their last-ditch effort to turn back the Allies and to regain the port of Antwerp in Belgium. This was the largest ground and air battle ever fought, and Trierweiler was at the front edge of the assault along the Luxembourg frontier. This was the first action for the 9th Division. The 3rd Artillery headquarters were pounded by German shells, and Trierweiler's CCA was forced to withdraw "several thousand yards to the left," but successfully formed the "right anchor of the Bulge."[2] By the 22nd, the Germans were stalled because of fuel shortages and strong pockets of American resistance.

Trierweiler's next letters do not reveal all that was going on; however, the news of the battle was reported in the papers back home.

December 22, 1944

. . . *Now to continue on in my letter answering. Maybe sometime I will be able to get caught up with you. I must say it is much easier to write when you have a letter to answer. . . .*

We live mostly on canned and dried foods. Some times on "C" and "K" rations its all good food tho and if varied a little bit does not get too monotonous. Thank you Joan for your fine letter. Daddy will write to you again when he has more time. I am glad that you had a very nice birthday and that you like your "Shaggy Pony" book. Now you take good care of your dollie because Daddy wants to see her when he comes home. I hope that Santa was very good to you all and that you had a very nice time. Now be good boys and girls for daddy. Will you?

Thank you Jack for your letter. I will see what I can do about making you a beanie when I get the shoe tongues and the rubber. It will probably be a long time until you get it back because Daddy is so far away and it takes a long time to get a package over here and then back to you. I wish that you could read to your Daddy in the evenings. I know that you read very nicely. Jim I am afraid that it is too far to send you a bunny rabbit. Daddy is very proud of you and the way you are so good to your baby sister. It is very fine of you to take care of her. Daddy wants you to always take good care of her and Joan. You will now won't you? . . .

This letter been interrupted many times, so before I get

too badly muddled up, [I'll quit.] Its disconnected badly as it is.

Sending all my love to you all, Daddy

On December 26th, Trierweiler's CCA was ordered to turn "its positions over to relief units," but the orders were changed and they were instead to aid "in the relief of Bastogne."[3] The turning point of the battle was reached on this day when the Germans failed to take the city.

December 28, 1944

. . . It's the wee hours of the morning and I am on duty sitting next to a stove and trying to keep warm. I guess I am doing a fair job of it at that tho for it is the first time in a while that I have felt half way comfortable. In fact that inner spring mattress of ours would certainly look mighty inviting. I'll bet you would have a hard time getting me up a week later.

That old moon is sure bright these nights, clear as crystal and a brittle cold. The snow crunches underfoot.

They say that if a man does not take pride in his unit, there is something wrong with the unit or the man. Anyway I feel that I am justified in being more than proud of mine. When you do what was considered impossible and do it with flying colors and never a word of thanks from some. Well I am proud to be a part of this organization.

Honestly – I'll bet I smell like a goat. I did get a spit bath of sorts a couple of days ago and changed underwear. . . . The country is beautiful both day and night with a blanket of snow and the light and dark green of a patch of pine as a background. From almost any little hill top you can see the roofs or church steeples of little towns scattered around.

Well its getting closer to payday, that is something to look forward to mostly as a time to send money home. . . .

Guess I had better look around a little to see about a bed to crawl into in case I get a chance tonight.

Sending all my love to you all, Daddy

December 29, 1944

. . . Can you imagine anyone sleeping until the afternoon? Well I did today. I turned in about six this morning and caught up on a little sleep. I hope to get a little more tonight. The cold has kinda settled down on us. Its kind of a clear cold.

There isn't a whole lot that I can tell except that I am OK. I have had a cold which is much better now. . . .

The children around here all seem to have rosy cheeks.

Many times the complexion is not too good but they in general seem to be quite healthy. Sometimes I wonder how they can be when they step right out of the kitchen door in a stream of liquid that runs from the manure pile.

The country where I am at now reminds me a lot of Colorado & Montana, almost all of it is cultivated except where the forest are located. . . .

I fueled up my new lighter today and it is downing very nicely. I sold my Zippo to another officer for five hundred francs. That's about eleven dollars or a little more. I could see no use for them both. I guess your investment will return dividends, as I will send the money home to you after my next payday. What I wanted was a pair of combat trousers but the other fellow said that he would do his best to get me a pair if he could in addition to the money. I sure hope that he can do it. They are nice and warm.

There isn't much more I can tell tonight so I guess I will close.

Sending all my love to you all Daddy
Please excuse the crumpled stationary. Daddy.

Shortly after retaking Bastogne, Trierweiler's unit earned a respite and was sent to a rest area at Metz-Thonville, France. There he was reassigned as an intelligence officer for divisional artillery. Nine days later, he was promoted to Major.[4]

Somewhere In France
January 7, 1945

It looks like today was my red letter day – I received three packages and eleven letters. I received the vest and the boots today and both of them fit fine. Thank you so much for sending them to me. I assure you that they have arrived at a very good time. It's very cold here and everyone wears as much as they can get.

I have enjoyed the last two days very much. The place we are staying in is cold as we have a hard time getting the stoves to keep from smoking, so mostly we endure the cold and keep away from the smoke. . . .

I know that you have been wondering where I have been and what I have been doing. Some I cannot tell you, others not yet. There has to be a certain time elapse between an action and when it can be mentioned. You were correct in your guess of Trier. That is, I was close to there. I imagine that Echternach has been stated in the news. I have been in that place that used to be a city. I have also fought at Hallar,

Beaufort, and Saulborn. Yes it was tough, but I don't think that the Boche will ever forget that part of their attack. The only time that I was afraid was at night. That was nothing new. I have always been afraid of the dark. Please try and make our children understand that there is nothing to fear from the dark. There is no such thing as a boggie man. If we teach them while they are young that there is nothing to fear they will not carry with them as I do a fear of the dark. I had Hell drilled into me ever since I can remember and it was always a place of darkness. Darkness was made so that the evil could take place. I have never out grown it. I hope that our children can be different. It's a most uncomfortable feeling.

The division is now off the so-called secret list, and well it should be. I shall always be proud of it.

The music tonight was wonderful. Just heard Jack Benny for the first time in I don't know when. Its swell to be where you can listen to a commercial radio and enjoy a bit of relaxation. . . .

I think that this should be enough for one night, don't you.

Sending all my love to you all, Daddy

Somewhere In France
January 16, 1945

. . . There is a lot of commotion when you gather a bunch of officers and they start a bull session. That is what is taking place tonight so that I do not know how far I will go with this. . . .

I am enclosing an article reprinted [?] from the Stars and Stripes about the first phase of the breakthrough that we participated in. . . . I don't know what you will think of it but it gives a rough idea. The boys of this unit were swell and did a splendid job.

During one of our heavier engagements a protestant chaplain and his assistant served meals at all hours of the day and night, just whenever a person could take a few minutes off to gulp down a bite. They even served it to those that could not leave their task. The boys would do anything for him, they appreciated it and I don't mean maybe.

The radio is coming in good tonight and I am enjoying it very much when it quiets down enough so that I can hear it. . . .

I am well and gripping just as much as I ever did so you know that I am OK.

Sending all my love to you all, Daddy

WORLD WAR II

February 14, 1945

. . . I think that this is the first letter that I have typed to you. Are you surprised? I happened to be in headquarters and as my pen is dry . . . thought that I would use the type-writer instead. Something is wrong with the power unit that supplies the current to my room and so I am spending the evening here where it is light. I received another V-mail from you today. . . .

By the time you receive this letter it will be about our anniversary. You know that I will be thinking of you at that time. This will be our first one apart but I guess we can stand that if we can spend the rest or at least most of the rest of them together. . . . I had a chance to visit Reims a while back and went through the cathedral there. It is quite nice, but what is outstanding about it is its age. It is certainly well con-structed. It seems that the older ones are of better construction than the new ones. It reminded me a lot of Westminster Abbey but of course there are no people buried under the floors. The windows are beautiful. . . .

No I do not want you to send me any candy. We are given a ration over here that is quite sufficient. The things that I really want I will ask for. I know that the mustard sardines are going to taste good when I get them. Today was swell. It was nice and warm. Those days seem to be few and far between, but its me that has been spoiled by too much living in the good old United States. I don't know just how close I am to the bottom of this sheet but maybe I had better call it quits for this time.

> Sending all my love to you all, Daddy

Germany
March 15, 1945

. . . It is now after one o'clock and I am supposed to have my relief come on now but I think I will let him sleep a bit as I am not sleepy and there is not too much doing at present. Maybe this bottle of wine that I got a hold of has something to do with it, but I rather doubt it. It is good wine tho. Some of the best that I have tasted over here. I am sending two packages home tomorrow, I hope. One of them contains a fly-ing jacket with a note to please dry clean and return. I would like to have it dry cleaned, and I mean cleaned, as it is quite dirty, but keep it at home for me until I call for it from you. If I can find a box I want to send home my flying boots. They are both presents from the Air Corps when I was flying with them.

In case anything should happen to me I want Dad to have first priority on anything of mine that he can use. I don't think the shirt I am sending will fit him, but I hope OK. If it does it's a present from the old country . . . I don't know Honey. I may lead you a rugged life when I get back. I have done without so many things for so long that I may insist that my family does likewise when I return. Actually the only [thing] that really counts is the love that we have for each other. Basic isn't it, but how true nevertheless. A person can do a lot of things if he or she knows that some one else has faith and will back them to the end of the world. That's how I feel. I do not bow down to anyone and state my views as I see them. I know it hurt me a lot of times but at least I can hold my head up and know that I have not curried favor. I certainly want my children to do likewise. They do not have to step back for anyone or anything. Do teach them that for me, please. As long as they do what is right and just they have no one to fear. . . .

No I never got into Germany when I was at Echternach. But all of that is in our hands now, just as much more will be before this is over with. I think that the average German looks at [us] as tho to say "How could this have happened to us?" Well it can and it . . . [did], and that is not the end and it will [not be] until they are completely whipped. Do not feel sorry for them. I have seen enough to never be sorry for them as long as I live. Some will forget I know but I never shall. I would like so much to talk to you in person without [the] restrictions necessarily imposed by censorship. It would help a person a lot. Sort of a mental release. Oh well some day I will be able to and won't want to then. Funny isn't it or is it. Tell the children to be very good and to mind well for you for Daddy may be home soon (I hope) and then they will have to answer to their Daddy. Guess I had better close for this time.

Sending all my love to you all, Daddy

March 18, 1945

. . . I have another V-mail from you today dated Feb 22. Have been wondering how you are, and if you are working too hard. You know you can do a lot of damage to your health by working after an operation. I sure hope that you have someone helping out all of this time. . . .

I see by the papers that McAuliffe is now a Maj Gen. The unit received a presidential citation. Too bad a few more of those could not be passed out.

This last bit that we did was nothing like the break

through. This time we were doing the dishing out and it was plenty. . . .

I am very much afraid that the army of occupation will not be in Luxemburg. I don't think that very many know too much about what, where or when it will be. . . .

My promotion party has not taken place yet due to unforeseen circumstances that you already know about. . . .

Sending all my love to you all. Daddy

May 3, 1945

. . . It seems that I have misplaced my air mail stamps so I am afraid that this letter will go by slow mail.

I am enclosing some old German Marks that the kids may like as souvenirs. They are worthless but maybe they would like them to play with. We stabilized the German monetary system in 1923 or 1924, I forget which, and any money that was issued prior to that time is of no value. Actually their money is that in which we are paid is no good here because we are not permitted to purchase anything from them. The only thing money is good for here is to play poker, send home or so that someone can purchase an item or so for you when he is in some other country and then the marks have to be changed to francs before they can be spent.

The Germans sure learn fast. They know that we are not permitted to give them anything so they have eggs that they offer to exchange for cigarettes, chocolate and the like. The kids give that old V sign for victory and then ask for chocolate, gum or cigarettes. They smile very nicely and steal anything you have when your back is turned.

Things are looking much better in Europe. It should not be too long until the fighting is over with. The one thing every one is thinking about is getting home. I am very much afraid that there are going to be a number of disappointed people, for it is impossible to just put up stakes and leave here. It will be quite some time before everyone gets home.

Sending all my love to you all, Daddy

May 19, 1945

. . . There is a slight lull in officer operations at the present time and I thought that I might be able to get off a few lines to you. I do as much work after supper it seems or any other time so I don't think that I am letting down.

At long last I can tell you where I am at the present time. I am located in Munchberg, Germany. I don't know how small a town your map shows but maybe it is on there. It is about 20 miles from the Czech border at the country's bound-

ary which is farther west. We are quite a ways north and a little east of Nurnberg. I do not think you will have much trouble finding it. Bavaria is a very pretty portion of Germany. The people live well, have nice homes, gardens, clothes, etc. It is hard to believe that we are in a country of murderers. Of course the stock answer is "We did not know such things were going on." It is very difficult to believe that any people in such a beautiful country could ever be anyway but friendly. Seeing is believing and I have seen plenty. . . .

> *Sending all my love to you all, Daddy*

May 21, 1945

. . . *Well the censorship lid is officially off and we can now write about almost anything that we wish except troop movements and such.*

I have told you our location and as best I could about the country. We have come a long ways from our starting point. As you guessed, we crossed on the QUEEN MARY and land[ed] in Scotland. Had a train trip down to around

Vehicles of 9th Armored Div, 1st Army, cross pontoon bridge at Limberg, Germany, March 27th, 1945. (National Archives)

Salisbury England and camped out there on the plains. After crossing the channel we . . . camped in the so called "hedge rows" of France near where the invasion landings were made. It was a long trip up to Luxemburg which was our next stop. From there on you know pretty much where I have been from the newspaper clippings. The breakthrough was terrific. I hope that I never again experience such as that. The rest of the fighting was no fun but I shall never forget the German offences. I am not permitted to give you the statistics but I can say that the portion of the division that I was with did, I think, more than their share of the fight[ing]. When the offensive came we were kicked back a few thousand yards, held, and then pushed forward. The Germans lost almost a complete division to us there. Then we went to Bastone. The road in had to be opened and kept open. We opened it and kept it open. There are a lot of things the newspaper men do not know. We attacked and advanced and then ran smack into Hitler's finest picked troops, the Fuehrer Brigade. It was like hitting a stone wall. We . . . gave all we had and broke up one counter attack after another. Then . . . that was the beginning of the end of the Germans. They started to retreat and recoil from our attacks. They never regained the initiative[?]. Tomorrow this division receives champagne [from] the Supreme Commander and permission for appropriate celebration as a result of being the first division across the Rhine. We set the stage for the last act. From then on there was no stopping the American armies.

There are of course many things that I have left unsaid, but do you wonder why I am so proud of my division.

Had hoped to write more, but have been called back to duty.

Sending all my love to you all, Daddy

Munchberg, Germany
May 27, 1945

No, we did not reach the Russians. We were the foremost element and were stopped so that an infantry division could make contact lightly. There is too much punch and drive to our division. We do not mind so much but it would have been nice to say the first across the Rhine and the first to contact the Russians. It makes no difference now tho, since it's all ended. Leipzig was really surrounded by German antiaircraft guns. It was one after another and batteries of eighteen and more. Would much rather face them tho than their artillery. . . .

World War II

So all the children have the chicken pox. I can just see you going slowly mad and getting gray hair. One at a time is bad enough but to have three at once is too much of a good thing. . . .

Sending all my love to you all, Daddy

May 31, 1945
. . . It is a lovely evening after a night and day of rain. I felt too cooped up in the office today and so spent at least half a day on some investigations. In the course of events I looked over an old castle. Part of it was built in 1380 with additions and modifications since. It was quite a pleasant place and had a wonderful view. They had quite a collection of antiques and many very old paintings. You would have loved to go thru. At the present time they have about 50 orphans and are caring for them there. There is a very nice chapel located in the court yard. The family is catholic.

There are many places here that have not been touched by the war, of course by the time our armies had reached this far the Germans had pretty well gone to pieces. The primary damage down here was done by Boches. Even the nice places are not modern as we know [it]. No central heating systems, inadequate sanitary facilities and the like. Of course it does but it isn't like our own country. . . .
I managed to get a hair cut today. It was too long and now it is down to regulation (my regulation). . . .

Sending my love to you all. Daddy

June 27, 1945
If I ever get out of Europe I will never want to came back here again. Their standard of living is so much lower than our own. Here the women do the work and they really do. The men are the baser subject only to the government.

About my liquor. The 20 bottles cost me the whole sum of six dollars. That is about the price of one bottle in the States at a regular liquor store. So maybe I did not spend too much for it. The battle dress was much more. Incidentally I still have most of it left. I am sure a hard drinker, and I don't think that we will be able to get any more when it is gone.

Send all my to love to you all, Daddy

June 29, 1945
Ever since we crossed the Rhine, especially, there has been a constant migration. People going home or at least [to] some place else. You have to see it to believe it. Walking, begging

rides, pushing hand carts, pulling wagons, riding bicycles, driving horses. Millions of them and one hell of a mess. Germany certainly had them fixed up royally. I don't see how they could have mixed people up more than they did. Some of them appreciate what you try to do for them others damn you.

A person can not imagine the cross-current of feelings between the nations here unless he has experienced it. It seems that no matter how they are treated by a common enemy they still hate each other. . . .

We have had no trouble with the German people here so if you are worried about my safety, just forget it.

Sending all my love to you all, Daddy

Camp San Antonio, France
September 4, 1945

I guess I have seen Germany for the last time. We crossed into France last evening and spent the night in Metz. We came on this camp today. This is a tent camp. It has no showers, no running water, no working facilities. In fact, no nothing, but it is the next step in the process of going home. I think that shortly after I arrive in the States that I will get a thirty day leave. How do you want to spend it? You might do some thinking along that line and set up a few tentative plans. . . .

Sending my love to you all, Daddy

Camp Calais, France
September 22, 1945

Please do not expect me to be unchanged when I arrive home. I am afraid that you may see a difference — that is one reason I have dreaded [coming] home. There is something that I want you to remember and that is the fact that knowing that I had love to back me is what brought me through. Now don't worry it's not as bad as all that but I want you to forgive me any mistakes that I may make.

For instance, a Person is rather blunt here when it means getting a job done, regardless of whose feelings it might hurt. I have worked hard on myself since the end of the war here to overcome some of these things. I hope that I have succeeded. So please forgive me anything that I might say or do that may seem to you out of the ordinary, when I arrive home. I feel that with help I can become again the person I once was, poor tho that may have been. All I ask is a little patience.   May I? . . .

Sending all my love to you all Daddy.

WORLD WAR II

PFC JOSEPH W. DUNCAN
COMPANY G, 309TH REGIMENT, 78TH INFANTRY DIVISION

"I was in the 78th division, 309th regiment, company G, I was a rifle-man." Joseph Duncan said this proudly because his 78th infantry divi-sion, the lightning division as it was known, was one of the most illus-trious outfits in the European Theater. Duncan was drafted into the serv-ice of the United States Army on July 5th, 1944. Prior to induction at age twenty, he had worked for two years at the Hudson Motor Car Company in Detroit.

The Battle of the Bulge

Duncan gave a vivid account of his experiences in this battle:

> Up there in the Hertgen forest, . . . it was all big [trees] . . . [It] start[ed] getting dark about 3:30 over there. These trees were so big, you know how it gets dark. We were there thirty days and then we started moving for the Rhine taking little towns on the way. And then we had a lot of pillboxes to blow up. And at night nobody could get out of the hole. We had a little pan we'd pee in and dump it over the side. You can't get out of the hole because they would shoot you.

During the Battle of the Bulge Duncan was, " . . . in the same hole for thirty days. No showers, no hot food. . . . We had heavy overcoats, boots, but . . . if you didn't change your socks everyday, you'd get frost-bitten feet." The conditions were extreme. Duncan also spoke of the food, "Oh . . . there was a candy bar, a sandwich, a cookie – I like[ed] the candy bars . . . they were rich, high in calories. And once and a while, they would bring up a hot meal for us on the frontlines." These "K-rations" as they were called were the only sustenance for the soldiers. The other difficulty for the soldiers was staying awake. Duncan explains that the watch shift "was three hours on . . . and there were three of us." Fortunately, enemy tanks were never a concern, "it was too cold. The tanks couldn't run."

Besides the extreme cold, psychologically it was hard for some men to stick it out in a foxhole. One restless Marine lieutenant near Duncan's foxhole became too impatient. Duncan remembered the Marine announcing: "You guys that are bedding down, you listen to me tomor-row were getting out of here." Duncan added, "So we woke up real early, . . . you don't slept too good with water in the ditch. He [the Marine] said, 'follow me' and he jumped up and zing! He never moved again. They dropped him right where he was. In about twenty minutes another patrol around the back and shot them out of there."

As Duncan found out, the heavily wooded, snowy terrain of the Argonne Forest was a hotbed for sniper fire making the advance of Allied forces a slow and tedious process. Duncan thought the Battle of the Bulge was a major turning point in the war. ". . .when we got to the Rhine River and we crossed that, that was the end of Germany. Because for miles they'd [the Germans] be walking back home — threw their rifles away."

From there the 78th moved towards the Rhineland. Duncan explained the purpose of the German pillboxes and how Americans destroyed them:

> The Germans had built three pillboxes, one here, one there, and they guarded each other. They were all concrete reinforced steel. And we'd . . . put snowsuits on. I never went on a raid like that. Because they didn't have enough sheets to wrap around me. . . . A [German] guard would be on the other side walking around all three of them. And they [the Americans] had him timed, you know when he'd come and the guy would go up with that wire, you know. Put it around his neck and tighten it up. Most guys who did that could talk German. They would say [to the Germans in the pillboxes] 'Hey Fritz, how you doing?' and he'd [to the American] say 'Well Okay' he could talk German. And then they'd go up to the door and put the dynamite in and just blow them to pieces.

Having reached the Rhine, the lightning division prepared for the second objective of the campaign: cross the Rhine into Germany. Allied forces were extremely worried about the Germans blowing up the dams and flooding the countryside. Duncan recalled, "I was up to the dam . . . yeah we guarded that and we'd go measure the water every night. They were supposed to blow the dam but they never did." When the 78th crossed the river, Duncan noted that, "the night we crossed the Rhine the engineers . . . had put . . . two planks with a little rope across there. And here I am with a rifle and stuff on my back . . . a sleeping bag and stuff and I had my arm . . . [on] the rope there. And the more you walked on there . . . guys had mud on their shoes . . . it was just like ice. Guys were slipping, falling in and I can't swim. . . . "

One of the first two infantry units to set foot on German soil, the 78th, now had the slow task of capturing one town after next. They

> went from town to town. Just . . . a lot of towns they'd put white sheets in the windows. They'd get us out in the open and then poured it to us. So then I was with the forward artillery man and he called in . . . we had maps with gridlines on them . . . he'd say, 'we're at 49,45 . . . cross section so and

WORLD WAR II

so . . . let's have the big ones, the one fifty-fives. And the guy would say, 'they're busy now' and he said . . . 'hey, when I meet you I'll kick you all over the place, give me them fifty-fives!' Last time I looked that way I was lying on the ground all I could see was splinters flying in the air. Then they say, 'give me three rounds' for zeroing in. . . . To the left, to the right, to the center. And [when] *they get it centered he says, 'let them have it.'*

After taking a town, Duncan said, "We looked for the best house to sleep in. We'd take the furniture, throw it around, sleep on the couch, sleep anyplace . . . on the floor. . . . But you always had one guy on guard, because they [the Germans] were sneaky – [They'd] sneak back . . . into town, after night. . . . "

While in Germany, the 78th captured a total of 45,581 German prisoners. Duncan said that he took prisoners to POW camps. He recalled one event in particular:

. . . [O]*ne night the guy said, 'we captured a couple Germans, take them back to the* [camp] *to interrogate them.' We had people back there that could talk good German. So I was taking them down the trail and it* [was] *cold...that's why I hate this snow here. I came to* [a] *roadblock and there was a tank there . . . and* [to] *everybody they say, 'Hey Joe,' (even if you're Mike, you're Joe to them). They said, 'Hey Joe, where you taking them guys?' I said, 'Back to the CP.' They said, 'Why don't you leave them here we'll take them back." I said, 'Boy, that's mighty kind of you guys. It's getting near supper time anyways.' You know if you're not there when they serve the food it's all gone. I said, 'Okay, make sure they get to the company headquarters.' So I started down the trail and I heard them pull out that fifty caliber* [gun] *on top of the tanks and I started to run. They never took them to no CP. Wiped them right away. I didn't want to hear them scream.*

Another horror that Duncan remembered from the war, was when his regiment liberated a concentration camp.

Well, we went and took it and the Germans ran. They had their dogs and they were running through the woods . . . they took their German shepherds because they got attached to them. So then we called for an air strike and he told them what part of the woods they were running through. He says, 'We'll take care of that.' And you could hear them machine guns on the airplanes, they didn't run very far. And when you

*see a guy like that you don't care . . . when they starve a guy
like that. I didn't want to go inside the fence because they
stunk and most guys had messed all over themselves. They
were sick . . . we moved on. We had to go and then they called
in another unit like medics. Give them shots because when
you get that skinny you can't take solid food for a while . . .
it would just come back up on you. . . .*

On May 2nd, 1945, during one of the many risky town sieges,
Duncan was hit in the right shoulder by shrapnel from a field artillery
shell. The shell was probably about the size of a baseball and was made
of burning hot metal. Duncan said in addition that:

> *. . . they took me in a stretcher, put me in an ambulance
> and took me to a field hospital . . . when I got there guys were
> screaming, 'Don't cut my leg off!' and 'Don't cut my arm off!'
> So I said to the nurse, 'Do I have to listen to that all night?'
> She said, 'No, you'll be in Paris tomorrow.' She grabbed one
> of them needles and 'zoom.' I didn't want to lay there listen-
> ing to that screaming and hollering, 'Where's the clergy man,
> I'm a good boy!' and all of that.*

Duncan was allowed a week of recovery in Paris. "During the day we
were at the hospital getting checked out by the army doctors. But at
night, you could get out." When Duncan was completely healed, he
returned to the front lines. At that point, his outfit was approximately
fifty miles from Berlin.

By the time the 78th had arrived in Berlin, the Russians were already
there. "When they [the Germans] surrendered, the Russians said, 'You
guys stop, we'll take it.'" Duncan remembered that the Russians were:

> *raunchy ... killers. We didn't fool with them. The way they
> were brought up over there* [in Russia]...[they were] *scary
> people. . . . And boy, they* [the Russians] *did* [take Berlin],
> *just flattened it like a pancake. And then, we rode in on
> trucks. . . . They had these big apartment houses there. This
> company would be there and this company would be here. We
> relieved the 82nd Airborne there. Russians were there...they
> were living across the river over there. The neighborhood we
> were in was nice. We had heat, hot water, could take a show-
> er whenever you wanted.*

Duncan often wrote letters home to his parents. Whenever they
asked him when he was coming home, he said that he did not know, that
it all depended on the number of points a soldier accumulated. "You got

so many extra points for being overseas. I think it was seventy or eighty points to come home." After a stay in Berlin, the 78th was shipped back to the states in what Duncan called, "a liberty ship — Kaiser built them."

Duncan was honorably discharged on May 16th, 1946, at Camp Atterbury, Indiana. At the end of the war, Duncan was awarded with the following decorations: the EAME Ribbon with three bronze stars, the Good Conduct Medal, the Purple Heart Medal, the Victory Medal of WWII, and the Army of Occupation Germany Medal.

Like most veterans, Duncan was reluctant to speak of the war when he returned home. The only person he told his experiences to was "his dad" because "strangers – they don't believe some of the things." Duncan said that when he tried to talk about the concentration camps at home, "nobody believed me. They were more worried about the baseball games and football games. Unless you were there you can't imagine what it is."

LIEUTENANT HAROLD EDWIN KREN
466TH BOMB GROUP, 8TH AIR FORCE

Harold Kren entered the service in California. After extensive training in B-24 heavy bombers, he arrived in July of 1944 at airfield number 120 in Attlebridge, East Anglia. By January 1945, he had completed thirty-five missions with the 466th Bomb Group. During this period, Kren reported that his bomb group was "shot full of holes . . . [we] had emergency landing types of experiences. We came close to a couple of mid-air collisions – close enough that it scared the bijeebers out of me. . . . "

> *The first mission out of the box for me was to fly to Brunswick in Germany and to drop some bombs and come back and I have got to say, it was a wonderful first experience although I didn't really realize that until after the third mission. It kind of goes like this. We departed, we assembled, we flew to Brunswick, en route the weather was nice. We saw some flak. It was low. It was far in front of us (by far I imagine half a mile to a mile). It never really got to us, we dropped our bombs, we turned around, we came back, we didn't see any fighters, we saw (as I recall) no flak on the way back (although if we did see it, it was no more impressive than what we saw on our way in and around the target), and we landed. And I thought, "Boy, this is just great. I wonder what all this business about flak is and fighters and what have you? We'll get this out of the way in no time and be on our way home. . . .*
>
> *It was our third mission that we went to Hamburg. . . .*

Hamburg changed my attitude about the ease of flying combat 100%, or 180°, if you care to look at it that way. We had flak. The flak was radar directed; it was extremely accurate, it was heavy. It was everything you could think of that would make a mission unpleasant. . . . We survived the mission. We were not shot full of holes; we were scared, but here's where the pilot came in. This is one of the reasons I . . . developed so much respect for our pilot, Niles Hartung. He had listened to, and he had paid attention to, and he [had] heeded the advice we had been given about what to do under these circumstances, and he was able to maintain formation – and we were flying, of course, off of somebody's wing – the second or third mission. . . . You're not leading anything, you're flying off a wing. Nonetheless, he was able to do evasive action sufficiently [and] maintain formation [so] that we got through this whole mess and that characteristic, that quality he showed us many, many, many times over. Well, that was the mission to Brunswick and that was the mission to Hamburg and that was probably – those two represent probably the two extremes – the easy and the tough. In between, I would say, was everything else.

We had a mission, interestingly enough, where we were carrying one hundred pound bombs – . . . they might have been (I think) . . . fragmentation bombs. Now, these bombs were loaded in such a way. . . . it went roughly like this: In order to get the maximum load over the target, the bombs were loaded three per bomb station from the bottom up (the upper ones only had two because there wasn't quite clearance for three), but the point being –I mean, the end result being that you had [counting] 3-6-9-12-24 and 2-4-6-8-24 . . . forty bombs that you could drop. The problem was that these fellows that were hung three to a station in the lower racks had a great tendency not to release. . . . And sure enough, half of ours didn't. We had twenty bombs stuck once – we got to the point of bomb release and we released our bombs. Twenty of them went out (the ones from the front racks, interestingly enough) and twenty of them (the ones in the rear racks) . . . piled up in the bomb bay. Now this is not a terribly difficult situation, except for a couple of points – they have nose and tail fuses on them and the ones in the upper racks . . . that fell down and were jammed against the ones in the lower stations, managed to, of course, jam the control cables so the airplane was for a bit of time out of control.

It was out of control in straight and level flight, fortu-

nately, but unfortunately once the bomb release point had been reached and the bombs dropped, the entire formation turned to return to base, but we continued straight forward because the pilots were not able to control the aircraft. And this went on, they tell me, for about fifty miles straight on into Germany while all the rest of the formation was going its merry way elsewhere. The one thing, of course, that you don't want to be in a situation like that is a lone aircraft – a lone bombing aircraft, because you are 100% dead meat as far as fighter aircraft are concerned. Well, the pilots were able to get control of the aircraft finally, were able to call in fighter cover, and we got turned around and headed back toward base – still fairly deep [in] Germany, of course. Problem being, we had all these bombs that [were] rattling around back there and this led us then to the next problem they presented, and that is their nose and tail fuses had become fully armed by now – that is, they were impact type fuses. They were designed to go off when struck and they were ready to do it if anybody wanted to strike them.

As the bombardier, it was my job to [go] back and do something about it. So there I was on the catwalk . . . about . . . six to eight inches wide and nothing between me and the ground down there, [some] twenty-odd thousand feet, but open air, no parachute, of course, because you can't wear a parachute and work back there at the same time – and once those little problems are out of the way, then it becomes fairly simple – you simply have to unscrew the fuses, dispose of them because they'll still explode – dispose of them without striking them somehow and then rassle the bombs out – and I mean rassle. . . . Well, we got it done. I worked on it for awhile myself and my co-pilot got free from what he was doing and between the two of us [we] managed to get everything out of there and fly on home. . . .

Kren also complimented the P-51 Mustangs, which had the "capability of escorting us essentially all the way to the target as well as back again." By late 1944 and early 1945, Kren stated that the Allied air forces had pretty much established air superiority; he only encountered in the German jet interceptors two or three times. This was "probably December or January of 1945" and that "was a very impressive sight."

Another unforgettable mission for Kren occurred

sometime in the late summer or early fall, we had flown a mission and we were returning over Holland and everything was peaceful on the way back and our fighter cover decided

*(with consent, of course) that they would go on down on the
deck and seek out what they could in the way of targets of
opportunity. We were by now nearly to, if not over the
Zuidersee on the way back to England.*

*They had no more than left then a flight of three
[German] ME-109s . . . came down from above someplace. . . .
[They] made one single pass through our squadron of six B-
24s, and when they finished this single pass, there were only
three of us left. Now, why those three instead of the other
three or another three or why we were not hit rather than
somebody else, I have no idea. I am just pleased – grateful I
guess would be a better word – that we weren't. . . . This is
not a pleasant kind of thing, and it was the price of inatten-
tion because we had all goofed off – all of the gunners had
backed off of being alert. I was sitting up in the nose turret. I
am sure I was not alert. We were just droning our way home
and we paid the price for it.*

If enemy aircraft weren't hazardous enough, friendly craft could be
just as dangerous:

*We're on our way back – we were in fact over England
and had just absolutely miserable weather conditions. It was
the sort of thing where you had – oh, you might have had 100
yard visibility at best. . . . You simply couldn't see what was
going on and the formation evaporated. . . . It just scattered
to the four winds as it were. Now, this didn't mean that we
couldn't find the base and land, but it meant that everybody
had an awful lot of clutter of other airplanes to get through
en route to doing it. And at one point we were probably at a
couple, [around] three thousand feet. . . . We were all strain-
ing to see . . . in this pea soup fog and . . . another B-24 cut
in front of us. I'm sure [it] missed us by no more than fifty or
sixty feet – lucky, you're darn right! I wasn't scared, I was
absolutely petrified! But, it takes skill and it takes luck and I
say unashamedly, I think we had both.*

Following the successful invasion in June of 1944, Patton's Third
Army began its race northeast towards the German lines. To keep the
Third Army moving, the Second Air Division, according to Kren, was
ordered to

*. . . stop flying bombing missions for a period and . . . fly gas
and maps to Patton's Army. Now by and large, this meant
flying at a 1000 feet to some point behind the lines, dis-*

charging your gas and turning around and coming back. I flew only one of these missions. . . . It was a very interesting thing. I flew to St. Dezier, which was fifty or sixty miles behind the lines in Nancy and Metz. Nothing special. We flew there and got to stay there overnight, sleeping in the aircraft and eating C-rations, which was okay. We got into town just as curfew was tolling and so our excitement . . . was to find an ice cream shop that hadn't quite closed and buy as much ice cream as we could consume on the spot, which was a pretty goodly amount; chat with the owners in Spanish as best we could because the owners were Spanish refugees from the Spanish revolution in the mid-'30s, and get on back to the base and the next morning take off and find our way back. . . .

This type of flying was a piece of cake for Kren; however, the situation became substantially more serious with the beginning of the Battle of the Bulge in mid-December. Kren recalled his crew

. . . flew seven missions in nine days during that time. . . . The Bulge was in small part made possible and lasted as long as it did because the weather was totally miserable. There was absolutely no flying for about two – two and a half weeks – and when it finally broke, then everything that could get in the air went into the air and we had the sight of B-24s (and I suspect [B-]17s as well) flying low level, 5,000 foot bombing missions. We bombed in an effort to, what they called, "interdict" the transportation capability – that is to say we bombed rail lines, actually crossroads to try to take out the highways, to try to take out the rail transport up in Bulge area, things that ordinarily [would] not be deemed worthy of bombing, particularly by strategic bombing forces, and very difficult to hit. Anyway, as I say, we did – it was seven missions in nine days starting the 23rd of December and ending the 31st, and at least six of the seven (if not all seven) were to the kind of microscopic . . . but important, kinds of targets that I tried to describe.

Kren completed his thirty-fifth and last mission over Rastatt, Germany, on January 7th, 1945. He also flew on missions to:

Hamburg, to Karlsruhe, to Mainz, Magdeburg, Osnabruck, Berlin, Karlsruhe again, and Koblenz. . . . and that's really pretty much of a thumbnail sketch of heavy bombardment combat . . . as I experienced it. I don't think it's at all unusu-

al for the time I was there. There were indeed a lot of casualties. . . . Airplanes blew up – I saw them do that. They were shot down – I saw that. People were killed, wounded and taken prisoner, and so on. This didn't happen with us. It didn't happen because I think we had a skillful pilot, a skillful co-pilot . . . a good navigator, and . . . a fair amount of good luck and not the least of all of this, I might say, you can attribute to the ground people who [took] care of the aircraft and armament and kept them in good flyable condition.

After the 7th of January 1945, I got orders to return to the States and did so and wound up . . . in Midland, Texas, where there was a refresher school for returned bombardiers. . . . [I] spent a year there having . . . been assigned to a ground school instructor's job, and then to ground school administrative job, and finally, went off active duty . . . in November or December of '46 at Mather Army Air Field. . . . I stayed in the reserve being quite convinced that there would be another good-scale war in my lifetime and I would be ordered up – turns out I wasn't, but I stayed in the reserve, and maintained my activity level and retired . . . in September of 1980.

LIEUTENANT FRED FEHSENFELD, SR.
354TH FIGHTER GROUP, 353RD FIGHTER SQUADRON
9TH AIR FORCE

Fred Fehsenfeld flew a remarkable eighty-six combat missions in P-47s and P-51s in the European Theater. He had "always liked to fly," and so he enlisted in the Army Air Corps. After extensive training, he "got in the convoy" with twelve other pilots and "we went across the north Atlantic to England. . . . We had a couple of scares because the Germans had submarines, and we were worried about getting torpedoed, but to my knowledge we didn't lose any of our convoys."

"When I got there . . . I went to a place called Stone in England and . . . we stayed there for maybe a couple of weeks . . . and then we were flown over to Paris, France. Paris had just been

Lt. Fred Fehsenfeld, Sr. (Courtesy of Fred Fehsenfeld, Sr.)

retaken by the Allies and so we stayed in the Rothchild Château outside Paris."

Fehsenfeld remained there for about three days, and then received orders to go with six pilots to the front near St. Dezier, France, where they joined the 354th Fighter Group and the 353rd Fighter Squadron in the 9th Air Force. His unit acted mostly as ground support for Patton's Third Army; Fehsenfeld remembers that on one occasion they "shot down fourteen or fifteen [German] airplanes that crashed around Patton. . . . General Patton got in his vehicle, went right to our airfield. . . . He was really impressed with us."

Fehsenfeld had joined an illustrious group of fighter pilots. Unfortunately, his first mission did not go quite as he expected it would:

> Well, my first experience in aerial combat. . . . I was flying with Colonel Eagleston, who was leading ace of the 9th Air Force in WWII, and I was the element leader and he was the flight leader, and . . . I saw a P-38 which was a photo or a reckee aircraft and . . . at least a dozen Focke-Wulf 190's were trailing behind it, and I called them out. . . . 'Bandits at . . . about 11 o'clock high,' and so he said, 'okay, let's tally ho, let's go get them!' . . . The airplanes were coming down right across in front of us – apparently the P-38 pilot was busy taking pictures of the front lines and was unaware of the FW-190's getting ready to shoot him. Eagle pulled into the FW-190's as they were coming by and he shot and blew one of the FW-190's out of the sky.
>
> I had been taught how to lead – you always have to lead, and so I did the wrong thing. I turned left and fortunately when I shot at the German, he pulled out of the line and so I followed him down. . . . I made up my mind that I was really going to try to do as good of a job as I was taught to do, and so . . . he dove away and I followed him. . . . I was thinking at the time . . . I finally want to make a German pay for yanking me out of Purdue University, and I was really going to get him. . . . I put on full power and I'm going as fast as a P-51 can in a dive . . . so I was just waiting to get about a thousand feet away from him to shoot, and . . . the pilot . . . dropped his wheels and flaps, and all of a sudden I was looking at the gun sight and the airplane was getting very big, because he is now [going] 200 miles per hour and I'm going almost 500 miles per hour. . . . And so, I didn't know what to do, but . . . I was really going to annihilate this guy, and when I went by him, I turned real tight to the right, and I looked back and he had his wheels and flaps up, and he had 20 mm canons, and they were being fired at me, and you could see

the tracers, and the tracers would come at my plane and because I was turning so tight, they'd always go behind my tail. And I was so scared, I yanked back on the stick and I did a snap roll. And then I yanked back . . . with the stick again and did another snap roll, but finally I got back on his tail, and . . . I squirted again and he bailed out. But I went from one minute where I was really the killer, [to] the next moment where I was going to be killed. And so the emotional thing was quite great.

Combat flying did not come without enormous stress. The 354th Fighter Group was comprised of some very aggressive fliers, according to Fehsenfeld; Aces such as Eagleston, Beerbower, Dahlberg, and others took enormous risks.

The average pilot of the 354th . . . always looked forward to the missions hoping maybe he could shoot down some aircraft, or be effective on some kind of ground device, occasionally the only thing that really made you worry is strafing the airdromes, and we averaged losing twenty-five percent of the aircraft that strafed an airdrome, so what we used to do is we knew where the airdrome was, and we get out at about thirty miles and get right on the deck, I mean right where the propeller was practically tickling the grass, really low, under the radar, and when we got within sight of the field, everybody put full power on, and whatever was in front of you, you shot, and then we never went back to make a second pass. The reason for that is that one of our very famous leaders . . . Major Beerbower, did a second pass on . . . a German airfield, and he strafed it and pulled up and did a 270° turn because he saw some FW-190's in the woods, and when he came back, why they blew him out of the air, so we just had a rule to strafe airdromes only once, [because] the Germans were firing a lot of anti-aircraft weaponry, and . . . you flew through those rounds and . . . if it happened to hit you, it hit you. . . . So that was really a scary mission because if you had sixteen [aircraft] going across, then only twelve would come out the other side. . . .

We flew in elements of two: . . . the wingman and . . . a flight leader, and . . . there were four flights in a squadron and three squadrons in a group . . . and we always flew in mutual support. . . . Both elements are looking to see if anybody is attacking from the rear . . . if we see attacking German aircraft, we yell, 'Break!' And then, as fast as we can, we turned to attack the German aircraft.

WORLD WAR II

On March 15th, 1945, Fehsenfeld assisted in shooting down a German aircraft; a month later on April 16th, he shot down two planes and in doing so saved his wingman's life. For this he earned a Silver Star and a promotion to 1st Lieutenant.

> What happened is, I was leading a flight . . . and we ran into seven aircraft. We were flying east, so we came up behind them and I said, 'forget about the wingman thing, and each pilot get behind an aircraft,' and I said, 'let's ease up on them, if we start shooting way out then you're in for a big dog fight.' Well, we went up and pretty much I think everybody was able to shoot down an aircraft. . . . I was circling and my wingman said, 'I'm at 11 o'clock low, and I got a Focke-Wulf 190 on my tail,' and 'could you help me?' So I dove down, he was right on the deck, and I fired at him and hit him, and then he tried an old trick that I had [had] pulled on me in the previous battle, of cutting the throttle and putting down his flaps and his wheels, and if you are going at 500 miles or 450 and some guy slows down to 200, I mean, you go right by him, and then he's behind you, and then he starts shooting at you, and I had that happen once. So when he did that, I saw it and I did a very sloppy barrel roll . . . [it] was almost at right angles to the line of flight, so it really slows the aircraft down quickly and I slipped in behind him and I shot him with considerable fire power, and it was . . . obvious he was going to go down, and he was still doing only 220, 230 miles an hour, so I just pulled up by the side of him. . . . I could see him, because I had put my wing nearly into his cockpit, and the guy was working hard trying to keep his aircraft up in the air, smoke was just roaring out of it. And he was at about 500 feet, and he blew off his canopy (the Germans had a canopy that would blow off), so he blew that off, and bailed out, but he was only at 500 feet, and his parachute only came out about halfway and he went kicking into the woods. And if he had just pulled back on his stick, and had gotten some altitude, and then went out of the aircraft, he'd still be alive today.

Battle of the Bulge

Fehsenfeld remembers that they were involved in "one of the bigger battles of World War II."

> Von Runstedt had attacked and broken through our lines and . . . penetrated back into France, substantially. . . . We absolutely had terrible weather, we were used to flying in bad

215

weather, and we had really no good instrument approaches, but we did have a way – we had some mountains, they weren't huge mountains, but we were able to use our radio fixes in order to know where to come and let down so we didn't crash into the mountains, but this weather was really bad, and it was . . . about the week before Christmas. We just couldn't fly. . . . Then on Christmas day in 1944[5] it broke and we flew our first mission on Christmas day, and once we got in the air, we were able to stop the assault by dive bombing and strafing planes. We had a couple ways of doing that, we could fire .50 caliber machine guns at Tiger tanks, but it wasn't too effective unless we could hit the thread, knock the thread off. We found that we could carry napalm bombs and slide them into the tanks and when the petroleum jelly burned, it would get the tank real hot and then the German soldiers would have to jump out and then our infantry could shoot them. And occasionally we'd tried skip bombing with 500 pound bombs, but it wasn't too effective because it hit and a lot of times it would just skip over the tanks, but we were able to stop them and of course any ground troops we could annihilate, so that's the way we were able to stop Von Runstedt at the Battle of the Bulge with the very able help of the infantry.

"Heil Hitler, in case we lose"

Humor was a great tension reliever for these pilots under the constant stress of combat flying. Fehsenfeld clearly remembered one of his lighter moments:

We had a droll sense of humor and so when we used to walk by other pilots, we would up our hands and say, 'Heil Hitler, in case we lose!' So one day I had flown three missions and an old gentlemen in a flying suit came by, and I just held up my hand, I was weary and said, 'Heil Hitler, in case we lose,' and this shocked expression came on the guy's face, and I thought oh, that's unusual.

[Later] that night and we were all in eating our dinner . . . our CO [Glenn Eagleston] said, 'all enlisted men out of the mess hall! . . . "There's two things I want to talk to you about,' and he said, 'Dahlberg, (who was one of our pilots) you shot down a British aircraft today, and they are really hot.' (He was a very eager guy and . . . we didn't like to fly in front of him because he had shot down two British aircraft. He shot down quite a few Germans too, but he was an awful

aggressive guy, and he didn't pay much attention to see whether you were friend or foe.)

And then he said, 'who was the guy that went by the commanding general of the 9th Air Force and said 'Heil Hitler, in case we lose?' I kept silent. As we were all going out, he said 'Fehsenfeld, come here.'

So I said, 'Uh-Oh.' So, I went over. . . . He said, 'the general wants to fly tomorrow. You are going to be his wingman.' . . . And he said, 'I'll tell you one thing, we don't want to . . . lose him, so if we run into enemy aircraft you make sure you protect him. If we get into areas where we have a lot of flack, you fly under him,' which means I would get the flack, but I said, 'Yeah, I got the message.'

So . . . I was a little worried he might recognize me. . . . The next morning I got up real early and I went down (and we had back parachutes and we had a helmet and then we had our oxygen mask), so I hung my oxygen mask so about half of my face was covered, and I started to get in my airplane and Eagleston called again, . . . 'Fehsenfeld, come here.' So I went over and here is the general and he said, 'general, this is your wingman and he's a good pilot and he will take care of you.' And so the general held out his hand and I shook his hand, and I didn't say a thing about saying 'Heil Hitler, in case we lose' or anything. So anyway we got in the aircraft and we flew and he was very eager to shoot down a German aircraft and quite often he would say, 'Bandits 11 o'clock high,' and I would call and say, 'general, those are our fat little friends the P-47s,' and he said, 'Oops, okay.'

I found a train and showed him where it was and he went down and strafed it. When you shot at trains, lots of times the engineers would let off steam, so you'd think you did a lot of damage. We usually strafed the cars because they carried ammunition a lot of times. So you wanted to shoot way out because we've lost quite a few planes that got in close and shot and then the munitions blow and when you flew through your wings just collapse on your aircraft. So we pulled up after that and then we saw a diesel German train, and so we went down and he shot that, so . . . he shot two trains while he was in the air, but we didn't see any enemy aircraft.

Twenty-five years later Fehsenfeld met Eagleston at a reunion. Fehsenfeld inquired whether he remembered the incident with the general. To this Eagleston replied: "I knew you were the guy that said "Heil Hitler," and so I knew that you would be feeling a little guilty and you would make sure the general didn't get killed."

WORLD WAR II

Last Official Mission

By the first of May, Fehsenfeld's unit was moved from Ober Olm to Ansbach, Germany. Then, on May 7th, 1945, when the war in Europe ended, Fehsenfeld's combat missions changed from armed patrols and reconnaissance to demonstration flights:

> One of the unusual things that happened to me was that I actually . . . flew the last official mission in World War II in Europe. . . . I was leading our squadron, which was . . . sixteen aircraft. And our job was not to shoot at anybody, but to go dive over where we knew some prisoner-of-war camps were, and then we dove over them and we did barrel rolls and aerobatics to build up the POW's morale because . . . if you have been a prisoner of war, why you know, your morale gets down. And so I did that, and I was telling this experience just recently to our group [the Pioneer Mustang Association] . . . and a guy held up his hand and he said, 'I was in the prisoner of war camp when you came,' and he said, 'I looked at you. You were yellow nose P-51s, okay?' and he said, 'to see those Yellow Nose come over . . . it really made a difference. The Germans – there was a lot of shooting still going [on] around our camp, and we were all worried they were going to shoot us, because the war was over. . . . The P-51s came, . . . the gates opened, and we just got out.'

After the POW camp flyover, Fehsenfeld related how he spotted approximately fifty to seventy Focke-Wulf 190s, that were still flying. What should he do about these planes? The German crews

> . . . flew in gaggles . . . [whereas] we always flew in flights of four. . . . They all fly off one pilot's [wing]. . . . And so, we were told not to shoot them. So, I said, 'I'm going to take these aircraft back to Ansbach and I'll have them land, and maybe they will give me credit for fifty or some aircraft [shot down] or something.' So anyway, I told everybody . . . 'you all stay up above and I'm going down [to] try to communicate with the guy (you couldn't talk on the radio or anything) and if they start shooting . . . 'you start shooting.' So anyway, I went down, flew [on] the guy's wing and he looked at me and nodded his head, and . . . I pointed the way we were going – we were going right at Ansbach, and he nodded his head, but as we were going toward Ansbach, we went by Munich . . . all these aircraft went down and landed at Munich Airport. Some of them didn't . . . put the wheels down, and landed in the

grass. I sent eight pilots back to Ansbach and I said, 'let's go land,' to the other eight pilots. There was a major there that was in the Quartermaster Corps or something, and Germans all lined up and were saying, 'Heil, Hitler' and all that kind of stuff. He said, 'Wow, that's all over, the war's over, you shouldn't do that!' And we're are looking at him . . . and some of our pilots . . . wanted to get their side arms. . . . They all carried P38's or Lugars or something like that and we decided maybe we could talk four Germans into maybe flying back to our airbase, which is only . . . sixty or seventy miles away. . . .

[While] we were working on the aircraft, a DC-3 landed and a full colonel came up and he said, 'What are you doing?' and I said, 'Well, we are trying to get four of these aircraft and take them back to our airbase and even though the war is over, we are probably going to Japan, and we'll fix 'em up, and then we'll go up with cameras, and have dog-fights with them and see how good we are and we will put our pilots in the Focke-Wulf 190s. He said, 'well,' he looked at me (and I was in a flying suit, and I didn't have any rankings) [and he said,] . . . 'what's your rank, soldier?' And I said, 'I'm a 1st Lieutenant,' and he said, 'We are grounding all these aircraft. We need them for intelligence.' . . . I didn't say anything, we all got back in our P-51s and flew back to Ansbach. So, when we got there, I told Colonel Eagleston what had happened, and he said, 'well . . . that's great. Tomorrow we will . . . load up with Jerry cans of high octane gasoline and we'll go down there and we'll find four guys and fly the aircraft back.' So I said, 'okay.' . . . I flew down on a P-51 and we all . . . landed in Munich again.

. . . We got there and now there's a major in the military police and he . . . just wouldn't give us the airplanes unless we had some kind of orders, so Eagle looks at me and said, 'this is your idea Fehsenfeld!' (and it wasn't my idea at all – it was his). And he says, 'Go back to XIXth Tac and get some orders, so that we can get four of these aircraft. And tell him Colonel Eagleston wants them. . . . '

So I flew to where XIXth Tac was; [but] . . . the war was over and everybody's not there, so I can't get any orders. Well, Eagleston was a real strange kind of guy, and [if] he gives you something to do, you are supposed to get it done. So I went back . . . to Ansbach and talked to our assistant of operations officer and he said, 'Okay, . . . I'll write you up some fake orders for these Focke-Wulf 190s, but you tell Eagle that they are fake, and don't leave them with anybody or I'm going to *go to jail.'*

So he knew how to do it. He got on the typewriter and gave me orders, so I flew back and got Eagleston and said, 'Hey, Jimmy Keane typed up these orders because I couldn't find anybody, so be sure and keep them.' So he went over and showed them to the guy and he said, 'Okay, you

Lt. Fred Fehsenfeld (l) and Harry Primrose. (Courtesy of Fred Fehsenfeld, Sr.)

can take four, but . . . I want a copy of the orders,' and Eagleston said, 'I'm sorry, this is the only copy of the orders I've got, but when I get back, I'll send you something. . . . '

Flying these illegal planes back to Ansbach was yet another challenge. Because Fehsenfeld had been gone two and a half hours, the other volunteer pilots had already acquainted themselves with the controls on the German planes. Fehsenfeld had to be a very quick study:

> *. . . they got me in a 190 and they are trying to explain to me about how to get the landing wheels down, there is a whole series of handles up in front and he said, 'grab that handle and pull it,' and I pulled it and the hood blew off so that scared the heck out of me, so they said, 'come on, we'll get another 190' (we had a lot of them). So I went over and climbed into another 190 and he says, 'it's easy, you take off, you know how to do that, you just push the throttle forward, and it had a stick and rudder pedals, and it was conventional in that sense, and when you get up in the air you push EIN [in] and the wheels will come up and you fly and when you are ready to land, you push AUS [out] and the wheels will come down . . . if it doesn't, there is a handle right up here. You pull that handle.'. . . He said, 'we've got to get going,' so they helped me get it started. . . . The first two got off alright, the third guy had problems and he bellied his in, and I got it up so I'm flying and I'm trying to push EIN to get the wheels to come up, . . . but every time I let go off the throttle, the*

throttle would come back all the way and the airplane would loose speed. So . . . I put the stick in between my knees and I'm looking for a friction control that we had on our [aircraft] and there isn't any. So I looked down on the bottom of the aircraft and there is a narrow, little knob, and you take your foot and [push.] I was able then finally to tighten it up so . . . I could get the wheels up. I pushed EIN and the wheels came up.

We had two 51s flying with us, taking us back, because we had no radio, and about that time some 51s from the 8th Air Force showed up, and they saw three of these 190s flying and fortunately, we had the two 51s from our outfit flying with us. . . . As we were flying back, we did barrel rolls as well as loops. It was really great. The first two aircraft went in and landed, as I glided down [to] land. I had been told to bring it in at 120 kilometers per hour. Well, that seemed reasonable to me. I didn't know what a kilometer was, and so I came down and I pushed AUS and [the landing controller] gave me a red light, the wheels wouldn't come down. So I went around again, and pushed AUS again, and [the controller] still gave me the red light. So I climbed up 6,000 feet, rolled the canopy back, and then I pushed AUS and . . . remembered something about pulling the handle, there were four of them as I recall, and so I grabbed one and I could feel something, so then I came in, and lined up on the runway and they gave me the green light, the wheels were down. Whew! So everybody's lining up along the runway sort of looking at this crazy guy trying to fly this 190 and land it, and because I had made so many passes (I made two passes), and . . . they were all saying, 'well, what if Fehsenfeld's going to really screw up here' and . . . so I said, 'I'll show everyone, I am going to bring it in at 120 kilometers.' Well, 120 kilometers is only 72 miles per hour, and the airplane stalls at that and I should have been up, oh probably close to 160 or 170 kilometers. . . . So I got about fifty feet above the ground . . . and I started bringing the nose back and it stalled. And so, when you are in an aircraft stalled you put on full throttle and . . . the only thing that you can control the wings with (the ailerons won't work in stalled condition), [is] . . . the rudder peddles, and I walked the rudder peddles down, and bang! I hit hard and then I start taxiing the thing and it really taxied hard and I couldn't understand why until later when I got a picture of me taxiing in with a flat tail wheel.

By the time the war ended, Fehsenfeld had flown eighty-six missions.

He was recognized with an Air Medal with three Silver clusters and with the Silver Star for saving a wingman's life and shooting down German planes. After returning to the States, he returned to Purdue University, where he graduated as a mechanical engineer. For a short time after that, he worked at the Rock Island Refining Company in Indianapolis. Fehsenfeld later joined his family's small business, which eventually grew into a fairly large company.

◈

PRIVATE FRANK COONEY
RIFLEMAN IN COMPANY A
359TH REGIMENT, 90TH INFANTRY DIVISION

Frank was living in Southern Troy, New York, at 562 Second Street when America joined World War II. He "had gotten out of high school a little over a year before, in Catholic High in Troy" and was working for Bear Manning Company. "They made abrasives or sandpaper. That's where I worked until I went in the army." Cooney was drafted in October of 1943, and was placed into the infantry as a replacement. "The invasion of Europe was planned apparently for June of '44 . . . so they were getting a lot of 'cannon fodder' for the invasion." Cooney, a city boy, had never fired a gun before, but "by the way they trained you, I qualified as a sharpshooter." The army was "quite skilled in training people like me . . . because they get low quality people, like me, and yet they can develop them and train them into useful products."

After seventeen weeks of infantry training, Cooney and his division were shipped to Europe in April 1944. He landed in Scotland, continued his training in Somersetshire in southwestern England, and finally embarked at Falmouth for Utah Beach and the D-Day landings. Cooney shared few details about his initial combat experiences on June 6th; rather, he summed it up by saying:

> It's a short time of terror and a lot of time of boredom. You're not fighting constantly. A lot of times you're just walking and just waiting. The army is just great for 'hurry up and wait' . . . and then you start fighting . . . you're too busy to be scared at the moment, although you are scared. I was scared plenty. But you're awfully busy too. You're trying to survive.

Cooney somehow managed to survive from one day to the next:

> After I landed, we were on the coast, so we were just pushing our way inland. And some of it was very slow going. In the early part the terrain was very hard to fight in – there

were these hedgerows. It was all country [and] *farm land. . . . I remember crawling through a ditch of thorns, and I didn't even feel them. . . .*

When I was in the infantry (which was most of the time), we didn't dig big foxholes. We didn't have time; we weren't ever in a spot that long, we were always moving.

For two weeks, while he was on loan to an artillery group, Cooney sought shelter in artillery foxholes. One in particular "was like a grave. . . . It would be about as long as yourself because you would sleep in it." One night, when he was in one of these deep foxholes, "there was some powder up on the ground . . . and this shell came over and hit the ammunition, which was just above my hole and that went up in a huge flame and I was laying in the hole; I couldn't get out of it." The explosion killed another soldier near him, so Cooney was appreciative of his found foxhole.

On August 16, 1944, while in northern France, Cooney sought shelter in an abandoned German foxhole. "They had nice deep holes, because they were in position for a long time." Unfortunately, the Germans returned, and Cooney was captured. He was first marched, and then was carried by truck across eastern France to Chalon. From there he was sent on to the first of two prison camps in Germany.

Cooney was never sure from then on whether or not he would survive:

When I first got caught, one guy was going to shoot me and he didn't because another guy stopped him. . . . If it weren't for this German sergeant, I would have been dead – he was ready to shoot me. And another time, we were walking along the road . . . they had a bunch of us, a bunch of prisoners not too far behind the front [lines]. *The Americans and Brits . . . had airplanes in the sky all the time, which meant if you were a German, you had to watch for it. So we were walking along a road and there was a British plane. He went by and started to make his turn . . . and he started heading for us and he was going to strafe us. He did strafe us. Normally you don't stay on the road when you see something like that coming at you. But the German sergeant, he made us stay on the road. And sure enough, at the last minute, I dove for the side of the road. I didn't care what he was going to do or say and we all did. The machine gun bullets, they went right by me, and they hit the sergeant – the guy who made us stay on the road – they got him. But the rest of us were shocked to death, we got up. That was a scary experience because they got some of the guys. . . .*

WORLD WAR II

> [The British pilot] *couldn't tell – we looked like Germans to him . . . we were prisoners of the Germans, but with the German army.*

Once Cooney and the rest of the American prisoners reached Chalon, they were taken by train to a camp at Lindberg [Limberg] near Frankfort. "That was a POW camp that was like [Camp] Upton, New York. It was a big one where all the POW's were coming in from the Western Front. And I stayed there a couple of weeks." From Limberg, Cooney was transported by boxcar – "fifty guys to a car" and "you might be in there for days. . . . Planes would come over and some of them would strafe the railroad yards. And we didn't know it at the time, but the Air Force had been warned about strafing boxcars, because POW's were in them. Of course, at the time we didn't know that, and here we are locked in a car, and you hear all this shooting going on outside. We were scared then."

After Limberg, Cooney was moved down south to Moosberg, which was about thirty-five miles from Munich. Cooney described both of these camps:

> They had a lot of barbed wire around them. Couple of double fences and all that. They [had] guards and dogs, everything to keep us under control. And then we had some barracks. In fact, I had never slept in a building from the time I left the States . . . until I got captured. Because all the time I was in England and France, we were living outside in tents, or less. . . . The weather wasn't that bad until I was down around Munich. Then it started to get wintry, but we had barracks then. Although the clothing wasn't too hot, because I got caught in the summertime and I just had summer clothes on. So I didn't get anymore and I lived in those clothes. Later in the wintertime, the Red Cross helped us some. They got us some clothes and I had a little French coat. And it wasn't too warm and it looked funny. It looked like a dress – it had a flared skirt, but anyway it gave some warmth.

Food was also limited:

> We were hungry all the time. That's why I would look forward to one of those K-rations. We didn't have any rations. Our main ration was a piece of black bread. The German soldiers used to carry that, too. That was their ration. It's bread that's very dense. They'd issue it by the kilogram. They would issue . . . so many loaves of bread to the barracks, and it would be cut up and divided amongst us. So we'd get a piece of bread, and we'd get some potatoes, mostly white potatoes. But we were always hungry in camp, so morale wasn't too

224

WORLD WAR II

Liberation of Stalag VII A — Moosburg, Germany — April 29, 1945

Similar photos at the National Archives identify this camp as "Stalag 7A Moosberg following liberation of prisoners by the 14th Armored Div., Third Army, on April 29. The Camp, which contained the largest number of Allied prisoners of war liberated at one time, had 29,284 prisoners, 14,891 of whom were American. More than half of the American prisoners were officers, mostly from Army Air Forces, April 29, 1945." [This photo identifies 2nd Lt. R. T. Sewell, Jr. It was placed at WWII Memorial, Washington, D.C., Memorial Day 2004] (Courtesy of Kathryn Lerch)

> good. Again, I was thankful to be alive and you didn't know how long you were going to stay alive, because the country was being bombed all the time, especially if we went into Munich. We went into Munich a lot, and we were always subject to being bombed.

Escape was never a consideration for Cooney, "because I didn't have anywhere to go. It was almost impossible for somebody like me, or most of us, because we didn't speak the language. We were deep into Germany . . . so there was nowhere for me to go, and if you don't speak the language, you're in trouble."

Liberation became a hope in mid-April as Allied forces "squeezed Germany from both sides." Since Cooney's camp was in southern Germany, it was one of the last to fall. Cooney remembers distinctly, "it was a Sunday morning and an American fighter plane came over, and he started barrel rolls and maneuvers, trying to indicate that our liberation was near. [See Fehsenfeld's account about fly-over.]Then a fight started.

225

World War II

We had some SS troops guarding the camp, and they put up a fight and it went on for a couple of hours. But we were pretty safe – we were inside the camp, and then when the fight stopped, it was over – the Americans came in. . . . I think it was an American armored division." The camp was in deplorable condition: "They had at least 10,000 prisoners in that camp, because they brought prisoners from all over Germany down to that camp . . . so there was an awful lot of us. . . . " Fortunately, the Americans promptly established waterlines to the former prisoners. The Germans, figured Cooney, had "been fighting for four or five years" and they "didn't have the equipment. . . . We could see the contrast between what the Americans had and what they had. It was very noticeable." Cooney remembers the date that he was freed: the 29th of April. "Our V-E Day was when we got liberated. That's when the war was over for us."

After liberation and a couple more weeks in Moosberg, Cooney was flown to Reims, France, "where we got cleaned up and fed. And then we went up to Le Havre, which was on the coast of France, to a camp called 'Lucky Strike.'" Cooney was one of 58,000 men to be processed through this camp. He finally sailed home via New York City, where his ship was welcomed by "fireboats with the hoses spraying them all over, and there was a ferry boat with people waving and all that. It was a good welcome. We didn't have a parade or anything, because we weren't the first, but we were welcomed. And that wasn't what we were looking for – we just wanted to get home."

Upon returning home, he had a seventy-two days leave and then Cooney joined some other former POW's for their final processing and paperwork at a camp in Lake Placid, New York. "I got out in December, a couple of weeks before Christmas, which was great."

Cooney returned briefly to the factory where he had worked before the war, but through the G.I. Bill, he was able to graduate from college with a degree in engineering. Cooney reflected on his wartime experience: "There is nothing like combat to teach you important things. Survival – your main job and important job was to survive, and I did that. . . . But once you get in these life and death situations . . . it really focuses your attention – teaches you what's really important."

STAFF SERGEANT LEONARD ROSE
459TH BOMBER GROUP, 15TH AIR FORCE
POW STALAG LUFT IV

Leonard Rose, or "Rosie," was almost eighteen when he enlisted in February of 1943. After extensive training, and because he knew all about the weapons, aircraft and bombs, he became an armor gunner on a B-24 crew. Eventually, "they put us aboard ship and took us overseas and we

226

WORLD WAR II

landed in Oran, North Africa, and we spent about a week there and then they finally transferred us up to the Mediterranean to Italy . . . where my base was . . . and I was with the 459th bomber group, . . . with the 15th Air Force. . . ." Rose's bomb group flew missions over Yugoslavia, Hungary, Poland, Czechoslovakia, Romania, Germany and France – with a fifty percent loss of bomber crews, according to his recollection. Not only was it dangerous flying, but as an armorer, Rose also had the dangerous job once the bombardier said 'bombs away,' he had to "make sure that one had not hung up" in the bomb bay, because "we couldn't land with it, and so I'd have to get up out of my turret and go into the bomb bay flying at 25,000 feet. . . . I always had a screw driver with me and I could reach up to the tackle, trip it and the bomb would fall out." As if this was not scary enough, Rose also completed seven missions over the Ploesti Oil Fields in Romania. These oil fields were indispensable to the German war effort and well defended.

> We'd go out and bomb it and then in two or three weeks they'd have it back in operation again, and basically I mean we'd get up close to that [and] all hell would break loose. I mean the anti-aircraft – the sky would turn black, and we would probably loose half of our airplanes, and we'd bomb them, go back home and probably a week or two later we'd be back up there doing the same thing all over again.

For the B-24 crews, stress was always a part of their lives:

> They'd get you up out of bed 3:00 in the morning and you'd go eat and get briefing, then you'd get in an airplane and you'd go out and bomb somebody and you'd come back. And seeing as you had no oxygen 'cause you were flying at high altitude, it would just wear you out. We'd get back 2:00 or 3:00 in the afternoon and you'd just go to your tent and you'd just sack out and somebody'd come wake you up 3:00 the next morning, and you'd do the same thing all over again.

Rose flew in combat for forty-two days, beginning with his first mission on July 17th, 1943, On August 29th, his thirtieth mission, his plane was shot down over Yugoslavia. He was effectively out of the war, but now had a new kind of stress: "all you could think of was survival and you just had to survive." Rose recounted,

> We were on our way to – trying to get back to Italy and we bail out. We run out of fuel and we run out of engines and so we parachuted out and we ended up landing in Yugoslavia. There I was captured by the Croatians and the next day they

*turned us over to the Germans, and then the Germans took us
from there to Budapest, Hungary and put me in an old prison
that was 1,000 years old.*

*. . . I spent three weeks there in solitary confinement, and
then after that they put us in box cars, and took me due north
to what is now Poland, but then they put us over to Germany,
and . . . [we] were in a prison camp and they had 10,000 of
us there. . . . [Since] we were all enlisted in the bomber crews
because when your crews got captured by the Germans, they'd
send the officers to a different camp than they did the enlisted [men], and then that's where I ended up in Stalag Luft IV.*

POW Experience

Boredom, as well as food and home, was constantly on their minds
while prisoners of war:

*We were in Stalag Luft IV which is up in Northern
Poland and we were all sergeants or above. I was a staff sergeant and there was no work to be done 'cause there was no
work there, and so basically it was just I would play cards
and some of them would [have] classes on languages and
we'd have guys that spoke a foreign language – we'd try to
learn the languages.*

*[We] read whatever we could. We were locked up a half
hour before it got dark and we were kept locked up until the
next morning. It'd be a half hour after it got daylight, so in
the winter time up there we were locked up for probably sixteen, seventeen hours a day 'cause . . . daylight wasn't very
long up there. . . .*

The Stalag Luft IV Prison Camp looked "like a city," according to
Rose. "Take two square blocks and put barb wire around them – that's
how big it was. . . . At one time there were 10,000 of us." Life and survival was tough in the camp; the food was basic, the Red Cross packages
were few and far between. "They would feed us maybe for a meal just
boiled potatoes. And there would be days that we would have dehydrat-
ed soup, cooked melon, barley. . . . " Although the Stalag Luft IV camp
was evacuated, Rosie remained imprisoned. Worse than prison was the
forced march across Germany ahead of the Russians – a trek that Rose
remembers all too well.

Death March

Then, come February the 6th . . . we could hear the

Russian big guns. The Russians were moving west and so then they [the Germans] decided they would evacuate us out of our camp, and so on February the 6th 1945, they started walking us out in groups of about 200-250. . . . There were about 8,000 of us at that time . . . and we were going to walk this over the end of old Germany and [they'd] put us in another prison[er] of war camp. . . . They'd said we'd only be on the road three or four days, but it ended up three months we'd walked. I'd walked over 600 miles and we never was in a heated building again. We slept in barns and fields, side of the road, and there were days we didn't have food and there was days we didn't have water and we drank out of ditches, ate snow. . . . [When] I went overseas I weighed 155 pounds and [when] I got home one year later, I weighed 92 pounds. . . . We never had our clothes off in three months and we were completely covered with body lice. Finally I ended up – I started out 170 miles northeast of Berlin and I ended up 90 miles south of Berlin and we had made a big circle around Berlin. . . .

I got liberated with the Russians and they locked me up for thirteen days and I thought they would take us to Russia and I didn't want to go, so on the thirteenth day of May 1945, we went over the wall that night to survive. . . .

We walked all night because we knew that if we went west we was finally getting to Allies, and so come daylight we got scared we didn't know what to do. So there was a big pine forest there. . . . So, what was another day without food and water when it's already been three months? So we just crawled up in that pine forest in a big pile of pine needles and just slept all day. . . . Then, we got out that second night and we ended up walking between twenty-five and forty miles in two nights. . . . Then come daylight the next morning well, we got to the Mulde River[1] and it so happened that the 69th Infantry Division had a pontoon bridge [set] up [as] a foot bridge and they had a sentry on each side, and so finally we got there and they sent us across the bridge and so that's when I got back to the Americans. . . .

That was the day that Heaven couldn't be any greater, because they took our old clothes off and burned them. . . . I don't know if it was a barber or not – he had a set of electric clippers and they just took us outside the tent and . . . and shaved off all the hair off of our bodies to get rid of the lice we were still covered in. And that day I had four hot showers, good American food, changes of clothes, delousing and . . . when we went to bed that night I said 'Lord, Heaven couldn't

*be any sweeter than this!' 'cause that was a day I'll always
remember.*

◈

Sergeant Edward Eugene Leitem
Battery B, 995th Field Artillery Battalion
Third Army

Ed Leitem served as a platoon sergeant with a combat engineering
battalion from January through May of 1945. His platoon was responsible for constructing fixed, floating and Bailey bridges across numerous
river crossings into Germany. Later, while moving across Germany,
Leitem was wounded when his platoon was engaged in combat on the
26th of March near St. Goar. [Shortly thereafter, (and most likely the
highlight of his military experience) he was personally awarded a Purple
Heart, in the field by General Eisenhower.]

Leitem, along with Patton's 3rd Army, continued a rapid movement
eastwards and they soon reached the outskirts of Weimar. (North of
town, where there was once a grove of trees, under which the great
German writer, Goethe, paused to reflect and write, there was instead the
infamous prison camp of Buchenwald.) While Cooney's camp at
Moosberg was horrible, nothing can quite compare to the horrific scene
which greeted members of Patton's Third Army when they liberated this
camp on April 11th, 1945.

This letter shares Ed Leitem's personal account to his father, Carl, of
what he heard and saw first-hand. Be forewarned, this descriptive
account is not for the squeamish.

17 April 45
Germany
    Dear Dad,
        *I certainly do wish that I had learned to speak German
when I had the chance. However, I have improved my French
very much and am able to make out very much better than I
ever expected. Almost everywhere I go I am able to find someone who speaks French so we get along all right. There were
lots of times when it made a lot of difference being able to
talk to these Heinies.*
        *I met a Frenchman when I visited that German Slaughter
House. He is the basis of almost all I am going to tell you
about that place. I believe every word of it too as you could
immediately tell upon listening to him that he was perfectly
sincere in all that he said, he did not try to put over any elab-
orate tales but plainly stated the blunt facts just as they hap-*

pened. One was impressed by his obvious earnestness and wish to give nothing but the facts. I cannot tell you yet what the name of the place was but all the places were the same or nearly so.

First of all I will tell you what the Frenchman told. Incidentally there were many more prisoners there and each and every story was amazingly similar which goes to prove the truth of the story. As far as the remaining prisoners knew between forty and sixty thousand Poles, Russians, Czechs, French, British, and American prisoners had been executed after torture in this place. During the month of February of this year close to three thousand were killed for sure. Torture consisted of many kinds all of

Edward Leitem receiving promotion from unidentified officer. (Courtesy of Harriet Campbell)

which I will not attempt to enumerate but will leave to your imagination. A favorite torture was to make these men stand at attention for a period of hours; if they moved they were made to stand an additional hour, if they moved in that additional hour another hour was added on and so forth. I actually talked to a man who in December of last year stood practically nude for a period of 36 hours. At intervals during that time he was beaten by the guards, at the same time he was given nothing to eat or drink. The barracks, if you could call them that, were never heated. The beds were nothing but boards nailed along the wall. Usually no covering and very little clothing was provided. The clothing that was issued was clothing that had been taken from the prisoners that had been killed that day. The guards made sure the prisoners knew it too. Before the dead men were burned, in fact sometimes before he was dead, a certain piece of him was cut out. The Heinies made soap out of these pieces and gave it to the pris-

oners to use for washing. Naturally this was almost impossible to do for I know how I would feel if I had to use soap that was made out of a friend. All this time a systematic system of starvation was in effect. Food, when it was served, was hot water with maybe a few carrots or potatoes cut into it. I'll tell you later the effect of this. Sanitation was practically nonexistent. The quarters remind one of nothing so much as a very dirty pigsty. Each barracks had a man in charge, who was assigned to keep order in his little group. He was in every case a tyrant who held the lives of his men in his hand to have them do anything that he wanted on pain of death. The things these men did are not fit for a decent person to even think about. It seems impossible that any human being could do the things these guards did. . . . Besides being starved, beaten, and frozen these poor miserable semblances of humans lived in constant fear of death. They all knew that sooner or later they were to be killed, but the instinct to live still kept them with some hope. When the Allied Armies drew near the prisoners were all promised death. Only the unexpected arrival of the Americans saved the few who are alive today. Even the arrival of medical care cannot prevent some from dying. They have been starved for so long that they cannot eat and despite the efforts of the doctors they continue to die like flies. While I was there three more died. As I write this I have no doubt that some more are dying. . . .

Now for what I actually saw. We approached the crematory and entered the small miserable courtyard. In the yard was an unforgettable sight. A rude wagon stood there piled high with dead bodies. There must have been close to a hundred piled up, but they were so thin that it was not much of a load. It was impossible to believe what we saw. It seemed incredible that any human being could get so thin and still live. It is no exaggeration when I say that they were nothing but skin and bones. Every ghastly detail was plainly visible because they were all naked. The joints looked huge in comparison to the rest of the wasted body. Hip bones were so prominent that they seem to be about to come through the skin. The ribs were merely a bit of skin stretched over a box of ribs. They were so emaciated that they could have lain out in the sun for a week without any evident decomposition. There was nothing on them to rot. Upon closer investigation it could be seen that each and every body had been brutally beaten. All the backs of the bodies were horribly scarred, in some cases the wounds had never time to heal. The heads had been shaved and were a mass of scars. Some of the dead had been shot but others had been hanged from a scaffold, which stood in the yard. They must have been very busy because the rack was built for six hooks. The ones who were hanged were not dropped but merely hung up until they strangled to death. All the bodies were not adults, these children showed the same signs of ill treatment that the others showed. Unmentionable things had also been done to the bodies, which I will not name.

We entered the crematory where we saw six furnaces. The fire had gone out and the half consumed bodies of several humans could be seen in the ovens. As the bodies were burned the ashes dropped though and were collected in the basement. A large truck could not have hauled all these ashes away in three loads. In fact just before I arrived a truck had hauled three loads of ashes away and there were still that many left at least. When you consider that the ashes from a body can be put in a small box about the size of a cigar box, you can see that a huge number of bodies had passed through the ovens. In the same basement was another room with hooks suspended from the ceiling from which men had been hanged and beaten to death with a huge knobbed, blood soaked club, which is still here. There are also places you can see where vast numbers of men have been shot down in cold blood. The cobblestones are soaked with blood. It looks as if automobiles had been drained there only the discolored spots are not oil but human blood. We also could see the living skeletons in some of the barracks. They were too weak to move and despite all the efforts of modern medicine there were slowly dying before our eyes. They had suffered so much that the look in their sunken eyes seemed to convey the impression that death would be a welcome visitor. From nearly two hundred pounds to less than forty pounds is unbelievable but absolutely true. Many, many photographs were taken there both by official photographers and ordinary soldiers. I only hope that these pictures, terrible and indecent as they are, can be released to the public of all nations in the world. It is an undying condemnation of the Germanic Race, any country and people who would condone such barbarity cannot by any stretch of the imagination be considered among the civilized people of the world. A person cannot think of any reason why anyone would want to perform such acts.

I have not completely covered the thing but I hope it will do a little toward making you feel towards the Germans the same way I do.

Please keep this letter. If you see any dumb so and so who is not yet mad at the Germans, show it to him and perhaps he will change his mind. I only wish I could be able to describe the scenes I saw with a better word picture, but this will have to do.

Write often.   *Love, Ed*

FRANK MICHAEL GRUNWALD
CZECHOSLOVAKIAN HOLOCAUST SURVIVOR

"I was about seven when the Germans walked in. They took over the whole country of Czechoslovakia . . . in the spring of 1939." At that time, Frank Grunwald was living a very comfortable and privileged life. He was a member of an upper middle class family.

> *My dad was a doctor and he practiced medicine. . . . We lived in central Prague in a really nice residential section in a big apartment (a two and a half bedroom, living room, big living/ dining room, library). . . . Dad had an office in the apartment, so the apartment had seven rooms, because two of them were part of his professional office (a waiting room, a separate restroom for the patients and an examination room for the patients). So, the patients had two rooms and a restroom, and we had the rest of the apartment. It was a very comfortable kind of scenario. . . .*

Grunwald's parents were both well-educated. "They spoke French, German, Czech, and English. . . . They were heavily into art and music." The senior Grunwald "had a lot of hobbies," including photography and mountain climbing. Music was also important to both of his parents; both enjoyed playing the piano. Although Grunwald did not take up the piano until he was older, he was enthralled with drawing and painting from a very young age. At every opportunity he would "steal" blank insurance forms from his dad's office and, "I started drawing and . . . drawing and painting."

All this changed, though, with the arrival of the Germans. Grunwald remembered that his parents were upset, but he "had no clue politically" and "did not understand what was going on." They often concealed their discussions from the children by speaking French, which neither he nor his brother spoke.

The German occupation of Czechoslovakia, and in particular Prague, occurred in mid-March of 1939. Grunwald remembered seeing a German gun emplacement along the river and about a year later, in 1940,

WORLD WAR II

> *We had a SS man in his uniform, and his wife came over to look at our apartment. And I clearly remember them walking in . . . just barging in. . . . They didn't say hello. . . . My mother didn't say hello, or shake hands. Of course she figured if they walk in and are not courteous to say hello, she is not going to respond. . . . So they walk in and look around. And so about a month or two later we were expelled from our apartment. And we had to move into a totally different section of Prague and live with some distant relatives of ours. We were just forced to live in a group with other people, because the SS basically . . . took over our apartment.*

Grunwald and his family stayed in Prague, but the "whole Jewish situation" became progressively worse in 1940.

> *Two or three months after the Germans came in, you saw anti-Jewish propaganda everywhere. . . . Well, I still remember newspapers with anti- Semitic propaganda talking about 'Jew feeds his horse with bread. . . . ' There was a shortage, it was the beginning of the war, there was a shortage of food, so right away the accusations about a Jew feeding his horse bread. This was part of the propaganda or [signs displayed] on storefronts 'Jews not allowed.'*
>
> *Shortly after they looked at our apartment and expelled us, we were told we had to wear a star of David on our clothing. Everybody had to do that if they went outside. You were a marked person basically. And we were also told that we could not attend public schools. . . . I was just starting second grade in the fall of 1939 and after that I didn't have any formal education. I missed most of my elementary school education. We had some secret meetings, some small groups of families that got together and kids, and we had some that you might call "undercover" private home lessons. It was very sketchy and not very well done. The formal education for me stopped when I was seven years old.*

Grunwald related how the situation grew increasingly difficult for his family.

> *We were marked people and we had to wear a star of David. We were now living in a place that was not ours, we were just living to survive somewhere. My dad had to stop practicing medicine because he lost the office and everything was taken away. Shortly after that we heard that the Jews are being transported into a temporary accumulation camp where*

they would bring everybody in and decide what to do with them. . . . And there was a town maybe a couple hours from Prague, an old Czech town. One of those old walled cities. . . . It was called Terezín (Theresienstadt was a façade. It was a "spa town" designed to impress the International Red Cross and the ruse worked and comprised smaller sub-camps, such as Terezín). It was named after Marie Theresa, who was one of the leaders in the kingdom during Hapsburg Empire in Austria. So Terezín was like a walled city where they brought all the Jews . . . that they found in almost any part of Czechoslovakia.

Grunwald was transported with his family to Terezín in mid-July of 1942. At this time, Grunwald did not know about the existence of concentration camps, and he doubted that his parents did either.

Our family was given a notice to be at the railroad station at a specific time. We and about 4,000-5,000 other families. And we were transported with just a couple suitcases, whatever we could grab. . . . They moved us into this walled city and it was locked. It was also the first time that we were really separated from our parents. . . .

The men were separated from the women. And the children were put up in one of the public schools. So they put bunk beds in the various classrooms and those were our living quarters. And Terezín was a tough place. It was not really a concentration camp the way you would imagine. It wasn't as austere. Because you were still living in a city environment. And most of the city was run by Jews. We very seldom saw an SS or German walking around Terezín. . . . There was a limited amount of food, a limited amount of water, there was a limited amount of supplies, clothing and stuff like that, so it was very tough from that standpoint.

Grunwald and his family were held at Terezín for about a year and a half. It was not a terrifying experience, but very limiting. There was some improvised education for the younger children and some free time.

During that year and a half, again we had very, very poor education. We had some educational classroom environment, but very little. . . . I did a lot of drawing and a lot of walking around outside. A lot of drawing and sketching. . . . And we did have some classroom work, perhaps two or three hours in the morning. I think we wasted a lot of time. We did a lot of activities like chorus, singing. . . .

I did see my parents virtually every day, because it was a relatively small town. We played and watched soccer games. We had a fair amount of food, but also when you are young, you don't require a lot of food. That's one of the advantages of being ten or twelve years old, you don't necessarily require the same calories as someone who is thirty-five or forty years old. It was very primitive. We never bought any new clothes. Everything was very minimal, extremely minimal.

And when we were in Terezín we slowly realized that it was only a temporary place. It was a staging area. It was a staging area for people to be transported somewhere else. And we didn't know where that somewhere else was. It was all kept secret. And I remember one of the boys in my room came to me crying one day saying that his grandmother and grandfather were being transported somewhere out of the country, out of Terezín. . . . They were going east and he was very upset and he was crying and he said that his grandmother committed suicide when she heard she was going to be transported out of Terezín.

On December 14th, 1943, the Grunwald family was reunited so that they could be transported from Terezín to Auschwitz on December 15th. Their transport, the first of two December transports, left with 2,504 prisoners. The next transport departed three days later.

We were told to get ready, that we were going to be shipped out by train. So, the whole family and about 2,500 other people were put on the train . . . and we were on the train for two and a half days . . . and we had no clue as to where we were going. We had no idea.

We were in a cattle car for two and a half days and we arrived at night in Auschwitz in Poland on the 17th of December. . . . This was kind of an eerie experience. . . . There were all these big floodlights on this very primitive railroad platform and then you had the SS with the dogs. . . . A lot of shouting, a lot of directions in German: get out, do this, go this way, go that way. Immediately the few suitcases . . . the few personal things we had were all taken away. 'Just, leave your stuff here, leave your suitcases here' and we were directed to walk for about twenty . . . or twenty-five minutes from the railroad station . . . to a completely closed-in by electrical wires camp where they had these huts. These [were] big long huts which might have been fifty, sixty yards long, maybe a couple hundred feet long by thirty feet wide with bunk beds on each side going down the length of the hut. This we found out soon was a family camp. This particular segment that we

> *were in was what the Germans called 'Familien Lager,' . . .*
> *[or] 'family camp.'*

After the war, Grunwald found out this Familien Lager had been set up as a model camp. As with Terezín, this camp was also meant to impress inspectors from the Swiss International Red Cross.

> *We were one of the few thousand people, perhaps six to eight thousand people, that were put in this family camp. Children, middle-aged parents, including grandparents, to prove to the International Red Cross that all Jews are well being taken care of, that nobody's being killed. That the young, as well as the old, and that the families are being kept together, that they're not being separated. . . . The Swiss [must have done] . . . a terrible job, inspecting, because they must have been   blind. . . . There were all these other camps all around us, all these other segments of Auschwitz all around us where people were segregated, where you only saw women, where you only saw men. There were gas chambers a quarter of a mile away from us; there were crematorium a quarter a mile away from us, so these people that came in to inspect must have been totally crazy, totally blind, or they didn't want to see what they didn't want to see because the Germans basically took them into our camp and showed them 'You see how we are treating these people. They are all together, the men, women and children and are all being well taken care of.'*

While most children, elderly men, and women were selected for the gas chambers shortly after arrival, Grunwald's family was spared because of timing.

> *Of [the] 2,500 and another group of 2,500 – total of maybe six or seven thousand, out of the hundreds of thousands that came in, we were saved, only because we came in at the time when they knew that the Swiss were coming in from the International Red Cross and they wanted this exemplary camp to be put together.*

Upon his family's arrival at Auschwitz,

> *My dad and my brother and I are put into this one big hut – big barrack and we are up on the upper bunks trying to keep warm under these military blankets. My mother was in the female part of the same camp. She was not that far away,*

and we could see her during the day. Basically, we had nothing to do. We were just surviving in this barrack, crowded in. We were given one piece of bread about two inches thick and a bowl of soup. That was our daily diet. In the morning we were given a cup of coffee . . . it tasted a little bit like coffee but it was all artificial. Our daily diet was probably about 150-200 calories a day. . . .

About three days after we arrived (and by this time we've got our striped uniforms on) . . . we are true prisoners. We are now officially behind the electrical wire, we are tattooed, we are shaved, we are hungry, we have the striped uniforms on and we are totally stuck. We realize . . . this is it. What's going to happen now? Nobody knows. Now the reality sets in.

Grunwald's Benefactors

It wasn't long before the monotony of camp life set in and Grunwald became bored. He remembered:

So I'm walking around, trying to entertain myself somehow and I walk to the front of this barrack, and in the front [are] a couple of rooms. On each side as you walk in through the main door, there is a room on the right and there is a room on the left – a small room, maybe twelve feet by twelve feet. And I look through the . . . door that's got a glass window in it and I see this young woman. This really pretty woman [is] . . . maybe 22 years old, drawing. She's got an easel and she's doing a sketch of a face, of a person. And with her is a friend of hers, another young lady, and I'm looking through the window, because I'm just so curious about what's going on here . . . there is a work of art being created here. So the young woman sees me looking through the window and she says to me, 'come on in. . . . So I open the door and I go in and there is a little wood stove in there so the place is really comfortable and warm and she's got food and she's got coffee and you know, this young lady is really special. She's got some kind of special connections. So I befriended this woman, whose name is Dina and Dina is an artist. . . . She came to Auschwitz with her mother and her brother in the September transport from Terezín. So she was there since September and now it is December of 1943.

Dina had also come from Prague, where she had studied art. During her three months at Auschwitz she had made "some really interesting connections."

WORLD WAR II

> *She's an artist and she befriends a German prisoner, not a Jew, not an SS, but a prisoner, whose name is Willy Brachman. She and Willy Brachman become very friendly; they become boyfriend and girlfriend. Willy Brachman is from Hamburg, Germany, and he's thrown into prison by the Germans because he did something – some petty crime when he was . . . a young man. They had something on him so they took him to Auschwitz, which was really not the right place for Brachman. . . .*
>
> *So Dina and Brachman have this romantic relationship and Brachman has a lot of power, because he's German, he's not Jewish. And the Germans – the SS make him kind of the overseer of this camp. So he's a prisoner, but because he's German, he certainly has got a lot of power and they give him the responsibility to be in control of this particular family camp. He's like [a] top dog in this family camp. . . . Not only is he a nice guy and a strong personality, [but when] he and Dina meet . . . he realizes that Dina is an artist and he introduces Dina to Dr. Mengele.*

Because Mengele did not have a color camera and he wanted to record the features of "some special prisoners," or Gypsies, he asked Dina to paint color portraits. While she sat painting portraits, it occurred to her that Grunwald could be helpful to her and to Brachman. Grunwald was certainly lucky. There were tasks he could do. If Brachman has

> *got messages he wants to give somebody, if he has things he wants me to bring to someone, if he has information that I need to go and give somebody, he uses me as his messenger. . . . So I am suddenly part of the camp elite. Because suddenly I am shedding my striped uniform, I'm given a pair of really good boots that go up to here* (motions just below knee) *that Willy Brachman was able to get from various places in the camp from people that arrived — there were thousands and thousands of pounds — millions of pounds of clothing that was put away in warehouses and that prisoners that had access to that were able to smuggle into the camp. So if you had the connections, anything was available, even in Auschwitz, if you had the connections. So because Willy Brachman was one of the top dogs among the prisoners, he had the connections, so he got me the beautiful riding pants — wool pants that looked like I would be riding a horse and those boots, and a nice shirt, or jacket or whatever.*

Grunwald remembered his parents were pleased with this opportunity:

They were thrilled because they suddenly realized that I'm not starving anymore and that I'm dressed probably better than anybody else in the camp except for Willy Brachman maybe. And so, suddenly, I'm not a big shot, but I have this privileged position in the camp. . . .

By this time, though, all of the inmates of the Familien Lager knew what was going on at Auschwitz. "We know what's happening because we see various groups of prisoners coming in and . . . they sometimes put them in barracks very close to our barracks . . . but they don't want anybody to communicate with them and they don't want them to communicate with us, but I sneak in there with a couple of other kids at night and I find . . .the Hungarian Jews that just came in the night before. The next day after I sneak back," they have gone to the gas chambers.

Fortunately for Grunwald, Dina was protected because she had an "elite relationship with Brachman and Mengele." Others in Dina's September transport to Auschwitz were "told they were being shipped out to Germany. And we found out that after they were shipped out they were all gassed."

July 6th Medical Inspection

The relative protection of the Familien Lager ended for Grunwald and his family in 1944. He remembered this day with particular clarity:

Suddenly, July 6th of 1944 there is a general call for everybody to go through a medical inspection. And they start sorting us out. . . . We were told there was going to be a selection process, that Mengele wants to see everybody . . . that's 2,500 to 3,000 people that were left in this camp. And I frankly didn't know what was going on. I didn't put it together why we were being medically examined by Mengele and two or three of his assistants. And so we went through the selection. It was very quick. They looked at you and said, 'You go this way' and he may look at someone who is fifteen years old and push him the other way. So what you had basically was a procession of people, ninety percent naked because they wanted to see everybody's bodies because they wanted to make sure nobody was seriously ill or whatever. And he would direct the people that were older than fourteen and healthy one direction. If you were sixty or sixty-five you were in deep trouble with Mengele. So, all the other elderly and super-young, less than fourteen years old were going in one direction and all the healthy ones and middle-aged were saved.

But I did not notice at this point that this is what he's

doing. So, I'm already selected, and I'm standing now among the eight years old and nine years old and the eighty-five year olds. So, I'm on death row but I don't realize it. My brother is also on death row, even though, at this point, he was sixteen. Because my brother was born with a congenital limp (he was born with one leg that was a little bit shorter than the other) and as soon as Mengele realized that this kid is limping, even though he's in good shape and he's healthy, he's out of here. So, my brother and I are both on death row. . . . Suddenly, out of nowhere, comes Willy Brachman. . . . He comes from nowhere and he comes very quickly and just appears. He grabs me and he moves me about ten feet over into the other group of boys fourteen and older and then he disappears.

Grunwald was saved by Brachman's quick intervention.

So, I'm now in the 14-16 year old group of kids and most of them are Czech, they all speak Czech. I know several of them. We get moved out of this camp . . . into another camp, which is now a men's camp. . . . My mother decides to stay with my brother. My mother knows that my brother is stuck. And my mother basically refuses to leave him. So she stays. My father gets moved out, also to another camp, not the same camp where I was. . . . Approximately six days later all the people: my mother, my brother, all the young people, all the eight, nine, ten year olds, all the mothers that stayed behind with their children – they all go to the gas chamber. They're all killed on the 10th of July.

I saw my father later on . . . even though he was in another camp, another section of the camp. . . . I knew that he was totally distraught. . . . He was a wreck, a total wreck. And at that point I suspected . . . I had an idea of what happened. I didn't really want to face it but I already realized that . . . this disaster occurred.

By December of 1943, conditions on the German Eastern Front were deteriorating. Camp authorities decided that it was time to move the remaining older, healthy prisoners closer to Germany – perhaps to work in German factories and to escape the Russians. Rumors of a impending move spread through the camp. Grunwald, who knew his dad was still alive, hoped to see him again before they were separated.

I see him in a group being taken to the railroad station. . . . I was able to find a pair of shoes that I knew would fit my dad and I was able to find an overcoat somewhere. . . . I had a couple packages of cigarettes ready; I had an overcoat, and I had this beautiful pair of shoes. I was ready to throw them over the barbed wire and I see him walking and I . . . threw the coat over, and he got the coat. And I threw one shoe over. It went over and I remember throwing the other shoe and anyway the shoe got stuck up on the wire. (It was not a tragedy. I found out a year later that he had good shoes.) But it haunted me, that shoe, just haunted me. . . .

Labor Camps

Around January 20th, 1944, Frank Grunwald (now twelve years old) and his dad were marched out of Auschwitz some thirty miles distant to the rail station. They were loaded on railcars and sent to different camps. Frank was conveyed across Czechoslovakia to the infamous labor camp at Mauthausen, Austria.

Mauthausen was a "category three" camp, which was designed by the Nazis to work Jewish prisoners to death in the stone quarry. Two other sub-camps for Mauthausen were Melk and Gunskirken, and Grunwald was moved back and forth between these three camps, which were all located in Upper Austria, a short distance from Linz.

We arrived in Mauthausen, which was the camp in Austria on the 23rd of January. So it took us three or four days to get there because we walked for two days and we had another about two days by train. We were in Mauthausen for only about four or five days and from Mauthausen we went by train to another camp which was also in Austria which was called Melk. . . . Mauthausen was frightening because when we arrived in Mauthausen (it's a famous concentration camp), Mauthausen had a stone quarry. Right below the camp was a stone quarry and there were hundreds and hundreds of American prisoners, American Army and Air Force prisoners and British prisoners and French prisoners that died in Mauthausen because of the quarry. The Germans had them working in the quarry and of course they didn't feed them properly and they didn't clothe them properly and they just died working. They killed them just through hard work. So Mauthausen was a real killer of a camp.

Mauthausen was a strange camp because it was up on a mountain and you had to walk these stone steps that were built by the prisoners from the stones in this quarry and these steps just went up, on and on and on and on, [Be]cause we were weak, we didn't have that much to eat and we had trouble going up those steps. And . . . I recall that these were the steps to heaven . . . I could have sworn that there were 250 steps. But I went back to Mauthausen about six years ago, and there are only about sixty steps! And to me, it was like 300 steps! Because for me to go up those sixty steps was absolutely a killer. . . .

Surprisingly, prisoners sometimes became the victims of other prisoners. Grunwald remembered one particular occasion shortly after his arrival at Mauthausen, after he had befriended a "bunch of young kids my age" and two "young Jewish Polish dentists." They must have felt sorry for him because they "kind of took me under their wing." At this time,

we were all standing in line to go to the showers in Mauthausen and it's late in the evening in January and it's freezing out, it's like twenty five degrees outside. We are waiting outside with just our very lightweight clothing and we had prisoners approach us that were already in Mauthausen for maybe several weeks or a couple of months and they said to us 'You're going into the gas chamber - give us your clothing.' So suddenly these two Polish guys that I'm with – these nice guys – one of them starts crying. And I realize why he's crying I realize what these guys just told him, that we're all going to die. I don't particularly take it too seriously at that point and we went into the showers. They were showers; they were not gas chambers and we got out of the showers soaking wet and with very little clothing on us and we went outside again and we finally ended up in some barracks. But some of the guys didn't have any shoes because they gave them away to the guys who were lying to us.

We were in Mauthausen for just a few days and then we were transported to Melk. . . . I remember Melk clearly because looking down from the concentration camp at Melk you could see this beautiful Baroque church. It's a famous church in the city of Melk, and it's gaudy Christian Baroque. . . . I remember looking at this church from the outside, from the camp.

In the 1990's, when Grunwald revisited this region of Austria, he visited Melk Abbey. Memories of the now extant labor camp flooded back to him:

We went there . . . and walked through the church and I thought, 'my God, all this was here while I was starving just about a quarter of a mile away!' To think of the contrasts, between what I had and what was happening here, then I

244

look up, where the camp used to be, and there is nothing there, it was just all wiped out. Just all demolished. We were in Melk, and we did absolutely nothing, we were just basically slowly starving to death. We didn't really have to do a lot of work, we didn't have any activities in any of these camps.

Grunwald stayed at Melk for a couple of months, and then, "because they didn't know where to put us . . . we went to one camp [and] back and forth to another camp." Eventually he returned to Mauthausen, but around April 27th, 1945, he was marched to yet another camp called Gunskirchen, near Rombach.

We were outside of Linz, the Austrian town . . . in a very very small camp outside the village of Gunskirchen. . . . We started walking the 27th and got there around 30th of April . . . and Gunskirchen was an absolute disaster. . . . It was a camp that had no running water; it was in the woods, it was hidden from the main road. We were lucky that anybody would ever find us there after the war. It was a bunch of very primitive huts that the prisoners were living in. I don't know if there were 10,000 prisoners in Gunskirchen or 2,000. I have no idea because everything was so dark and hidden. All we kids (I was twelve at that point) [and] everyone else was either thirteen or fourteen. I was the youngest. What we did was hang together and we said, 'Let's see if we can go in here and stay in one of these huts.' We opened the hut and it's crowded and smelling and there are dead bodies all over the ground, and we said, 'no, we're not going to sleep here.' So we had a bunch of blankets and we made . . . a very primitive tent out of the blankets and we slept outside. . . .

For about three or four days we slept outside and the last couple of days there are no food deliveries. So we typically got a bowl of soup and a piece of bread, very similar to what we got in Auschwitz, only a little bit less in Gunskirchen because we didn't get any coffee in Gunskirchen. It was simply a bowl of soup and a piece German pumpernickel bread, which I recall as being moldy. . . . Your pumpernickel bread was moldy, so if you . . .[hit it], it would turn into dust . . . it was the mold that was flying through the air. . . .

Liberation

In early May of 1945, Upper Austria came under the control of the American forces. On May 4th, Grunwald celebrated the arrival of the 71st Infantry Division in Gunskirchen. Mauthausen was liberated the next day.

Then . . . [by] day number six and day number seven no food [came], nothing. And the last day which may be day number eight we hear very early in the morning – maybe like five in the morning – we hear machine gunfire and really heavy firing, really heavy small arms firing. And the first thing that comes to your mind is, they're shooting the prisoners. Always in any situation you are worried about your own life. . . . You don't think about the war, you are a prisoner [and] you are surrounded by a bunch of German military that are guarding you, so you figure, they must be shooting the prisoners. Well, then there is silence. There is no machine gun fire for a couple minutes, and then maybe half an hour or an hour   later . . . it's [about] seven o'clock in the morning, and I see three or four of these German military that were guarding the camp standing in this clearing. I see them standing and holding a white flag, just a white rag, a sheet or something. And then about three minutes later I see the first American soldier coming. . . .

I could tell — first off, I see these guys holding a white flag. . . . They don't have their guns, nothing, they're just standing there. I knew they were not Germans, they were dressed totally differently from the German soldiers.

With his liberation, Grunwald was naturally euphoric.

I was in heaven. But the first thing we did . . . was attack this little wooded building, no bigger than ten feet by ten feet, and it was filled with red beets. So we go in there and just crash into this building and we grab some of these red beets, which is great because they are mostly sugar and water, so they are easy to digest. And we eat the beets. After that, the GI's guide us down to the main road . . . about 600 yards away . . . and then they want us to walk to the nearest town. We can't walk really, we are too weak to even walk. . . . So they pick us up on military trucks and take us to this town, and then they stop at a German warehouse. And when we look inside the German warehouse there are a bunch of boxes of rice, boxes of sugar, boxes of flour. We can't eat any of that stuff, it has to be cooked. So they give us all this stuff and we can't eat it. So there is not much we can do with it. So they take us by truck to the nearest town, the name of the town was Wels.

An American hospital was established in Wels. Here Grunwald and many other former camp inmates spent time as they recovered their strength and waited for transportation back to their homelands.

As luck would have it, though, Grunwald's father had also survived the camps and was liberated by the Americans. Upon liberation, he assisted the American doctors and served as a translator for them. The Americans showed their gratitude by loaning him a car (which they had confiscated from a German) so that the senior Grunwald could return to Prague to search for Frank. In Prague, he located some recently repatriated Mauthausen prisoners who told him where to find his son. Frank vividly remembered how they reunited:

> *My dad and the rest of us in the family had sort of a standard signal — [a] whistle. . . . And so I'm on the second floor in the school talking to one of my friends. And suddenly I hear this whistle, I look up and right away I know it's my dad. . . . So we meet and hug and everything, within a half an hour . . . I'm out of there. We are in the car and we are driving back to Prague. So all the way to Prague, we get over the Austrian border and we go into Czechoslovakia, we are hungry so we stop in a little country farmhouse. It's like ten o'clock in the morning, because we left early . . . that day. We walk into this farmhouse and my dad . . . say[s] to this woman, 'can you give us some breakfast? We haven't had anything to eat.' So she makes about fifty scrambled eggs, and you know it's the first time I've had scrambled eggs in about three years. So we just feast on these scrambled eggs and just three hours later we are in Prague. . . .*
>
> *We could not move into our apartment right away. I don't know who was living there at that point . . . so we stayed with our maid. This is our maid who has been in our family for forty years. This is a woman that came to work for my grandparents, for my mother's parents and who helped bring up my mother. She was a Czech orphan and my grandparents took her in. She became really part of the family, so now she knows everybody is gone, except for my father and me. So she says, 'Well, you live with me.' She was living on the second floor of a private home outside of Prague in a very nice apartment. So we stayed there for about three or four months, and it took us that long to get our property back, our apartment back, and find some furniture to put into the apartment. And that summer we moved back into the apartment. So that's the story.*

Fellow Auschwitz prisoners Willy Brachman and Dina also survived the war. Dina was repatriated, along with her mother, back to Prague and Willy Brachman returned to Germany. Although Dina's connection to

World War II

Brachman was lost, a mutual friend helped Grunwald reconnect with Dina many years later in the United States. Grunwald regretted, though, that he was never able to get in touch with Brachman in order to thank him for saving his life.

Although almost sixty years have passed, Grunwald does not believe that he can ever forgive the Germans for what they did. "I still feel angry that people could be so cruel to destroy other people," and yet, "I don't think I would want to hurt them." Survival was possible for Grunwald because of some extraordinarily good luck and because of his inner strength, which could be attributed to his family upbringing. When the anti-Jewish persecution became heinous, "we were told to keep our chin up and retain our pride and confidence, be positive and no matter what happens, retain our dignity. And we'll get through this the best way we know how. That was the philosophy."

Private Stanley J. Fleszar
806th Tank Destroyer Battalion and
G.F.R.S. Replacement Pool, France

Letters remain the essential link between civilians on the home front and soldiers far away on the battlefield or a the prison camp. This was particularly true during World War II when others forms of communication were costly or non-existent. If a soldier does not receive letters, his morale and fighting effectiveness becomes a problem. Similarly, loved ones at home become anxious if they hear no news.

Stanley Fleszar was deployed to England near the end of 1943, and following additional training in a tank destroyer battalion, he moved over to northeastern France in November of 1944.

Although there is only one extant letter for Stanley Fleszar, what he includes in that letter to his sweetheart, Dora Lee King, speaks for all lonely soldiers.

Private Stanley J. Feszar.
(Courtesy of Patricia Bozek)

Dear Sweetheart:
Ain't you got no paper?
Ain't you got no pen?
Ain't you no envelope
To put my letter in?
Has ya lost my address?
Lost me letters too?
Don't you know I'm wondering
Why I ain't heard from you?
Is ya mad or somethin'?
Or maybe . . . digging a well?
Is ya gonna write tonight?
Ya is? Gee, that's swell!

WORLD WAR II

END NOTES

[1] The Mulde River was tributary of the Elbe River in east central Germany.

[2] Trierweiler's family and military history is based on an interview completed with him by a family member, Dionne Wilson, in 1987. The interview is in the possession of the family.

[3] Trierweiler interview, 1987.

[4] Trierweiler interview, 1987.

[5] The weather cleared miraculously on Christmas day. This was the first opportunity that allowed the Air Force to fly bombing missions in order to help the beleaguered American forces on the ground. They targeted primarily German connection lines and electrical lines.

[6] Mauthausen, by mid-April, was in a state of chaos because of the influx of thousands of additional prisoners who had been hastily brought from other German camps as the Germans attempted to move their slave labor away from the invading Russian army.

Korean War

THE KOREAN WAR, beginning in 1950 and lasting until 1953, was the attempt of the United Nations, working with the United States, to repel the invading North Korean Communists from democratic South Korea. The North Koreans invaded on June 25th, 1950, and soon after, two UN resolutions were passed supporting the use of force to "restore the international peace and security in the area." On June 27th, President Truman authorized the use of United States troops in South Korea. General MacArthur was the unified commander. Although the war eventually ended in a stalemate, the progress of the Communist advance was stopped at the 38th parallel. More than 34,000 Americans were killed and more than 103,000 were wounded. The total casualties on all sides equaled almost one million.

Two who served in this "military police action" were Dr. Bruce Meyer in 1951 and Murray Freed in the infantry in 1952.

⬧

LIEUTENANT (JG) LEO BRUCE MEYER
FIRST M.A.S.H., X CORPS, US EIGHTH ARMY

Dr. Bruce Meyer and his wife, Marjorie, were residing in California, when Meyer was called to serve. He was assigned to the 1st M.A.S.H. or 1st Mobile Army Surgical Hospital as their orthopedic specialist. The Korean conflict was already seven months old when Meyer arrived at the 8th Army Headquarters in Pusan, in southeastern Korea. First impressions were not good. Pusan was "a real hell hole – dirty and much civilian confusion." Meyer's final destination via Taegue, was Andong. The 1st M.A.S.H. had been established there a few months earlier.[1]

The majority of his personal letters were addressed to his wife, whom he often called 'Peety.' His numerous letters give insights into the life of soldiers serving in remote areas, often close to the danger of the front lines. Doctors and nurses in frontline M.A.S.H. units were considered "combat" personnel. As such, they fulfilled the typical year's service in only six, yet interminable months. For Meyer, this was the experience of a lifetime. He welcomed it as a way to gain medical experience, but as this hard existence persisted, he became more and more anxious to get home.

KOREAN WAR

[Pusan]
January 16, 1951
Dear Peety, . . .
I ended the letter abruptly last night expecting our train as poor as it is to leave but we sat in the station all   night. . . . About midnight a trainload of N. Korean prisoners pulled in next to us. What a howling mob that was. Most had practically no clothes & the temp at least 30°. A few obviously hadn't survived the train ride. They were all herded by S. Korean soldiers to a prison camp nearby. . . . Our train consists of about 500 troops headed for Taegu & our boxcar full of officers. The army's inefficiency at this point amazes me. Have seen navy personnel here & in Sasebo & certainly envy them. Boarded the hospital ship REPOSE docked here in the harbor & they sure lead a different existence. Our experiences last night were an eye opener & we are still in Pusan. . . . Though conditions will prob[ably] get worse the further away from Pusan we get I personally think it will be easier at least for me to do with less. Food seems pretty good – better than I expected esp[ecially] with "C" rations. . . .

Finally, after countless delays, Meyer's train departed. There were 600 troops aboard, with about fifty to sixty men per car. Meyer was able to sweet-talk the train commander into letting him share the commander's compartment, where he found a soft cot warmed by a pot-bellied stove.

[en route to Andong, Korea]
January 22, 1951
On leaving Pusan yesterday the weather was blowing a gale and freezing. Was beautifully clear though and have put some kodachrome in my camera for the countryside. For part of the trip we traveled along the east coast in full moonlight. . . . It was quite pretty with little thatched-roof fishing villages on the shore. Today the countryside consists of dry barren hills. . . . There are very few trees, mostly pine higher up on the ridges. In the valleys are villages surrounded by dry rice paddies. They are very primitive, made of mud and straw. Lots of children around too. Surprisingly enough there are many apple orchards about too. Any water about is frozen solid. There are many ice cycles on the train, so you can see it's cold. That army sleeping bag is really warm, what with it being down (duck) with a canvas cover and an Army blanket liner. Am going to guard it with my life.
Oh yes, we have a little Korean house boy in this car to clean up, make coffee and do the chores. Never had it so good!

252

KOREAN WAR

. . . During the night we unloaded soldiers long the way and picked up a few. We're heading for the end of the line today. Here is a map:

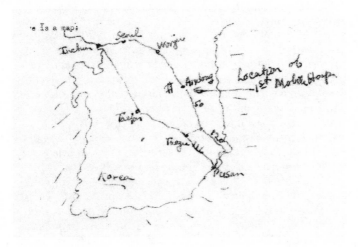

. . . Most of the boys over here are anxious to get home and feel we're wasting our time in this no good country. They are always anxious to get news which is something like a luxury. They say there are lots of refugees on the roads further north but we haven't seen any yet except the many in Pusan. . . .

As Meyer's train neared Andong, he disembarked with his gear.

[Andong, Korea]
January 21 or 22, 1951
. . . Here at last with the 1st Mobile Army Surg. Hosp. (1st M.A.S.H.). . . . As our train pulled into a siding some 5 miles out of Andong I noticed a group of tents & ambulances on some high ground beside some rice paddies the whole little valley surrounded by a high ridge. I hollered to the group & asked what unit it was & sure enough it was the 1st M.A.S.H. & so I piled off the train into the rice paddie & lugged my stuff into camp sierra club style. Hence I got in at 3 PM instead of probably at 8 tonight. Met the commanding officer, was shown around & have recently gotten settled. As I mentioned before I hadn't met many acquaintances here in Korea yet. Well I made up for it here. Bill Crepps who I

interned with was here & in addition were <u>two</u> boys with whom I went to Columbia with John Wilsey & Bill Scott. Apparently Crepps had asked Scott about me some time ago & little did they think I would be with them here. You see it's been quite a reunion. I woke Crepps up from sleep today & he was quite surprised needless to say, see he has a fox hole under his cot & here apparently is a little Gorilla activity in these parts but our unit has a pretty good guard. The nights are clear & moonlight is full. You can visualize the set up here perfectly as it is practically just like the Sierra Club – tents, sleeping bags, chow out of mess kits & cups, some time of lavatory & living out of field packs & dufflebag. . . .

Medically the hosp has about 140 beds, & is now treating med. cases as well as surg. ones. There are about 16 nurses & 14 medics with about 100 corpsmen. Surg. is emergency type & primary treatment cleaning up wounds & casting fractures, no elective stuff or corrective, plenty of ortho[pedic] which I will prob[ably] do most of since I'm the <u>orthopedist</u> in the group. Have a portable X-ray unit, generator plant, water supply, surgery, laboratory & is quite well equipped. Evacuation is by helicopter & fortunately in this spot by train. Pts [patients] don't usually remain more than 3 days. Lots of stuff comes thru including Prisoners of War. . . .

<u>Addendum</u>: This unit is apparently one of the first of its kind. They have seen & done lots of surg. so far. I expect to learn quite a bit I guess. Save this letter and see if I feel as eager in a few months. Will gather more history of the unit & put you up on it later.

January 23, 1951

The first day on the job – did quite a bit of surgery on gunshot wounds. Get a number of pts daily & lots from Guerilla activity. Because of that we are moving to a more secure location tomorrow. At present we're out in the hills all by ourselves. Tis much prettier out here whereas in town its quite dirty. Moving day tomorrow means up at 5 A.M. Our move, however, is only 4 miles.

January 24, 1951

. . . We moved from our last location to a school here in Andong. Of course its much dirtier but its safer. We really were sitting ducks with all the Guerillas around. It's amazing no one bothered us. Some South Korean soldiers guarded us & the marines came out a couple of times but I understand they drew straws. We were in a little draw surrounded by hills. . . .

Last night slept in a barn. No water, windy & cold. We final-
ly managed to get a tent tonight. It seems med. officers here,
theoretically the most important part of the unit come last.
Have found out there are some "8" balls around realize more
than there is the <u>Army way</u> & the <u>Right Way</u>. Surgery booms
daily. There are lots of gunshot wounds, many of which are
self inflicted surprising enough. Have been doing a fair
amount of surgery. . . .

January 28, 1951
. . . Just finished spraying the tent, sleeping bag, clothes
with DDT powder! Heard that the Chinese are having an epi-
demic of Typhus. . . .

January 29, 1951
. . . We're supposed to move again one of these days fur-
ther north about 50 or 60 miles. It's kind of a mess moving,
but more to see. It seems you just get settled, a few boxes
around your bed to call home & eat off of & we're on the dusty
road again. Can't figure this war out yet. . . .

On the last day in January, Bruce Meyer wrote to his father:

January 31, 1951
. . . We're intended to be a 60 bed mobile surg. hosp. but
now operate 200 beds & take medical cases as well. The lat-
ter is made up of pneumonias & frost bites primarily. The sur-
gery is practically all orthopedics with gun shot wounds &
fractures & I'm the chief of Orthopedics so needless to say
have plenty to do. Am happy though to be doing my special-
ty. . . .
We move quite often & tomorrow we're slated for anoth-
er, further north near Wonju to support the 7ᵗʰ Division.
I can't say that I dislike this sort of life, but would rather
be doing it in the Sierras. . . .

Chechon, Korea
February 4, 1951
. . . We have moved from Andong, about 90 miles fur-
ther north & since our new location we've been pretty darn
busy. Got 6 hrs sleep out of 48 but managed to sleep in all
day today. It seems that every time this unit gets a shower set
up or candy & cigarette rations we move. The ride up here was
over a winding mountain dirt road not unlike our trip viz New
Mexico. And in fact the country was very much the same.

Crossed a mountain range & now the mountains are higher around us & snow covered. In fact there is snow on the ground around us now and of course it's much colder too. Riding up in the back of us & ambulance was dusty & unfortunately I managed to get a little car sick. Most of the towns we passed were burned to the ground & some were still burning as we passed. Had the hospital come up one day & the rest 2 days later. There must have been about 30 trucks in our convoy. The towns here have been completely evacuated of all Koreans. Lots of the troops are living in the crude Korean houses, but we have pretty much of a tent village except for surgery which is in a bank building.

We have now acquired 4 helicopters & they have been landing in front to evacuate the more serious cases.

We're located in a valley now. The mountains are very pretty with the snow. The rumor is . . . that we're to move again – this time to Wonju. . . .

You would laugh if you could see me. I have an "empire" all of my own. Have a box fixed up as a table next to my bunk, a platform to set my duffle on, & a rope to hang stuff. We've really got it made. Ah yes, what a life. . . .

February 7, 1951

. . . A few of the fellows went up to Wonju today to see about a location for our hospital when we make the next move, which will probably be soon. It is another 30 miles up to the line.

We received a few patients last night who had been prisoners of the North Koreans and were released because of their wounds and inability to keep up. They seem to have been treated pretty well and apparently did not suffer. They said the Koreans expect to push us out by the end of the month. Sure can't figure them out. . . .

Here is another bit of every day life in Korea – a conscientious soldier DDTing himself instead of using a bath·powder or even taking a bath. I'm getting quite used to mine out of my helmet. . . .

"Operation Roundup" began on February 3rd, 1951, when the I and X Corps, United Nations and Republic of Korea forces moved north from Wonju. What they did not anticipate was a massive infiltration and attack by the Chinese forces moving south on February 11th.

The Chinese objective was Wonju, where five important roads intersected. Wonju was centrally located in a valley at the east-west geographical center of Korea. It was about thirty miles north of Chechon, where the 1st M.A.S.H. was located. The Chinese utilized Mao's principles of warfare: strike at night, strike while the enemy is moving, and use encirclement and massive force, etc. The end result was an enormous battle, planned by the Chinese and unanticipated by the Americans.[2]

February 11, 1951

. . . I was about to mail that little box of film back to you today and was writing a note when all <u>hell</u> broke lose. An ammunition dump about a quarter of a mile away exploded. The concussion was something. When we realized what had happened we looked outside and saw a huge cloud billowing into the sky. It wasn't long before ambulance loads were dispatched and pts arrived, one with his whole lower jaw blown off. We rushed him into surgery and had begun working when a second and even larger explosion occurred, this time breaking all the windows in surgery and practically knocking the pt. off the table. I was just starting a transfusion on him at the time. From then on, 4 o'clock to now about 9 P.M. things began to pop with a continuous din of exploding shells. Every now an then you could hear one pass overhead. Small shell fragments occ. hit the tents. Also a dud mortar shell landed next to our generator. After dark the sky was lit by fires and exploding flares and shells a sight almost equal to the fourth of July display in Oakland. Our ambulance crews were near the amo train when the second blast occurred and the men were knocked out of the trucks but none seriously hurt. Of course we had quite an influx of pts from the blast area and there are more no doubt who are still in the area that are not able to be reached. No one knows how it all started.

Some of the men did heroic jobs in getting a few of the amo trains out of the immediate area. Things have quieted down now. About an hour before it all happened the hospital had been ordered to pack up to move to Wonju. We had evacuated all our remaining patients and had actually packed some of the quip[ment] when the mass came in. Needless to say there was some confusion in getting things running but all the serious ones were separated and minor injuries taken care of afterward. Some fun.

Apparently we are going to move one of these days up to Wonju. Don't know whether it will be any better as far as setting up a hospital but it will be closer to the front and I think evacuation will be easier, esp. by air. There is a C-47 strip there. . . .

Meyer soon realized that there was a massive battle occurring just to the north. The defense of the Wonju line began on February 13th and lasted until the 18th. Casualties started coming in soon, and when the final casualty numbers for the battle of Wonju were calculated, UN and US forces had approximately 2,000 casualties, and the ROK had 9,800.[3]

February 14, 1951

. . . *At the present time the receiving tent is empty. Hope it keeps that way for another 12 hrs at least. Most of the boys of last night siege will do pretty well. Some of the elbow injuries will have to have their elbows frozen in one position though their bones are shattered so. The fighting still seems to be going on up ahead, about 25 miles, but between somewhere there a roadblock by the Chinese which means the patients are being evacuated another way. I suppose that is the reason for the lull now. This apparently has been the most number of cases that the 1st M.A.S.H. has had since they have been over here. Actually for that number of casualties we need a lot more help, especially in surgery.*

Blood certainly makes the difference between life and death for most of these boys. When you realize that all of the blood over here is type "O" which is given so that in emergencies it doesn't have to be typed or crossed with the patients. People with "O" are called universal donors – can give to anyone. When they are injured a litter bearer has to crawl out to get him and drag him back to an ambulance or jeep, dress his wounds, then there is a delay because of enemy fire, and a long rough motor ride back to the clearing station and then back to a mobile hospital like ours for emergency surgery. Usually that takes at least 18 hours, sometimes 3 or 4 days. Most of them don't get anything to eat during that time because they are always expected to have surgery and no one knows when or it isn't possible. That together with pain and bleeding one can realize the shock they suffer the treatment for which in these cases of war wounds most surely is blood. It is excellent treatment in the cases of infection which invariably set in after a day or so waiting to get evacuated. After seeing some of these wounds and being amazed how good shape they are in under the circumstances I know the difference in the blood they get in the forward stations. I guess many people don't realize it but lots of blood is being used and needed.

. . . *Our daily routine is pretty much the same every day. The hours are very irregular though. When there is work you work, when you sleep you sleep, night or day. I haven't changed my underwear since I got here. Getting pretty well* acquainted with them by now. . . .

February 16, 1951
4:30 A.M.
Once again I am keeping late hours and have a few minutes to get off a letter to you . . . Needless to say have been busy. It seems that when the U.N. is on the offensive we're busy. I started at the job Wednesday morning and it is now Friday morning with three hours sleep. Surprising enough I don't feel half bad. Last

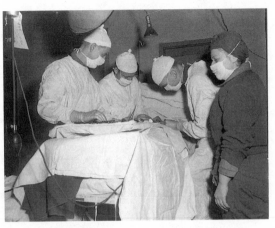

Frontline operation: Medical corps team of First Mobile Hospital, X Corps, Korea, performs frontline operation on battle-wounded soldier. (L-R) CPL Bob Crain, surgical technician; Lt. (jg) Bruce Meyer, Navy Surgeon; Capt. John J. Wilsey, Surgeon, and Lt. Marie Smarz, Army Nurse Corps, February 14, 1951. (National Archives)

night was another of those that tear your heart out. Saw some mighty pitiful sights. Apparently from the news broadcasts the UN can claim a victory from the fighting up around Wonju. Hope so as we had to pay for it. . . .

February 16, 1951
. . . Managed to get some sleep today do my washing clothes etc. It's nice to get a fresh start on life. I'm on the night shift now 8 to 8. When it's quiet I get some sleep or reading done. Another addition to the outfit was an officers' mess today – real tables with a cloth on them and service. Have almost forgotten what it's like to have such comfort. Needless to say it makes a meal after working much more enjoyable.

No incoming mail today. That term over here usually means enemy artillery fire. Out going mail is the other way around. Our artillery has been pounding them out since dark. Sounds like thunder off in the distance. It is cold tonight too. The wind howled today and old man weather tried to have it snow a little. I just walked over to the surgery and smelled fried chicken – quite a treat for these parts. Had some and it was delicious. . . .

After the siege of the past three days one can really appreciate what those poor kids have to go thru. I don't envy them at all. . . .

February 18 , 1951

. . . Got a batch of prisoners of war in tonight for treatment. Most of them we evacuate down the line to Pusan. There is enough to do here without taking up time for them. Of course if there are emergency measures we give it. . . .

The defense of the Wonju line ended on February 18th and on the 20th, Gen. Matthew Ridgway began the counteroffensive, "Operation Killer," which was intended to deny the Chinese an opportunity for new attacks.[4]

February 21, 1951

. . . Has been a good day in more ways than one as hit it hard again. Am at the end of another stretch for some time without sleep and just can't wait to hit the sack. We were lucky tonight and it is all quiet on the eastern front. You can tell from the misspelled words that I'm not doing to well. Wanted to stay up to catch the 12 o'clock news but the radio isn't working. . . .

This experience here is something terrific but I sure wouldn't want to go thru it again. Well, dearest, I had better get of to bed before I drop. Some 30 hours is kind of long. Stopped by the chow tent: fried chicken & cherry pie good! good! good!

February 22, 1951

. . . Am standing waiting for the next case to start so will take the time to bat out a letter [on a typewriter] *to you. Outside the rain is coming down in buckets and has been all day. You can imagine the roads and paths with six inches of mud, puddles in the tents with small streams running through them. None of the tents had ditches dug around them hence crews were in the rain tonight digging. . . . Went over to the chow in the mess tent a little while ago and there were six inches of water standing on the floor. Had a steak though so was worth standing in it. . . .*

Seems that all the business we are having tonight is self-inflicted wounds. That is the way it goes – after a big battle – lots of the boys seem to get cold feet. Of course they are all called accidental – all gunshot wounds of the feet or toes. . . . Oh yes, our liquor ration arrived yesterday. Each one of us in the tent, 10, now has about three bottles of whisky.

Should have a good party one of these days or nights. The only trouble is I am on night duty.

Meyer's next letter indicates his growing appreciation for his M.A.S.H. experience:

February 23, 1951
4:00 A.M.

. . . This experience is worth its weight in gold though it is nothing anybody likes. I have seen more traumatic surgery already than I could otherwise see my entire life. During that battle for Wonju and Chechon the casualties just piled in here. It was a matter of running around from one to another getting people out of shock with blood transfusion after another. I couldn't have gotten this experience in the Navy. You just don't see it there in such great numbers. . . .

All of our supplies are coming into us by air. Daily a half dozen flying boxcars (C-19) come over, circle, and then come in low and like laying an egg out of their open rear end are dropped the supplies with parachutes. They fly over at 1000 feet. Been getting lots of fresh meat and chicken. Also have had eggs every morning for breakfast. I have had no less than four each meal. We have been in Chechon some time now and are getting quite well set up. Kind of expect we will be here a while longer too.

The big rain seems to be over now. It left the place a sea of mud though. Things are pretty well in control again what with the aid of sand and gravel from the creek bed. . . .

February 25, 1951

As usual we have been going full blast right around the clock. It seems when you are the only hosp behind some 60,000 men on the offensive you can't be anything else. Just can't seem to get ahead. We're supposed to take care of prisoners too but so far we just let them wait until after the G.I.'s but of course there is no end to the G.I.'s. Was happy to receive some help today – a British doctor, & another medic from one of the charming companies in town that made four working today & then there are three on our shift tonight. In addition to the British there is a Dutch & French med[ical] unit in town now. Of course they aren't operating as med unit though.

February 26, 1951
9:00 A.M.

Another onslaught last night. Now have 350 patients

theoretically should have 60. Did 22 in surg. last night. Off to bed. . . .

March 3, 1951 [first letter]

. . . General Ridgway of the 8th Army and Gen Arnold of the Tenth Corps were here yesterday to present a Bronze Star to one of the nurses. She apparently made coffee in a pea can during an ambush or something. At any rate she is another one of the lame brains in the unit and it is kind of sickening to think she got a citation like that when all the boys in the front have to about let themselves get killed for nothing. Did you see the article in Time a couple of weeks ago (19th) about the Silver stars and Bronze stars passed out during the Korean War for nothing? This is another example, only worse. . . .

March 3, 1951 [second letter]

. . . I think I mentioned that spring was in the air in my last letter. Was all a mistake. For the past two days it has been cold as you know what. Crack an egg and before it hits the pan it is frozen. It must be below zero. There is ice inside of the tent and my corner is right on the open tear so the wind just howls in. . . .

March 8, 1951

. . . The day before last we didn't do much until about 5 in the evening & then I started on probably one of the biggest casts I've done so far – a laminectomy. A chap was shot through the spine severing part of the cord. Since it's orthopedic & neuro surgery I got the job. Had to expose his cord & cut away the cord fragments imbedded in the spinal cord. Bob Cordell worked with me & it took us until about 2 A.M. to finish – some 6 hrs. The chap did pretty well & we sent him on down the line today.

Yesterday after a late start did only a few cases & then tried to get a shower but when we arrived at the unit the dern thing didn't work & so not it's been 6 wks since I've had a shower & probably will be much longer. In the evening, Charlie Reimers, from Philadelphia, Bob Cordell from Baltimore and I decided we should have a party since we missed each the two nights previously. It started out kind of slow but by midnight it was a knock-out drag-out affair. I sure enjoyed my beer & Canadian Club chaser – the first I've had since being here & needless to say have felt very unstable today. Was lots of fun though. Fortunately we got the chief nurse in on it as today the Col. wanted to know the reason for so much noise during the wee hours. He couldn't quite read the riot act to her as the party was held in her "office."

March 9, 1951

. . . Another new addition to our officers' mess was made today – a larger tent. Probably will be used for parties & as a rec[reation] hall. With all the tents they have put up around here would think we were going to stay permanently. Acquired 4 helicopters today also. Maybe they will make up for our not moving as they can get the pts down pretty quickly. . . .

March 11, 1951

. . . Almost had another laminectomy to do today but

Helicopter pilot prepares to take off for the 1st Mobile Army Surgical Hospital, Chechon, Korea, with the wounded men enclosed in the stretcher attached on the right side, March 10, 1951. [This was after the battle of Wonju, during "Operation Killer".] (National Archives)

managed to get the patient out by helicopter instead. We have four of the humming birds with us now. Yesterday they flew over to get a shower in the dern things. Actually with the roads as muddy as they are it is much safer in the air. Will have to take a ride in one of them one of these days.

KOREAN WAR

March 13, 1951
    . . . Tomorrow may be able to get off in a helicopter to see the countryside from the air. I still think we're going to move soon. . . .

    From the news our boys up ahead haven't made contact with the Chinese yet. I wonder what we're going to do when we reach the 38th this time. Prob[ably] make it in a few days. . . .

[Chechon]
March 15, 1951
    . . . Yes, we are still in Chechon, and don't know when or if we will ever move. It seems the 8th Army wants us here and the 7th Division wants us up ahead. Who knows, we don't.

    There is something very frustrating about sitting here day after day. One wants to get up and to go but there isn't any place to go. You don't dare go wandering around in the hills very much and we haven't got much to do around these parts. Mind you I haven't begun to complain about the let up in business yet and am still enjoying it. We get up late and just putter around. Spend some time in the mess hall. Also have a cocktail hour before dinner. . . .

March 18, 1951
    . . . We really have an <u>empire</u> now. All of us got up this A.M. & finally decided to do something about our tent. We got hold of the outside detail – a sergeant & about 15 koreans - & a <u>new tent</u>. Down came the old torn one, the ground was leveled & all the dern rocks scraped away. After the new one went up it was stitched around the sides to keep water out & then below and then believe it or not we layed a floor of <u>bricks</u>. What with the idea of being here a while we went all out. It's about time after 6 weeks in a pig pen. We even have the inside arranged so we've got more room. . . .

    Heard a nice complement today. The 10th Sta[tion] Hosp in Pusan said that of all the M.A.S.H. hosp in Korea the work they get from us is the best. . . .

    I guess people have to have something to talk about & let their imagination & subconscious desires get away from them. Anyway since the 1st M.A.S.H. is really the original of its kind & a relatively young organization, the rumor is that we are going to be sent to Europe with the other troops. That's an example of how screwy rumors get around. . . .

Korean War

March 19, 1951

 . . . *The news wasn't too encouraging this eve. MacArthur thinks we ought to cross the 38ᵗʰ & the 10 P.M. news reported enemy contact on center & east front. Maybe we'll be <u>busy</u> again soon. I think though that we're going to stay in Chechon a while. . . .*

March 21, 1951

 . . . *Took a walk over to the Xth Corps headquarters after lunch. The place is really <u>ultra</u> <u>ultra</u>. All their tents are lined up perfectly. They have three large white flag poles & believe it or not, 2 new Chevrolet sedans. Those are the first cars I've seen in a long time & here in Chechon. They have a small airstrip with a few L-5's & a couple of avions for the generals. There is plenty of brass around there. . . . Was all set to go up to Wonju in the helocopter but Col. Dubay decided not to go so I had to drop out again. . . .*

Lots of troops have moved into town now since our arrival 7 weeks ago & the place has changed quite a bit. There are many tents & new developments. . . .

March 22, 1951

 . . . *Just going to start a letter before the eve mail arrives & I go to another movie. Spent a quiet day making a few consults & playing bridge. We have developed the practice of cocktail hour at 4:30 before dinner now. All the goodies you send come in real handy – cheese, salami, tuna fish, sardines, etc. The <u>orange juice</u> we use concentrated as a mix for an orange blossom cocktail. Works very well. The cheese crackers & plain one all good too. . . . Have been listening to the short wave on Cordell's radio & getting far away places like Hawaii, L.A., N.Y., Australia, Scotland, England, China, Russia, Philippines & Japan. . . .*

March 25, 1951

 . . . *Here it is Easter Sunday, raining and me with very little to do. Got up this morning, did an amputation of a prisoner's arm and then went to church. Was held on Chapel Hill down by the rail terminal. . . . The pulpit was draped with a red parachute used to drop off supplies from these flying boxcars. After church, baked ham for lunch and this afternoon reading and writing. Yes, it has been raining since early this morning without letup and of course the ground is a sea of mud. . . .*

Can't you see us sitting or lying on the cots in our test

with the rain drops pattering on the roof, a five gallon can of laundry boiling on the stove, and the purr of the generator outside. Every-now-and then someone gets up, goes outside to the john to break the usual run of things. The movie tonight is a picture we saw together <u>All the Kings Men</u>. I don't know whether I will get up enough ambition to go to it or not. I hear we have a couple of more P.O.W's coming in with fractured femurs. Of course these are all dirty wounds and I guess we will have to take care of them. Some of our G.I.'s can't understand why they have to lie in the same ward with these prisoners who get the same care as they do. Here they are sleeping in the same tent with those they were shooting at and those who were killing their buddies. I guess you can't blame them a bit though for their feelings. . . .

March 26, 1951

. . . Today makes 6 mo in Korea for most of these guys & so a party is in the making. I'm on surg call tonight so shall be a good boy. . . .

March 28, 1951

. . . Had one of the Koreans give me a haircut today – not bad – at least it's out of my ears.

We have been playing records from "South Pacific" all day. You would think you were in the States on a Sunday afternoon the way you can hear the music coming over the camp. . . .

They have set up a rotation plan now giving 2 points/month for combat troops & 1 points/mo for others. One needs 12 points to get back to the states. Fortunately a M.A.S.H. is considered <u>combat</u> so that should mean 6 mo. Practically everyone in the unit is eligible but there is no word when the business will start. . . .

April 2, 1951

. . . A couple of days ago I went thru the surgery log book and copied out all the cases I have done. It amounted to 193. . . . About 150 of them were done in Feb. though as we haven't been very busy since then. I hope it don't get busy either. I have seen all of that stuff that I want to. . . .

April 3, 1951

. . . Haven't done much the past few days but we keep expecting more to happen. At least though there is no contact with the enemy. The radio claims a large accumulation of

troops north of the 38ᵗʰ. The weather has changed enough
now so am wearing summer fatigues. It's not very warm yet
but does get a little humid when it rains. . . .

On April 5ᵗʰ, Meyer expected to have to rough it again soon – after
all, "we ought to earn those 2 points a month" as "combat troops." In
addition, Meyers mentioned the repercussions for MacArthur, who had
created a hornet's nest when he crossed the Yalu River.

April 10, 1951

. . . Rumors have it that we move in about a week.
Supposed to be another party tonight for our departing nurses
too, Gad! Had a bit of excitement last night when someone
tossed a hand grenade in the area – no one was hurt though.
Apparently they caught 4 fellows A.W.O.L. from their units
since Feb. . . .

April 11, 1951

. . . What did you think of the news today – Truman's
relieving MacArthur? Ridgeway is a good man & he sure will
take the bull by the horns too. I think Mac was dealt a low
blow though. I imagine he will retire now – He should. Britain
will be happy about it. Wonder if Mac will stay in the Far
East or maybe become ambassador to Japan.
We still stay in Chechon — ? ? ? . . . The Chinese are
being pushed back slowly but no real push has occurred. . . .
We have an improvement in our movie tent, too. New
benches, sand on the floor for dryness & warmth & the seats
are on an incline so more in the back can see without stretch-
ing their necks. Before you would get trench foot just watch-
ing the movie.
There hasn't been much business these days. In fact I just
have two patients on the ward now – a cut finger (infected) &
a chap with vague shoulder pain. . . .

April 16, 1951

. . . As you can see I am still in the fair city of Chechon,
or what' left of it. At the present though we are really rear ech-
elon & have been for a few weeks. We are apparently being
held in reserve until our namesake town Chechon is cleared
out for us. The inactivity of late March and April has been
wonderful & as far as we are concerned would be happy to
just sit here & bask in the sun daily. . . .
The 2ⁿᵈ M.A.S.H. has just arrived & we have had an
opportunity to get acquainted with their nurses as they were

*with us a few days awaiting the arrival of their doctors &
men. Rotation has begun – some of our nurses have left
already. We hear that a few doctors also are on the way. Tis
good news. . . .*

*What do you think of the MacArthur deal? His arrival in
the States & Congress should be interesting. . . .*

April 17, 1951

*. . . Signs are becoming evident that we shall move soon
– maybe a week or so. The Col wants to scout a site today &
a few of our excess tents are being taken down. . . . At least a
move will make the time pass faster. Heck, May is practically here, and by the end of May I am look[ing] for my
orders. . . .*

*An advance party left yesterday to scout out a new loca-
tion for us so maybe we'll be on our way again soon. . . . Has
given us an advantage to get lots of supplies north over the <u>dry</u>
roads before the rain. There are no railroads beyond Chechon
yet. I think also [—-?] has postponed the expected Chinese
offensive. They have also done quite a bit of work on the
roads & bridges. Ridgway is moving ahead slowly & always
securing the rear so we don't get too far ahead of ourselves.
We have lots of foxholes dug around now for possible air
raids. . . .*

April 20, 1951

*. . . Just listened to MacArthur's speech before Congress.
Reminded me of the famous one that Churchill made. He
really put it over dramatically and eloquently. I do feel that
the principles on which Truman acted are right though. The
matter might have been handled diff[erntly] by having a
joint staff conf[erence] instead of relieving Mac completely. It
is certainly true though that all defenses are in the Far East &
we certainly can't limit this war to Korea & expect to lick the
Chinese. It could go on forever while we stood guard on the
MacArthur line. Maybe tho if we reach a point we will have
gained a strong enough advantage for peace talks. It looks like
we are entering a very interesting & crucial era in world history. Will be anxious to see the reactions around the world to
Mac's & Truman next few talks. There is prob[ably] quite a
strong "Mac for President" faction in force now isn't there. I
certainly hope he doesn't "fade away" like the old soldier he
spoke of. He is too political a man & one with a head on his
shoulders & who acts on the power of his convictions. I felt
proud for this man when I heard him. I hope I can feel the*

same after Truman finishes. I don't think I'd ever heard him speak before. It's just life. . . .

The order today was <u>wear</u> <u>steel</u> <u>helmets</u>. We're really combat troops again. The usual air raid precautions. . . .

Meyer's unit received orders to move closer to the 38th parallel. To move a whole hospital unit was a logistical challenge and rife with hazards – especially when driving over the mountainous dirt roads at night.

April 21, 1951

. . . Well, we're still here but not for long. Got the word this aft[ernoon] to hit the road. Party is leaving early tomorrow & I'll be going in a day or so with another group. We're going to set up in Chunchon this time. Apparently they have taken the Hunchon Reservoir so here we come. No one wants particularly to go to work on battle casualties but we're all getting tired of just sitting around. . . . We probably should be in our next location for quite a while. There will be two M.A.S.H. units behind us to move before we will. . . .

Meyer's unit was now located about twenty miles from the front lines.

April 22, 1951

. . . Surprise! I came on the first "wave" & am now in Chunchon, 6 miles below the 38th. It's really a much more beautiful spot. The town itself is demolished by our bombing but we're on the outskirts, across a large river in what was an old school yard. Chunchon is in the center of a large plain surrounded by high mountains. We have a beautiful view & have also a few trees which is a blessing. The ride up needless to say was dusty & our faces looked like we'd used <u>Max Factor</u>. Took some Kodachrome which you'll see. We left about 5 A.M. this morning & arrived about 3 P.M.

The sites were quite mountainous all the way & surprisingly pretty. We passed many streams rushing over rocks almost like the Sierra. On the other hand too we saw quite a lot more of the ravages of war. Many tanks, trucks demolished & burned along the roadside – old gun implacements & foxholes. Practically all the villages & towns were leveled by burning or shellfire.

Was a kick to see the pet names on all the vehicles that passed us – "Hadacol" . . . "Mighty Midget" etc. Also along the road were caution signs like the Burma Shave deals. "Don't pass on hills – if the MP's don't get you the Buzzards will" CHARMS, charms, charms. "<u>Charms</u>" are a package

*candy the army passes out of which everyone is tired of. Now
we have a somewhat disabled (to say the least) character in
the unit here who thinks he is being very generous when he
offers . . . "Charms anyone?"*

*. . . Once again we can hear the sound of artillery &
bombing. The Air Corps has had a busy day as we have seen
many planes in the air. . . . Apparently we have to be careful
of land mines around here as they are all over the place. . . .*

*Was busy today pitching tents etc. We were all set for
patients & they came piling in at noon so will be back working around the clock again. I've been out of doors in the sun
seeing that tents got up so will work in surgery tonight on the
night shift. Sounds like the Chinese broke thru a little. We
have quite a nice hosp. set up – all in tents this time but it's
dusty as our trucks have churned up our front yard. . . . You
should see the dust cloud when the copters land. They have
been bringing in a few today too. . . .*

April 25, 1951

*. . . If you received my last letter yet you are prob[ably]
wondering what we're doing in Chunchon. Well, shortly after
finished writing to you I went over to get busy on a load of
casualties that came in – must have been 75 in all – when we
received word to evacuate all patients & pack up & leave ourselves. About 10 patients had been to surg[ery] already &
they had to be moved too. We had just gotten the place set up
& functioning since noon when at about 10 P.M. we had to
tear her down by moonlight. The catch was tough we had no
trucks. Ours were all in Chechon waiting to bring up our nurses & a few other MD's & equipt. They had just gotten there
apparently & had to turn right around & come back the 80
miles of mountain road for us & we got a few from the 2nd
M.A.S.H. that's here in Hoengsong. The trucks pulled in
about 2 A.M. & the first convoy was on its way by 4 A.M. The
rest of us awaited more trucks & were on the road by 6 A.M.
yesterday morning. We retraced [?] our ride back here to
Hoegsong where we have been camping until we're reassigned
to a new location which will apparently be back further in
Wonju again where we were supposed to be once before way
back in Feb. Such is life with the 1st M.A.S.H..*

*I guess we arrived in Chunchon just as the Chinese broke
thru & I hear that now where our hosp[ital] was there are
many tanks & artillery lined up along the river behind which
would have been firing over our heads again. Looks like we
got out just in time. Sounds like Chechon all over again except*

at Chunchon we were able to get out & at Chechon we could-
n't if we wanted to as the Chinese apparently had the road
blocked.

The road back here was a continuous line of vehicles but
fortunately the roads were in good cond[ition] & weather fine
– sunny & moonlight. Am surprised the Chinese air corps did-
n't take an opportunity.

It is amazing with so much stuff to move & with so many
trucks to keep going that things run so smoothly & with so lit-
tle trouble & accidents.

We had a little excitement en route when our convoy got
in on a little ambush. Had no trouble tho & got into
Hoengsong here about noon. . . .

The boys have worked hard & long under hard
cond[itions] & deserve credit.

Got mail in last night . . . also your <u>delicious</u> box of cook-
ies. Good! Good! Good! . . .

We stopped at the 2nd M.A.S.H. which has the most
beautiful camp site in Korea – on a slight rise above the river
with grass & trees. We just lay down & slept & GI's had to
pitch a few tents for the night. There was a shower unit set up
across the river from us where we realized how good it can
make you feel to get the dust off.

Our orders have been changed so many times that past
few days that we just sit tight until we hear the same one
twice. Our trucks have loaded & unloaded at least a dozen
times in the past 4 days. . . .

Wonju, Korea
April 26, 1951

Are you able to follow me on a map? As you see we're
back in Wonju. . . . Haven't had any business yet . . . but if
the Chinese keep pushing maybe we will be at the front again
soon too. . . .

Our ride down from Hoengsong last night was only 7
miles long so went quickly. They have the railroad completed
into Wonju now so at least is easier to get supplies up this far.
The road is the toughest between Chechon & Wonju too.

10th Corps H.Q. has moved back too. Saw them on the
road tonight. They were the ones too who said we shouldn't
have moved from Chunchon. Apparently our strategy is to
retreat slowly at the same time killing them off.

Have been interested in reading the reports in magazines
& papers of the feelings around the world regarding the
MacArthur-Truman episode. It seems that most here feel that

Truman prob[ably] acted in the right direction. Most of us feel that eventually we will prob[ably] have to fight this war like MacArthur wants to but that we aren't ready yet and that the longer we can wait the better we will be prepared.

This present Chinese push may be the deciding one though. . . .

April 27, 1951

. . . Today it rained, first in quite a while but not hard. Just settled the dust & washed the tent. The Chinese are still pushing but mostly on Seoul now. The central front seems contained. . . .

Got another liquor ration in today. When it rains it pours. . . .

April 29, 1951

The Air Corps was busy overhead again today – also dropping supplies and our troops pulled out of Chunchon leaving it completely to the Chinese, they're closing in on Seoul too. A queer war alright. . . .

Each town over here in central and northern Korea is in a huge valley surrounded by mts and you have to go over mountain roads & passes to get from one to the next – like going from Calistoga to the ranch. . . .

Our 1st M.A.S.H. enlisted men (EM's) were severely beaten in baseball tonight by the ambulance co[mpany] attached to us. . . .

May 2, 1951

. . . My night calls got me up . . . last night, too. The poor devil was really clobbered last night when he stepped on a land mine here in Wonju – lost both his legs & a hand. We have gotten a few more cases today but most of them the usual civilian accidents, traffic ac[cident] etc. . . .

Got a little good news that promotions may be out soon too. I should be up for one.

Am getting more & more anxious to be on my way home. This inactivity here has made it such that we hate to do any work at all. We all need a change to pick up moral & do efficient work. If I get to Oak Knoll I'll prob[ably] see the patients I've taken care of here. Will be an excellent opportunity to complete ones experience in handling battle casualties & see the follow-ups. If I'm lucky & is going to work out that way & my military service will be worth more than any civilian residency would have been. . . .

KOREAN WAR

May 5, 1951

> We had a terrific rain yesterday & it seemed on acre or about 3 acres drained into our tent. It ran through like a river. Had we not had sand on the floor the place would have been a sea of mud. We had to get out & build a dyke around the tent. Today it cleared up and was able to take a sunbath this afternoon.

> We dug ourselves a hole in the tent for a cooler for the beer today. The stuff tastes pretty good in this weather.

> We're kind of getting sick of the Marines around us – a bunch of scroungers & cocky individ[uals]. There are a few Marine pilots here too who fly observation planes & copters. They spend most the time buzzing the nurses' tent by 10 ft. As far as I am concerned they're a bunch of damn fools. One slip & they would make a mess of the hospital.

> . . . Haven't more news about getting home. Just keep hoping that it will be soon. . . .

May 8, 1951

> . . . . Last night Scotty [?] had scrounged 42 lbs of steaks so it was the occasion for an officers' steak party. There was plenty of liquid too & had to put a few people to bed. Oh yes. I ate 5 steaks & were they good! I don't think I slept at all last night – too much meat. Just lay there thinking of getting home.

> This morning we had to get up early for another formation & even had a parade yet & at least we passed in review. The occasion was the presentation of two D.F.C.s to two of our copter pilots for an evacuation mission they flew in March one night out of the mountains. There [are] a hell of a lot better boys than these damned Marine pilots. We're all fed up with the Marines right now. . . .

May 9, 1951

> . . . Today was one of our hottest yet & we had to go into surg[ery] with another little Korean kid who stepped on a land mine. He was "clobbered" but the feat was something. Perspiration just poured off during the operation and there is always a fly or two around. Well hope I'm not here when it gets really bad. Were busy last night with 3 other land mine victims. It sure pays to stay on the beaten path around here. I understand the Chinese are vanishing again above the 38th but laying mines again as they go. These [are] some of the worst wounds we have to take care of. . . .

Korean War

May 11, 1951

. . . Today we put our mosquito liner up & have the tent sides up so we're practically out of doors. . . .

The officers team played again tonight & we really were hot 19 to 5. I'm playing catcher – Crepps was pitcher. I hit a home run with the bases loaded tonight.

Afterward I did one of the cases I operated on about 10 days ago – a Korean boy with a gun shot wound of his arm. I had to close the skin tonight & also took a big lump off his fanny. The operating situation is terrific now. We're doing everything in tents now — & by the middle of the day it's hot as blazes – one sweats a gallon doing a case. Then there are flies buzzing around too. At night tho its cooler – moths & Daddy Long legs are always falling into the wounds. . . .

P.S. You should see our surg. ward – like a pediatric ward with all the Korean kids we have who have stepped on land mines. They're pretty sick little devils tho & are well behaved. One of their mothers came in the other day dressed in typical poor Korean clothes, draping white cloak with a baby tied on her back. The little thing began to cry & she stopped and nursed it rite in the ward in front of the GI patients – what a riot. Then there are the little guys who make pee pee in front of everybody at the movies. Such is life. . . .

May 14, 1951

. . . Tis a dreary rainy day & the mist is hanging around the hills again which seems to be so characteristic of Korea. It seems the Chinese are all poised for another offensive & have timed it well with the weather. They have been setting up quite a smoke screen the past week also to conceal their movements by setting forest fires.

Dex and I had quite a time with one of our little Korean pts this morning. Was time to change his dressings & cast. Well, we found the dressings crawling with maggots. It's quite discouraging but the wound itself was surprisingly clean. Maggots tho brought by the flies eat up all the dead tissue and are one of nature's way of doing a surgical debridement. In the old days they uses to put them in the wounds purposely for that purpose.

Got quite a kick out of the little kids on the ward today – 5 of them. Their mothers & brothers & sisters were visiting them & were all smiles. One little tiger's little brother is always around feeding & keeping the others covered up all the time. They're learning bits of English too a "Good Morning" & doctors names. Am going to have to get a picture of them the next sunny day. . . .

Korean War

May 19, 1951

. . . *Yep, we're busy again – the armors fire, the planes go overhead – the pts come in – such is life! . . .*

P.S. Note new address – they changed the number of our M.A.S.H. to the 8209.[5]

May 21, 1951

. . . *Was only mod[erately] busy last night & saw another movie after finishing up. . . . If we get finished tonight I think we have a Western but business may be better as I think the Chinese attacked again. The 2nd Division seems to be catching hell constantly. . . .*

There have been quite a few planes landing 10 miles up at Hoengsong. I think it almost equals the Berlin Airlift. . . .

Hongchon
May 25, 1951

Well, we're no longer in Wonju. We came back up the road this time stopping here instead of going the next 25 miles to Chunchon which was just recaptured today. Came up last night & are already comfortably situated in a little valley with a nice sheltering hillside behind us that is covered with trees & shrubs. The site here is more country like & quite pretty. I think it is the best site we have had. We kind of expect to be busy, but the news has the Chinese retreating. The signs of war here are little more fresh here & will take some pictures. Tomorrow is the day after which I can expect orders but heck it may even be a month yet before I get them. Replacements don't seem to be coming very fast for medical officers. For EM's they're coming in now. Our ambulance company with 80 men has 100 replacements. Our M.A.S.H. with 120 men got in 108 replacements. So you see the men will be getting back soon. It won't be long now though. . . .

We took a walk today while the hosp was being set up. Saw the remains of a jet fighter strewn over about ? mile, five graves marked by G.I. letters in some old gun emplacements, prob[ably] GI's too, and an old Korean shrine with a bombed out roof. The inside of the building was very colorful with all sorts of designs. An interesting place which I'll get a picture of one of these sunny days. . . .

May 28, 1951

The tail end of another busy day – and I do mean busy. It's coming in here at the rate of 400-500 a day – surgery going full blast all the time – ambulances coming and going from front lines to us to air port & evacuation to hosp in rear. We're so swamped now that we take care of only those who are so bad they can't go further or who couldn't travel without great difficulty. And the news has the Chinese retreating on all fronts. You'd never know it from the looks of this place. I guess an army suffers more on offense than defense tho. . . .

May 29, 1951

. . . And we thought Chechon in Feb was bad! Gad! That was child's play. Beginning to get a little tired but it will have to let up soon. We have been blessed the last few days with good weather & hence have been able to air evac[uate] pts who can travel as we're able to get to only about 1/2 in surgery. . . .

I have a weeks beard & must shave tonight also am kind of smelly too & look like a butcher. There's no sense changing clothes tho as one gets dirty the next minute. . . .

May 31, 1951 [first letter]

. . . We're still pretty busy but are working with only 5 surgeons (3 at night & 2 in the day). We're doing all the abdominal cases with just a corpsman helping now & can get more thru that way. The rain has come and gone too & practically flooded us out. It's quite humid here now too. Nothing ever dries out. Our plaster casts aren't setting very well either.

We're supposed to have more doctors come in today from the 11th Evac[uation] Hosp for temporary duty. Maybe they are Cordell & my replacements??? We're short now with Reimers in Japan on R&R, at a time like this too. . . .

May 31, 1951 [second letter]

Well . . . the end of another day & tomorrow the beginning of another month. I can't say I'm at all excited about the last but of rumor I've heard once again in the true army way I won't be leaving until the end of June at least. . . . I won't say more because the damn army changes their mind every day. . . . Well another bitch, the Navy, Cordell and I are now the only Lt's around here. Everyone else has been made captain or better. Many have been in the service less time than we have & will behind us in school & just finished their internships.

Well enough bitching. We're still busy & the poor devils keep coming in all shot up. The radio news keeps saying we're meeting no resistance too – what a crock — — — — ! . . .

Talk about getting plastered – just finished putting a colored boy in a plaster vest, lft arm, hips & both legs in a cast. Could have been simpler to have dipped him in plaster alone. . . . Many seriously wounded amounting to about 1100 pts in a week. . . .

June 5, 1951 [first letter]
. . . I've been kind of out the past couple of days . . . with diarrhea, cramps, & the grippe. Am better now tho & getting back to eating again. Back on night duty too which I think I like better than days. It looks like business might get a little lighter from now on – I hope. We certainly have a surgical ward full of sick cookies though. . . .

June 5, 1951 [second letter]
. . . Have this dern typewriter tonight so will bat one off to you if you can stand deciphering it. It misses and skips a few beats now and then as you can see. Was fortunate in having a quiet night last night. . . . The peace talk doesn't seem to be getting anywhere. The line is around the 38th again and I don't expect will go much farther but they are still meeting resistance. I don't think we could go much farther without heavy losses. . . .

Our surgical ward is a much pleasanter place now as we have evacuated many and others haven't made it. Was quite a mad house for a while. During this last siege we were so busy that we began to do all the cases by ourselves – that is one doctor and a corpsman on the bellies and all. They are real long and complicated cases too that ordinarily at home three surgeons work on so you can see how things are going. Getting along quite well that way too, certainly no worse and can accomplish much more. In the past ten days of some 1200 patients run through the hospital and 200 of the most serious ones operated on we did 36 abdominal wounds, lots of chests and large bones. Once again the blood is keeping these guys alive. Some get anywhere from 6 to 12 pints apiece so you see how it is needed.

We had an interesting fire here today. One of the gas drums had leaked into a small stream running thru our camp and someone threw a cigarette into the . . . stream. The whole stream for about 50 yds went up in flame. No one was hurt fortunately.

Reimers came back from R&R last night so now we have 8 surgeons whereas we only had 5 during the rush. There is a Swedish Col here wanting a little experience for a short time. . . .

June 10, 1951

. . . Here we sit relatively idle & spend the time bitching about the food, rotations, life in Korea and the army in general. Someone manages each day to mark off a day on the calendar nailed [?] on the inside of our tent liner and it's getting steadily closer to the end of the month. I manage to get up for breakfast these days but purely only for survival. The other meals have been so poor lately that have to eat something & even breakfast isn't very palatable anymore. Almost immediately after breakfast tho I'm back in bed until lunch unless something better gets me up. . . .

Went to sleep the other night with the patter of rain on the roof of the tent – quite a lullaby. . . . I haven't much other news not even about any promotion so time marches on. . . .

June 13, 1951

. . . As I am on call and feeling my oats again, I didn't go back to bed but hiked up on the ridge behind the camp. From there got a terrific view of the surrounding valley, the M.S.R., & the airport. I sat up there quite a while thinking of getting home & what we will do. It certainly will be exciting again & I can hardly wait. . . .

And today I slept thru breakfast but had to get up at 9:00 A.M. to see my pts. Didn't get back to bed either so I'm improving I guess. . . .

June 16, 1951

. . . And today marks the end of another week leaving prob[ably] just a week & 5 days left. Yesterday the first surgeon replacement arrived & there is supposed to be an orthoped on the way. When he gets here I'll treat him with kid gloves. We were saying that it looked like we were going to have to wait until the present freshmen med. students graduated but things look like they are beginning to move now. . . .

What are you going to be wearing when I first see you? Probably something I've never seen you in. . . .

June 18, 1951

. . . Keep crossing the days off the calendar here & it's getting closer. I'm on nights again now & have been blessed with some good weather too. . . .

I haven't let myself make definite plans until I actually get orders, more or less keeping fingers crossed, but when they come I'll go hog wild.

June 20, 1951

    . . . *Today at noon a Lt Col spoke on the radio just before the newscast & said at 1:00 P.M. there would be an important message for everyone. Well, everyone waited eagerly thinking, — Peace? War with Russia? Atom Bomb, etc. & at 1:00 came the news – we had to turn in all our script money for a new type. I guess they wanted to catch unauthorized persons script. I had $12.50. I haven't been paid for the past two months as I had my pay record picked up thinking I was leaving. The allotment I assume continues through. . . .*

    Wilsey was promoted to major today & one of the nurses to 1st Lt. Ho-hum & Cordell & I still remain " j.g." Such is life. Everyone in the unit has been promoted now. . . .

June 22, 1951

    . . . *The Col. gave a party last night & there was quite a gang there. I was on call & had quite a busy night with a couple of truck wrecks & an appendix to take care of. . . . One of the nurses whose husband is here in the infantry has him visiting her & the Col gave them a tent right in the middle of the camp. There is a big sign in front – "Out of Bounds" They're "poor kids" too. . . .*

June 24, 1951

    . . . *The time of departure ever getting closer, only 4 more days if things go according to Hoyle and that means only 1 more day on call as O.D. Here's hoping! . . . Tomorrow is the 1 year anniversary of the Korean War. What a mess. Am glad things have been quiet lately. We hear medical replacements are arriving. Hope to see them soon. . . .*

June 26, 1951

    . . . *Yep, still have no orders yet – maybe tomorrow or next day. I've got to give a talk tomorrow. The Hongchon Med. Society, composed of 1st M.A.S.H. doctors. Gad! I guess we have nothing better to do though. I think if my orders come I'll get stinking drunk & be in no shape to talk. The usual stuff today (everyone's doing well for a change – at least now) sunbathing, reading, shower, dinner & tonight Al DeMateo is making Pizzas for a M.A.S.H. party tonight.*

    I've about given all my stuff away & when I do leave, if ever, won't have a thing to carry but my tooth brush. . . .

June 28, 1951

    . . . *Just another day in Korea and the same as every other. . . . no orders. . . . I gave my little dissertation yester-*

day to the "Society" of quacks & it went over quite well. . . .
Crepps & Wilsey got word that their departure will be delayed
a couple or so weeks. . . . The time goes slowly when we're idle
like this but it's better than treating casualties. . . .

Tokyo
July 2, 1951
. . . Well, things happen fast when they do. It was only two
days ago we were sitting in the tent in Hongchon waiting for
lunch & cussing the fact that we hadn't gotten orders yet &
had heard that the other Navy personnel had left when our
orders . . . arrived and that was 11:00 A.M. By 2 P.M. we were
on our way with all the goodbyes behind us. We went by jeep
30 miles to Chunchon, again where we caught a flying box
car (C-119) 20 min after we arrived & made a short hop west
into Seoul to land at Kimjo while they unloaded a 2 ton gen-
erator. That little job took about an hour & we were off again
for Japan landing 2 hrs later in Ashia Air Base on the north-
ern end of the Japanese Isl. along the west coast above Sasebo.
There we were – lunch in Korea, dinner in Japan. We stayed
overnight there & had a delicious steak dinner before catching
a DC-4 [3] or C-47 to Tokyo yesterday that flying took about
7 hours as we made quite a few stops en route & is about 600
miles. Another Cook's tour of Japan, this time by air. Came
back out to Camp Drake where we have been in Jan. & now
are awaiting trans. from here. Will get our luggage this after-
noon & get into clean clothes for a change. Hope to have time
to get down into Tokyo or Yokohama before leaving to do
some shopping. . . .
My orders read for <u>Oak</u> <u>Knoll</u> & have 15 days leave after
I get to the State! You might have an idea where we could live.
I expect to return by boat & we have to go back to Sasebo by
train to get the dern thing, so that will be the 3rd time up &
down the islands. . . .

Sasebo, Japan
July 5, 1951
. . . Arrived last night – 2 nights & 1 day after leaving
Tokyo. Looks like we will be here at least until the 11th & may
be longer before getting a ship, so don't count on that 2 ?
weeks I told you. . . . Was wonderful talking on the phone to
you. . . . Cordell & I placed the calls at about midnight &
stayed in a little Japanese hotel, sleeping on the floor on mats
& quilts to wait. Had to take our shoes off & all to walk thru
the place. . . . I'll write or telegraph just before I leave when I

find out what ship or where we'll arrive. . . .

July 9, 1951
        . . . After having spent the last 3-4 days here in Sasebo killing time & mosquitoes & bottles, we have finally gotten shipping orders – We're to leave tomorrow 10 July on the GEN. WILLIAM WEIGEL a Navy transport for San Francisco. Will probably arrive in about two weeks making it about 24th July. Apparently the boat docks at Ft. Mason by the Marina, & we're taken then by ferry boat to Camp Stoneman for processing. I don't know how long the latter will take – maybe a day. Stoneman is up near Travis above the Carquinas Bridge. I don't know if you can meet me at Ft. Mason or not or at Stoneman. If you can be at Mason. I'll try to be up at the front of the boat. . . . Maybe we can celebrate in S.F. & stay there when I get in or go up to the Ranch. You might make some reservations if we stay in S.F. . . . As I said we will have 15 days leave before Oak Knoll. Just two weeks! It will be good to get home. You can let the folks know. . . .

        Well, Peety Girl, am loving lu more & more & sure am going to hug the dickens out of you. And the next time you will be there. Kissing, Peety

SERGEANT FIRST CLASS MURRAY FREED
45TH INFANTRY DIVISION, X CORPS, EIGHTH ARMY

Murray Freed was twenty and living in Detroit in February of 1952 when he was drafted. At the time, he owned a gas station with a partner. He had been married for only three months. In only twenty months, he was trained, shipped to Korea, and sent home.

Freed spent four months training in Pennsylvania and then was shipped to Japan, where he trained for a few more months before arriving in Korea in the late summer or early fall of 1952.

Freed first arrived at a place called Anchor Hill in North Korea on the Sea of Japan. Freed remembered, "I was really scared. I didn't know what to expect. . . . I'll tell you this, I was scared as everybody else was most of the time I was there. But when push comes to shove, your fear gets buried and . . . you automatically do what you were trained to do."

Freed remembers what it was like fighting in the hills of Korea with support from the U.S.S. *Missouri's* artillery. "I felt sorry [about] all the terror we produced for the people [the shells] were landing on. It was . . . unbelievable. And I was lying in my bunker and every time one of those shells landed, I shook. Because the ground just trembled."

But Freed rarely knew where he was. " . . . [W]e were never really told where we were. . . . [A]ll we knew really what was happening fifty feet to your right and fifty feet to your left. We were in trenches most of the time. The only time we left the trenches is when we retreated, which happened, or when we went out to the hill in front of us to kick them off of it."

Freed described a typical day in the trenches:

> *We'd be in there twenty-four hours a day. At night we would stand out in the trench, we had guard duty. . . . [O]ne man from the bunker at a time would stay out in the trench and listen and watch. [W]hen your time was up, you would wake your replacement up. You would go down in the bunker and wake him up and he'd come out and he'd stand there. And it was very cold . . . just terrible cold. . . . They used to bring . . . hot meals. They had, we used to call them 'chogi trains.' . . . They were Korean service corps workers. . . . The Korean army was there also. So were the Greeks and the French and the English and the Canadians. It was . . . the United Nations. . . .*
> *During the day, we would constantly be working on our*

Sgt. Murray Freed with pistol. (Courtesy of Murray Freed)

fighting positions. . . . Filling sandbags with sand and mak-
ing them more secure. . . . At night, and sometimes during the
day, we had to go out on patrol. That was loading up with
ammo and taking your weapon and putting your helmet on. . . .
We used to wear an armor vest too. . . . At night you'd go out
on anywhere from two men in a patrol to . . . a squad of eight
men. And when I was on machine gun crew, we'd . . . have to
take the gun along with us. . . . After about six or seven weeks
on machine gun, I told the squad leader that I didn't want to
be on the machine gun crew any more, I just wanted to be a
rifleman. So I became a rifleman.

Even during the war there was humor. Freed reflects, "When men get
together under adverse conditions . . . we used to kid guys. One guy had
big ears and he couldn't get a cap to fit him. Only a bigger cap, and his
ears kept it up and he was a constant butt of jokes . . . in a friendly way."

Freed's unit was relieved by a ROK division and moved back to the
rear. He recalls his unit's losses; "We had taken about . . . forty casualties.
Twenty of them were from the platoon I was in." Away from the front,
they were given food and showers, and then trained all over again.

Freed moved back into action in February of 1953, but was not exactly on the frontline. "We were a blocking force. We were behind a hill that
had Americans on it and we were there just in case they broke through,
we had to take over, which didn't happen."

Freed's regiment was relocated and assigned to guard a prisoner of
war camp on Koje-do Island off the coast, where the Communists prisoners were kept. Freed recalls his experiences on Koje-do:

Our regiment went down and we did guard duty there.
We were guarding the prisoners. The prisoners, some of them
were very docile, they were the ones who actually surrendered
the first chance they had. . . . There was one compound of
prisoners that were dyed in the wool Communists. They
would kill you if they could. And in fact while we were there,
they did kill some South Korean military police and our com-
pany was one of the companies that had to go in and quell
the . . . riot. It was pretty bloody.

Freed recalls that sometimes nature was the enemy. "We landed [on
Koje-do] in the morning, and that night, a typhoon hit the island. . . .
We had these two and a half tons trucks. They were blowing around like
pieces of Kleenex."

Freed's regiment was moved back to Korea for the rest of the war.
About a week before the truce was signed, he was part of a horrible battle.

KOREAN WAR

. . . They threw us into the hole to block the Chinese. . . . We weren't even on the main line. We were out in no man's land. Most of my company was wiped out there. I lost a lot of friends. . . . We had sixty-eight men killed and thirty wounded. In about five or six hours. . . . We had . . . a little over five hundred dead Chinamen on the hill with us. I found some of my men with their arms tied behind with barbed wire and they'd shot 'em in the back of the head with shotguns and taken all their heads off.

When the truce was signed the troops pulled back to the lines that had been agreed upon. About six weeks later, Freed was allowed to return home. He went to Fort Sheridan, north of Chicago, and stayed there for a few months until he had enough time in the army to get out. Freed recalls what happened when he came back to America. "We had to sit in an orientation, which was absolutely ludicrous, on how to behave in a civilian environment. I didn't know what they thought we were going to do, go around shooting people or attacking them."

Freed related how he was treated after returning from the war:

I went to a restaurant with my buddies . . . and we sat down and we ordered from the waiter . . . The owner, he walked out and he looked at us. . . . I was in the 45th Infantry Division. . . . We still had the division patch on our jackets. . . . He came in and he [said] 'you know something, . . . I was in that outfit you were in . . . in Italy and southern France in World War II.' . . . He wouldn't ever, ever let us pay for a meal or a drink in that place. We were treated nicely.

Freed reflected on the role of the Korean War. "The Korean War . . . was the start of the downfall of communism. In only three years, we lost almost as many men in Korea as we did in ten years in Vietnam. There are still over 8,000 people missing."

"You know what they call the Korean War?" he asked. "It's called the Forgotten War. Because really the only people who remember it are those who were there and their families."

Korean War

End Notes

[1] Description of medical mission and duties of M.A.S.H. units in the May 19th, 1951, issue of *Stars & Stripes*: "This was a hospital that could move at a moment's notice to handle non-transportable patients at divisional clearing stations and prepare them for evacuation. . . . After a man is wounded he is usually under their care within three or four hours," or less time if evacuated by helicopter. "When a patient is brought in, his wounds are cleaned and dressed, and then he is DDTd and prepared for surgery. X-rays are made if it is necessary to locate bullets or shell fragments. Next he is carried in a litter to surgery where as many as eight operating tables may be working at one time. The surgeons . . . work from one table to the next until the tent is cleared, taking only a few minutes time out while waiting for ambulances to arrive. After surgery, the patient is moved to a post-operations tent where he rests until he can be moved to rear areas by plane or hospital train. . . . Ever heedful of its mission of mercy, M.A.S.H. units also treat civilians from villages and surrounding countryside and prisoners of war."

[2] For a detailed account of the battle for Wonju, see J.D. Coleman, *Wonju: The Gettysburg of the Korean War*, (Washington, D.C., 2000).

[3] For a complete summary of casualties, see *Wonju*, p. 157.

[4] For more details regarding the offensive movements by the American Eighth Army, see *Wonju*, pp. 242-258.

[5] Meyer is referring to the May 19th, 1951 article about the 1st or 8209 M.A.S.H., which represented a new way of treating soldiers' wounds. In another unidentified article (probably published Stateside), "Treatment At 8209 M.A.S.H. Resembles Bellevue General," gives more details about Meyer's unit. "There are 13 doctors on the staff, aided by 17 nurses and the 120 male enlisted technicians." The hospital has been functioning constantly from Chechon to Hungnam . . . and last February [1951], the

Chinese got within miles of the hospital before it beat a hasty retreat to safer ground."

Vietnam War

THE VIETNAM WAR lasted from 1959 to 1975 and involved the North and South Vietnamese and the United States. The conflict revolved around Vietnam, which had been separated into North Vietnam and South Vietnam after the completion of the First Indochinese War, when the Vietnamese claimed independence from the French. North Vietnam was run by communists, who hated the French, and South Vietnam was populated by those who supported the French. The United States became initially involved when the South Vietnamese government requested military assistance to help them repel the insurgent Viet Cong guerrillas in the south. The United States' investment was in concurrence with its political philosophy, which was based on the "domino theory." This theory predicted that if communist North Vietnam took over South Vietnam, communism would sweep throughout Southeast Asia. Communism had to be contained in the Cold War world.

Perhaps another reason that America became involved was because of devout, if misguided, patriotism. In August 1964, two American destroyers were attacked by North Vietnamese torpedo boats in the Gulf of Tonkin. This changed the complexion of the war. Consequently, the amount of American military forces present in Vietnam increased from a few thousand advisors in the late 1950s and early 1960s to approximately 500,000 combat and support troops by 1968. Protests of the war, both at home and abroad, escalated along with the scope of the war. The seemingly irresolvable war ultimately led to a change in presidential administrations. A welcomed truce was brokered in 1973 and the majority of American forces came home. South Vietnam was eventually overrun by North Vietnam in 1975.

Six officers and enlisted men shared their letters and stories from Vietnam. This special group, whose service spans most of the Vietnam War as well as different branches of the service, tells amazing stories. Some were sustained by their strong faith while a few were disillusioned by the war. One of the first to serve, during the early part of the conflict was Chicagoan William Catching.

VIETNAM WAR

Sergeant E-5 William Catching
First Infantry Division
1964-1967

The United States Armies that served in the Vietnam War were composed of the most African Americans to serve in any American war. Although African Americans accounted for only 11.0% of the United States' population, they made up 12.6% of the soldiers deployed to Vietnam. Sergeant Catching was just one of the proud African American soldiers who enlisted to serve his country. Catching was immediately thrown into combat with an infantry platoon. This baptism by fire required him to rely intensely on his religious faith.

Sgt. William Catching. (Courtesy of William Catching)

Arrival

I cannot forget when we left from O'Hare airport in Chicago and we took a . . . charter flight . . . to Vietnam. We stopped in Hawaii. We stopped in the Philippines, and then we were in Vietnam. I remember when we landed, I could smell sewage – I could smell jungle [and] *it smelled like things were rotting. It smelled different. It smelled like the alley did in Chicago when the garbage wasn't picked up.*

I remember being told that we were not to speak to anyone, that we were to stay together, we were not to drink any of the water, and we were then moved into an area where we were all given a rifle, two clips of ammo, and we were loaded into what they call two and a half ton trucks. We used to call them deuce and a half, and we were all told to face outside and stand in the back in what was considered the cattle car. It's just a truck with railings around three sides of it. And we were to face out with our rifles pointing out, and keep our eyes open for any Vietnamese who appeared to be hostile. And if we saw that, we were to fire on them or shoot. So, right away you get to a country. You've never been there, and then you're told that you have to be very careful and you're given a rifle. The reality of being in a place that is hostile . . . to you was very real very quickly.

I remember when we landed at the airfield, at the destination where I would be stationed, which was a place called

*Phuc Vinh, thirty miles, I believe, southeast or southwest of
Saigon. There was a very small Christmas tree and it had tin-
sel on it, and it looked like a Christmas tree that somebody
would throw away at the end of Christmas, that the garbage
men would pick up, but there was this little bitty tree out on
the runway. And the wind was blowing, the dust was blowing and the tree looked kind of lonely, kind of like how I felt
arriving in Vietnam on . . . Christmas Day 1965.*

Only five days after he had arrived in Vietnam, Catching knew that
he would be tested. He contemplated how he would face the challenge
of battle and survive:

December 30, 1965
Dear Mama and Family,
*. . . Over here a man really learns that he needs God and
if he doesn't have God with him he is really in sorry shape.
You know mama, I really don't mind going on these operations because I am [at] peace with God and I know He will
take care of me. It seems funny because at night when I'm
tired and falling asleep on guard or when I'm being shot at
out there I can just feel him all around me. It's kind of hard
to explain but I know He's there and I'm never really afraid
out there.*
*I carry the Bible you gave me everywhere I go and believe
it or not it gets read ever as often. I also carry the rosary
Hortense gave me and at night when I have to stay up I pray
the rosary to stay awake. . . .*

The New Year had barely begun when Catching found himself face-
to-face with the enemy for the first time:

*I had my first encounter with combat, New Year's Eve of
1966. I had been in the country for a week. We were out on
a holding patrol in which we were assigned to establish a base
camp around a very important bridge. We were to dig in and
secure the bridge so that our supply trucks could be protected
at that bridge site. There was a highway nearby called
Highway One and Highway One ran west of Vietnam, and it
was a huge supply line for anyone who could maintain it, and
basically the American forces maintained . . . Highway One
because we had the ability to do that.*
*The equivalent to Highway One would be the Ho Chi
Minh trail, up in northern Vietnam, which is basically the
same idea but the Ho Chi Minh trail was a little jungle path*

that the North Vietnamese used to continue to bring their supplies in from North Vietnam. It was a very rugged kind of trail. . . . The United States military used to bomb and disrupt that path as often as they could. . . . The Viet Cong would try and booby trap the highway, put landmines underneath the roads, in the dirt so that when trucks passed and rolled over the landmines they would detonate the landmine, which had a pressure sensitive cap. So, our job was to make sure those types of land mines were not deployed on Highway One especially around the bridge.

Well, New Year's Eve night we were in our secure position, and I heard what sounded like a couple firecrackers and I looked around our perimeter and saw a couple flashes of light and the next thing I knew it was like all hell broke loose. There were tracer rounds which are bullets that have a phosphorus kind of trail that give you the ability to see where the round is going, machine guns use them a lot. A phosphorus round or a trace round is every fifth bullet and when you have machine guns, that way every fifth bullet you could see a streak, as it moves through the night sky, you could see where the bullets are going. But we had been attacked by a small Viet Cong force. It was my first experience of being involved in combat. I didn't even fire my rifle. I was in awe of what was going on and I didn't see a target so I didn't fire. So it was kind of something that was surreal. . . . It seemed like I was watching an Army movie on TV in Technicolor, but I was in that midst of this.

My next experience in combat was . . . [when] we were on a trail. One squad was on sort of an infiltrating mission to just infiltrate into some jungle areas where there could be some Viet Cong forces [and] we happened to surprise another squad of soldiers that were Viet Cong, coming the other way. Turn a corner and in the jungle you can't see very far ahead of you, [be]cause it is very thick vegetation, so a lot of time you have these little paths and you don't see around the corner because it's just impossible to. The guys that were leading our patrol turned the corner and lo and behold, there was a guy that was leading a Viet Cong patrol coming the other way. And it was kind of comical because it was frightening, because he turned around and ran and the other guy ran back the other way, and we were told to retreat to a secure area, where we were to create a perimeter and secure ourselves. And what you do is that you lay in a circle with everyone's feet pointed towards the center of the circle, and your rifles pointing out, and just wait and see what's going to happen, but *before we could do that the Viet Cong had already put three mortar rounds in our position . . . and I remember being lifted off the ground. It felt like three or four feet when the explosion hit the ground, and then it hit again and we got lifted off the ground. That night we laid out in that rubber tree plantation while our friendly forces (the Navy) shot artillery rounds in to protect us. So we had to lay there all night and wait until morning. . . . [while] the naval artillery protected us.*

The conditions continued to get tougher, according to Catching:

. . . The biggest fire fight . . . [occurred] one night [when] I was on a listening post with a small group of us. A listening post is where you station yourself out ahead of your perimeter or your line of fire that your base camp establishes. And you're kind of out there about a hundred to two hundred yards from where everything is secure and your job is to be listening for any movement coming towards your friendly line. That particular night we were attacked by a large force of Viet Cong, who felt our battalion was going to be out on patrol, but we weren't. So, the Vietnamese intelligence was wrong, and a small 500 to 600 force of Viet Cong attacked a fully equipped, a fully armed, a fully prepared US Army force, which we were.

I remember being caught in the cross fire of both our troops and the Viet Cong and the bullets were falling in our position so close that you could feel the dirt flying up around you and hitting you in the face. It was a very scary experience because we weren't able to fire back because the bullets that were being fired from both sides were so low that if you were to raise up from where you were laying, you could be hit by either friendly fire or enemy fire. So, we lay there all night with these bullets flying across us and I was afraid, but I had a strong faith in God, which I still do, and I said a prayer and started looking at the stars in the sky. The next thing I knew it was morning. I couldn't believe what had happened, because I knew I had [fallen] asleep, but I think I was so frightened that I passed out and I think that was a very merciful thing of God to let happen to me, because it was very scary and I knew I couldn't have just fallen asleep with all of that violence so it was sort of a night of hell. . . . I remember waking up or opening my eyes and it was just a beautiful summer day with the birds and jungle noises filtering in and it was like nothing had ever happened. That morning they

U.S. Army field map for Vietnam. (Courtesy of Nick Vawter)

piled up bodies of Viet Cong all over the place. We had destroyed their forces and I had experienced my very first live . . . firefight.

Friendly Fire

I can vividly remember one night we were on the outside of a swamp where we had camped . . . and we were going to go in the swamp the next morning. . . . Well, that particular night we had a mortar round or rather an artillery round that was supposed to land outside the perimeter of where we were . . . and it landed short exploding not far from where we were, which meant that the fragments of the artillery round showered down on top of us. And I can't forget how scared I was because, in a pitch black dark night in the jungle, when you have a flash of light like that, it blinds you, and for the next – it seemed like forever – but probably [was] ten or fifteen minutes I couldn't see anything, because I had been blinded, and I had night blindness. Everyone else did too. But I could hear people moaning. I could hear people calling out for help, but I couldn't see anything. We had to wait until that night blindness went away before anybody could be helped. It turns out that we had three or four people who were injured pretty badly that night.

Mines

The very next morning we moved into the swamp and I was standing on the edge of the swamp and a couple of people who I was very close to, were in the squad ahead of me and they were heading into the swamp to begin our search and destroy mission. And there was a huge explosion and it was a claymore mine that went off. A claymore mine is a mine that is fired towards a group of men and our claymore mines that we had were factory made and had been filled with one hundred, at least one hundred small steel pellets

*with composition explosion behind it. And when it exploded
and burst, it would throw out pellets up to one hundred yards
ahead of it. The Viet Cong had similar weapons, but they
made them. What they would do was take glass, nails, bolts,
anything that was sharp and could injure somebody and pack
those into these little explosive charges. When you got close
enough they would detonate these things and they would just
sort of blow out in front of the people walking. [On] that particular day, that mine went off and killed one of my best
friends and somebody I was very fond of. That made me very
angry, because I saw them carry his body back to the helicopter and it reminded me of a limp rag. He'd been blown – I felt
like he'd been blown to pieces. He was really a nice guy; we
were stationed in Washington D.C. together, and he was the
pitcher on our softball team, and he was a good pitcher too,
he was a fun guy to be around. But, he was dead and he was
only eighteen or nineteen years old. It really made me angry.
I wanted to kill somebody that day. If I could've just killed
somebody I would've felt better I guess, but that's the way it
happens sometimes. Turns out that there was nobody to fight.
They blew up a few people and ran. By the time we were ready
to move on, they were gone. That can be very demoralizing.
You see people around you getting hurt, but you can't do anything about it. . . .*

*I prayed. I trusted God to keep me safe, and I didn't rely
on any luck. But some people did. . . . I still to this day don't
believe that your lucky, in my world and what I learned is
that you can either be blessed or not. Being blessed in God is
far better to being lucky at a crap table in life.*

Enemy Under the Ground

Then, seven months into Catching's term of service, his platoon
moved to an area called Lon Bin in order to fight a large enemy force.

*Our job was to go and fight it, though this was very hard
because the Viet Cong used to build large complexes underground since our planes and our technology to find them was
very good. So they had no way of building base camps that
were visible, because they knew they would be detected. They
learned how to build their camps underneath the ground and
when we would go in these areas, we would have to go and
find these camps. We had men who were called tunnel riders
and they were usually small men, who could get in these tunnels, and follow them to whatever dead-end, or room, or*

whatever was in there, and a lot of times when these tunnels were discovered and slaughtered and examined, there were small hospitals underground, weapons storage, and food storage, it was just life underground. But this particular day, we had discovered a tunnel complex that the Viet Cong[1] had built. . . . I was carrying a radio that day and reporting in and as we were standing on the road I heard a shot fired and I felt pain in my arm. I had been shot. The minute that I felt the pain, there was a large volley of bullets and rifles firing; I was being pinned down. Apparently they were targeting me because I had the radio. . . . My squad essentially was able to return the fire and got them to retreat and they saved me. I had a bullet wound in my arm and I had several other bullets that had also hit me, but because they were ricochets off the dirt or a tree they did no harm. Other bullets hit me in my foot and one hit me in the back of the radio. They didn't penetrate my shoe and my radio pack. . . . I was met by a helicopter that same day that took me out of Vietnam, I believe it was June 27th of 1966. And that was the last combat action, the day I was shot.

Catching, though wounded, was able to write home the same day:

Dear Nita,
. . . On June 27 I won myself a medal I never wanted to get – a Purple Heart. While we were searching out a Viet Cong base camp we got into a fight and good old me got that right through the left forearm. Boy! Did that ever smart! I've been in the hospital now for four days. It wasn't too bad of a wound. No broken bones but I did get some muscles torn and I think a nerve. My thumb is very hard to move but I guess they will take care of that. . . .

Following the war, Catching thought long and hard about what had happened in Vietnam. He anguished over the senseless number of casualties and the war in general:

The very frustrating part of what we did, was that we were not engaging regular North Vietnamese forces. The soldiers that we found ourselves in the midst of battle with would wait for us to walk through their areas in the jungle, and they would wait very quietly, and they would take the opportunity to ambush us, and fire into us as we were just walking corps. We would try to kill two or three of them and then they would run. Well, if you're walking through the jun-

gle and you're getting shot at, the first thing you do is you drop to the ground so you can figure out where everything is and who's firing, and then you're ready to start thinking about how you're going to engage the enemy. By that time, the Viet Cong had already left. It was very frustrating and they knew it. Because the idea was to give you the impression that you were fighting a ghost, someone who was there but wasn't. They didn't want to have a big fight, they just wanted to harass you and pick us off one by one, so with that scenario being the primary way in which we ended up in engaging the enemy, other then if we just walked into a fire fight. I saw several people that I knew well who were shot one way or another and were part of our group.

After Catching was wounded, he was patched up and sent home. He wrote his mother after departing Vietnam:

July 10, 1966
Dearest Mama,
. . . Mama you just couldn't imagine how good it felt when I got off the plane [in Okinawa, Japan]. *The air was so clean, the grass and trees smelled so good and I guess there was just a sense of freedom in the air. It sort of put a person's mind at ease to know that he didn't have to worry about being shot at or being blown up at any minute. . . .*

Catching had originally considered a career in the military, but with loosing a close friend and seeing good men destroyed because they "indulged in too much pot," or drank too much, he began to reconsider his choice. Leaving the military, though, did not provide a solution to his problems. Catching concluded:

No one comes away from a war without being affected, some kind of way. And those of us who have survived, we carry some emotional scars, but, life goes on. You have to refocus yourself and do the best you can, to get over that and try to live a meaningful, wholesome life after that, but a war's an ugly place to be.

Catching also found that going back to a normal life was virtually impossible: "It's kind of strange that you have an experience like that over three years . . . [and] then one day everyone goes back to doing what they were doing before they joined, and then your life changes again." For him, readjustment was very difficult.

Post-traumatic stress hit me very hard after the war. . . .

I had to go to counseling for a while because of my nightmares. I had this recurring dream where I was a prisoner and the officer that was my captor would place a .45 caliber pistol to my head and fire it. I still wake up, right about the time that he is firing the gun. It was a recurring nightmare, just being shot in the head and not being able to do anything about it. But, as I worked my way through that with counseling, what I found out was that maybe it was because I felt helpless about stuff, that I had no control over things. That dream eventually went away and I'm glad it did. I began dreaming in ways where I was fighting back and I wasn't a victim of my circumstances or a victim of life. And once that started happening I knew I was okay, that I could protect myself, I wasn't vulnerable, and I would be okay.

Catching concluded, that although one might be depressed or confused about why one fought in the war, one must also

learn how to be grateful for having the opportunity to be born in the United States of America. What it means to have the opportunity to do whatever you want to do with your life, in spite of the fact that there was segregation and racial prejudice and things like that. . . .

Once you've gone through [a war] and you've survived, you never want to give it up because there's too much – there's too many lessons, too many life lessons that you learn. . . . If you can use those lessons in a positive, constructive way, then you have a better life. You understand other people better, and you're not naive about saying something happened because you had to face some very tough decisions in a very critical time and that is a way of growing you up, maturing you in a way that other people will never ever experience.

CAPTAIN JOHN B. REINHARDT
(FIRST TOUR) 196TH LIGHT INFANTRY BRIGADE,
(SECOND TOUR) 361ST AERIAL WEAPONS COMPANY
1967-1968

In 1967, John Reinhardt was very busy, as he balanced three part time jobs while being a full time student at Ball State University. Unfortunately, he became sick while in college and lost his student deferment. To avoid being drafted, he enlisted, and eventually completed extra training at Officer Training School. For his first term of service in

Vietnam, he was assigned to the 196th Light Artillery Brigade and was a platoon leader; for his second term he was an assault helicopter pilot in the "Pink Panthers."

Reinhardt remembered the circumstances of his first arrival in Vietnam:

Capt. Reinhardt (left) with fellow soldier. (Courtesy of John Reinhardt)

> [It] *was terrifying for me. We arrived again, early in the morning as I did at Ft. Campbell, and we were on an Air Force cargo plane basically. And the pilot came on saying, 'you know, we are now entering a hostile area, blah, blah, blah. We will now be making our approach at an abnormally steep angle. In the event of an emergency. . . . ' As we looked out the windows, we saw nothing but puffs of smoke. We didn't know what it was. . . . And a long story short: we landed, the doors were opened and the first impression was one of the most ungodly smells I've ever smelled in my life. And that was Vietnam. The second thing that hit us was the heat. It was just unbelievably hot. And then the third thing as we kind of all just got off the plane and didn't know what to do, was the recognition that the puffs of smoke really wasn't anything the way of incoming, it was just the normal process of burning human waste every morning. They had fifty-five-gallon drums, because there was no plumbing or anything, they were just outside latrines and they pour diesel over it and burn it, and it's got this ungodly set of fumes and smell. So that was my introduction to Vietnam in the first twenty minutes.*

Reinhardt had trained to be an artillery officer, but he stepped up and took an infantry leadership position when the former platoon leader was killed. However, this new position soon led only to dangerous times for Reinhardt, despite his excellent leadership skills. Reinhardt was thrown into a new type of role and had a close call, one which left a lasting impression on him.

> *Probably the worst experience was when . . . we were attached to a mechanized infantry outfit, which had what they called armored personnel carriers. They were . . . small*

tank-like vehicle[s] that would carry a squad of infantry. And for whatever reason, they sent us out of range of artillery support and the only thing we had was tactical air [support] to really bring in heavy armament on them. And we got into a couple of pretty big firefights, but the bottom line is that the place that we had to pass through, they had mined with very large bombs. And the sight of a twenty-ton . . . armored personnel carrier going up in the air twenty or thirty feet and killing everybody on it, including all the people that were sitting on it, was amazing. And the thing that made it much more surreal at the time was I had literally just gotten off of that vehicle five minutes before. For whatever reason, . . . God said it wasn't my time. And we lost three more vehicles that same day. Most of the people killed were with the mechanized infantry outfit, although our infantry guys that were riding on it oftentimes they were maimed or eardrums blown out. . . .

During his first tour, Reinhardt found that the atmosphere was very serious, what with the constant stress from carrying out missions against the North Vietnamese Army and the Viet Cong. For Reinhardt, "there is a tremendous amount of boredom, waiting for something to happen." One such event occurred

in a very mountainous region. We were going into an NVA base camp. There had been huge numbers of B-52 strikes the night before, and we were going in to see if they had done any good. And, very thick jungle, it was . . . slow going. . . . If you could go fifty yards in ten minutes you were doing good. En route, you were trying to be cautious. . . . [O]ur point man . . . literally turned a corner and walked head-on into a point man from the NVA. Both of them totally armed, ready to go. Both of them looked at each other, turned around and ran. And nothing happened for almost a minute. And then all hell broke loose with a firefight. But, I mean these two guys, absolutely scared the daylights out of each other by coming face to face probably not more than ten feet away from each other and [both] turned and ran.

Despite the hardships that Reinhardt and his platoon faced, there was a great sense of camaraderie. One of the most significant and satisfying jobs Reinhardt ever had was leading the infantry platoon.

Everybody did what they had to do. As an artillery officer, when I was doing my job I didn't have time to protect myself. But there was always someone from that infantry company that made sure that "60" was taken care of (that was my call sign). . . . And a group of people that had two years of high school, Ph.D.'s, we had a pro athlete, a pro baseball player — a real cross-section of people; blacks, whites, Asians, the whole bit. And when we were together there, there wasn't anything that could split it up. And that experience taught me more about people and the fact that we are not all white, and all that, because I had not been exposed to a lot of minorities growing up. I had never lived with minorities growing up, and that was a real eye opener.

By Reinhardt's second tour in 1968, the morale had changed in Vietnam and the anti-war movement was becoming stronger at home. The camaraderie he so fondly mentioned was beginning to erode. Other troubles were also brewing:

A lot of the rear area units started experiencing race problems . . . drug problems, things of that nature in '68. By the time I got back over there for my second tour, it had gotten so bad. One, because it was clear that we were pulling out and that we weren't going to win the war and nobody wanted to get killed. . . . But the bottom line is we had more deaths due to heroin overdoses than we did to combat losses. You could buy a vial of heroin for $5 that was 97% pure. And they would lace it with one or two joints, believing that . . . at eighteen-nineteen-twenty years old, you could stop whenever you wanted. You didn't stop. Two or three of those and you were hooked. You were a heroin addict. And we had kids run through mine fields, get their legs blown off trying to get to it and buying more. Kids shot and killed each other rather than get caught. We had a terrible set of experiences as related to drugs.

In 1972, Reinhardt served as an Army Aviator with the "Pink Panthers" of the 361st Aerial Weapons Company. One particular mission was memorable:

Probably one of the most astonishing things for me was flying over a ridge . . . and seeing row after row of Communist tanks coming at us and going into a real intense environment. We flew all across the border missions. We were in Laos, Cambodia, and all those various areas, and what were called special operations were studying operations, it was all Special Forces and CIA. And that was the start of the real downfall of Vietnam then, when the traditional, Viet intensity envi-

ronment weapons came across the mountains and just crushed the South Vietnamese.

During his second tour, Reinhardt attempted to keep a diary, but this did not last very long because he flew increasingly more dangerous missions. For example, on one mission, Reinhardt flew in to pick up a team of soldiers whose extraction helicopter had been shot down. This move was almost unheard of, because the Cobra attack helicopter[2] that he flew could not take off very well. Reinhardt also flew another rescue mission to pick up a downed F-4 pilot. Most of the missions, however, were classified. Reinhardt recalled one of these special missions:

One team in at Docseang [had] a 'Daisy Cutter.' This was pretty amazing. It is a 10,000-pound bomb that's got a detonator so that it will go off somewhere between fifty and 100 feet above the ground. And it will blow an LZ [landing zone] that we could put a team in, and then we went in. And we also dropped what I will just call an incapacitating gas. We went in and then kidnapped high-ranking NV officers and used them for ransom later. You won't be able to find much about that, but that was fairly common. That was a normal mission for us.

```
0 ot
1
2   02:30
3   01:00      RAT F
4   06:45      Downed F/4 Pilot
5   01:00      NOTHING
6   03:00
7
8   01:00
9   02:30
10  04:30    TacE 2 Teams  BIRD ODCU   LOW POWER
11  03:25    TAC E HALO TEAM South
12  02:00    58 CAL HITS ON A06
13  05:30    TAE E MINN. T/R PROBLEM
14  05:00    3TAC Ei  HYD FAIL. VERY LUCKY IT.  TO MAX
15  06:00    2TAC E's A02 EXP 200 RKTS
16  Down
17  01:00    NOTHING
18  02:35    A02 1 Team 200 DkSeang
19  01:00    NIGHT
20  05:00    A09 Daisy Cutter  OUTSTANDING SHOW
21                   TYPHOON
22                   NO FLY
23
24  04:10    A02 GOLF COURSE
25  No Fly
26  No Fly
```

Page from Reinhardt's flight diary. (Courtesy of John Reinhardt)

Not all flights were as dramatic as this. Reinhardt remembered some stunts helicopters crews would participate in.

We did what we called "string training." And this was a

method of inserting as well as extracting people from a helicopter on a rope. . . . And we had a special rig that had D-rings on it and you would hook into that and it could yank you out if you got shot down or if you were a special forces guy and we were extracting a team. We would hook up. The Huey

Photograph of villagers taken by John Reinhardt. (Courtesy of John Reinhardt)

would hover up and then fly off with you, and you would be at the end of the string spinning around. The pilots all wanted to do it, too. So we did and the guy that was flying the Huey that day, took four of us and dumped us in a river, bottom line. And then he took us up to about 4,000 or 5,000 feet. All I know is I've never been colder in my entire life. [Y]ou are flying at eighty knots and you are holding onto each other so you don't spin and I'll be darn[ed] if he didn't – he dropped us and cut the strings, dropped the strings right in front of our commanding officers, right in front of his what we called 'hooch,' where he lived. And here [are] four dripping wet, frozen pilots that are fifty miles away from where our aircraft are, laying in front of Colonel Bagnall's front door. And he didn't say too much. He waited until dinner that night and came into the club . . . and played the whole thing up. He knew his boys were having fun, but he would certainly appreciate it if they would keep their dirty laundry out of his backyard. He went on and on, but he was a super commander. He later became a three-star General and was commandant at West Point.

After flying several successful classified missions, Reinhardt returned to the United States. The conflict in Vietnam was ending and the troops were being pulled out. Reinhardt's service in the United States Army ended back at Ft. Campbell, Kentucky, where he was a captain assigned to the 101st Airborne Division. He resigned his commission on July 15th, after six and a half years in the service.

Today John Reinhardt is married and has two children, both of whom are in the United States Army. Reinhardt was awarded several medals and citations: a Silver Star on his first tour, a Distinguished Flying Cross on his second tour, a couple of Bronze Stars, twenty-plus air medals, one or two V-Devices for Valor, Whitney's Cross of Gallantry, a Purple Heart, a Combat Infantryman's Badge, and several campaign ribbons.

⬥

WARRANT OFFICER 2ND CLASS, EDWARD KOROSHETZ
155TH-ASSAULT HELICOPTER COMPANY, US ARMY
1968-1971

Like Captain Reinhardt, Edward Koroshetz was trained on assault helicopters. He was deployed to Kam Rahn Bay. As a young man, Koroshetz struggled in school. He decided to join the Army as a helicopter pilot. He had grown up in a military family and had been told stories by his parents, who had been in World War II. His father had been a boatswain on a naval submarine and his mother was in the WAVES. With the advent of Vietnam, he decided that it was time for him to serve too. Koroshetz realized as soon as he arrived in Vietnam that this was a whole different experience:

> *Climbing on the bus I saw bars and screens . . . and I don't mean typical window screens – I mean wire, heavy wire mesh, spanned wire mesh across all the windows so no one could throw any grenades in the bus. . . . That right there got me a little concerned, and it just so happened I was sent from there to Le trang. . . . Le trang had gotten hit the night before we got there. There were barracks that had been blown up.*

Koroshetz described his responsibilities as a warrant officer:

> *. . . I was assigned to a . . . slick platoon, which was a troop-carrying helicopter platoon of the 155th. I was what you call a pilot. It's more like a copilot. Each helicopter was a UH1. Each had a crew of four (the aircraft commander, the pilot, which would be a copilot, the door gunner, and the crew chief), so I was the pilot. . . . You knew how to fly the helicopter before you got to Nam, . . . but in Nam you learned how to stay alive in the helicopter. So there you trained with the instructor pilots in a different unit, and you learned how to fly the combat and contact that your unit flew.*

Koroshetz described their specially outfitted aircraft and missions:

VIETNAM WAR

We inserted troops into LZ's, which are landing zones. Bad guys were sitting out there and shooting at you as you were coming in. I was the first. For approximately a month and a half I was in the slick unit and got shot at. The ship got shot up several times and there was an opening in what we call "guns." It's a gun platoon, which in this assault helicopter company we flew the old Charley Model, UH1C. It was a ship, called a 'hog,' which carried large rocket pods on each side. The other was a mini that carried small rocket pods on each side, mini guns hanging off of them like gattling guns. There was another one, which was called a 'Hog Frog.' A 'hog' meaning with the big pods for the rockets and a 'frog' meant it carried a 40mm grenade launcher on the nose. [We were] not supposed to do that, we bastardized the aircraft – put it on and it eventually tore the aircraft apart because it was a stress to carry it, so we flew it that way. So the first month and a half in country I was with the slicks. The next, from that point to eight months in country I flew gun ships with the 155th. My call sign was "Falcon 4" and I was aircraft commander. The unit rotated home and I had seven and a half months in country. I didn't have eight months, so I couldn't rotate back home with the unit and they reassigned me to a unit up in the Da Nang, Marble Mountain, which was a 282nd. Their call sign was "Alley Cats," so I went up there and finished off my tour from December through about March, I was two weeks off of finishing my tour and I flew with them and I was "Alley Cat 4."

These missions were extremely dangerous and many casualties were expected.

Any assault helicopter company took casualties, lost a lot of good friends both from combat and from aviation accidents. You're flying in an environment that you wouldn't normally fly. When troops are in contact and they need support, there's times when you fly and you're flying through the clouds trying to get to some place and they're things that we used to call cumulus granite. In other words, it's a mountain sticking up inside and you can't see it and you're trying to work your way through and fly into the mountain. A lot of guys lost their lives because of aviation accidents, not just because of the bad guys shooting. . . . My unit, . . . when I was there... lost two pilots, a crew chief and a door gunner. . . . The guys, the crew right across the hooch from me, that was a medivac crew – they came up from the coast and flew

*. . . two weeks on and two weeks off and they rotated them on
out. The crew across the hall of the hooch, they got killed.
They went into an LZ to pull out some dead people [and] took
a B-40 rocket in the cockpit and just rolled right over the side
of the hill killing everybody.*

*[T]he unit lost some, but we didn't take as many losses
as when I went up to the 282ⁿᵈ in Marble Mountain. We took
a lot more losses with that unit, but it was different types of
flying. We invaded Laos up at that point and when we went
into Laos in early 1971. . . . I remember sitting on the bunker
up in Dong Ha watching the helicopters being slung back that
were shot down and every night you saw maybe a half dozen
to a dozen helicopters being brought back that got shot down
and those were the ones that they could recover, that's not
including the ones they blew up, so we took some very heavy
losses when we were into Laos.*

Koroshetz and his crew also took hits while on missions:

*[The] first time I got shot up (the helicopter got shot up,
. . . not . . . my personal body), we went into an LZ and this
was the day . . . two pilots got killed. I was flying what we
used to call "ash and trash." "Ash and trash" was darlock
sector [where] you flew around into different villages [and]
re-supplied. I was a slick pilot at that point – copilot. We re-
supplied different firebases in the villages helping the indige-
nous, the locals. Sometimes we'd fly the chief of the village
out and take him someplace . . . that day.*

*We had come back to the compound on our strip in Buon
Me Thuot to refuel. We had lunch and word came out that
one of our ships went down. The call sign for the slick I was
with was "stage coach," so one of the stage coaches went
down. We went on out, we circled and . . . it's an unwritten
code . . . that [when] someone gets shot down, you keep going
in and pulling them out till you get every one out. You're not
going to leave anybody behind, your not going to leave anybody on the ground. . . . There were instances where you put
a helicopter in and it gets hit and you put another one right
back in; it gets hit [and] you put another one right back in
until you get everyone off the ground. You don't leave them
behind.*

*This one, we went in. We were chosen to go in first. We
got in there, bad guys, and these were NVA, they weren't
Charley [Viet Cong]. Bad guys all over the place and we were
in Cambodia; (officially we weren't in Cambodia at that*

time) . . . so we went on in, we got door gunner and the crew chief out. They'd been laying on the ground for about fifteen to thirty minutes. We got them in. Bad guys were chasing them. . . . Everything around the helicopter was blowing up, the tree line in front of us, took rounds in the helicopter. I was the copilot. I was light on the controls the aircraft command-er was flying. The crew chief and the door gunners were in the back firing their M-60's, they were throwing grenades out on the ground at the bad guys, 'cause they came out underneath us, and I had a little White Owl tipped cigar stuck in my mouth when we went in (it wasn't lit), I just had it in my mouth and by the time we had come out I had eaten the hole cigar. I chewed the plastic tip and the cigar. I was that scared I would say. When it's happening you react, later on you're scared, you're not scared when it's happening, your just react-ing and your doing it and afterwards, it gets to you and you go back to the compound (the airfield) that night and we'd go get drunk, and we'd go fly the next day. That was my first time.

Koroshetz was directly involved with placing soldiers on the battle-field and then evacuating them. Thus, the bond between soldiers was especially close:

You're closer to people you're in combat . . . then you will ever be to anybody in your life — your brothers, your sisters, your family or anything else. The bond you have between you and a few other select buddies. You may go back, you know, you may end and you've gone your own way after Vietnam but there's still a strong feeling. . . .

After the war, Koroshetz attended Georgia Tech, where he received a degree in civil engineering. He was one of the first American civil engi-neers to go into mainland China when it was re-opened to Americans in the 1970s.

LIEUTENANT MICHAEL T. BURNS
443RD TACTICAL FIGHTER UNIT, "SATAN'S ANGELS"
U.S. AIR FORCE
1968 AND 1972

Well, when I was a boy I can recall watching World War II films, watching P-51s rolling inverted and diving through the clouds wondering how wonderful that would be to do that . . . in R.O.T.C. . . . . I qualified for pilot training. . . . . I always wanted to serve my country, ... [Therefore,] I volunteered, I wanted to fly jets.

After training in Oklahoma, Arizona, and completing survival school in Canada and the Philippines, Burns departed for the Far East. He flew out of Ubon, Thailand. "It was hotter than blazes, I mean it was very humid and this air base is . . . scraped out,. . . . It's all pretty flat. It's very primitive. There's a house for the officers' club, there's a place for us to sleep called a 'hooch,' and the flight line where the hangers and where the jets were kept."

After about one month and eighteen missions in Thailand, Burns and his fellow co-pilot, Major Crumpler, were shot down over North Vietnam.

I was shot down on my eighteenth mission. And some of those were the kind of missions where they drove you up . . . about 20,000 feet and they vectored you around and tell you to drop bombs now. And you just release your bombs through the clouds and somebody on the ground was planning, you know, a target down there that they wanted you to hit. But most of the flights were flying around at about 5,000 feet driving up and down roads looking for anything moving. There was one or two times where we were bombing something in a valley, blowing up a bridge and we went down and I was flying with a guy, a Thunderbird pilot actually, and he went down in this valley, just under the Mach, and dropped the bombs and pulled out about 7 G pull out, and . . . we got below the hills and . . . I could see this white tracers of a fifty caliber. He was right even with us, but he wasn't leading us. And I could see the bullets coming out but going behind us. But this guy just hauled ass through that valley . . . I had a couple of other missions like that until the last one when I was shot down.

For Burns, this event was certainly his most memorable experience of the Vietnam War. Burns related what happened next:

We were on an armed reconnaissance with one other F-4. We were two, lead was out about one mile ahead of us and . . . we were driving up and down this road at about 3:00 o'clock in the afternoon and my front-seater, Major Crumpler, said he saw some guns at the base of this hill, down to our

*right, so we jacked up the airspeed and we rolled in at about
5,000 feet and as we came down, lining up on the guns – we
got pretty low, the guns were at the base of the hill and . . .
the hill was probably about a thousand feet. Anyways, we
released the bombs about that time, all the tracers came up,
and they were red and they say the red ones are 35mm . . .
and I could feel this thumping on the bottom of the airplane.*

*We pulled out well over five hundred knots, right over the
trees, right over that hill, and as we pulled out and banked, I
looked back to see where a bomb hit. The last two-thirds of
the airplane was a ball of fire. I couldn't see the tail and I
don't think Crumpler noticed that we were burning. I mean,
he was getting ready to make another bomb run. So I told him
that we were hit and head for the South China Sea . . . to the
right, to the east. So we headed for the South China Sea and
started driving that airplane and when we got to about eight
thousand feet, at one point, one of the engines died, it was
just zero. The other engine was on after-burner and we got
real slow, about two hundred knots, and then the airplane
jerked down real hard and jerked up real hard, threw us
around in the canopy and then it just fell out of the sky. I
mean it just fell, because I could see the earth go by, then the
canopies, then the blue sky, then the earth. Then we ejected
and I came down through the clouds . . . in a wide open field.*

Burns made " a perfect parachute-landing roll," and then his survival
school training clicked into action:

*I rolled my chute up and hid it. And as I was down there
I could hear this rat-tat-tat-tat. It was coming from all
around. It was gunfire way out in the distance and they were
shooting in my direction. So I couldn't see anybody. . . . There
weren't any trees around, . . . so once I hid the chute, I got my
radio out and I pulled out the antennae. I called the other airplanes up there someplace. . . . I said, 'this is Burns, I am on
the ground and I am okay.' And the voice came over and said,
'we didn't see your chute. Give us a reading from that smoke
in the hills.' I looked over at the hills . . . and there was a
black column of smoke rising and that was our F-4 burning.
So I took my compass out and dropped it on the ground and
it said 045. So I said, '045 about 2 miles.' He said, 'head
west. We will try a pick-up in the morning.' So I started running to the west, and if you ran for two weeks day and night,
24 hours a day, you might get into the hills, but it was hope.*

So I started running to the west and at some point I got real tired and I looked down and I still had my G-suit on, the fast pants we call them. So I had to unbuckle that, throw it in the weeds and I kept running.

I could still hear this gunfire, this rat-tat-tat-tat, from different directions and so I saw this one bush, a huge stand of bushes, so I crawled into it and I pulled all the weeds up behind me that I bent like they teach us in survival school, and I sat there. It got as quiet as this room. And I could see the sun, sort of coming down, you know just slowly going down, time is passing. I took my .38 out. . . . And I figured if there is someone between me and that helicopter, I'll use it. But I didn't need it. So I put it in the dirt next to me and I just waited. Then, I don't know how much time went by – some, and then I heard this crackling noise behind me. So . . . I turned around to look and there was this little Vietnamese man, looked like about sixty with a black T-shirt, black shorts. He would take two cautious steps into the weeds coming right towards me and then he would bend down and look through the reeds, through the stems of the bushes, and he didn't see me.

And he would take a couple more steps and finally his eyes met mine. He was about ten feet away and his eyes got real big and he kind of fell backwards and started screaming and as I turned around about five guys –Vietnamese– piled through the bush. They had crept up to it and were standing right on the outside of it. They . . . jumped through the bush and I was looking up the barrel of four or five AK-47s. They have great big barrels like a nickel or a quarter. So, that is how I got captured.

Captivity

Burns and Crumpler were led off to a rural, locally-run underground prison for almost a month. All of this seemed like a dream to Burns.

There was a couple of days where I think I didn't have enough water or something. I thought I was in a dream. We walked through the night. Walked and walked. Then they tied us up and we would have to wait and then we would get up and walk some more. They took us to a hooch and . . . every building was underground. Only the roof was above ground. The walls of the hut – the mud – they dug out. . . . I had a cave about five feet deep and three feet high. And that is where I stayed for twenty days and Crumpler had a cave on the other side of the building. I do remember there was a little family of frogs back there and they sat right up over my shoulder. . . . I was about six inches from them. We were eyeball to eyeball. They were my only friends for twenty days.

They dragged me out and tied me to this pole, same as Crumpler. They would have a show-and-tell. The whole village would walk through and that went on for about twenty days. . . . They took turns guarding us. Somebody was suppose to keep us alive and I remember this one guard came in, and I have to tell you about this guy . . . he was like . . . a Vietminh soldier, like a professional jungle soldier. He had these spindly legs like a runner, shorts, blue T-shirt, he had a rice sack, a roll of rice, they wear over one shoulder, that was his food, an AK-47, a shock of black hair, high cheek bones. His eyes were just barely open, just slants.

And he came in to this place where I was held. I saw him coming in. He threw everybody out. He just shooed them all out. . . . I was watching this and then he came over to my cave, got down in front and he motioned me out. And so I came to the opening of the cave, and he took out a bar of tobacco. It is just a hard bar, and some . . . white paper and he took out a big knife and he scraped off tobacco in this piece of paper. He actually took two pieces of paper – he scraped off tobacco in both. He took mine. He took one rolled it up like an ice cream cone kinda licked it, glued it and handed it to me. Then he made his. Rolled it up, ice cream cone, licked it, and then he found a match, lit my cigarette, lit his, and we stood there smoking and just looking at me, wasn't evil, wasn't mad.

He was just looking at another soldier. It was quite a moment. Then when we were finished with the cigarette, he kind of went, . . . 'everything okay?' And I said, 'okay.' He said, 'get back in there.' Then he let everybody come back down. He was my guard for a couple of days. Then after twenty days, . . . another guy came down, a F-105 pilot, Grover James. He bailed out at about 600 knots and his leg was broken. It was stiff. And he looked like he had been burnt. I thought he was, I didn't know what had happened to him. He looked awful, but the three of us started north. And we could only drive at night because there are F-4's and F-105's up there driving around trying to blow up trucks on the roads and that is where we were now. So we came to a village after about two days and they stopped and they took me off the truck and pushed me into this one village.

They kept pushing and everyone was screaming and it was dark and there were torches and they shoved me into this hooch and it was all dark and smoky. I could see a lot of forms in there and they pushed me over to the side of it and there was a body on the ground and they were shoving me down and it was an American. And he had a cast on his one leg and . . . a cast on his left arm I think, and his right leg. (It was opposite.) And he was lying there and his other hand was covering his eyes. He was lying on his back and they wanted me to take care of him, so they shoved me down to him and I got down close to him and people outside screaming and kind of forming up and he mumbled something. I got closer, I said, 'are you okay?' And then he mumbled something else and I said, 'I can't hear you buddy.' I said, 'are you okay?' He said, 'do you like parades?' And . . . he thought, we were going to be paraded through this village. And that was the first words out of his mouth. Bobby Fat became a very close friend. He just had a way of looking at doom or looking at disaster and . . . coming up with these one-liners. He was great! . . .

They just wanted me to wipe his butt, to clean him up. He was . . . a mess. He was lying in his own shit and they didn't want to touch him and so that is what I did. I nurse-maided him for a couple of years really. And he was a pris-oner for five years like me. When he got back [home] his financée that he left was waiting for him, and I was his best man about a month after we got back, if you could believe that. But then the four of us – they trucked us up to Hanoi and we arrived at the Hanoi Hilton, downtown Hanoi, thirty-five days after I was shot down.

" The Hanoi Hilton"

In Hanoi, at the infamous Han Lo prison, Burns' first cellmates were other injured pilots:

My first cell was with Fat and James because they were both injured and I wasn't and I could take care of them, so I would carry them to the washroom, you know, fireman's carry. Once a week we would go throw water on ourselves. We arrived in August. Lots of interrogations [except for the wounded.] They would drag me up there and talk to me all the time and we heard coughing. . . . We knew this place was full of Americans, but we couldn't talk to them. We were not allowed to talk above a whisper, then January '69, we were just in our cell. It was freezing. We could hear this [gong]. (The Vietnamese have a noon hour at 11:00 o'clock), they ring a gong and the whole town goes to sleep for two hours. They take a siesta. At 1:00 o'clock, the gong rings and everybody wakes up.

Burns had his first opportunity to communicate with others in the prison in mid-January of 1969.

Learning the Code

The gong went off at 11:00 o'clock . . . about mid-January '69, and got real quiet, and after a while I could hear [whispered], 'cell four get under your door, cell four.' And it was across the hall, dark hall [so] that you have the picture. There was a guy named Jerry Marble. He was a captain in the Marine Corps. Captain Marble – he was under the door whispering, yelling for us to get under the door. And that was the first contact we had with anyone. So Fat got up in the window, stood on James, to look out and see where the guard was and I got under the door, it is about a 2" rise from the door to the floor, and I could look across the hall – this dark hall, and I could see this . . . bald head, and bright shiny teeth, and bright eyes, and Jerry Marble. He was in there in solitary confinement.

. . . He was smiling at us and he asked us who we were, when we got shot down, what was going on in the world. Then he told us the tap code and said practice it, memorize it and get on the wall tonight. We could hear this thumping and bounce and things that made no sense to us. But we practiced the tap code and that night we were ears to the wall after the guards cleared out and we could now talk. We were now communicating with the rest of the prison camp. You could talk to the next cell, they talk to the next cell, the next cell, and word would get around – conversations – everybody would know who was there, who the ranking officer was. Everybody knew what the ranks were, down to the lowest, and who was being tortured. It was an amazing system – it worked all night long.

Vietnam War

Life in Prison

When I first got into that prison camp, . . . it was all gray. It [was] like purgatory almost. It felt like life ended. Well, it doesn't, it's just you've got to make the big adjustment, either quit or you just kind of adapt to it. And they kept me in a small cell for a long time and then I was with these two guys who were wounded for a month or so, and then they moved us, . . . (Fat, James and myself) into "Thunderbird Ford" and that is where we stayed, I think, for about a year or [a] year and a half.

I remember that first time they walked me down the hall down the . . . courtyard to Thunderbird. . . . I thought, 'God, where is everybody?' I could hear sneezing and . . . coughing, and . . . hear men's noises, and I could hear the loud speaker. They had a loud speaker in every cell, and there was this tired old man. It sounded like reading. He was an American. He was a POW reading about how the glorious war was going in the south and how we lost 10,000 men today and had eighteen airplanes shot down and he sounded, (I just thought to myself), 'God, what did they do to that guy?' It sounded awful and well, I got used to it. . . . They put us in cells, 9x9, 9x12. There were several different camps. . . .

. . . At the Hanoi Hilton, downtown in Thunderbird, it was a 9x12 room. There was the three of us. Our bathroom is a black bucket. It's just a bucket . . . and we called it the 'black stallion,' but that is . . . what we used for the bathroom. And they would come in the morning, God, 6 o'clock or 5:30, open that door, we would have to stand up, bow; somebody would take the bucket out, full to the brim, walk down to the— there was a rack with a hole in this place to dump the bucket in. . . .

Then they'd put three bowls of soup down and slam the door and leave. And then we tried to communicate all day. . . .

Food at the 'Hanoi Hilton' was minimal; it varied from boiled pork fat to French bread:

Well, basically it was soup twice a day. . . . But from November or October until like March it was boiled greens and pork fat – little pieces of pork fat with the hair sticking up. And then, from March through the summer up until late October, it was boiled pumpkin with pork fat, a loaf – a small loaf, a small like a half or a third loaf of bread. The French were there for sixty some years, so it was their bread. I am not sure where they got the bread. They had these bole weevils – we called them little black bugs in there that guys just ate because they said they were dead. It was probably protein anyway, so that was our basic food.

During his more than five years of incarceration, Burns lost more than twenty-five pounds. The food situation was so bad that he remembers talking about food: "First, it was food. We just dreamed about food to the point where . . . "it would create an illusion that there was almost too much."

Adjusting to Prison life

Well, the first year I was getting used to being in prison camp. [It] is extremely difficult where you are cut off from everybody. I mean, it is not that you are in jail and you can go out in the courtyard and you can talk with one hundred guys. You are in – you are in this cell with one person for a year and a half, or maybe a year with two people. You can't talk above a whisper. There is no TV. There's no distractions, just you. You're stuck there. And you can tap on the walls to the cellmate next to you. And you'd better be careful.

For Burns, adjustment to being a prisoner was difficult – all kinds of thoughts and dreams ran through his head – whether retaliation and even hopes for escape:

That first year, I felt, I thought I was full of rage. How I could be kept there. . . . If someone had thrown an automatic weapon through the cell bars, . . . there is a point in that first year where when they opened the door, I would have run out shooting and just trying to take as many people as I [could], because that is how I felt. . . . Well, at some point I started adjusting inside about this long-term event that might be coming up and tried to adjust my inner clock so that when it happen[ed] I [was] going to be together. I'm not going to be coming apart. I'm going to just keep my head and keep working on the future and taking care of my friends and staying in close touch with my comrades. That was probably the biggest thing.

It was equally tough for Burns' family. For eighteen months "all they knew was that I was shot down and there was some garbled information about whether they saw a chute or not." Only after an outside organization had visited the prison, was Burns able to write a very brief note to his folks assuring them that he was fine. After that initial letter, he was able to write "once every four or five months a six line letter. You can . . . [say] you're fine. You really can't say very much. You can't talk about what is going on around you."

To pass the time . . . and to keep their sanity, Burns and the other prisoners kept their minds as sharp as possible. Burns remembers, they

> talked about every single thing you can think about in your life. . . . Talk about God and religion and I soon found out there was a lot of bright people out there. . . . Some of them had European commands and they just remembered lots of things and so I learned poetry . . . I learned Shakespeare. We told movies. There was a guy who was a butcher once, before he was in the navy and he could draw a cow on the floor with a rock and we talked about the pieces of meat and . . . spent hours discussing the pros and cons.
>
> There were a couple people who knew wines and where they came from, the different parts of France, and Germany and Italy. And they knew this stuff and so we spent hours listening to that and talking about it. . . . People taught math. People knew the Bible up, down and forwards, so that was something else that we talked about. A lot of days were this: . . . they'd open the doors at 6 o'clock, put the food in. Somebody would go empty your bucket, the shit bucket, bring it back, and close that door and that was the last thing that would happen in your life until about 6 o'clock that night when it opened again and they'd take those two bowls and set down two other bowls and slam the door. So you had twelve hours somehow to pass with nothing but yourself and maybe one person, or maybe two if you're lucky. Twelve hours and the time went by like . . . a second seemed to take an hour. . . . I could lay at the back of my bed . . . and with my head, I could look up through the glass out across the wall, outside of the prison and there was a tree, a full green tree on the outside of the prison. And this one summer, I think it's 1969, I watched that tree in the morning, when the light came up, I just stared at it for hours and I could see that when the sun came up, that Hanoi sun in the summer, and just beat that tree, I could see it actually wrinkle, I mean actually droop under the beating of that sun. At least it appeared to me. I

*mean that's how we'd pass time. And in the morning it would
be all spritzed up again with the dew. . . .*

Humor worked wonders. Although Burns cannot remember any specific humorous comments, he does remember "Grover James, [who was] one of my favorite people in all of the world. His one-liners. . . . There where times when I held my gut and laughed as hard as I could   quietly. . . . "

Homecoming

With the truce in 1973, Burns and the other prisoners were released. He came home from Vietnam in mid-March 1973. For a year he had a tough time readjusting. Although " I promised that I would stay in the service, I promised myself for one year to the day 'cause I knew I was getting out . . . I had no idea what I was going to do." After getting out of the service in 1974, Burns went back to study at Notre Dame University and then went on to law school.

The Vietnam War and his years of imprisonment made a tremendous impression on Burns. Reflecting back almost thirty years later, Burns is still not sure why he was even in Vietnam. "I don't know what the war was about. I don't know why we spend so much treasure and blood, this blood letting we do every twenty or thirty years and so I've gotten a . . . very cynical outlook about the United States in war anywhere."

Burns' greatest test was being a POW: "I've had to look at myself, come face to face with myself . . . in a cell, . . . where there is no place to hide. That's . . . quite an education." Although Burns opted not to remain in the military, most of his friends did stay in the service.

End Notes

[1] Catching described the Viet Cong: "There is a difference between the Viet Cong and the North Vietnamese. The North Vietnamese soldier was a regular soldier like I was, who had a uniform and was trained formally in military combat. The Viet Cong were South Vietnamese civilian forces; men and woman who were loyal to North Vietnam's cause, and they were called 'the men in black pajamas,' because they used to wear black uniforms [that] looked like a pajama top and a pajama bottom. They were like militia men, they were like revolutionary fighters, they were just people who believed that the North Vietnamese purpose in South Vietnam was right and they were loyal to North Vietnam."

Vietnam War

2 The Cobra Attack Helicopter Reinhardt flew was created for Vietnam, because a fast, armed helicopter specifically loaded with powerful weapons was needed as an escort for unarmed choppers. Vietnam was the first war where the United States instituted aggressive helicopter transportation (needed for dropping troops quickly and effectively in remote Landing Zones) and helicopter warfare to destroy Viet Cong and NVA establishments in the dense jungle.

The Gulf & Iraq Wars

OPERATION DESERT STORM began on January 18th, 1991, when a Coalition comprised of the United States and thirty-one other nations declared war on Iraq. This was in reaction to Saddam Hussein's invasion of the neighboring country of Kuwait. The First Persian Gulf War lasted less than two months, and a cease-fire was declared on February 28th. Although the issues with Hussein had not been completely resolved at that time, some believed that more should have been done to remove Hussein from power. Instead, it was hoped that imposition of UN sanctions and the resulting economic hardships would force Hussein to comply. When tensions flared again in 1993, air and cruise missile strikes were directed against military targets in Iraq. Overall, the first Gulf War was a military success for the Coalition Forces because Hussein's forces were driven from the sovereign nation of Kuwait. It was hoped that Hussein would comply with the order to eliminate certain weapons from his arsenal.

In the spring of 2003, however, it was believed that Hussein once again posed a threat, and had in his possession a variety of "weapons of mass destruction." Consequently, the Coalition Forces, including the two major powers, the United States and Britain, acted to interdict Hussein. Operation Iraqi Freedom, which was launched on March 20th, 2003, had a broader mission than the first Gulf War. Its objectives included the rapid deployment of military forces into Iraq in order to remove Saddam Hussein from power, to locate and disable WMDs, and to provide ongoing peace-keeping security while a new government was established. Although the military portion of the mission was declared "officially" over on May 1st, 2003, American troops remained in Iraq through 2004, deployed in and around Baghdad, in the Sunni Triangle, and in the North; in the South, Coalition troops secured southern parts of Iraq around Basra, in an effort to protect oil pipelines. With the official military offensive finished, the next tasks included eliminating pockets of radical, armed resistance and helping the Iraqis form a stable new government.

Two officers who served during the Gulf War were Major John Hightower and Dr. Steve Wintermeyer; a third officer, Dr. David Barrows, was in the Iraq War. All of these men were involved in a military effort that was very different from Vietnam. In the Middle East, the US has shown that it has the ability to commit forces far from home rapidly and effectively, aided by state-of-the-art high-tech military machines and equipment.

GULF & IRAQ WARS

MAJOR JOHN P. HIGHTOWER
THIRD BATTALION, 35TH ARMOR, 1ST ARMORED DIVISION
US ARMY

John Hightower graduated from The Citadel in Charlestown, South Carolina, and entered the US Army in 1987. He was stationed in Germany. When the Gulf War began in 1991, he was deployed to the Persian Gulf. There, he served as a lieutenant and tank platoon leader of a unit that operated seventy-ton M1A1 tanks. To get ready to fight a war in a distant, desert land was a logistical challenge. According to Hightower, getting heavy equipment and support vehicles to assembly points in Saudi Arabia was complex:

> *Now a 70-ton tank, getting it from Germany to Saudi Arabia, is kind of a tough proposition. When you've got 54 of them to move, it can be pretty hairy because most roads won't support that kind of weight, so what you have to do with those tanks is put them on trains, and have them taken by train to a port, where they're put on ships and then they have to sail all of the way around Europe and down through the, Strait of Hormuz and into the Red Sea and around Saudi Arabia. . . . Flying from Germany to Saudi Arabia takes about six hours, but it takes about a month and a half for your equipment to get from the train to the ship, and for the ship around through the Mediterranean Sea and down around the Saudi peninsula to Saudi Arabia. . . . To make a long story short, we ended up in a place called Al-Jabal which was a tent city they had set up near the port.*

Thus, when Hightower and his platoon arrived at Al-Jabal, they had only their basic weapons, rucksacks, duffel bags, and gas masks with them. In the meantime, the troops trained, got acclimated to the brutally hot desert weather, and found ways to pass their time. "We watched . . . [movies], we played cards. . . . You would get really good at cards, and we had this one boom box, but the guy who brought the boom box was an idiot. He only brought like two tapes with him to go in the boom box, and I've got to tell you, to this very day, I can sing 'Friends in Low Places' to you." While waiting for Operation Desert Storm to begin, troops also practiced their language skills and learned how to deal with the native Iraqi population.

Hightower remembered how they trained with a psychological operations team:

. . . they had these tapes of Arabic speakers who had record-
ed phrases like, 'Give up . . . Come surrender and you won't
be hurt.' Or, 'Come surrender and we'll give you food, and
send you to the rear, and you will see your families again.' So,
rather than go in and just shoot everybody up, we would roll
in. We would stop just outside their weapon's range, and we
would send these guys in this little truck with a bullhorn on
top of it, out there, and they would play their tape. And you
know what? It would work.

Hightower spent more time waiting for action in the Gulf War than he did in action. "First of all, let me tell you that the ground war only actually lasted for four days. The basic battle plan was to move out and if anything got in your way, kill it." Yet, because the mission was direct-ed against Hussein and his sons, as well as the Ba'athist Iraqi govern-ment, Coalition Forces had no quarrel with the peaceful Iraqi citizens. Hightower remembers "more prisoners were taken, than lives taken."

After much time spent organizing and training, Hightower and his platoon moved forward into their first of a series of three important engagements which comprised a plan of battle, referred to as the 'Great Wheel.' This involved the carefully coordinated movement of 6,000 vehicles from east to west, in an effort to destroy Republican Guard Iraqi forces.

On February 25th, Hightower and the 1st Armored Division began its advance towards al-Busayyah. The division's brigades moved as a flexible front – as a "modified division wedge" that was spread across a twenty-six kilometer front. The advance, though, was slowed by increasingly bad weather. Dust storms reduced visibility and forced the troops to use "thermal sights to scan the area around them and drivers used night vision devices to maintain formation."[1] The commanders knew that for-ward momentum was their key to success and the brigades spent the night "pounding the Iraqi defenders" with artillery. The dawn attack on al-Busayyah on the 26th, amounted to little more than a skirmish, but was significant in that it was the first combat experience for the 1st Division since World War II.[2]

I fought at a place called Al-Busayyah. . . . I fought in
at least three fights while we were out there . . . all in the
space of those four days. Each one of them was pretty much
the same, but one of them was at night, and that was pretty
wild, to fight at night.. . . . Al-Busayyah was one of them.

The next objective for the 1st Division (in the VII Corps) on February 26th, was to advance towards the Republican Guard. This involved a coor-dinated 90° turn to the east by a massive number of vehicles and 145,000 men; the corps then had to cross another 50 kilometers of desert to reach its objective. Weather continued to be abysmal, though, with visibility near zero. Air cover was largely impossible and the corps would "have to feel its way toward the Republican Guard." Yet, the blind race had to be rapid so that the Republican Guard could not escape.[3]

On February 27th, the 1st Division with a front of 350 M-1 tanks, continued eastwards towards the Iraqi Medina Division. This tank battle would be the largest since World War II. Numbers of tanks and firepower determined the final outcome of this battle along the Medina Ridge. The VII Corps had the advantage: Iraqi shells habitually landed short at 1,800 meters, while Bradley tanks fired at a safer range of 2,400 meters. This effectively finished the battle for the Iraqis. According to Hightower,

> We pretty much just rolled over them there, and then we fought again at, we fought the Republican Guard. . . . The Tawakalna Republican Guard division. . . . And then we fought once at night, and I think those were the Hammurabi Republican Guards. All of these fights were kind of out in the middle of the desert.
>
> I fought at a place called Khamisiyah, which was a big —we found out later— it was a big chemical weapons dump for those guys (The Army sent me a letter later saying that I 'might' have been exposed to chemical agents).

Hightower talked about fear while he was in the war. He mentioned that he was never scared in terms of fearing for his life, but he was scared that he would make an error in a situation that called for critical decisions.

> I was more afraid of saying or doing something stupid in a tense situation with my soldiers watching, than I was about me personally getting shot or anything like that (I did get shot at a couple of times. The funny thing is that you're not even aware of the bullet going by until after it's passed you. It sounds like a bee buzzing by).

Fortunately, Hightower suffered only a minor, non-combat injury during the war. There were others who were less fortunate. According to Hightower, "the Purple Heart is the award that you get when you don't duck fast enough. That's the one you don't want to get."

Hightower did not get a Purple Heart, but he was "awarded the Southwest Asia Service Medal just for basically being in the combat zone. . . . I got two foreign decorations. One was the Kuwait Liberation Medal, which was awarded to us by Saudi Arabia, and the other was also called the Kuwait Liberation Medal, but was awarded to us by Kuwait. . . . I received the Bronze Star, which is a combat award."

Hightower made many sacrifices to be in the military. "You spend a lot of time away from home. You spend a lot of time away from your family, depending on the job, so that is a sacrifice you make. There is a financial sacrifice, too

Hightower's time overseas was full of trying experiences. Luckily, the time spent preparing for the war greatly outweighed the time spent in actual combat. He works still with the United States Army, as a Military Intelligence Officer in Georgia.

※

CAPTAIN STEVE WINTERMEYER, M.D.
46TH COMBAT SURGICAL HOSPITAL
US ARMY

In 1981, when Wintermeyer was attending his first year of medical school, he applied for an army scholarship in order to pay for his education. This scholarship meant that the army would pay for his last three years of medical school as long as Wintermeyer did his residency training in the army and then served for three more years. This obligation led to his serving in the Gulf War in 1991.

Shortly after learning of the Iraqi invasion of Kuwait, Wintermeyer recalled how he kidded around with some of his friends about the probability of any of them being sent to the Gulf. It was not such a long shot, though, and soon Wintermeyer had to prepare for deployment. He said his good-byes from Fort Devens, Massachusetts, on October 18th, 1991. "I didn't know what to expect. I had never been to Saudi Arabia, Iraq, or Kuwait before. I figured it was probably going to be hot, I knew it was going to be sandy, and I didn't know much else."

"We flew over on a plane, but our equipment was sent over by ship . . . so there wasn't a whole lot for us to do initially." Because of the equipment delay, they stayed in a Saudi Arabian staging area for ten more days. The daytime temperatures were about 100° F and they ended up playing cards most of the time. They were given some training manuals on medical and environmental issues in the desert and a book on Arabic sayings. The men were also given "amazingly comfortable" cots, mummy sleeping bags, (which they thought were ridiculous until they experienced the desert's night time temperatures), and uncomfortable boots. In this staging area, an old quarry called 'Cement City,' they tried to figure out their assignments.

It was decided that our job was to be the hospital for the
24th Infantry Division (Mechanized). A division has twenty
thousand troops with tanks. They had set up their location in

the middle of the desert in Saudi Arabia, about one hundred miles south of Kuwait. Our job was to go up, set up our hospital just south of where they were, and become their hospital. That's what we did from the end of October until early January. . . .

On Wednesday, January 17ᵗʰ, 1991, a bombing campaign was started with massive air and missile attacks. At this point, Wintermeyer and the others of the 46ᵗʰ Combat Surgical Hospital changed their mission.

In January we tore everything down and loaded it onto trucks and then we drove up to a location very close to the Saudi-Iraq border and sat there for awhile. It was off of what was called 'Tapline Road,' a major road that bordered Kuwait and Iraq in Saudi Arabia. We were there for about a month waiting for things to happen. Then on February 27, the ground invasions started. The troops (82ⁿᵈ Airborne Division, 101ˢᵗ Airborne Assault Division and 6ᵗʰ French Division) went into Iraq and twenty-four hours later we were told to drive in too so we all got in the back of the trucks and drove in. We drove in a convoy for twenty-four hours, siting in the back of a truck, exposed. We had no idea where we were going except into Iraq and it finally got to a point where it was like a pioneer setting the American west, 'Oh, this looks like a good place! Let's stop here!' So we set up our hospital and our job at that point was to have the hospital set up and be able to take patients in four hours. We moved quickly.

This was a scary time for the men in his unit, remembered Wintermeyer:

The night that we moved into Iraq when we were told at two A.M. that we had four hours to get in the trucks. We were clueless and didn't know what was going on. Before we left, we were in the tents and this was the first time that we had actually thought and considered the fact that something could happen. I had to decide what should be done if I got killed. I spoke to Joe, Jim and Jeff, the three physicians I supervised, and told them that Joe would be in charge if I got killed. . . .

During his deployment to Iraq, there were about twenty physicians in the 46ᵗʰ Combat Support Hospital. Wintermeyer recounted that there were "about three internists, one General Medical Officer (GMO), two orthopedists, four surgeons, two obstetricians, one radiologist, and a hospital commander who was also a doctor. There were also about forty nurses, three pharmacists, and a few other people. All of these people were on a Professional Filer (PROFIS) List and they had a regular job during peace time and then got sent over."

The PROFIS List was a list made up of about sixty or eighty people who held regular day jobs who, if the combat support hospital ever got deployed, would come along.

Capt. Steve Wintermeyer (back row, no helmet) with colleagues just before departure into Iraq. (Courtesy of Steve Wintermeyer)

Wintermeyer was Chief of Medicine and Ambulatory Care for the 46th CSH. He also assisted in the physical set-up of the hospital, which consisted of DEPMEDS equipment, canvas tents placed over modular frames.

> It was all tents . . . and you would build the middle frame and you could make it modular. The way that we set ours up was that near the approach from the road that people would take, the emergency room entrance would be the first thing that they would come to. Next to that was a walk-in clinic, an x-ray trailer, operating rooms, intensive care units, and a number of wards for other patients. It was basically these modular metal frames that people could put up and then the canvas tent material that we would put over it.

Once the hospital was established, daily activities quickly became routine:

Wintermeyer on his cot wearing his gas mask. (Courtesy of Steve Wintermeyer)

A typical day, for example, after we had set up our hospital, would be breakfast from six to seven and then a morning formation at seven thirty. Then I had a call schedule set out for the four people that I was in charge of; me, the two internists, and the general medical officer. I would make it so that one of us was responsible and would be available in the emergency room, one would be available in the clinic area, one would be available in the intensive care units, and one would have the day off. Typically the person who had the day off would still be over in the hospital doing something because it can be pretty boring. We would be there all day until dinnertime. A big treat was, after eating dinner, people would go to mail call and hopefully receive mail from home and then generally go back to tents. If you were one of the people on call, then you would be in the hospital. Lights were out at ten o'clock. We had electricity for the tents so you could stay up and read or play cards.

Wintermeyer commented that the medical care was outstanding:

If a soldier was hurt on the front line and needed more care, then they would be sent back to either a Mobile Army Surgical Hospital (M.A.S.H.) or a Combat Support Hospital, (CSH unit pronounced "cash"). We had an emergency room that was open all the time. As a hospital, we were almost a full service hospital, open twenty-four hours a day. We would sleep in the hospital during call nights and when we weren't on call we slept in our regular tents, which were about two hundred yards away from the hospital. If anything happened and they needed reinforcements, they sent someone over to the tents to wake up some more doctors. . . .

The ER in action in the 46th CSH. (Courtesy of Steve Wintermeyer)

Wintermeyer's time in Iraq, though, was not without tragedy. "The other toughest time was having colleagues get killed in motor vehicle accidents. One was a friend of mine and in the unit next to ours. . . . It was hard."

Finally, on Wednesday,

February 27th, President Bush, Sr. suspended offensive combat and laid out the conditions for a permanent cease-fire. Wintermeyer remained with his hospital unit in Iraq, where they continued to accept patients. Wintermeyer's unit returned to Saudi Arabia in early March of 1991, and from there, they flew home.

Wintermeyer still practices medicine. Looking back on the first Gulf War, he recognizes that "We were very fortunate with this war. I had a good group of people to go with, people that I worked with before and knew. . . . I was awarded the Bronze Star for Service and the 46th CSH was awarded an Army Meritorious Unit Commendation Medal, which reflects the quality of the people I worked with. It was a somewhat easy war. We were victorious, it was short, clean, and few died. Most wars are not going to be like that, so we were very fortunate. It was a popular war, not like Vietnam. All I was asked to do was my job. I just had to be a doctor and do my job by providing medical care.

Lieutenant David A. Barrows, M.D.
2nd Assault Amphibian Battalion, 2nd Marine Division

Dr. David Barrows reflects on his personal experiences while serving as a battalion surgeon with the 2nd Assault Amphibian Battalion in Kuwait and Iraq from February through May of 2003:

> *As a child and young adult, I had read many a book on military history and found it fascinating and intriguing in an academic sense. To experience war first hand applies the human element of emotion and the attempt to fathom the chaotic and seemingly random events to the foundation that one has constructed in his or her mind from histories, lectures, and training. In doing so, this creates an occasional surreal perception of events amplified by the physical toll of the environment, strenuous work, long hours, interpersonal relationships, ultimately controlled by decisions of leaders based on real or perceived information. Involvement in war creates vivid, indelible memories of the experiences whether they were the events or the perceptions thereof. As the old saying goes, there is no substitute for experience; that most certainly is the case of war. I cannot possibly do justice to describe war at the fundamental level despite the fact that I took 3000 pictures and wrote over 400 pages in my journal during my deployment. Many people are more qualified to describe the purpose, strategy, tactics of this conflict, and I must defer to them in*

that. What follows is my attempt to convey my perceptions and experiences of the war.

Granted, not being a Marine or Soldier and instead a physician and noncombatant Sailor, makes my version unique. It is augmented by the fact that the 2D AABN only billets one physician, whereas, all infantry battalions billet two. This view is augmented by the fact that I had no contact with other physicians during the combat phase.

In this photo-essay, Barrows shares some of his personal photographs, journal entries and comments regarding his time in the Persian Gulf.

Lt. David Barrows MC, USNR, Battalion Surgeon, 2nd Assault Amphibian Battalion at pause, east of Baghdad. (All photos courtesy of David Barrows)

'Feb 9, 2003 – Definitely one of the longest days of my life. Filled with many emotions. I almost don't know where to begin. I left Camp Lejeune Friday night. It was very hard to say goodbye to Liz. I love her very much and hope to see her again. I love her smile.'

So began my journal that I kept each day of the deployment. Rereading through it a year later, instantly resurfaced a plethora of vivid memories. Even though we happened to be deployed exactly 100 days, the actual amount of time spent certainly seems incongruous with what we experienced. The physically demanding environment, the long hours, the continuous emotional roller coaster, fear of the future and unknown, and the unquenchable thirst for a bit of information as to what we were to do or where to go in a veritable desert of facts faced daily by all, elongated our perception of time.

. . . As a surgical intern at Cottage Hospital in Santa Barbara, California, I was doing pre-rounds on my patients . . . and heard the fateful words "a plane has crashed

into the World Trade Center" through the bedside speaker of my patient who was asleep so early in the morning. . . . As soon as the second plane hit, I had the feeling . . . that I would be going to war with the Marines, and not to sea with the Navy as I desired. Sure enough, seven months later I found myself billeted to the 2nd Marine Division stationed in Camp Lejeune, North Carolina.

At Camp Matilda in Kuwait

Barrows spent forty days at Camp Matilda before his unit headed north into Iraq on March 21st, 2003.

I arrived with the battalion's rear party on 9 February 2003. . . . We joined elements of the 1st Marine Division in Camp Matilda in the Kuwaiti Desert as we gathered gear and prepared for what we all knew to be the inevitable assault to the north. We rapidly settled into camp life within about a week with an established routine.

Rising at about 0530 local time we conducted personal hygiene tasks, followed by breakfast in the chow tent, where we endured long lines for monotonous meals of Wheatabix (so aptly nicknamed "Colon Blow" by the Marines), slurpy eggs, cardboard sausages, and floppy half cooked bacon, with a touch of grits (so pleasantly provided by the desert wind)! Our day continued with conducting various preparation tasks mixed with periods of waiting, followed by "lunch on the boulevard" consisting of one of 24 specially prepared government gourmet meals: MRE's! [Meal-Ready-to-Eat]

What I quickly noticed about the "boulevard" was its uncanny similarity to pictures of tent cities of the American Civil War I had seen in my father's books as a child; fundamentally, warfare never changes – just the faces and the colors of the uniforms!

By about 1600 local time, we fell into one of a few categories: worn out from preparations, bored, or both. This inevitably led to the afternoon ritual of the second chow line. A distinct difference emerged with the line with respect to its morning brother. It developed into the fundamental social event of the day. Many a tale was spun during this time and friendships were developed. Those [with] whom I stood in line . . . are now some of my closest friends!

As our month went by, Marines began to individualize

Camp Matilda with Cobra helicopters, February 2003.

Chow line at Camp Matilda, March 3rd, 2003.

Entrance to Enlisted AAV tent.

their abodes, and the junior enlisted members of the 2D AABN became quite creative.

Each of us, whether Sailor or Marine, were ultimately part of a team that required us to accomplish our preparatory tasks no matter how menial they sometimes felt. As far as the medical department went we organized our gear to have it easily accessible in trauma kits for combat situations. The corpsmen carefully filtered through the gear and compressed it to a manageable size to move forward with. In the meantime Motor Transport Platoon prepared the vehicles.

I was nervous about moving forward because of the

"hoopty" that the battalion was providing me to be my ride! I was slated to be in the low-back 1035 ambulance with a Marine and a Corpsman. Not only were the canvas and other structural items on their last legs, so was the engine. Fortunately, a few days before our departure, the

997 and Hoopty #1 at Matilda, February of 2003.

Hummer gave up the ghost as it belched out large columns of black smoke! Fortunately, we were provided with a brand new Hummer ambulance from 4th tracks that we put our old canvas and gear on – we now had the ultimate sleeper! My Chief Petty Officer and a Marine Corporal who turned out to be an extremely valuable medical resource (paramedic as a civilian) drove the newer 4-patient ambulance.

Moving into Iraq

After a month of preparation, Barrows and his battalion were ready to move forward. "Everyone had the sense that something would soon occur, whether it would be Saddam backing down or us assaulting. Somehow, no one seemed to believe in the former – all waited for Bush's ultimatum that came on 17 March (Washington, D.C. time). We knew that we would make our move quickly after that. . . .

"The 2D AABN, along with the rest of 1st Marine Division began its grim march to the north at about the time of the President's speech. As a person who had been a civilian all my life until about 8 months before the war, a sense of awe filled me."

Barrows made notes in his journal on March 19th prior to the assault:

[We] passed miles and miles of Hummers, Tracks, LAR's (actually Light Armored Vehicles (LAV's) of the Light Armored Reconnaissance Battalion) all bristling with weapons – quite impressive [and] the vast majority of [Marines reflected] a sense of quiet grim determination. Later that evening while in our position near the Iraqi board-

er, I reflected on my observations and let my thoughts catch up with me: Sitting here in my hole . . . just made me feel really weird – a doctor among warriors – just kinda hit me. . . . How different from California!

Coalition forces poised to move into Iraq.

On March 21ˢᵗ, when the assault began, Barrows recorded more impressions:

> *As I lay down in my hole, I looked north and watched an almost endless bombardment of out going artillery. It was impressive, I definitely would not want to be on the receiving end! My mind is kinda numbed right now. I never thought I'd be in a war—It still has not sunk in. It will probably take some time. It is now 0450Z and we have just begun our march north to Iraq. How long will I be there? . . .*

Barrows remembers with great clarity their battalion's entry into Iraq:

> *At this time the fear of the unknown crept in as I sat there alone in my thoughts. The fluid situation and minimal communications added to the uncertainties. At the same time, I had a feeling of a sense of security of being with one of the most elite fighting forces in the world, the US Marines. This tempered my uncertainties. I knew that the men in the holes spread throughout our preparation site likely were undergoing the same thoughts and emotions. Speaking with many later proved that my supposition was correct.*
> *Speaking as a physician, one recurrent thing frustrated me the most—a lack of information—and this acutely revealed itself the first evening of the war as I lay by myself looking north. My ambulance . . . provided minimalist accommodations, including a radio mount without radios! As the war progressed this frustration mounted, especially for some-*

one who depends on detailed information to function as a physician. . . .

Barrows was not the only one frustrated by the lack of information.

> *One of the guys"* [gave him] *a good laugh when he said, 'I feel like a mushroom – I'm kept in the dark and am fed shit.' Granted, it is impossible to give everyone a comprehensive background on the situation; it's impractical, not necessary, and sometimes downright dangerous. As the war progressed, I calmed myself by accepting the lack of information while on the move, and instead turned my efforts to observation of the situation, and people through my pictures and my writing. Fortunately, I did receive a daily update at our nightly battalion meetings. . . .*

Through the Breach into Iraq

> *Our section moved across the Iraqi boarder on the afternoon of the 21st of March. The trip through the sand berms took quite some time. As I took pictures of the crossing, my vehicle partners and I reflected on the significance. I vividly remember my corpsman that sat behind me, HA Gibson,*

Crossing the last sand berm while looking north from Kuwait into Iraq.

blurt out 'Ooooh Shit, here goes.' I let out a good laugh and remembered what my dad had always joked about when I was a kid: 'Papers, we don't need no stinking papers' came to mind as I reflected on how I didn't even possess a passport, and here I was an invader. Such thoughts lightened the tense situation.

Tension was created by the uncertainties of the war, but those occasional "bright spots that we all strove to enjoy" relieved this. It took us, "away from the sobering predicament we found ourselves in. One such experience came the night after we crossed the border as we slowly proceeded north . . . plodding along slowly for several hours." Barrows wrote in his journal:

As we were moving to the . . . site, we stopped all of a sudden. We were passed by a herd of twelve camels running south –I thought at first they were troops jumping out of a vehicle a couple ahead of us running toward us, because they were behind the air intake to the engine and I could not see them too well with the NVG's (Night Vision Goggles). It was amazing to look at them with the NVG's – there were even two baby camels running behind mama – quite cute!

As Barrows' battalion continued towards Baghdad, he took photographs whenever possible:

As a company, we initially underwent combat as we passed north through An Nasiriyah proceeding in the direction of Al Kut. An Nasiriyah was a hornet nest of Saddam's Fedayeen [a paramilitary group] *(aka friends of Saddam). They intended to prevent the Marine advance, however this ended up in a significant amount of carnage on their side. The Headquarters and Services Company* [H & S] *of the 2D AABN was the first soft skinned convoy to cross the Euphrates River going through An Nasiriyah. In the process we passed the remnants of the vehicles of the ambushed Army convoy made famous by Jessica Lynch. As we went through, we sustained our first casualty, as one of the Gunnery Sergeants was struck in the helmet by an AK-47 round. Luck would have it he was only temporally knocked out – that made my job easy! As we drove down the main drag of An Nasiriyah, the Marines of Taskforce Tarawa guarded our convoy by providing suppressive fire against the disorganized enemy attacks that occasionally came from both sides.*

Looking out over canal and date farm located north of An Nasiriyah and elementary school in small town north of An Nasiriyah.

Now I mildly scold myself for not taking more pictures of the event. I have to refrain from that, because that was my first taste of combat and I had no idea of what to expect. So many things I wanted to take pictures of, yet they will only remain as indelible images on my mind. As we zigzagged through the city and crossed the bridges we began to see the obvious carnage of war. Many Iraqis met their death in vehicles head[ing] south from the direction of Al Kut to support the fighters in An Nasiriyah. Essentially as an observer, I was appalled by the gruesome contortions of their bodies and faces and those that were dismembered. Many of the Marines had never seen dead bodies in their lives. As a surgery intern, I had seen my share of blunt and ballistic trauma; however, I had experienced it in a clinical setting. Outside the structured sterile environment of the hospital the carnage made my veritable cast-iron stomach turn a bit!

The day after passing through of An Nasiriyah, . . . one of my most surreal experiences occurred. It so happened that a very severe sand storm occurred such that the lighting produced an atmospheric tone of bright orange red. I noticed that it imparted a sepia flare to the photos I took. An uncanny similarity existed between my pictures and those taken by an Army medic friend of mine who served in Vietnam. It seems a stroke of fate provided me the opportunity to photograph similar subjects – water and rice paddies with palm trees. They were identical in the two sets of photos taken 30+ years apart! At that point I began to contemplate whether this current war would develop into a political nightmare like the Vietnam War. As we were assaulting toward Baghdad I wondered how we would do at winning the "hearts and minds" of the Iraqi people occasionally. I reinforced those thoughts every time I came upon a school, for it is through education of the children can one truly alter the course of a nation, whether for good or bad.

Undeniably one of the most stressful days of the war took place the day after we drove through An Nasiriyah. At the end of it [the town], we found ourselves at the tip of the spear with a section of LAR cut off from the other elements of the division behind us. As we left our position in the morning, a large complement of Iraqi fighters assaulted our right flank in a spoiling attack. I was on the west side of the roadway standing outside my vehicle commenting to my vehicle partners how slow things were going when it occurred to me that a group of Marines at the crest of the road were firing to the east in concert with one of the tracks. I calmly got in the Hummer as the convoy started to move. It wasn't until a day or two later when I reflected how I responded to combat then and as we moved north. I was amazed that this was pretty much the reaction of all the Marines – methodical calmness. I believe excellent training and exhaustion both helped this. A few nights later, a group of Iraqis unsuccessfully tried to fire rockets into our position during the night. I had dug a shallower than usual hole for protection twofold; the ground was extremely unforgiving and I was completely beat. The rockets' blasts woke me. . . . I merely lay there on my back, reached over, grabbed my Kevlar and flak, dragged them over my face and chest, respectively, and fell asleep.

On April 3rd, Barrows moved closer to Baghdad, but not without incident.

For me the first such personal test occurred after moving out of the An Nasiriyah area as we headed north toward Baghdad via Al Numiniyah. Not a one of us knew what to expect with respect to suicide bombers during our assault. We were warned of the potential. . . . As we were headed north, we came upon a large group of locals that were waving at us in the distance. Based on our experiences in the towns behind us, we were wary of the fact that some might wave and greet us one moment and then try to shoot us in the back the next moment after pulling an AK-47 out of their long gowns. As we continued our approach . . . as the guys were running up and climbing on the American

A typical sleeping hole, where Capt. Hall collapsed exhausted after digging pit and being on watch the entire night before!

Local Iraqis greeting the H&S Company as it drives off a major highway.

*vehicles with no fear, a child about 11 years old came to mine
and reached in (my window). He did not realize I had a condition 1 off-safe pistol aimed at his belly – that was one of
the scariest moments . . . all he wanted though was . . .
Charms [candy]—which I gave to him. . . . Reflecting on the
event later, I am happy that the child never saw me pointing
the pistol at him through the canvas door of the Hummer.
Instead he will hopefully remember an American giving him
candy! I will forever be relieved that I never had to pull the
trigger in self-defense. However, this sobering experience
forced me to personally consider the horror of war and the
fickle turns of fate that alter peoples' lives.*

Observations of Iraqi Life, under & after Saddam

*As the war developed, so did my impression of the coun-
try and the people. World politics aside, Saddam Hussein's
regime proved a disaster to the casual outside observer. The
longer we were there the more disgusted I was with the des-
pot. Poverty was noticeably rampant; an inexcusable symp-
tom of the tyrannical regime. The average person we came
across appeared to be hungry, for the vast majority gestured
for food. This perception may have been skewed by the fact
that many Iraqi likely realized that Americans brought good
food in the form of "Meal Ready to Eat" (MRE). The housing
both in farmlands and Baghdad was by American standards
low. The majority of buildings in the towns to the south were
mud huts with flat roofs made of palm trees. The streets of
Baghdad were not much better. Granted, with the war going
on the situation was likely worse than usual. However, one
noticed trash everywhere, dumps were uncovered piles of trash
just outside the towns that exuded the worst possible stench,
the buildings were in various states of disrepair, and the street
maintenance was minimal at best (not considering the
American tracked vehicles damaging the pavement). . . .*

On April 7th, Barrows and his H & S Company moved into Baghdad.
"At the time of our initial invasion, my impression of the average Iraqi
was that he or she welcomed the Americans. At numerous locations [we]
were greeted by a smile, a wave, and a word or two of English. They
became more prevalent and forceful as we moved toward Baghdad and
eventually entered the city from the northeast." In his journal Barrows
wrote, "Yesterday, after a couple of hours pause, we finally moved north
into the outskirts of Baghdad. There were thousands of people lining the

streets. Many people yelled 'very good' to us. One yelled 'doctor' to my Hummer! Another yelled 'congratulations.' Also, a guy screamed to HM1 (James Cartier) 'Saddam!' and at the same time motioned with his fingers as if he was slitting his throat!"

The vision of the 1st Marine Division was the concept of "no better friend, no worst enemy." As such, it was part of our mission to "win the hearts and minds of the people." In the spirit of achieving that vision, we would greet and wave to all we encountered driving along, however, we remained wary and had weapons at the ready should the need arise to use them. On of my most vivid memories of this occurred as I

Lt. Col. Stuart Harris waving to local Iraqis.

was with the Battalion Commander, Lieutenant Colonel Stuart Harris. I happened to take the following picture of him waving to people in Baghdad. Serendipitously, I captured his face in the mirror of the Hummer.

After encamping slightly to the east of Baghdad, we finally moved in to Baghdad from east side of the city. Many of us were on edge, because we did not know what to expect. As we went along, we were pleasantly surprised by the fact that the locals were predominantly doing one of three things while they greeted us with enthusiasm: fleeing, watching, or looting! Everywhere we went in Baghdad that day and after, we were constantly reminded of the regime we came to depose by the numerous murals of the tyrant. During the assault, I was impressed with the Marines, in that the only defacing that I observed was that of the multitude of murals depicting Saddam Hussein. Different units would tag the murals, and others would drive by and change the tags! I happened to snap a shot of one such picture that said 1st Tanks on it.

By mid-April, Barrows' unit settled in the northern Baghdad area.

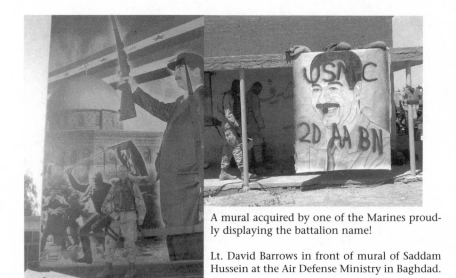

A mural acquired by one of the Marines proudly displaying the battalion name!

Lt. David Barrows in front of mural of Saddam Hussein at the Air Defense Ministry in Baghdad.

Our company did not move. We accomplished our mission by sending our teams. I did have the opportunity to tag along on a mail run to our other two companies in Baghdad supporting two different regiments.[4] By that time, 18 April 03, things had begun to calm down, and I wanted to at least get a view of Baghdad before our unit was moved out, so as to complete my experience of the war and for historical benefit. As our small convoy delivered mail to various former Iraqi military and government locations that we were occupying, I began to form an opinion of how shoddy the military infrastructure was, and how obvious it was for us to easily overcome them. Our first stop of the morning was the Iraqi air defense ministry. I was amazed at how shoddy the construction was of everything – there were pictures of Saddam everywhere. All the classrooms gave a feel of a preschool, except the subject matter was air defense. I picked up a book on air defense. It was about ballistics, bullets, RPG's and such.

Another soldier found a different kind of souvenir:

To contrast [to] what the average citizen endured, one of my corpsmen . . . attached to Bravo Company, 2DAABN, acquired a gilded teacup from one of the presidential palaces

Mail was delivered to Bravo Company of the 2D AABN while it was stationed in central Baghdad at one of the former Ba'ath party locations. The exuberance of the men could be seen on their faces the instant our Hummer convoy rolled in with the bags of mail.

Teacup from one of the presidential palaces in Baghdad.

in Baghdad. He, as well as numbers of other Marines and Sailors who managed to go inside the palaces were amazed by the wealth and gaudiness of the estates.

By the 18th [of April] in Baghdad the resilience of the Iraqi people began to show; the locals had begun the process of putting their lives back together, despite the occupation. Driving along, we passed street vendors selling cigarettes, fruits and vegetables, a true to life butcher shop right in the middle of the street (hence the American service members' endearing term, "streetmeat"). All of these observations rein-

forced my appreciation for life thousands of miles away in the United States. . . .

Life as the Battalion Surgeon

We moved on to Ad Diwaniyah south of Baghdad, where our battalion regrouped prior to redeploying to Camp Lejeune, North Carolina. We ended up living on an Iraqi military installation – a complete pit of a place. Everything was of the shoddiest construction; more proof that the military was not quite up to the task of resisting the United States, for Saddam Hussein was spending too much money on teacups and not weapons!!! . . . Life in Ad Diwaniyah became more bearable. We had latrines and showers. . . . The problem that did arise however, was that with such a large concentration of people, trash and waste rapidly drew the vermin – in particular the fly! Every time one went to the latrine, they would fly off the human waste and crawl on your rear-end! This, in addition to landing on your food a couple hundred meters away, led to a serious health problem – diarrhea. This lead to the renaming of our location as Ad Diarrhea, instead of Ad Diwaniyah! The majority of the battalion, including myself were struck with the viral illness, a kissing cousin of Norwalk Agent, the virus that has struck many a cruise ship over the past couple of years.

From a medical standpoint, this problem did put us in a bit of a bind. I used all of my IV fluids and all of my anti-diarrheal medications. I was fortunate enough to be able receive IV fluid replenishment supplies.

As a division we were extremely lucky, we did not have any significant medical issues grip the battalion until we reached Ad Diwaniyah. If we had been struck with such a diarrheal illness as we moved northwards during the assault, life would have been miserable, and we likely would not have done things as quickly, thus increasing the casualty rate. Our lack of such problems on the way up can be attributed to the fact that we began healthy in Kuwait, and once we moved forward, our only source of food was sealed MRE's, and we were moving so fast that we were not stagnating in our own waste—one of the advantages of speed.

As a physician for a division battalion, my primary job entailed triage and stabilization, due to the minimal supplies we actually moved forward with. God forbid we actually had run into a heavy combat situation with multiple casualties, it would have been difficult to get easy access to our supplies, because they were in one 7-ton truck in quadcons 6 feet off the ground! Furthermore, we would have rapidly gone through what we had if it came to trauma. I did not trust the resupply system, from what I observed in some cases, and I was very glad we did not have to try it with the medical supplies during combat. Fortunately, H&S Company was blessed with minimal casualties, limited primarily to a couple of serious falls and vehicle accidents. These were technically easy to take care of.

The most significant medical challenge faced occurred north of An Nasiriyah, when H&S Company was charged with moving a large group of enemy prisoners of war. Approximately eight of them needed serious medical attention. As a physician, I was frustrated, because I did not have the supplies to definitively care for them and the combat situation did not permit immediate evacuation. So my corpsmen and I did the best we could with what we had to take care of them. This experience made me appreciate the wealth of the American medical system, where supplies are veritably at your fingertips.

. . . When it came to medical care in the field, [I was] extremely proud of my 18 corpsmen. Most of them were 19 to 21 years old and led very well. . . . For guys who were essentially just out of high school, I was impressed with their dedication and application of what they had been taught in Navy Corps School. . . .

Returning Home

At the conclusion of 100-some days' service to Iraq, Barrows remembered some comments by one of the men in his battalion, CWO-2 Diggs, who had already completed numerous tours of duty. Diggs said, "There are three very good feelings when you return. The first is when you actually touch down on the runway at Cherry Point – all the Marines cheer and clap their hands. The second greatest feeling is the bus trip to Camp Lejeune, going down [highway] 24 and arriving at the gate. . . . [then the third and] the best feeling is making eye contact with your wife – the greatest feeling in the world. I can't wait for that time. . . . "

David Barrows' military deployment to Iraq concluded May 16, 2003 and a year after his return from Iraq, he reflected upon the value of his wartime experiences:

. . . They were valuable for many reasons – maturity,

patience, inner calmness, greater understanding of the human condition all factor into the equation. Furthermore, I believe they have helped me become a better physician. . . .

War answers a fundamental question that I believe exists at some level in anyone who joins the military, that is, 'does one have the fortitude to face the uncertainty and trauma of war and come through better for the experience?' For each person this response is different. Speaking from my life since the deployment, it was valuable for me and has opened opportunities to me immensely.

Finally, as an eternal optimist, I hope that one-day Iraq will become prosperous. I would be curious to return in twenty years to see how the place improves . . . .

END NOTES

[1] General Robert H. Scales, Jr., *Certain Victory: The US Army in the Gulf War*, (Washington, D.C., 1993), 240. See pages 238 to 245 for details of the 1st Armored Division activities.

[2] *Certain Victory*, p. 243.

[3] *Certain Victory*, p. 247.

[4] Regarding the mail, Barrows wrote: "Although I cannot possibly speak for everyone, I did notice that a few things were vital to our emotional well being. I found comfort in writing letters to my wife, family, and friends regularly. I began doing this upon arrival in Kuwait and continued to do this throughout the duration of my time in Iraq. More uplifting however, was to receive mail! Naturally, letters, more than packages, provided more sustenance to the soul. Once we began our drive north, our first mail call occurred on day 20 of the war! Everyone felt bad for those who got nothing. Conversely, I received a glut of 20 letters – it was difficult to savor the letters. Not knowing what lay in the future everyone read their letters immediately!

Besides letter writing, many people were surprised by the simplest gestures. My wife left a surprise for me when I got to Kuwait." Barrows noted in his journal on February 25th: "I opened my book bag and opened my surgical book and I found that Liz had stuffed a couple of pictures of herself at the wedding into the book and that made me feel very good. I had to show the guys. It lifted my spirits and made me more than ever want to be home with her."